FRAGILE DIGNITY

Society of Biblical Literature

Semeia Studies

Gerald O. West, General Editor

Editorial Board:
Pablo Andiñach
Fiona Black
Denise K. Buell
Gay L. Byron
Jione Havea
Jennifer L. Koosed
Jeremy Punt
Yak-Hwee Tan

Number 72
Board Editor: Jeremy Punt

FRAGILE DIGNITY
Intercontextual Conversations on Scriptures, Family, and Violence

FRAGILE DIGNITY

INTERCONTEXTUAL CONVERSATIONS ON SCRIPTURES, FAMILY, AND VIOLENCE

Edited by
L. Juliana Claassens and Klaas Spronk

Society of Biblical Literature
Atlanta

FRAGILE DIGNITY
Intercontextual Conversations on Scriptures, Family, and Violence

Copyright © 2013 by the Society of Biblical Literature

All rights reserved. No part of this work may be reproduced or transmitted in any form or by any means, electronic or mechanical, including photocopying and recording, or by means of any information storage or retrieval system, except as may be expressly permitted by the 1976 Copyright Act or in writing from the publisher. Requests for permission should be addressed in writing to the Rights and Permissions Office, Society of Biblical Literature, 825 Houston Mill Road, Atlanta, GA 30329 USA.

Library of Congress Cataloging-in-Publication Data

Fragile dignity : intercontextual conversations on scriptures, family, and violence / edited by L. Juliana Claassens and Klaas Spronk.
    p. cm. — (Semeia studies / Society of Biblical Literature ; number 72)
    "The collection of essays is the result of the collaboration between the Protestant Theological University in Kampen, Netherlands and the Faculty of Theology at Stellenbosch University, South Africa"—Introduction.
    Includes bibliographical references and index.
    ISBN 978-1-58983-895-6 (paper binding : alk. paper) — ISBN 978-1-58983-896-3 (electronic format) — ISBN 978-1-58983-897-0 (hardcover binding : alk. paper)
    1. Dignity—Religious aspects—Christianity. 2. Dignity. 3. Life—Religious aspects—Christianity. 4. Violence—Religious aspects—Christianity. 5. Family violence—Religious aspects—Christianity. 6. Families—Biblical teaching. 7. Church work with families. I. Claassens, L. Juliana, 1972– II. Spronk, Klaas. III. Series: Semeia studies ; no. 72.
    BV4647.D5F73 2013
    241'.697—dc23   2013022944

Printed on acid-free, recycled paper conforming to
ANSI/NISO Z39.48-1992 (R1997) and ISO 9706:1994
standards for paper permanence.

Contents

Introduction
L. Juliana Claassens and Klaas Spronk 1

Part 1: Hermeneutical Framework

The Hermeneutics of Dignity
Frits de Lange 9

Response
Gerrit Brand 29

Figuring God and Humankind: The *Imago Dei* in View of Anthropologies in the Old Testament
Hendrik Bosman 39

Response
Klaas Spronk 57

The Givenness of Human Dignity: A Response to the Essays of Frits de Lange and Hendrik Bosman
Beverley E. Mitchell 65

Part 2: Engaging the Text

A True Disgrace? The Representation of Violence against Women in the Book of Lamentations and in J. M. Coetzee's Novel *Disgrace*
L. Juliana Claassens 73

Response
Dorothea Erbele-Küster 91

Birth as Creation under Threat? Biblical-Theological Reflections
on Assisted Reproductive Technologies
Dorothea Erbele-Küster 101

    Response
        Charlene van der Walt 117

Human Dignity, Families, and Violence: The New Testament
as Resource?
Jeremy Punt..127

    Response
        Magda Misset-van de Weg..147

A Fragile Dignity: Intercontextual Conversation on Scripture,
Family, and Violence
Elsa Tamez..159

Part 3: Engaging the Context

Dignity in the Family? Analyzing Our Ambiguous Relationship to
the Family and Theological Suggestions toward Overcoming It
Petruschka Schaafsma 169

    Response
        Robert Vosloo 189

Empowering Those Who Suffer Domestic Violence: The Necessity
of Different Theological Imagery
Anne-Claire Mulder..199

    Response
        Mary-Anne Plaatjies van Huffel..219

Family and Its Discontents
Cheryl B. Anderson 227

Missing Links in Mainline Churches: Biblical Life Stories and
Their Claim in Today's Family Preaching
Ciska Stark..233

Response
    Ian Nell 251

"Household" (Dis)loyalties and Violence in Judges 14 and 15:
    Dignity of Gendered and Religious "Others" in a Dialogical
    Theological Praxis
    D. Xolile Simon and Lee-Ann J. Simon 259

Response
    Leo Koffeman 273

Honor in the Bible and the Qur'an
    Gé Speelman 281

Response
    Yusef Wagid 303

Fragile Dignity: Family, Honor, Scripture
    Monica J. Melanchthon 309

Reflections on Reflections: Rights, In/Dignity, In/Equality,
    Faith—The Bible as Universal Medicine?
    Athalya Brenner..319

Contributors...333

Introduction

L. Juliana Claassens and Klaas Spronk

In her book *Frames of War*, Judith Butler reminds us of a reality we know all too well: human beings are vulnerable, prone to injury, disease, and death. From the moment we are born, our survival depends on what Butler calls "a social network of hands" (Butler 2009, 14–16). Most of us are born into families that provide a child care not only to survive, but also to thrive. Family thus serves as the space that protects life. However, in many instances today, the family has unfortunately become the space in which human life is prevented from flourishing.

This volume focuses on the notion of human dignity and particularly on how this concept relates to those instances in which families or society at large fail to protect human life and human dignity. The collection of essays is the result of the collaboration between the Protestant Theological University in Kampen, Netherlands and the Faculty of Theology at Stellenbosch University, South Africa. The essays reflect both on theoretical aspects of the notion of human dignity and on its social ramifications. Together they constitute an extended case study on in/dignity in and around the family as well as on the performance of dignity—or, as will be evident from this volume, quite often indignity—in wider communities.

The title of this volume, *Fragile Dignity*, captures the paradox that, on the one hand, human beings are endowed with an inherent dignity as creatures created in the image of God (Gen 1:26-27). This "eccentric existence," as David Kelsey calls it in his work with the same title, maintains that the call to respect human dignity is not related to an individual's intellectual or physical abilities, but is rooted in the individual's relationship with the Creator God (Kelsey 2009, 289–90). This dignity is thus inherent in all human beings regardless of race, class, sexual orientation, intellectual abilities, or other traits. On the other hand, however, this dignity is also a fragile dignity, as is evident in the continual violation of human worth, and as is particularly evident in the ugly face of violence inflicted on and affecting individuals and groups at home and in the public sphere.

Recognizing this fragility of human dignity led the two universities to come together in dialogue. Even though we come from very different contexts—North versus South; developed versus developing world—the internal boundaries in our respective contexts are already more porous: as other European societies, the Dutch, for example, must learn how to negotiate the presence of immigrants in their midst, and South Africa, with its complex apartheid history, is still learning to negotiate complex race relations.

Building on a six-year collaboration that comprised yearly conferences alternating between our two institutions and focusing on various aspects pertaining to human dignity, these two Faculties of Theology engaged in dialogue, responding to one another's contributions in the form of responsive letters—the salutation and greeting contained within each response suggesting something of the personal relationship involved in the act of intimately engaging with one another's work. For us, these North-South and South-North dialogues were a great example of theology as encounter, according to which we face one another in our differentness, asking difficult questions of one another, and coming to see ourselves in a new light. The Russian literary theorist Mikhail Bakhtin describes the value of dialogical engagement to reveal new dimensions of a particular topic: When two people look over each other's shoulders, they inadvertently occupy different positions and hence look at the same thing in different ways, thus complementing and mutually enriching each other's perspective (Bakhtin 1986, 7; cf. Holquist 1990, 21).

The dialogues that form part of *Fragile Dignity* indeed attest to the rich perspectives that emerged from the ongoing conversation between the two theological faculties from the Northern and Southern hemispheres. However, in light of the fact that the dialogical nature of words or texts implies that new voices continually may be recalled and may join to the dialogue—what Mikhail Bakhtin has called the *unfinalizable* character of the dialogical nature of the word—this volume seeks to model the importance of extending the conversation. Therefore, *Fragile Dignity* sought to add more voices to this conversation on family, violence, and human dignity. As a result, the initial dialogues were extended by including a series of external responses: four female respondents from different parts of the world (Beverly Mitchell from the USA, Elsa Tamez from Costa Rica, Cheryl Anderson from the USA, and Monica Melanchthon from India, who during the writing of this book moved to Australia) responding to the various sections contained in this volume, culminating in a third-level response to the book as a whole ("Reflections on Reflections") by yet another female respondent, Athalya Brenner, who splits her time between Israel and Amsterdam. These multilayered responses by respondents from very different contexts were crucial to the final form of this book, as they represent voices beyond the initial North-South dialogues joining the conversation on human dignity, attesting to the underlying conviction that the conversation initiated in this book on human dignity in our respective contexts is far from over.

Another key feature of *Fragile Dignity* is that it contains important perspectives with regard to the way one uses biblical texts in a normative conversation on the promotion of human dignity in contemporary contexts. This is evident from the overall shape of this volume. For instance, in the first section that constitutes the hermeneutical framework for this volume, the notion of the *imago Dei* cited above is problematized in the contribution by Hendrik Bosman, with response by Klaas Spronk, as it shows how biblical traditions present a variety of diverse and ambiguous perspectives on what it means to say that humankind is created in the image of God.

The contributions to this volume furthermore build on the assumption that the biblical texts are complex, ambiguous, and even messy, mirroring the complexity and ambiguity that constitute our contemporary contexts. This is particularly evident in the second section of this volume, "Engaging the Text," in which biblical scholars engage with the biblical text with an eye to context, both ancient and contemporary. Moreover, the interdisciplinary collaboration in this volume is reflected in the fact that it includes scholars who are not traditionally trained biblical scholars but who, nevertheless, sought to engage the Bible in their reflection regarding threats to human dignity in the context of family. One finds in the third section of this volume, "Engaging the Context," how practical theologians, missiologists, theologians, church historians, and educators engage with the context with an eye to the biblical text (and in at least one instance, the Qur'an). It is evident in many of the contributions that the biblical text functions not so much in a normative fashion, as a means of ending the conversation with an authoritative last word, but rather as a way to open up discussion to its transformative power. The biblical text may, for instance, function as a mirror of a society that, as one participant notes, sometimes produces a rather hazy image. Yet the scriptural traditions helped all the participants to discover who they are and what the (re)construction of human dignity might entail.

The essays contained in this volume relating to the theme of family, violence, and human dignity share the underlying assumption that life is precious; that humans possess an inherent dignity that deserves to be respected; and that human beings ought to be given the opportunity to flourish. However, these essays also consider those forces that prevent life from reaching its full potential. For this reason, quite a few of the contributions focus on the way domestic violence threatens the dignity of men, women, and children. This reality finds literary expression in the biblical traditions. (See, for example, the dialogue between Anne-Claire Mulder and Mary-Anne Plaatjies-van Huffel and the dialogue between Xolile and Lee-Ann Simon and Leo Koffemann.) Gé Speelman (with a response by Yusef Waghid) moreover considers this theme in the context of Islam, and L. Juliana Claassens (with a response by Dorothea Erbele-Küster) investigates how violence against women is used as a metaphor for describing the sociopolitical situations in both the Book of Lamentations as well as in the Nobel prizewinning novel *Disgrace* by South African author J. M. Coetzee.

In the process of compiling this volume, we gained a number of important insights. First, the collaboration reflected in *Fragile Dignity* proved to be an enriching experience for all involved. All were constantly surprised by the rich perspectives and new angles revealed by this interaction. For instance, it soon became evident that what we mean by family is not as self-evident as one would think in our respective contexts. In the same way, Jeremy Punt's contribution (with response by Magda Misset-van de Weg) reveals the complexity of and diversity in what constitutes the family in the New Testament traditions. This challenged us to also acknowledge the complexity and rich variety of kinds of family in our respective contexts of South Africa and the Netherlands. Blended families and families ravaged by HIV/AIDS; families torn apart by apartheid policies, and more recently by globalizing forces, have forever changed what we mean by family.

Moreover, the very notion of human dignity itself revealed many different layers of meaning as the contributors explored the concept from various angles. Throughout the consultation, it became evident that this term is much more complex than initially believed—something already introduced in the introductory essay that considers the hermeneutics of dignity (Frits de Lange, responded to by Gerrit Brand). Moreover, we grappled with questions of what dignity means in the midst of the tense Muslim-Christian relations experienced by some of Stellenbosch University's Nigerian students, or in the context of desperate women seeking to conceive by means of assisted reproductive techniques, and for surrogate mothers and potential egg donors.

Second, the theological engagement found in *Fragile Dignity* is a truly interdisciplinary venture as the dialogues quite often cross disciplinary lines. In his reflection on the role of universities in times of political transition, Stellenbosch University president Russel Botman (2011) argues that multi-, inter-, and transdisciplinary engagement is vital for solving the problems we are facing in the contemporary world, problems so complex that we cannot go at them alone. The same could be said about theology done in our globalizing context, in which it seems that the efficacy of the theology of the future rests on its ability to cross borders, both disciplinary and geographical.

Finally, the complexity and unfinalizability of these dialogues do not preclude the participations from working toward a common goal. It is evident that all of the participants in this project—both initial conversationists and respondents—are deeply committed to respecting the inherent dignity of all people, regardless of the ways in which we differ in race, class, gender, and so on. John Rogerson (2010, 193) is right when he says: "We become more truly human the more that we accept others as being truly human." The fragile dignity highlighted in this volume implies that people are engaged in an ongoing process of becoming more human. In allowing their fellow human beings the opportunity to flourish, to reach their full potential in the world, people may live into the *imago Dei* (Gen 1:26–27), in this way becoming the realization of God's purposes in the world (Rogerson 2010, 174).

This book is dedicated to the memory of our colleague Gerrit Brand, who sadly died before the publication of this book and whose life attests, amidst the fragility of our existence, to this ongoing quest to become more human.

References

Bakhtin, Mikhail M. 1986. *Speech Genres and Other Late Essays*. Edited by Caryl Emerson and Michael Holquist. Translated by Vern W. McGee. Austin: University of Texas Press.

Botman, H. Russel. 2011. Hope in Africa: The Role of Universities in Times of Political Transition. Keynote Address given at Talloires Network Leaders Conference *Building the Engaged University, Moving beyond the Ivory Tower*. Madrid, Spain, June 14–16, 2011. Online: http://scholar.sun.ac.za/handle/10019.1/20946?show=full.

Butler, Judith. 2009. *Frames of War: When Is Life Grievable?* London: Verso.

Holquist, Michael. 2009. *Dialogism: Bakhtin and His World*. London: Routledge.

Kelsey, David. 2009. *Eccentric Existence: A Theological Anthropology*. Louisville: Westminster John Knox.

Rogerson, John W. 2010. *A Theology of the Old Testament: Cultural Memory, Communication, and Being Human*. Minneapolis: Fortress.

Part 1
Hermeneutical Framework

The Hermeneutics of Dignity

Frits de Lange

Within the history of modern morality, one finds a complex set of interwoven, often implicit, meanings with regard to the concept of human dignity. I consider it part of an ethicist's hermeneutical task to try to make these meanings more explicit.

Furthermore, the concept of dignity can only be understood when its narrative structure is acknowledged. By using the metaphor of an old master's canvas, covered in several layers of paint, I first try to condense the historical dimension of the narrative to form a composite image. I further assume that "dignity" does not refer to some objective essence of individual human beings, but to a relationship rooted in social practices. Dignity is not a "value," understood as an abstract ideal, but the moral qualification of concrete practices of social recognition. As I will argue, the biblical narrative of the Good Samaritan exemplifies this relational dimension of dignity in a paradigmatic way.

The Rhetoric of Human Dignity

There is no such "thing" as dignity. As Ludwig Wittgenstein demonstrated, words derive their meaning from the social contexts and dialogical practices in which they are used (Wittgenstein 1953). When we "read" in humans an inalienable dignity, we do not discover some objective essence. Even speaking of the *inherent* dignity of human beings is the outcome of a process of social interaction that had lasted for a long time, going back long before Immanuel Kant, and that is deeply rooted in the Christian and classical-humanistic tradition. We may call dialogical practices such as these discourses. Discourses are sets of meanings, metaphors, representations, images, stories, or utterances with which people structure and give meaning to daily reality. Discourses are texts-in-action, and they have normative power. Those who have discursive power can impose their reading on others as "truth." By the power of their rhetoric, discourses may convince one that things are "really like this." Discourses have an "ontologizing," reality-creating function. Discursive power defines reality, creates truth, as Michel Foucault suggested (Foucault, 1972). On the one hand, discourse may have an oppressive effect by marginalizing groups or individuals. However, on the other hand, discourse may also increase people's freedom and contribute to the goodness of their lives (cf. Gergen 1994).

"Dignity" also forms part of a discourse. In fact, it belongs to two discourses: the discourse on justice and the discourse on human flourishing, which are two dialogical practices deeply rooted in the culture of modernity. Phenomenologically, a reference to dignity sometimes functions as an argument. However, more often such a reference is a cry for justice, an expression of pain. In bioethical debates it is used as a conservative rhetorical strategy while, when used in indictments against social inequality, it stands for change: reject all human trafficking and child labor on grounds of their human dignity! Talk about "dignity" never takes the form of neutral, factual statements such as "2 + 2 = 4" or "it is raining"; it is always embedded in pathos, in powerful emotions of anger, grief, or hope.

However hard it may be to find a sound definition of dignity as a concept, the violation of what it refers to is always accompanied by strong feelings of indignation. This accompanying emotion has important cognitive value: it provides us with knowledge about what is morally at stake (Nussbaum, 2001). Emotions play a visionary role in ethics.

A Performative Speech Act

Whoever speaks of dignity, acts morally. He or she commits a performative speech act. An utterance is performative when an expression's meaning consists in the act executed by it ("I promise you"), while a constative speech act refers to a state of affairs by saying how "it is" (Austin 1962; Searle 1969). A performative speech act, on the other hand, creates the reality it refers to; it has poetic force. People promise, they ask, command, request, invite, warn, greet, obey, or witness. To lament—the violation of human dignity, for example—is also a performative speech act, although it is sometimes hidden among factual observations. A lament refers to a fact but, at the same time, it functions as an appeal to the hearer not to accept that fact.

The rhetoric of human dignity has a strong performative function: it aims at bringing something about. One can distinguish between two types of performative discourses: a discourse on justice and a discourse on flourishing. In modern society, the former dominates the ethics of politics and the latter the ethics pertaining to the care system. The discourse on justice is often ignited by a "negative contrast experience" (Schillebeekcx 1980, 661) of injustice, that is, by a feeling of indignation due to threatened, infringed upon, or violated human dignity. For the cognition of justice, one needs dialogue and rational deliberation. However, a sense of injustice is expressed in a direct and unmediated way in its [justice's] contrary: "What an *in*justice!" Only the experience of injustice shifts the thinking of philosophers in the direction of the formulation of a theory of justice (Ricoeur 1990 31; 1995, 94).

An appeal to "dignity" in discourses of justice may be compared to the sounding of an alarm in a public building or to the "danger" alarm in an old mine: to those who hear the alarm it is not at first clear what wrong. However, it does alert or caution people: "Beware, someone's humanity is in danger!" (Agich 2007, 491). Together with the emotion, however, the far-reaching cognitive claim is made that borders have been trespassed and that dignity has been violated.

Afterward, philosophical theories and religious doctrines often give explicit meaning and expression to this archaic intuition and provide theoretical flesh to the frame of emotion. However, theory always comes later; theory follows life. Human worth, then, say philosophers (such as Immanuel Kant), is a distinguishing characteristic of the human species that deserves categorical respect (Kant 1978, 69). Dignity is awarded ontological status; it becomes rooted in the greater scheme of things. Though dignity can be violated, it can never be lost. In turn, theologians contend that every human being is created in the image of God and, therefore, possesses an inalienable, absolute dignity, rooted in his or her createdness. The emotions and intuitions come first and only then follows their expression in elementary theories of human rights. The elementary emotion in this type of discourse is indignation and the basic attitude it requires is respect.

A Discourse on Justice Versus a Discourse on Flourishing

But what does it mean to treat people according to their human dignity? In justice discourses that underpin human rights theories, human dignity is portrayed as a quality inherent in every single human being. Dignity is a permanent, universal, a priori, and absolute characteristic. It does not matter how young or old, strong or weak, wise or naive someone is. However much people may differ with regard to their dignity, they are all equal.

The specter of who or what belongs to the category of "human being" can be understood in a broad or a narrow way. Do embryos, germ or stem cells, DNA, or body tissue, for example, also belong to the category? Though the latter examples do not constitute human beings in the strict sense, we may treat them *as if* they do. Dignity might, furthermore, be attributed not only to the not-yet-living, but also to the other side of the spectrum, to the no-longer-living when we approach a corpse with reverence and require the respectful honoring of the dead. Though they have passed away as human beings, the dead are treated *as if* they still are living human beings.

However, a second type of dignity discourse may be distinguished. It does not revolve around justice but around flourishing. It focuses not on a shared, general humanity, but on individuality. Terminally ill and suffering children, homeless junkies, alcoholic homeless persons, elderly persons suffering from incontinence or dementia are all examples of people whose dignity is threatened because their individual human flourishing is frustrated. They are suffering because their ability to lead the kind of life they have reason to value is frustrated (Sen 1999).

In the latter discursive context, genuine concern about human happiness and self-actualization forms the leading theme rather than indignation at social injustice. However, indignation does feature, and it is in the emotion of indignation that a strong cognitive claim is put forward: this individual human being should have flourished; this individual life should have been "successful" in its striving after happiness (cf. the teleological structure of Aristotle's [1908, 1097a15–b2] concept of εὐδαιμονία). However, the budding beauty of this individual life has been stunted or has prematurely withered, and that is why someone leading such a life, someone with such a fate, deserves compassion.

In this discourse, dignity is apparently not understood as being an inherent attribute of every human being. Rather it is presented as contingent and transient—one may either gain or lose it. It is particular and comparative as well: one may "own" more or less of it at different times, live with more or less dignity than others. Not the injustice of society, but the finiteness and vulnerability of human nature, is primarily at stake. This discourse is also rooted in emotions that only afterward receive philosophical or religious underpinnings. Though people cannot claim a "right to happiness," they "deserve"—as Amartya Sen defends in his capability approach to ethics—the realization of their capacities that allows them "to lead the kind of life they have reason to value." Whether the claim is based on a human rights ethic (as is the case with Sen), or whether it is rooted in the religious conviction that we are all created in the image of God (as Christians say), it has far-reaching implications: every single human being is born to attain happiness, even if only a few do so in reality. Many lives end tragically, without anyone in particular to blame for it. However, despite this, a stubborn conviction prevails that the good life forms part of human destiny (cf. Aristotle, *Nicomachean Ethics*) at least in the humanistic and Christian traditions. If, due to illness or fate, nature does not live up to expectations of a good life, we should be compassionate and should see to goodness ourselves.

The performative attitude in this type of dignity discourse is one of empathy, compassion, and care—as has been propagated by the ethics of care for decades (Noddings 1984). No one is blamed (though it might be God or nature), but concern is expressed about the suffering of this person in particular: *ecce homo*, behold the human being.

In late modern society, the two discourses referred to above are embedded in different societal contexts. The discourse on justice dominates politics; the discourse on flourishing prevails in the world of care and welfare. The former is publicly oriented, the latter points toward dignity in the private sphere: dignity in public versus dignity at home (Tronto 1993).

Should we accept this dualism between private care and public politics? Do politics not need more compassion and do we not need more justice at home? Martha Nussbaum argues that both discourses are rooted in one and the same foundational moral experience (Nussbaum 2001). According to her, the emotion of compassion represents the common missing link between the discourse on justice and the discourse on flourishing. As a child grows into adulthood, he or she develops a sensibility for the needs and sufferings of others, and this lays the foundation for his or her later sense of justice. The ability to forgive oneself one's own insufficiencies, and to come to terms again with others, prevents children from entrenching themselves in their shame and anger. Mercy teaches them to care well for themselves and be attentive to the claims of others who are just as vulnerable and finite as themselves.

Is mercy perhaps the shared basis of both discourses? Or—as was already mentioned with reference to Paul Ricoeur—is the feeling of injustice irreducible and original, and will both the discourses need a complementary idiom, irrespective of their cultural or historical social setting? A detailed discussion of the latter question is impossible here.

The Objectivity of Dignity-to-Be-Acknowledged

Thus far one may conclude that the meaning of dignity is implicit in its use. An abstract definition of dignity, isolated from its social practices, does not take one any further. The negative contrasting experience of injustice and the empathic concern with a tragic life express the value attributed to human lives.

By situating dignity firmly within social practices, we take up a specific position in the ontological debate on whether human dignity is an objective characteristic or whether it only exists "in the eye of the beholder." Dignity, as I will argue below, is a practice of or exercise in recognition. Therefore, dignity is to be considered an objective, personal "characteristic" and, at the same time, a subjective "projection." Dignity is a relational good that is conceivable only within the interconnectedness of human relationships. It is inconceivable within a framework of a dualistic subject-object relations.

Accordingly, the objectivity of dignity should be defended, albeit in a well-defined and restricted sense. Although I argue for the epistemic relationality of dignity (there is no knowledge of dignity apart from human relationships), I at the same time defend its ontological objectivity (dignity exists, even if not recognized or acknowledged by an observer); it is objectively "there." In both types of dignity discourse, the claim is justified that the dignity-to-be-acknowledged is an objective "given." Even though it may be denied, negated, or violated, the dignity-to-be-acknowledged belongs to the ontological fabric of human nature. Dignity-to-be-acknowledged is part of being human as are the two legs we walk on. This does not mean that those who are missing one or even both legs have lost their humanity. They are still considered members of the species of bipods. The latter is true in the case of legs and one should extend the analogy: dignity can be violated; however, as a to-be-acknowledged-dignity it can never be forfeited. In essence, dignity belongs to the definition of being human.

What may the foundation of the latter claim be? The theoretical underpinning (or perhaps I should say, the rationalization afterwards) for the objectivity of dignity may differ. Three traditions may generally be distinguished in modern culture regarding this. (1) The Stoa connected dignity with reason, with the human capacity that distinguishes humans from (other) animals. In arguing thus, the Stoa went beyond Aristotle, to whom the thought of a general human dignity, an intrinsic good shared by all humans, was foreign. However, to the Stoa, dignity was also not a given but an *ideal*: only after lifelong spiritual training and practice may someone, regardless of his or her background or social class, control his or her passions and desires and subjugate them to reason. (2) The Christian tradition follows the Stoa, but goes a step further: because humans are created in the image and after the likeness of God (Gen 1:26–27), dignity intrinsically belongs to being human. But what does that mean? Depending on how the analogy between God and humanity was conceived, different *imago Dei* doctrines have been developed. Do human beings look like God physically, do they take after God with regard to their relationality, their mastery over nature, their striving for the good, or, as the Stoics already suggested, with regard to their rationality? However understood, in accordance with the broad Christian tradition, every human born of humans should at the same time be considered as having originated in God, and thereby sharing in some of God's holiness. (3) Finally, Immanuel Kant strips dignity of its theological roots and relates it to human autonomy—understood as the human freedom to impose on oneself a universal moral law by the use of one's practical reason. In principle, every single human being with well-developed rational abilities is autonomous, though not everyone is consciously using these rational abilities. To Kant, reason is not a psychological characteristic, but a moral quality: the ability to bind one's will freely according to one's own rationality (Kant 1978).

For the moment, what unites these views is more important than what distinguishes between them: in their objectivism they share an antirelativistic outlook. Dignity cannot be jeopardized, for instance, by saying that it represents a typical Western value that is not shared by other cultures. This objectivity provides a strong foundation to the human rights discourse. The claim is supported by ordinary language: the common way of saying that "dignity has been violated" presupposes that, in order to be violated, dignity has to exist and be present somehow and somewhere.

Once dignity is only considered as a subjective projection, its moral validity is solely relative to its observer. Dignity is then also not acknowledged, but only attributed. When dignity equals rationality, for example, then the moment patients suffering from Alzheimer's disease lose their cognitive abilities, they will also lose their dignity. One "has" dignity only as long as one's life is valued by others or by oneself. There is no dignity-to-be-acknowledged left when there is no longer any acknowledgement of dignity.

The subjective perspective occupies a strong position because it draws on the shortcomings of the objectivistic approach. Subjective recognition is per definition implied in the concept of dignity. For, once we attribute dignity to others, we cannot treat them in an indifferent or hostile manner without being inconsistent. We are wrapped up in a performative contradiction; we trespass the rules of the dignity discourse, to which the act of valuation and respect intrinsically belongs.

So, is dignity an objective characteristic or a subjective projection? I want to argue that it is both at the same time, because dignity can only be correctly understood as a relational good, a value that is realized in concrete practices of recognition. The subject of dignity is neither the isolated individual who "owns," "shows," or "acknowledges" dignity as a characteristic, nor the individual from whom it is "taken away," whose dignity is "violated." The dynamics between the three ontological elements of the concept of dignity exist concurrently and are interwoven: the human being who reveals his or her dignity (one: the subject) in the subjective act of recognition (two: the relationship) of another's objective dignity-to-be-acknowledged (three: the subject). Whoever talks about dignity should change his or her perspective at least three times.

Is human dignity an objectively given characteristic? The objectivity of dignity is only defendable within a relational context; it becomes visible and reveals its moral truth in social practices of recognition. Dignity exists solely as dignity-to-be-acknowledged and it reveals itself *sub contrario* when it is infringed upon by violence, humiliation, neglect, indifference. Per definition, human dignity is dignity contested.

Dimensions of Dignity: A Layered Portrait

Even more important than the ontological and epistemological status of the concept of dignity is its ethical content. The negative contrast experience caused by inflicted injustice and the concern with a tragic individual life may be the cause of indignation ("It's a shame!") and mercy ("*Ecce homo!*"). But do indignation and mercy also offer sufficient moral reasons for it? As a justification, these emotions alone do not offer enough. Why, then, do we strive for human dignity? To answer this question we shall have to construct a good story.

In order to reconstruct the story, one needs a long breath and a broad vision. Human dignity is a complex concept with a long history. The latter includes not only the Stoa, but also early Christianity. Not only the Renaissance and Enlightenment, but also the Reformation and nineteenth-century Roman Catholicism contributed to the richness and depth of this narrative (van der Ven 2004). Only by remaining cognizant of this complex history does one approach discerning the layered connotations of the concept of human dignity. One might compare the long narrative to an old painting. Human dignity is like a canvas on which an artist had applied layer after layer of materials (first the undercoat or primer, followed a second layer, the so-called underpainting, and then by successive layers of paint to produce the pictorial presentation). Over centuries, layers of meaning of dignity were added and merged to form one complex image. The image as a whole has a normative impact on any attentive and benevolent observer. Having intensely observed and absorbed the image, one's view of oneself and of others cannot be left unchanged. From now on, the dignity narrative will orient one's attitudes in life. However, the painting itself will remain defenseless and powerless vis à vis the passersby, who do not notice or heed its message and who remain indifferent to the picture.

Menschenwürde

The primer in the human dignity painting consists of the general dignity shared by every single human being. Whether we, with the Stoa, connect dignity theoretically to reason (Wildfeuer 2002, 40) or, with Christian faith, to the image of God, or, with Kant, to autonomy, the principle of equality expressed in it has a tremendous democratizing and anti-discriminating effect. To this first layer of meaning we owe the human rights tradition. Human dignity is not dependent on power, wealth, age, or merit, but is based on the simple fact that one is born human. Solely for that reason do we owe respect to others. This "primer" in dignity—I call it (with Nordenfelt 2009) *Menschenwürde*, because it is strongly rooted in European history and the German philosophical Enlightenment—is a powerful weapon to be used against discrimination of any kind. It can be used it in fighting, for example, racism, sexism, and ageism.

Merit

Another layer of meaning on the dignity portrait can be distinguished, namely the underpainting, which provides the first background contours, giving the picture a horizon. Dignity is not based solely on general human characteristics. It is also connected to the special social positions people occupy within a given society, and the reputation they derive from these positions. One might call this *social* dignity—as opposed to general *Menschenwürde*. I suspect social dignity to be a quasi-universal anthropological constant and not an exclusive or specific Western concept. In this meaning of the word dignity, people are not equal, but they are perceived to differ from one another. Someone deserves and acquires *dignitas*—a term coined by Cicero in his *De inventione* (2.166)—because of his or her social merit, and the latter may differ according to the type of society a person belongs to. In a hierarchical society, social dignity is linked to members' rank, standing, or class. One's value in the eyes of others depends on the status and position one occupies. In modern democracies, social dignity has been personalized and individualized. Status does not, first of all, depend on one's social position (though it still functions as a source of prestige), but on one's personal merit and on what one rightfully deserves. Social positions are no longer determined by background or birth, but by individual achievements (Botton 2004). According to the meritocratic ideal, one's talent and just deserts are the conditions for success. In order to gain prestige, one has to "make" it. While, in earlier times, having (ownership) and being (background) may have counted as the bases of status, doing is what counts now.

Identity

However, the dignity portrait is still missing an essential layer: the pictorial representation. There is a primer, there is a background and a horizon, but the personal touch is still lacking. Besides a general human dignity and a specific social *dignitas*, a personal dignity has to be distinguished. Next to one's *Menschenwürde*, one's ranking on the scale of social success, one's personal value, is an essential ingredient of one's dignity. Friends, partners, relatives are all cherished, not primarily because of what they do, have, and are capable of, but because of the unique persons they *are*. We value their incomparable character, personality, and life stories that made them who they are now. "That's the way I am…." "Exactly—and that's why I love you." When people are, by contrast, forced by their social environment to be different from whom they (in the deepest sense of the word) want to be, they experience this as a violation of their personal dignity. "You have to respect me for who I am" means as much as: "you have to acknowledge my uniqueness."

Personal dignity is based on someone's personal identity. During the course of one's life, the distinctiveness of one's personality crystallizes in one's unique life story. If we value an older man or women because of the person they have become, we not only admire what they did in their lives, but also what they have experienced, and what they have personally done with those experiences. This we may refer to as their character.

Character is not only a psychological category; it is also an ethical category (Kupperman 1995). Character belongs to the grandeur of being human: not to be held captive by one's genetic or social nature, but to distinguish oneself from it. One's identity—as Paul Ricoeur points out—not only includes substantial sameness (*idem*-identity), but also biographical consistency (*ipse*-identity; Ricoeur 1990). One's self and one's natural make-up (one's natural composition) are not the same thing. Respect for personal dignity is the recognition of the inner freedom with which one commits oneself, accepts responsibilities, and keeps promises. Most people's freedom to maneuver, to do, or to act is marginal. However, even in those who have almost completely lost all cognitive control over their lives (e.g., older persons living with dementia), an inner freedom must be recognized. Theologically, one may speak here of the ineffable mystery of humanness. Being created in the image of God does not mean that humanity shares a set of positive qualities with its creator, but that it shares in his ineffable nature. An important contribution of theology to the hermeneutics of human dignity lies in the development of an "apophatic anthropology" (Woodhead 2006).

Splendor

Is the narrative portrayed in the painting now complete? One might say so, but one may also add a fourth, final layer to the dignity canvas: the varnish that gives the image its brightness and brilliance. When speaking about dignity, the jargon of ethics is not enough; the language of aesthetics is needed to express the glory of humanness. When speaking about the splendid presence of dignitaries, the medieval philosopher Boethius (*Consolation of Philosophy* 3.4), calls to mind "the beauty of dignity." In contemporary philosophy of the art of living—drawing on the ancient Greek tradition of καλὸς κἀγαθός (Jaeger 1945, 13) —this aesthetic dignity is democratized: every single human being is considered capable of becoming a beautiful person, creating himself or herself into a work of art to be enjoyed (Nehemias 1998). Within the Jewish and Christian traditions, however, one already finds a longstanding tradition of the intertwining of ethics and aesthetics. "For thou hast made him a little lower than the angels, and hast crowned him with glory and honor," declares Ps 8:5. The sacredness of human beings is not recognized in their rationality, but in their beauty.

Mutual Vulnerability (The Good Samaritan)

For the recognition of the fundamental relationality of dignity, an understanding of the biblical narrative of the Good Samaritan is indispensable. The story and its reception in the history of care clearly seems at odds with an individualistic concept of dignity, which reduces dignity to a set of personal, positive characteristics, as is found from the Stoics via Immanuel Kant (1978) to Jürgen Habermas (1987) with reference to human reason, free will, and the human capability to communicate. The understanding behind the latter view is that only those with these characteristics possess human dignity and those who do not (e.g., the mentally challenged or demented elderly persons) lose their entitlement to recognition. Dignity is only reserved for those complying with the standards of "anthropological correctness."

In contrast to the above, the Good Samaritan invites us to an inverse perspective. Dignity is revealed in the relational context of human suffering and care. Paul Valadier expresses this dignity as follows:

> The human being is not venerable because of his [sic] special qualities, his noble and elevated characteristic, but, at the contrary, when losing the qualities of that elevated status. When he, having lost human shape, completely is surrendered to the care of his brothers and sisters in being human. (Valadier 2003)

The traveler in the story is not assisted because he is supposed to be a reasonable, free, communicative person, but because, wounded and moaning, he silently calls out for help. He lost his capabilities and is dependent on the care of others to restore them. He "owns" his dignity-to-be-acknowledged precisely by lying vulnerably by the side of the road.

The Samaritan affirms this dignity by spontaneously responding to the victim's call. The help he provides is an enactment of the recognition of the wounded man's dignity. At the same time, however, the victim's silent call for recognition occasions him to express his own inner, ineffable freedom-to-care. The Samaritan cares for the other, not because of his own altruistic or heroic moral characteristics, but because, taken up in the flow of the relationship of care, he cannot do otherwise. He could, of course, have done otherwise, "passing by on the other side" as the Levite and the priests did (Luke 10:31–32), but his freely offered compassion is born of an inner ethical necessity. He simply was not capable of not coming to the victim's rescue. The Samaritan's dignity consists in his spontaneous embodiment of the ethical ideal of caring (Noddings 1984).

A peculiar commonality arises between these two people in their asymmetrical relationship of power and dependency. In such a situation of unexpected intimacy, the awareness arises, as Ricoeur argues, that the other is as myself and I am as the other in the fragility we share (Ricoeur 1990). Mutual respect for humanity flows from the "indignity" that the Samaritan and the wounded have in common: their need and their being in need. The difference between their deprivations seems enormous, but in fact it only differs in degree, for their respective situations might quite easily change places. The condition of "woundability" of the one (the exposure to suffering), has turned into concrete woundedness to the other. The awareness that we are in need of each other, enduring the human condition "on all levels of existence, in particular in moments of grief, loneliness, abandonment, and fear for suffering and death," as Valadier writes, invites us to confirm one another's humanness in mutual compassion. Dignity does not refer to an individual quality, but to a negative "possession" that is only "possessed" in the desire for recognition and care by others. In the act of compassion, dignity is mutually affirmed in recognizing each other as fragile humans-in-need.

With the help of Ricoeur's phenomenological approach, one may try philosophically to come to terms with the odd reciprocity between the Samaritan and the victim, in which they mutually offer each other their dignity. In his *Oneself as Another* (*Soi-même comme un autre*) Ricoeur ponders the meaning of mutual, disinterested compassion in this kind of relationship, that is, when it is not affirmed by the equality of a relationship between friends. Between friends compassion means a mutual give and take, a linear reciprocity. One's self-esteem is spontaneously confirmed by the other. Friends know that no one can flourish on his or her own—happy people need friends, as Aristotle wrote. As "other selves," friends mutually bring out the best in themselves.

But what happens if when equilibrium between give and take is disturbed? Then only the asymmetry of a one-sided appeal for compassion remains. However, even in situations such as in the story of the Good

Samaritan, Ricoeur argues, a peculiar kind of ethical reciprocity arises. The other's "initiative" (the victim at the side of the road in the parable) makes an appeal to the Samaritan's goodness, liberating in the latter a hidden capacity to give, out of esteem (*égard*) for the other. The wounded man's powerless request for recognition demands a free offer of recognition by the Samaritan. The Samaritan subsequently does not care because of some moral duty or conventional norm; he acts out of spontaneous benevolence, closely related to his self-esteem and his own endeavors toward living a good life. He esteems himself as the one who maintains the ethical ideal of caring (Noddings 1984, 107). Although the victim could just as well have been "helped" by someone who acted due to social pressure or moral heroism, the essence of the affirmation of both the victim's dignity and the dignity of the Samaritan consists in the fact that in their relationship they mutually recognize their ineffable, inner freedom to care: the one to be expressed, the other to be restored.

The biblical narrative of the Good Samaritan has served as paradigm for practices of care throughout the centuries and still portrays the reciprocal dynamics of the care relationship. Even though it apparently depicts a one-sided act of mercy—confirming the asymmetrical relationship of one who cares and the one cared for—the iconography of the parable shows how the restoration and affirmation of human dignity is a mutual affair.

Representations of the story of the Good Samaritan are known to exist from the fourth century onward (for the following, cf. Bühren 1998). At that time, however, an allegorical interpretation, in which the Samaritan served as a model for Christ, was dominant and would remain so for centuries. The man is Adam; Jerusalem is paradise; Jericho is the world; the robbers are humanity's evil traits; the priest represents the Law and the Levite the prophets; the Samaritan is Christ; and the inn is the church.

From the Renaissance onward, however, more attention was paid to the story itself. The human drama in the scene was magnified. The corporeality, the drama, and the subjectivity of actors were allowed to speak their own language. The function of art changed as well as it was no longer understood as reflecting the reality of heaven, but as moving the heart of the observer; it aimed to entice him or her to have compassion.

A mature example of this emotional drama can be found in the painting of Giordano Luca Giordano (*The Good Samaritan*, 1685, Musée des Beaux-Arts, Rouen, France; images on the internet available). It emphasizes the first, asymmetrical moment in this relationship of care. Oil and wine become secondary to the distraught expression on the face of

Samaritan as he looks down at the naked, pale body of the victim that dominates the painting, covering, in full light, the whole width of the canvas. Not the face—invisible, tilted all the way back—but the naked, vulnerable torso is turned toward the viewer. Human dignity seems to linger only one-sidedly in the Samaritan's apparent dismay: Does a heart still beat in that chest, or am I too late to help?

The depiction of the story by Renaissance artist Jacopo Bassano (*The Good Samaritan*, ca. 1562–63, The National Gallery, London; images on the internet available) does not focus on the asymmetrical beginnings of the drama of dignity, but on its reciprocity. Here, however, the scene is about restoring the victim's autonomy. The Samaritan places himself under the latter's body and tries to raise him up. His bending down in compassion is apparently not an end in itself either; it is not a servile self-debasement, but is aimed at "resurrection." Is not the Greek word for human being, ανθρωπος, derived from ανα-τρεπειν, to "lift something up," "to raise high"? The human being is the creature meant to move about with "aufrechten Gang" (Immanuel Kant), to live upright in a *status erectus* (Huizing 2000, 214).

The best known depiction of the Good Samaritan is probably the nineteenth-century painting by Vincent van Gogh (*The Good Samaritan [after Delacroix]*, 1890, Kröller-Müller Museum, Otterlo, the Netherland; images on the Internet available). Van Gogh's representation is classical in the sense that here too it shows the Levite and the priest moving away. The opened and empty trunk points to the robbery that has taken place. However, the representation is special, because the hierarchy in the relationship of caregiver and victim is turned upside down. The Samaritan is just a common man with his sleeves rolled up and plain slippers on his feet. His horse is a mule and far from a regally harnessed steed. This is more a depiction of popular neighborliness, a horizontal solidarity of one person with another, rather than of an aristocratic ethic of beneficence. Even more than in the case of Bassano's painting, the asymmetry of assistance is turned around: those in high places and the humble trade places. As the Samaritan tries to help the victim onto the horse, the former, the one having pity, is located underneath the victim, and he clearly strains under the latter's physical weight. In fact, the image teems with exertion. The emphasis is on the enormous strain that the Samaritan is under to lift the wounded man onto the mule. The victim is the one who should sit upright again. While the victim clumsily holds on to the Samaritan, his stocky and awkwardly-positioned half-naked body is no picture of beauty or vulnerability, but merely of dependence. Apparently van Gogh sees an exalted person in the humbled one by alluding to Jesus' entry into Jerusalem.

In an asymmetrical power relationship an ethical equality is revealed. It does not happen naturally as in the give-and-take of friendship, but via a detour of inequality. "It compensates the initial asymmetry, which arises from the primacy of the other in the initial situation, by the inversed movement of recognition" (Ricoeur 1990, 222). It seems as if the victim can do nothing more than receive, whereas only the helper may take the initiative to act. Apparently this is true as the other is suffering not only because he or she experiences pain, but also because his or her capacity to act is destroyed. The victim has literally become a "patient," enduring the hardships of life. But, whoever engages others in genuine sympathy, "walking the extra second mile with them," *will receive something* in return, even though the gift might express itself only in some slender hands that ask to be held and cherished.

Sometimes the shock of sudden dependence on assistance is needed to reawaken the consciousness that one is oneself an "other" in need of help amidst many others, and this creates equality in ethical relationships: one moment one may be the deprived victim by the side of the road, and the next moment, the benefactor.

Caring for others in the awareness of sharing the human condition affirms one's self-esteem: it acknowledges one's inner freedom to care, the freedom to stay with and to help others or to abandon them, to follow the flow of spontaneous benevolence or to resist it. As Ricoeur writes, "This exchange authorizes to say that I cannot estimate myself without estimating the other *as* myself." Here "as myself" means: you also are someone with an inner freedom to care, longing for and striving as I toward a good life for and with others. "It results in the fundamental equivalence of the esteem of *the other as a oneself* and the esteem of *myself as another*" (Ricoeur 1990, 226; emphasis original). In the view of Ricoeur, equality means a resemblance, not identity, between us: we are *as* another, not: we are the other. The irreplaceability and uniqueness of the inner freedom to care for every single human being remains basic for mutual respect. When a person spontaneously cares for another, he or she esteems the other's personal dignity and, at the same time, expresses his or her own.

Ricoeur tries to capture in a phenomenological theory what the parable of the Good Samaritan tells in a story. However, though the relational dynamics of dignity is preeminently expressed in the biblical narrative, the classic tragedy reveals a comparable dialectic of suffering and care as well.

Paul Valadier refers to Sophocles, who makes Oedipus say: "Only when I am nothing, I become human" (Valadier 2003). Oedipus murdered his father, committed adultery with his mother—he lost his social *dignitas*, as well as his moral integrity. He is a hostage of his own guilt, and because he is unable to ever again look himself in the eye, he stabs his own eyes out. Oedipus is a human being stripped of social and personal dignity. But in this indignity he expresses his desire for recognition and care. As a main character in a tragedy, he appeals to the compassion of the spectator, and probably not in vain: sharing the same human condition, the spectator knows that he or she may be hit by a similarly tragic fate.

The characters in the classic tragedy are struck by adversity, but still keep intact a fundamental human dignity. Dignity and need are interwoven in a complex manner. In order to feel compassion and mercy, one has to become convinced that others may be subject to serious adversity without being responsible for it. Contrary to the Stoics, who argued that someone who does not conquer hardship rationally loses his or her dignity, Sophocles and other classical authors of tragedies are convinced that the fundamental dignity of a human being remains intact even when the world shows its most cruel side. In the tragedy, the appeal to people's agency is never abandoned—even when they are completely victimized and powerless. Humanness does not disappear, and the ability to do good remains even when everything else is destroyed (Nussbaum 1986).

Classical tragedies as well as biblical epics show that one split second often separates being all from being nothing. In one moment, one may be an in-control traveler, and in the next, one may lie close to death by the side of the road. The king's son may suddenly turn and become his murderer. A shared acknowledgement of the vulnerability of being human and of the dependency on others' care may invite us to a mutual recognition of possible goodness amidst suffering. If human dignity had to be defined instead of narrated, this formula would be a suitable candidate.

REFERENCES

Agich, George J. 2007. Reflections on the Function of Dignity in the Context of Caring for Old People. *J Med Philos* 32:483–94.

Aristotle. *Nichomachean Ethics*. 1908. Translated by W. D. Ross. Oxford: Clarendon.

Austin, John L. 1962. *How to Do Things with Words*. Cambridge, Mass.: Harvard University Press.

Bühren, Ralf van. 1998. *Die Werke der Barmherzigkeit in der Kunst des 12.–18. Jahrhunderts: Zum Wandel eines Bildmotivs vor dem Hintergrund neuzeitlicher Rhetorikrezeption.* Hildesheim: Georg Olms.
Botton, Alain de. 2004. *Status Anxiety.* New York: Pantheon.
Foucault, Michel. 1972. *The Archaeology of Knowledge and the Discourse on Language.* New York: Pantheon.
Gergen, Kenneth J. 1994. *Realities and Relationships: Soundings in Social Construction.* Cambridge, Mass.: Harvard University Press.
Habermas, Jürgen. 1987. *The Theory of Communicative Action.* Translated by Thomas McCarthy. Cambridge: Polity.
Huizing, Klaas. 2000. *Der erlesene Mensch: Eine literarische Anthropologie.* Freiburg: Kreuz.
Jaeger, Werner. 1945. *Paideia: The Ideals of Greek Culture.* Translated by Gilbert Highet. New York: Oxford University Press.
Kant, Immanuel. *Grundlegung zur Metaphysik der Sitten.* 1978. Frankfurt: Suhrkamp. First published 1785.
Kupperman, Joel. 1995. *Character.* Oxford: Oxford University Press.
Løgstrup, Knud Ejler. 1997. *The Ethical Demand.* Notre Dame, Ind.: University of Notre Dame Press.
Nehemias, Alexander. 1998. *The Art of Living: Socratic Reflections from Plato to Foucault.* Berkeley: University of California Press.
Noddings, Nel. 1984. *Caring: A Feminine Approach to Ethics and Moral Education.* Berkeley: University of California Press.
Nordenfelt, Lennart, ed. 2009. *Dignity in Care for Older People.* Oxford: Wiley-Blackwell.
Nussbaum, Martha C. 1986. *The Fragility of Goodness: Luck and Ethics in Greek Tragedy and Philosophy.* Cambridge: Cambridge University Press.
Nussbaum, Martha C. 2001. *Upheavals of Thought: The Intelligence of Emotions.* Cambridge: Cambridge University Press.
Ricoeur, Paul. 1990. *Soi-même comme un autre.* Paris: Seuil.
Ricoeur, Paul. 1995. *Le Juste.* Paris: Éditions Esprit.
Schillebeeckx, Edward, O.P. 1980. *Jesus: An Experiment in Christology.* New York: Herder & Herder.
Searle, John. 1969. *Speech Acts.* Cambridge: Cambridge University Press.
Sen, Amartya. 1999. *Development as Freedom.* New York: Anchor House.
Tronto, Joan C. 1993. *Moral Boundaries: A Political Argument for an Ethic of Care.* New York: Routledge.
Valadier, Paul. 2003. The Person Who Lacks Dignity. *Concilium* 2:49–56.

Ven, Johannes van der. 2004. *Is There a God of Human Right? The Complex Relationship between Human Rights and Religion: A South African Case*. Leiden: Brill.

Wildfeuer, Armin G. 2002. Menschenwürde—Leerfomel oder unverzichtbare Gedanke? Pages 19–116 in *Person—Menschenwürde—Menschenrechte im Disput*. Edited by M. Nicht and A. G. Wildfeuer. Münster: LIT.

Wittgenstein, Ludwig. 1953. *Philosophical Investigations*. Oxford: Blackwell.

Woodhead, Linda. 2006. Apophatic Anthropology. Pages 233–46 in *God and Human Dignity*. Edited by Linda Woodhead and Kendall Soulen. Grand Rapids: Eerdmans.

A Response to Frits de Lange's "The Hermeneutics of Dignity"

†Gerrit Brand

Dear Frits,

By pure coincidence I am reading your reflections on "the hermeneutics of dignity" at a time when I am also teaching an undergraduate course on human dignity with my colleagues Julie Claassens and Jeremy Punt. This course presented a challenge to us because it is officially called "Dogmatic Themes." In other words, we were expected to approach the concept of dignity as a doctrinal or systematic theological issue. Jeremy and Julie did so as biblical scholars and I as a systematic theologian.

The "danger," as we saw it, was that we could end up teaching a course on ethical rather than dogmatic themes. Of course, as soon as one puts it like that, one realizes that the distinction is problematic. Can there ever be an ethic without doctrinal assumptions? Is not all systematic theology ultimately about how to live a good life? Is that not why Calvin always asked of every doctrine what its "use" was—thereby suggesting that theological teachings are of no use unless they have ... well, some use (see Ganoczy 1983)? Particularly here at Stellenbosch University, the approach of my colleagues who teach Christian ethics has consistently been that of a "thick" ethical reflection that derives its very meaning and appeal from its thorough embeddedness in a rich theological framework and tradition (see, e.g., Koopman 2008). In fact, I am not sure whether the notion of a "thin" ethic (which, I assume, would have to hang in thin air) is even coherent, let alone desirable.

Nevertheless, some sort of distinction between dogmatics and ethics must be possible. Even talking about their inseparability already suggests this, for two things cannot be inseparable unless they are distinct. Here, Ludwig Wittgenstein—or at least Wittgenstein as some commentators understand him—has always been a great help to me. If faith is a "form of life" in which the meaning of human experiences and the demands of life are disclosed by means of a "language game" drawing on the models, metaphors, and narratives of a tradition (and if that language game can only be engaged in for as long as one assumes the veracity of certain truth claims—see Wittgenstein 1966, 53–72; Brümmer 2010, 3), then both the distinction between and the inseparability of doctrine and morality, or dogmatics and ethics, become clear. Therefore, your opening thoughts on rhetoric, speech acts, and discourses as they relate to the concept of human dignity immediately appealed to me.

However, it is precisely at this point that I also realized how much of a systematic theologian, rather than an ethicist, I am. Systematic theology as I understand it must always be aimed at truth—at "what is the case." Not only that, of course, but certainly that as well. A purely descriptivist theology in the sense of an account and analysis of what has been and is being said about faith—even if the analysis involves the attitudes or sensibilities associated with various religious ideas (see, e.g., Vedder 2006)—is not sufficient (Brand 2011, 24–26). (And as far as so-called nonrealism or antirealism in theology is concerned, I have never been able to see how it could avoid self-referential incoherence.) As a Wittgensteinian of sorts, then, my engagement with the form of life of faith is always also focused on the tacit presuppositions of this form of life (Brümmer 2010, 3)—the truth claims assented to, whether explicitly or implicitly, consciously or unconsciously, by those who participate in this form of life.

So, when the topic of human dignity comes up, at least one of the questions I automatically ask is: what are the truth claims presupposed in the language game (or in your terms: the rhetoric, speech acts, and discourses) of human dignity? In asking this question I am by no means suggesting that there are certain facts about *homo sapiens* that we may discover by simply observing specimens of the species and from which we can then draw conclusions about what ought to be valued and how life ought to be lived. Like you (if I understand you correctly), I want to start from the language game of ascribing and appealing to human dignity. My interest in the question of truth is not speculative, but hermeneutical. The truth claims implicit in a way of speaking and acting cannot be divorced from that speaking and acting. It is part of the *meaning* of that speaking and acting.

In a paradoxical way, then, the systematic theologian, in zooming in on the truth question, is trying to make sense of the practice, whereas, in zooming in on the question of what the practices ought to be, the ethicist is really clarifying the meaning of the assumed truth claims. To ask whether claims about the inherent dignity of human beings can be shown to be true or false in isolation from the discursive practice constituted by the truth claims, is to ask an unanswerable question. The question should rather be whether it makes sense, whether it is wise or advisable, whether there are good reasons, to *assume* that these claims are true.

In this regard, your comments about the possibility of acting or speaking "as if" (12) are insightful. On occasion, I have also defined faith as "living as if," and qualified it by expanding the definition to "*trying to* live as if," and even "*being moved or inspired to* try to live as if" (Brand 2005, 2007). However, in using such language I would not want to discard the notion of objective truth—not objective in the sense of evident to everyone or what can be (empirically) proved, but objective in the sense of true whether recognized as such or not. For me, the "as if" is intended to recognize that people can live—and in fact do live—on the basis of assumptions that they may not feel quite sure of, or even assumptions that they hope may perhaps be true. This was the great insight of Pascal (1671, 20 [VII]) for which he is so often derided. To live "as if" is not to pretend, but to stake your life on the belief, or the suspicion, or the hope, that something is in fact the case.

This is not something that only some people (such as so-called "religious" people) do. It is an inescapable aspect of the human condition. It is part of our inherent vulnerability and dependence as human beings—vulnerability, because we may be confronted with experiences of darkness, evil, and suffering of which we can no longer make sense in terms of the rhetoric, speech acts, and discourses (the language games) available to us, so that our "gamble" (especially when the stakes are high) may leave us destitute; and dependence, because we are not free to live on the basis of just any assumptions we choose, but depend (as you so poignantly illustrate with reference to people who have grown up without love) on experiences, communities, concepts, and traditions that are not of our own making. I completely agree with you that our dignity cannot be derived from our autonomy, if by autonomy we mean being in control of our lives. Autonomy is a good, something we may legitimately strive for (especially for others, or for one another), but it is not the basis of our dignity as human beings.

For me, one implication of the doctrine of the incarnation is that the image of God is also reflected in our vulnerability and dependence, since

God willingly took on our dependent and vulnerable humanity, thereby revealing a deep mystery about the being of God (see Labooy 2002, 303–5). This should be read as confirming the doctrine of creation, according to which, in the eyes of the Creator, creation is "good," and men and women are "very good" (Gen 1:4, 10, 12, 18, 21, 25, 31). Again, however, everything that follows from this collapses as soon as we try to escape from claiming, or suspecting, or hoping, that God *in fact* took on a human nature; that the divine being is in itself *in fact* not different from the God revealed in the Crucified One, that God is *in fact* the Creator, and that the world is *in fact* pleasing to God's eyes.

That we cannot somehow prove the veracity of such claims does not mean that they are not truth claims. In an earlier conversation you once mentioned Rorty in this connection:

> According to Richard Rorty ... the discourse of dignity, is not grounded in rationality but in emotions. Rationally [it is] not defendable. There is no evidence for their ontological reality.... There is no need for that either, Rorty says. In the end, moral convictions are not determined by rational theory, but by the sympathy with which one identifies with others. (De Lange 2010, 2)

It seems to me that Rorty—for example, throughout his *Philosophy and the Mirror of Nature* (1979)—fails to distinguish between truth and provability. Ironically, this makes Rorty an empiricist: something is true if it can be shown to be true (a classic case of begging the question). What reason could we have for believing that whatever is true must also be provable? Surely there are states of affairs that we cannot prove? And surely it is impossible to avoid making some assumptions about what some of those states of affairs may be while realizing how vulnerable those assumptions make us?

What am I getting at? I am getting to what seems to me one of your key questions: is there a sense in which dignity may be "objective" (14)? Is there a way to avoid the conclusion that ascriptions of dignity, being linguistic constructions, are purely subjective? From what I have said thus far, you will have gathered that my answer to this question is yes. At least, if we cannot answer affirmatively to your question, then we may as well leave behind all talk of human dignity. If talk about dignity is nothing but an expression of emotions or sensibilities, it follows that any concern for the recognition and defense of human dignity is merely a personal preference, similar to my preference for red wine or steak, something about which one cannot be right or wrong.

To this one may, perhaps, reply that people's preference for dignity talk is generally incomparably stronger than their preference for red wine or steak. This, however, will not do, because if the intensity of the preference is what matters, then an addiction to drugs, gambling, or violence would have to be considered as being at one and the same level as a concern for human dignity.

If we say (as you indeed do at one point) that human dignity "must" be upheld, we are assuming that this "must" applies to all people, whether it corresponds to their preferences or not. The suggestion is that it would be *true* that people ought to do so even if nobody did so or even if nobody accepted that they ought to do so. What could this possibly mean?

Let me get two red herrings out of the way. First, the fact that the word dignity "[derives its] meaning from the social context and dialogical practices in which [it is] used" (9), and that its meaning is therefore constructed, does not warrant the conclusion that "when we 'read' in humans an inalienable dignity, we do not discover some objective essence" (9). It may be true that we have not discovered such an essence (if "essence" is the right word in this regard), or that, though we may think we have discovered it, we are in fact mistaken, but if this were true it would not be because the word dignity is part of human language and has a history. After all, the word "gene" is also a word produced by people, a word with a history, a word that only came into existence fairly recently, and so on. Does it follow from this that genes have not been discovered, that they do not exist?

Second, the fact that utterances about dignity can be accurately described as "performative" (10) does not distinguish them all that clearly from other utterances. Speech act theory holds that *all* language shares with performative language the characteristic that when we speak we are "doing things with words" (Austin 1962), that the meaning of a sentence is its use. And one of the things we can do with words, one of the speech acts humans perform, is to make assertions.

Added to this is the fact (not sufficiently recognized by Austin and Searle [1969], to whom you refer) that speech acts never have a single function (10). Rather, any speech act has a multiple "illocutionary load" (Brümmer 2006, 105–42). Thus, the fact that a speech act involving the concept of dignity may be expressive in nature—a precondition for any performative utterance that "creates the reality it refers to" (10)—and perhaps in some cases even *primarily* expressive does not imply that such a speech act must lack a constative load (a truth value). One speech act may well express an emotion (which may help create a reality) *and* make a truth claim at the same time. The act of saying "I love you" is certainly both expressive and performative, but only if it is (in a complex manner) also true!

So, back to your question: in what sense can talk about dignity be more than subjective? (In my terms: how could ascriptions of dignity, or claims about our duties with regard to dignity, be thought of as true?) The centerpiece of your answer is that dignity should be thought of in relational terms (16). I find this answer on the whole compelling. It reminds me of certain reflections of Marcel Sarot's on models of the good life. The latter considers "objective" and "subjective" accounts of the good life and, although he recognizes important insights in both, concludes that "intersubjective" accounts succeed better in accounting for those insights while putting them in a more helpful perspective (Sarot 1999).

This also reminds me of perhaps the most widely known of all African proverbs. In the Sotho languages it is *Motho ke motho ka batho*, but equivalents exist in many other African languages. The proverb literally means that a human is a human through humans. In other contexts the word *ka*, which I translate as "through," is used in instrumental terms: one chops wood with (*ka*) an axe; you write with (*ka*) a pen; et cetera. In the concept of *botho* (*ubuntu* in the Nguni languages), which can be translated as "humanness," it would seem that humans (*batho* or *banto*) are the "tool," the "means," by which I am a human (*motho*). If I deny or threaten the *botho*, the humanity, of others, I thereby lose my own. If it is anything, dignity is a relational concept. (This also shows very nicely how performative language can also express truths.)

However, this raises another serious question: do I lose my inherent dignity when my community no longer recognizes it? You distinguish, rightly I think, between different uses of the word "dignity." Inherent dignity is the dignity we possess (or that it can be claimed we possess) by virtue of being human (9), but you also point out, in a way that I find very illuminating, that there is a type of dignity that we can possess in degrees ("more or less") (12): a dignity that depends on our status in society or our achievements (from whence the word "dignitaries," which overlaps almost fully with "VIP's"!); a dignity linked to our unique individuality (18); and a dignity relating to our beauty or splendor (20). Can any of these types of dignity be lost completely? This does seem to be the case if it is true that relations between humans are the sole basis of dignity. Put differently: can dignity rightly be regarded as "objective" if it is fully grounded in an anthropocentric intersubjectivity?

This question is not purely theoretical. I recently read an interview with Peter Singer (date unknown) in which he states quite categorically what he also defended in his *Practical Ethics* (1983), namely that to kill a baby is a lesser evil than to kill an adult. Singer's reason for saying so is fully consistent with his understanding of the basis of human dignity, of the "sanctity" of human life: an infant is not, as Singer puts it (referring back to his 1983 publication), "a being who is capable of anticipating the future, of having wants and desires for the future"; it "has no sense of existing over time." It is not yet aware of itself as a subject, as an "I" and, therefore, it cannot attach any conscious value to its own existence. Moreover, an infant generally has fewer social connections in the form of friendship and other attachments; its death will, therefore, affect fewer people as fewer people may attach value to its life. Singer qualifies this by pointing out that, since most parents love their babies, it would be a great evil to kill such a baby; it would constitute a great harm to the parents. However, parents who do not want to raise an infant—for instance, because it is seriously disabled—may have the right to end its life. It is clear that in Singer's anthropology human dignity is constituted exhaustively by the value we attach to ourselves and to others. There is no deeper, no more fundamental, basis for human dignity.

As a South African who regularly has to hear of horrific crimes perpetrated against infants—a phenomenon that says a lot about the breakdown of human relationships and the mutual valuing that ought to characterize it—I am left very uneasy by Singer's vision. When a baby is left at home unattended, and is kidnapped and dies in some unspeakable act of violence; when a baby is abandoned by its mother in a ditch or on a rubbish dump to die; or when a desperate parent decides to wipe out his or her whole family (an occurrence that, I am sorry to say, has become commonplace in South Africa)—when such things happen, does the fact that no one clearly really valued the life and future prospects of the infant in question mean that the infant had no dignity to violate? Am I wrong to feel—like Ivan Karamazov in Dostoevsky's *The Brothers Karamazov* (2009, 173-80)—even more outraged by such crimes and by the way society as a whole is implicated in them, than I do about crimes against adults (however horrific the latter might also be)? Is this not a natural human response? Is this reaction based merely on instinct, or is the instinctual (where it still exists) also the right and proper reaction?

The dilemma, then, is that although I agree that dignity can only be made sense of in relational and performative terms, I at the same time remain very uncomfortable with the idea that its existence ultimately rests on us humans. I want to believe (and I think you do too, Frits) that, even in a world where no one recognizes (even their own) human dignity any longer, every newborn child nevertheless *possesses* human dignity. If this can only make sense in a relational context, that relational context would have to be one that includes but also transcends human relations. *Motho ke motho ka batho*, yes, but only within a framework where the word for God, *Modimo*, is inseparable from its plural, *badimo*, the word for human ancestors—which suggests that God is the first Ancestor, the Father, the Mother, the source of our being.

More and more theologians are now suggesting that Jesus is aptly called the Ancestor par excellence (see Brand 2002, 115–46). This means that the God we meet in Jesus, the God who comes to us in vulnerability and dependence, and not our human forebears or the communities deriving from them, is the source of our being—*and of our dignity*. Even if I do not matter to other people, yes, even if I do not matter to myself, I still matter to God. When a human being is injured—even if neither that person nor anyone else is affected by it—God is injured. It is this God who posed that terrifying question to Cain: "Where is Abel thy brother?" (Gen 4:9) It is this God who insisted that we humans are "very good"—that we have splendor, beauty!—even if we ourselves fail to see this, or are convinced of the opposite. It is this God who values each one of us as a unique individual *coram Deo*. And it is this God who, in Christ, establishes a new community in which the "status" of its members rests not on achievements or social status, but on the fact that they are loved by God—and where, because it is a community of those who have been convinced of this, even the "least dignified" members are essential to the body (1 Cor 12:12–27).

Frits, as you rightly emphasize, human beings share in the ineffability of God (19). We can never fully say what it is to be human, what it is to be me or you, or what precisely our dignity consist in. However, we can claim that our humanity and our dignity derive from our relation to God who, as Barth so wonderfully put it, is the One who loves in freedom (Barth 1940, VI, §28). The question is: do we believe this? Do we really believe this to be *true*? "When the Son of Man cometh, shall he find faith on the earth?" (Luke 18:8).

I wish you all the best.

Your fellow searcher,
Gerrit

References

Austin, John L. 1962. *How to Do Things with Words*. Cambridge, Mass.: Harvard University Press.

Barth, Karl. 1940. *Die Kirchliche Dogmatik II: Die Lehre von Gott 1*. Zolikon: Evangelischer Verlag A. G.

Brand, Gerrit. 2002. *Speaking of a Fabulous Ghost: In Search of Theological Criteria, with Special Reference to the Debate on Salvation in African Christian Theology*. Frankfurt: Peter Lang.

———. 2005. Kuberklip: om te leef "asof" [Cuberstone: To Live "As If"). Cited 16 February 2012. Online: http://www.oulitnet.co.za/senet/senet.asp?id=25843.

———. 2007. Geen God of God-Geen? [No God or God-gene?] KKNK- Oop Gesprek, 1 April 2007. Online: http://www.givengain.com/cgi-bin/giga.cgi?cmd=cause_dir_news_item&cause_id=1270%C3%83%C3%9C&news_id=18684&cat_id=272.

———. 2011. Is *Fides Quaerens Intellectum* a Scholarly Enterprise? Some Thoughts on Confessional Theology at a Public University. *AcTSup* 14:20–30.

Brümmer, Vincent. 2006. Speech Acts. Pages 105–42 in *Brümmer on Meaning and the Christian Faith: Collected Writings of Vincent Brümmer*. Edited by John A. Hinnells. Aldershot: Ashgate.

———. 2010. Spirituality and the Hermeneutics of Faith. *HTS Teologiese Studies/Theological Studies* 66 (2010). Online: http://www.hts.org.za/index.php/HTS/article/view/891/1163.

De Lange, Frits. 2010. Working paper, Stellenbosch-PThU Consultation on "Dignity—At Home and in Public," 25–26 October, 2010. Unpublished.

Dostoevsky, Fyodor M. 2009. *The Brothers Karamazov*. Grand Rapids: Christian Classics Ethereal Library. First published in Russian in 1880.

Ganoczy, Alexandre. 1983. *Die Hermeneutik Calvins: Geistesgeschichtliche Voraussetzungen und Grundzuge*. Wiesbaden: Steiner.

Koopman, Nico. 2008. "Church and Public Policy Discourses in South Africa." Cited 16 February 2012. Online: http://ebookbrowse.com/churches-and-public-policy-discourses-in-south-africa-doc-d217486041.

Labooy, Guus. 2002. *Freedom and Dispositions: Two Main Concepts in Theology and Biological Psychiatry, a Systematic Analysis*. Frankfurt: Peter Lang.

Pascal, Blaise. 1671. *Pensées: Sur la religion et sur quelques autres sujets.* Paris: Guillaume Desprez.
Rorty, Richard. 1979. *Philosophy and the Mirror of Nature.* Princeton: Princeton University Press.
Sarot, Marcel. 1999. *Living a Good Life in Spite of Evil.* Frankfurt: Peter Lang.
Singer, Peter. 1983. *Practical Ethics.* Cambridge: Cambridge University Press.
———. (no date). Interview with Peter Singer. Online: http://www.princeton.edu/~psinger/faq.html.
Vedder, Ben. 2006. Hoe Godsdienst te Beschrijven: Rede ter Gelegenheid van de 83ᵉ Dies Natalis van de Radboud Universiteit Nijmegen. Online: http://webdoc.ubn.ru.nl/mono/v/vedder_b/hoe_goteb.pdf.
Wittgenstein, Ludwig. 1966. *Lectures and Conversations on Aesthetics, Psychology and Religious Belief.* Oxford: Blackwell.

Figuring God and Humankind: The *Imago Dei* in View of Anthropologies in the Old Testament

Hendrik Bosman

Introduction

When one person kills almost eighty unarmed people without any obvious remorse in Norway, a country renowned for its culture of human rights and cultural tolerance, the brutality triggers the renewal of age-old questions: What does human dignity entail? What is it to be human?[1] Presupposing that the Old Testament has any contribution to make will not meet with unqualified support. On the contrary, most critics may deny that the Old Testament has any contribution to make to this debate at all—a point of view with which a few scholars, such as John Rogerson, will disagree (Rogerson 2009, 171–72).

Can one perhaps contribute to this debate by scrutinizing the modern discourse on theological anthropology? At first glance, the importance of humankind's having been created in the image of God in modern theological discussion can lead to the impression that it was as important in biblical traditions (Curtis 1992, 389). However, one is somewhat taken aback when searching for biblical references to this idea, when it becomes clear that only three short passages in Gen 1–11 describe how we are created in the "image/likeness" of God (Gen 1:26–28; 5:1–3; 9:6).

This essay presupposes that different discourses on the nature of humankind can be found in the Old Testament, and that the differences

---

1. On 22 July 2011 Anders Breivik bombed government buildings in Oslo and fired at teenagers attending a youth camp on Utoya island, next to the Norwegian coast, causing the deaths of seventy-eight people.

among them are related to the diverging contexts within which the discourses evolved (Schüle 2007, 909). On the one hand, a distinction will be made between Priestly and non-Priestly traditions (especially wisdom literature) concerning a theological understanding of humanity; but on the other hand an attempt will be made to read diverging anthropological traditions as part of one canonical text (with special emphasis on Gen 1–3).

As Moltmann (1974, x) correctly assumed, any reflection on how the Old Testament views humankind will inevitably incorporate thoughts about who God is. This contribution on how to interpret the enigmatic concept of the "image of God" in the Old Testament is not only faced with the challenge of unraveling anthropological traditions, but is also confronted with the question how humankind "figures God"—in more (theological) ways than one (Walters 2008).

One is overwhelmed by the extensive research on humankind as created in the "image of God," which can be accessed by the excellent research surveys compiled by Westermann (1984) and Jonnson (1988). In this contribution special attention will be given to research from the past decade.

W. Sibley Towner (2005, 343) has written a clear and informative summary of the different scholarly proposals on the meaning of humankind created in the "image of God." Some of the more important suggestions include the following:

- The image of God can be traced in spiritual characteristics "such as memory, self-awareness, rationality, intelligence, spirituality, even an immortal soul" (e.g., Philo, Augustine, Aquinas, Schleiermacher, Eichrodt, and Fohrer).
- The image of God is found in the human ability to "make moral decisions, which presupposes free will and knowledge of good and evil" (e.g., Bromiley and Morrison).
- The image of God "can be seen in the external appearance of human beings" (e.g., Gunkel, von Rad, and Zimmerli).
- The image in question is displayed "when the human serves as God's deputy on earth, an idea often expressed in royal ideology" (von Rad, Wildberger, and W. H. Schmidt).
- Human beings are considered to be "God's counterpart or partner, the 'thou' which is addressed by the divine 'I'" (e.g., Buber, Brunner, and Westermann).

- The image of God in humankind "consists precisely in the division of humankind into female and male" (e.g., Barth, Bonhoeffer).

Towner's own and final remarks should be taken to heart (2005, 356):

> We neither are God's clones nor are we "miserable offenders," wholly incapable of good. We are God's creatures and chosen partners in the work of the creation. We are given ever greater opportunity to be bearers of the divine image, that is, positive, responsible stewards in the world.

This theological anthropology juxtaposes with more secular anthropologies, such as Marxism and existentialism, but despite the divergent points of departure there is a similar underlying engagement with what it means to be human (Fichtner 1978, 3). As Köhler (1956, 126–27) remarked: "It belongs to the very nature of every man [sic] that he should come to terms with life … that he endeavours to come to terms with it is of the very essence of existence."

Humankind as "Image of God" in the Ancient Near East

Middleton (2005, 95–129) critiqued certain scholarly suggestions regarding ancient Near Eastern parallels with the Old Testament understanding of the image of God and some of these will be discussed in more detail:

- The image of God as counterpart of the gods (e.g., *Epic of Gilgamesh*).
- The Egyptian *Instruction of Merikare* and the *Instruction of Ani* referring to humans being the images of a god.
- The practice of erecting statues of kings in distant parts of their kingdom to represent them there.
- The references in royal texts to several kings and a few priests as the images of deities.

In the ancient Near East, the king was often perceived as resembling the image of a god. This can be traced back as far as the eighteenth dynasty in Egypt during the second half of the second millennium (Curtis 1984, 80–90). However, one has to be very circumspect with generalizations in this regard because the early second millennium B.C.E. Egyptian *Instruc-*

tion of Merikare applied the image of God to all people (Walton 2006, 212–13). In the epilogue of *The Instruction of Ani*, it is the reason of humankind that resembles the divine (Ockinga 1984, 154).

Similar examples among Mesopotamian cultures emerge a few centuries later in middle- and neo-Assyrian texts in which the Assyrian king Esarhaddon is described as "the perfect likeness of the god," and in which a proverb, "man is the shadow of god," is used (Parpola 1993, 207).

The manner in which humankind is created in Gen 2 and placed within the Garden of Eden corresponds with elements of the Mesopotamian *mis pi* ("opening of the mouth") ritual, according to which "a divine image is created and then brought to life" (Schüle 2005, 20). Four stages can be discerned in the process of making a divine image (Walker and Dick 1999, 55–121):

- Craftsmen shape the material image/statue in a workshop situated in the temple district and the mouth of the image is opened as a symbolic act to indicate that the statue is able to breathe and that it is alive.
- From the workshop the image is taken through a harsh and wilderness-like environment before it reaches a garden located next to the river.
- In the garden the completion of the image takes place by means of a series of further mouth openings. The image is then left alone to be accepted by the gods as a true image of the divine.
- Finally, the image is taken from the garden to the holy of holies section of the temple of the god whose living image the statue represents.

On a life-size statue of a male found at Tell Fekheriye, dated late ninth century B.C.E., the Aramaic text at the back makes use of cognates for both *dəmût* ("image, likeness") and *ṣelem* ("statue"). This "parallel use suggests no significant differences of meaning should be sought between the two cognate Hebrew words" (Hallo and Younger 2000, 153–54):

> The statue of Hadad-yithʻi, king of Gurzan… this image he made better than before. In the presence of Hadad who dwells in Sikan, the lord of Habur, he has set up his statue.

Here the "image" indicates a statue that the king had made that "displays the features of the king. As such it can be identified to be the *dəmût*, the 'likeness,' of Hadduyitî. The statue as image "makes the king present in the face of his god, while he himself might be absent" (Schüle 2005, 10).

The concept of the *imago Dei* developed against the background of the ancient Near Eastern view of "divine presence in the shape of images" that was transformed by the Old Testament by substituting the statue with humankind as living beings becoming images of God (Schüle 2005, 11).

Humankind according to Priestly Sources in the Old Testament

In sharp contrast to ancient Near Eastern traditions where only kings and pharaohs represent the divine, the Old Testament seems to imply that all human beings are created in the divine image (Eskenazi 2008, 8). All three passages in Gen 1–11 that refer to humankind's having been made in the image of God are usually considered to be the product of the Priestly Writer:[2]

> Then God said, "Let us make humankind in our image, according to our likeness: and let them have dominion.... So God created humankind in his image, in the image of God he created them: male and female he created them.... God said to them, "…Have dominion over the fish of the sea and over the birds of the air and over every living thing that moves upon the earth" (Gen 1:26–28).

> When God created humankind, he made them in the likeness of God. Male and female he created them, and he blessed them and named them "humankind" when they were created. When Adam had lived one hundred thirty years, he became the father of a son in his likeness (*dəmût*), according to his image (*ṣelem*), and named him Seth (Gen 5:1–3).

> Whoever sheds the blood of a human, by a human shall that person's blood be shed; for in his own image (*ṣelem*) God made humankind (Gen 9:6).

---

2. Old Testament criticism has moved beyond Wellhausen's Documentary Hypothesis (JEDP), and I distinguish between Priestly and non-Priestly sources. The latter are usually characterized by their sapiential influences.

Although numerous scholars have reflected at length upon the creation of humankind in the "image of God," its exact meaning "remains unclear and contested" (Childs 1993, 112). In his magisterial commentary on Genesis, Westermann (1974, 203–22) argues that the "image of God" must be discussed in relation to creation in general and dominion in particular. Despite the impression that the *imago* of humankind entails some *similitudo* with the divine—as reflected in its dominion over all creatures—humankind must also realize that it forms part of creation, albeit in a special way.

The first appearance of humankind forms part of a series of creations that came into being due to words spoken by God. This is in stark contrast with many of the creation myths of the ancient Near East that describe how violent effort (*Chaoskampf!*) was required to create despite the forces of chaos opposing it (Arnold 2009, 44). Creating humankind through speech forms part of a broader pattern in Gen 1:1–2:3, where almost half of the verbs referring to divine action are "verbs of speaking," and this forms the backdrop to the observation that speech constitutes a "special characteristic of a human being" (Auld 2009, 261).

Prior to the creation of humankind several kinds of living creatures (domestic and wild animals, reptiles, etc.) were indirectly created by letting the earth bring them forth by means of natural reproduction (Gen 1:24–25). This indirect creation of animals is contrasted with "a uniquely deliberative decision" by God to directly and personally create humanity in his image and according to his likeness—making use of two related concepts that express the complexity and ambiguity involved with human creation (Blenkinsopp 2011, 25). Aune (2005, 261) argues that the use of two concepts suggest "a closer comparison" than the use of one concept, and that "image" implies greater precision than "likeness."

The creation in the image of God is articulated in royal vocabulary when "dominion" over different kinds of animals is indicated by the use of the verb *rādâ* (in both v. 26 and v. 28). It would seem as if the "image of God is about the exercise of rulership in the world" (Arnold 2009, 45). Blenkinsopp (2011, 26) argues against the assumption that the command to have dominion encourages the exploitation of animal life by pointing out that *rādâ* is used in both the Pentateuch and the Prophets to emphasize "the humane exercise of authority" (Lev 25:43; Ezek 34:4).

The ambiguous use of both "image" and "likeness" in Gen 1:26 differs from the chiastic structure of Gen 1:27 that seems "to give 'image' prominence over 'likeness' by not only repeating 'image' but also establishing it as 'the central hinge of the statement'" (Aune 2005, 261). In contrast to negative Mesopotamian perceptions of humanity, the Priestly writer advocates the dignity of humankind as a whole by the inclusive clarification "male and female he created them" (Blenkinsopp 2011, 26).

In Gen 5:1–3 we find the start of the *tōləḏôt* ("list of descendants") of Adam. This clearly resonates with Gen 1:26–27 by again stressing that humankind was made in the image of God and created male and female. Although *'āḏām* is used in the first two verses without the definite article, it is only the first instance that indicates that it is used as a proper name; in subsequent occurrences it refers to "humankind' (Alter 2004, 35). Thompson (2009, 146) suggests that another type of royal metaphor is used here in connection with the creation of humanity: the relationship between a father (Adam) and his son (Seth), born in the likeness and according to the image of the father. Like the royal dynasties of old, this list of Adam's descendants includes ten consecutive generations up to Noah. Despite the initial inclusive reference to humankind being male and female, no mention is made of any female offspring in the subsequent family tree up to Noah (Auld 2005, 260). In the whole of Gen 5 only Seth is described as being born in the likeness and image of his father Adam. Seth is born in the image of both his father and of God his creator, and this places him in what Arnold (2009, 86) describes as a position of "unfortunate bipolarity." The subsequent narratives related to the Flood and the Tower of Babel amply illustrate how fragile and tenacious the dignity of humankind turned out to be (Gen 6–11).

In Gen 9:1–7 we find God's fourth speech to Noah, which clearly echoes the thought and terminology of Gen 1 (Arnold 2009, 27). The favorable evaluation of being created in the image of God is again linked to aspects of royal dominion over every living thing, and is "appended to the legal dictum banning the shedding of human blood" (Blenkinsopp 2011, 27). All blood of living creatures—humankind and animals alike—is protected, since it symbolizes life, and may not be *eaten*. However, in the case of animals blood may be *shed* while the blood of humankind may not (Auld 2005, 260). The chiastic structure of verse 6 and the wordplay between "blood" (*dām*) and "humankind" (*'āḏām*) expresses "a system of retributive justice" (Alter 2004, 50). This legal principle of the *lex taliones* is "thereby given a theological underpinning, in the sense that acts of violence visited on the other … constitute a desecration or defacing of the image of God in the victim" (Blenkinsopp 2011, 27).

The use of the *imago Dei* terminology in Gen 5 and 9 indicates that neither the fall into sin (Gen 3) nor the Flood (Gen 6–9) undid the image of God in humankind—a matter that the Reformed Protestant tradition has to be reminded of in light of its rather bleak view of the impact of the events in Eden on humankind (Towner 2005, 351). On this topic Boer (1990, 37–55) refers to "the misnomer 'total depravity.'" Against this background it is all the more intriguing that the "image of God" as a theological theme played a very minor role in the rest of the Old Testament.

Reflection on humankind's having been created in the image of God should also take into consideration that the Holiness Code (Lev 17–26) repeatedly commands the Israelites to be holy because their Lord God is holy (e.g., Lev 20:26). Garr (2003, 238) therefore concludes that Israel must accordingly "actively represent God, God's holiness, and his separative modality of creation in the world."

Not only do descriptions of humankind in the Old Testament have a theological ring to them, but some depictions of the divine are anthropomorphic in character (Towner 2005, 350). In a prophetic vision of God rooted in priestly traditions, the enigmatic Ezek 1:26 describes "seated above the likeness of a throne … something that seemed like a human form." This vision is soon explained in verse 28 as "the appearance of the likeness of the glory of the Lord." It therefore seems likely that Gen 1:26–28 "draws on the older visionary tradition of the anthropomorphic deity but ultimately transcends it insofar as it omits any description of the divine" (Smith 1990, 102).

In the Psalter's first praise song framed by an identical confirmation that the Lord is our Sovereign and that his majesty fills the earth (8:1, 9), Ps 8:4 poses a question that still deserves attention today, since it forms part of a section that ponders why God is involved with mere human beings (Goldingay 2009, 154):

> What are human beings that you are mindful of them
> > Mortals that you care for them?

These rhetorical questions probably echo concerns prevalent in the religious community and do not take the relationship with God for granted. In response to the questions about humankind, the psalmist provides answers that are similar to the Priestly theological anthropology in Gen 1:

> Yet you have made them a little lower than God (divine beings/angels),
> > and have crowned them with glory and honor.
> > You have given them dominion over the works of your hands;
> > you have put all things under their feet. (Ps 8:5–6)

Some scholars have suggested that Ps 8 as a whole constitutes "an extended chiasmus," and that according to this structure verses 5 and 6 form "the key thematic verses of the psalm," containing the point of view that God is so great that there is no need for him to be mindful of humankind (Kraut 2010, 23). Once again there is a clear link in Ps 8 between the creation of humankind in the image of God and humankind's "godlike dominance over the natural world."

Having dominion (*rādâ*) over animals seems to be one important aspect of how Priestly theology understood the "image of God" to be manifested in humankind—this dominion has a royal quality, and it includes the totality of creation: air, sea, and earth (Ps 8:7–8). The chiastic structure Ps 8 has at least two purposes: "it demonstrates the parallels between God's dominion over the universe and man's dominion over the natural world," and it highlights "the essential paradox of man's place in the world and the glorious beneficence of the Creator who established mankind as earth's divine-like sovereign" (Kraut 2010, 24).

The use of the concept "image of God" by the Priestly writer is foundational for the establishment of a comprehensive, theological anthropology containing the following important functional and qualitative elements (Schüle 2005, 4–7, 20; Schellenberger 2009, 111–12):

- The general role of human beings as rulers over all of creation (so-called *dominium terrae*) can be gleaned from the royal terminology related to being created in the image of God. This resonates with the royal ideologies of kingship that can be found in both Egypt and among the Mesopotamian cultures.
- The particular relationship between male and female, implied by their both being created in the image of God. Despite the surrounding patriarchal society, the idea of equality between men and women might be alluded to in this programmatic introduction to Scripture.
- The relationship between God and humankind is more "democratic" because all people have the ability to be the image and likeness of God. This ability is not only reserved for royalty but is possible for the whole of humanity.
- As a cultic image represented a god in his or her temple, the human being represents the presence of God on earth. As creation comes to fulfillment on the seventh day, so humankind

represents God by resting on the seventh day. The emphasis shifts from sacred space (tabernacle or temple) to sacred time (Sabbath) and humankind's creation in the image of God makes this shift possible.

Humankind according to Non-Priestly Sources in the Old Testament

According to Gen 2 the Lord creates humankind (*'ādām*) "from the dust of the ground" (*hā'ădāmâ*) as part of what is often referred to as the Yahwistic rendition of creation (Towner 2005, 345):

> Then the Lord God formed man from the dust of the ground, and breathed into his nostrils the breath of life; and the man became a living being. (Gen 2:7)

Humankind is depicted here as a "living being" as a result of the "breath of life" that the Lord God breathed into the man he created.

The concept *'ādām* is a generic reference to humankind in general, and is never used in the Hebrew Bible in the feminine or plural (Sarna 1989, 12). Although humankind (*'ādām*) seems to include both male and female in the Priestly Gen 1, the account in Gen 2 distinguishes in more detail between male and female:

> And the rib that the Lord God had taken from the man he made into a woman and brought her to the man. Then the man said: "This is at last bone of my bones and flesh from my flesh; this one shall be called Woman, for out of the Man this one was taken." (Gen 2:22-23)

The creation of the woman from the rib of the man seems to be a type of aetiology of marriage. It forms part of a larger narrative that includes both Gen 2 and 3. This narrative describes how the harmonious order created in the Garden of Eden was destroyed by human disobedience (Childs 1993, 112-13).

Andreas Schüle (2005, 11) argues persuasively that Gen 2–3

> challenges the priestly position—which means that there are, according to the second telling of creation, aspects to human life that are not contained by the concept of the image ... such as the relationship between man and woman, the human quest for knowledge and the ability to defy God's command.

In contrast to Gen 1:28, according to which humankind is to be fruitful and have dominion, one finds in Gen 3 a description of humankind that indicates how human existence is cursed by pain, arduous labor, and mortality. Even amidst this less than rosy description of the plight of humanity in Gen 3, we find a remarkable assurance that God takes care of humankind by making clothes for Adam and Eve (Schüle 2005, 17).

It is, therefore, possible to read Gen 1–3 as a coherent whole without denying that some elements in Gen 2–3 (such as Gen 2:4b–9 and 18–24) are older than Gen 1 (Ben-Chorin 1986, 11). Carr (1993, 577–95) develops arguments by Westermann that an older (preexilic) tradition on the creation of man and woman was supplemented in postexilic times by a garden or paradise story in which Persian influences can be detected.

Furthermore, any theological reflection on humanity created in the "image of God" must also take into consideration the prohibition of images:

> You shall not make yourself an idol, whether in the form of anything that is in heaven above, or that is on the earth beneath, or that is in the water under the earth. (Exod 20:4; Deut 5:8)

It is not clear when cultic images were first prohibited in Israelite or early Jewish religious practice. Some scholars argue in favor of an early tolerant attitude toward the iconic representation of deities (Mettinger 1995); other scholars presume Israelite aniconism to be ancient (Schmidt 1990). The plundering Romans found no divine image when they sacked the Second Temple in Jerusalem, and the prohibition of cultic images probably goes back to vehement criticism of idols in Ezekiel and Deutero-Isaiah during the exile. This makes the probable coexistence of idol criticism and the formulation in the Priestly account of the creation of humankind in Gen 1 quite remarkable.

According to younger wisdom literature, the relationship between God and humankind is influenced by its seminal presupposition that the "fear of the Lord is the beginning of knowledge" (Prov 1:7) and that the "fear of the Lord is the beginning of wisdom" (Prov 9:10). Although the relationship between the Lord and humankind as his image is maintained, the distance and difference between the divine and humankind is highlighted.

The Priestly understanding of humankind as created in the "image of God' is thus supplemented by non-Priestly material that elaborates on what it means to be created a human being. Wisdom literature often describes how human beings respond to being created as part of a creation marked by order and mystery (Schüle 2005, 18–19).

Humankind according to Intertestamental Sources

According to early Jewish interpretation that employs language reminiscent of Gen 1 and Ps 8, the relationship between humans and the image of God should be understood as being similar to the correspondence between an original and a copy:

> He endowed them with strength like his own,
> and made them in his own image (Sir 17:3).

This reference to humankind's having been created in the image of God forms part of Sir 17:1– 14, in which the creation narratives of Gen 1 and 2 are merged with the Sinai tradition on the giving of the Ten Commandments (Exod 19–20). Emphasis is placed on the assumption that the image of God implies human authority over animals, and that this is comparable to the sovereignty of God in the heavens (Crenshaw 1997, 730).

As indicated in Wis 2:23–24, the image of God is rooted in the divine qualities of eternity and immortality (Janowski 2009, 414–15):

> For God created us for incorruption,
> and made us in the image of his own eternity.

It is possible that wordplay is involved in the way the author of the Wisdom of Solomon describes how "God created the human being in the image of God's own being (*idiotes*) or perhaps of God's own eternity (*aidiotes*)" (Blenkinsopp 2011, 26). To come to grips with this enigmatic remark, one should keep in mind that it forms part of the conclusion of a speech describing the folly of the wicked who do not comprehend the goal or destiny of God's creation of humankind, namely "incorruption" (1:16–2:24). "To sustain the bold claim for immortality, the author appeals to the powerful 'image of God' in the Genesis narratives" (Kolarcik 1997, 464).

Clear references to the possibility of some form of afterlife for human beings, and suggestions that being human entails having an immortal soul only developed in the late intertestamental period:

> for a perishable body weighs down the soul,
> and this earthy tent burdens the thoughtful mind. (Wis 9:15)

Conclusion

Anthropological texts in the Old Testament do not present a concise definition of the nature of human beings. In their dialogical structure they rather reflect the ongoing interaction between humankind and God that is constitutive of the former's humanity and that is realized "in God's presence" (Janowski 2009a, 292). One should, however, be very careful not to depict Old Testament anthropology as being exclusively transcendental in character. It should be appreciated as being constituted in the human body and shaped by the society within which it exists (Wolff 1974; Schüle 2011, 406).

Therefore, it comes as no surprise that humankind seems to be defined in terms of different—even contradicting—personal and social relationships (Walton 2006, 208–9):

- All people are made of dust and therefore connected to the ground and mortal (non-Priestly tradition).
- Due to the woman's having been created from the rib of the man, a strong connectivity exists between female and male (non-Priestly tradition).
- As "image of God," the whole of humankind is related to God and connected to creation. On the one hand, not only kings but every human being is created in the "image of God"; however, on the other hand, terminology emanating from royal ideology is used to describe how humankind rules over creation (Priestly tradition).
- In an imageless religion the "image of God" is qualified by the "likeness of God," thereby making the relationship between God and humankind less prone to idolatry (Priestly tradition).
- According to the non-Priestly traditions, the Lord planted a garden to provide for humankind, and did not demand slave labor from humans as in the rest of the ancient Near East.

The Priestly account of creation ends with the day of rest within which humankind as the "image of God" can exist in a sacred space (temporally as Sabbath and physically as temple).

It seems as if the earlier non-Priestly descriptions of humankind understood the "image of God" in a more physical sense whilst the Priestly writer spiritualized the concept by combining *dəmût* ("resemblance") with *ṣelem* ("image").

In the end one must acknowledge that there is no clarity about what the "image of God" entails, and that the mystery, or at least the ambiguity surrounding it, is maintained (Childs 1993, 569). From the brief overview of the anthropological traditions in the Old Testament given above it is evident that most biblical anthropology "turns out to be theological anthropology, which means that a human being is defined by his or her relationship with God and God's other creatures" (Towner 2005, 350).

This focus on the relation between humankind and God resonates with David Kelsey's recently published *Eccentric Existence: A Theological Anthropology*, in which his essential claim is "that human existence is 'eccentric' because it is centered on God and that this God warrants seeking wisdom" (Ford 2011, 47). To comprehend a human existence centered on God and rooted in personal embodiment as well as social context, one must allow not only Gen 1, but also Gen 2–3 and wisdom literature to inform our theological anthropology, which attempts to "figure God" in ways appropriate to the contexts we live in.

The atrocities perpetrated by human beings illustrate the fragile and vulnerable nature of our humanity. Old Testament anthropology is an important but pluriform reminder that being created in the "image of God" implies a resilient and tenacious dignity that is preserved despite the "fall" into sin, murder (Cain and Abel), violence (the Flood) and hubris (tower of Babel). "Figuring God" is an openended theological challenge to humanity—to incorporate the human being as a whole (body, soul, and spirit); male and female (despite the pervasiveness of patriarchy in many societies); engaging with asymmetrical power relations between rulers and the ruled (considering the economic chasm between developed and developing countries); and redefining dominion with regard to a creation that is on the brink of ecological devastation! The "image of God" positions humankind in the liminal space between fragility and greatness, rooted in the potential to reflect his image and to resemble his likeness.

References

Albertz, Rainer. 1992. Mensch II. Altes Testament. Pages 464–74 in vol. 2 of *Theologische Realenzyklopädie*. Edited by Gerhard Müller, Horst Balz, and Gerhard Krause. Berlin: de Gruyter.

Alter, Robert. 2004. *The Five Books of Moses: A Translation with Commentary*. New York: Norton.
Arnold, Bill T. 2009. *Genesis*. NCBC. Cambridge: Cambridge University Press.
Auld, Graeme 2005. *Imago Dei* in Genesis: Speaking in the Image of God. *ExpTim* 116:259–62.
Barton, John. 2002. *Ethics and the Old Testament*. 2nd ed. London: SCM.
Ben-Chorin, Schalom. 1986. "*Was ist der Mensch?*" *Anthropologie des Judentums*. Tübingen: Mohr.
Blenkinsopp, Joseph. 2011. *Creation, Un-Creation, Re-Creation: A Discursive Commentary on Genesis 1–11*. London: T&T Clark.
Boer, Harry R. 1990. *An Ember Still Glowing: Humankind as the Image of God*. Grand Rapids: Eerdmans.
Bunge, Maria J. 2011. Kinder, das Bild Gottes und die Christologie: Theologische Antropologie in Solidarität mit Kindern. *EvT* 71:165–78.
Carr, David. 1993. The Politics of Textual Subversion: A Diachronic Perspective on the Garden of Eden Story. *JBL* 112:57–95.
Childs, Brevard S. 1993. *Biblical Theology of the Old and New Testaments: Theological Reflection on the Christian Bible*. Minneapolis: Fortress.
Crenshaw, John L. 1997. The Book of Sirach. Pages 601–867 in vol. 5 of *The New Interpreter's Bible*. Edited by Leander E. Keck. Nashville: Abingdon.
Curtis, Edward M. 1992. Image of God (OT). Pages 381–89 in vol. 3 of *Anchor Bible Dictionary*. Edited by David N. Freedman. New York: Doubleday.
Eichrodt, Walter. 1970. *Man in the Old Testament*. SBT 4. London: SCM. First published 1951.
Eskenazi, Tamara C., ed. 2008. *The Torah: A Woman's Commentary*. New York: WRJ.
Fichtner, Joseph. 1978. *Man the Image of God: A Christian Anthropology*. New York: Alba House.
Ford, David F. 2011. The What, How and Who of Humanity before God: Theological Anthropology and the Bible in the Twenty-First Century. *ModTheo* 27:41–54.
Fretheim, Terrence E. 2008. Image of God. Pages 18–21 in vol. 3 of *The New Interpreter's Dictionary of the Bible*. Edited by Katherine D. Sakenfeld. Nashville: Abingdon.
Garr, W. Randall. 2003. *In His Own Image and Likeness: Humanity, Divinity, and Monotheism*. Leiden: Brill.

Goldingay, John. 2009. *Psalms I (Pss. 1-14)*. Grand Rapids: Baker Academic.

Gowan, Donald E. 1975. *When Man Becomes God: Humanism and Hybris in the Old Testament*. Pittsburgh: Pickwick.

Hallo, William W., and K. Lawson Younger, eds. 2000. *Monumental Inscriptions from the Biblical World*. Vol. 2 of *The Context of Scripture*. Leiden: Brill.

Janowski, Bernd. 2009a. Human Beings IV. Old Testament. Pages 292-93 in vol. 6 of *Religion Past and Present: Encyclopedia of Theology and Religion*. Edited by Hans D. Betz, Don S. Browning, Bernd Janowski, and Eberhard Jüngel. Leiden: Brill.

———. 2009b. Image of God. Pages 414-17 in vol. 6. of *Religion Past and Present: Encyclopedia of Theology and Religion*. Edited by Hans D. Betz, Don S. Browning, Bernd Janowski, and Eberhard Jüngel. Leiden: Brill.

Jonnson, Gunnlaugur A. 1984. *The Image of God: Genesis 1:26-28 in a Century of Old Testament Research*. Lund: Almqvist & Wiksell.

Kelsey, David H. 2009. *Eccentric Existence: A Theological Anthropology*. 2 vols. Louisville: Westminster John Knox.

Köhler, Ludwig. 1956. *Hebrew Man*. London: SCM. First published 1953.

Kolarcik, Michael. 1997. The Book of Wisdom. Pages 1076-89 in vol. 5 of *The New Interpreter's Bible*. Edited by Leander E. Keck. Nashville: Abingdon.

Kraut, Judah. 2010. The Birds and the Babes: The Structure and Meaning of Psalm. *JQR* 100:10-24.

Mettinger, Tryggve. 1995. *No Graven Image: Israelite Aniconism in Its Ancient Near Eastern Context*. ConBOT 42. Lund: Almqvist & Wiksell.

Middleton, J. Richard. 2005. *The Liberating Image: The* Imago Dei *in Genesis 1*. Grand Rapids: Brazos.

Moltmann, Jürgen. 1974. *Man: Christian Anthropology in the Conflicts of the Present*. London: SPCK.

Ockinga, Benno. 1984. *Die Gottebenbildlichkeit im Alten Ägypten und im Alten Testament*. Ägypten und Altes Testament 7. Wiesbaden: Otto Harrassowitz.

Parpola, Simo. 1993. *Letters from Assyrian and Babylonian Scholars*. SAA 10. Helsinki: University of Helsinki Press.

Rogerson, John. 1978. *Anthropology and the Old Testament*. Oxford: Blackwell.

———. 2007. What Does It Mean to be Human? The Central Question of Old Testament Theology. Pages 50–59 in *Theory and Practice in Old Testament Ethics*. Edited by M. Daniel Carroll. London: T&T Clark.

———. 2009. *A Theology of the Old Testament: Cultural Memory, Communication, and Being Human*. London: SPCK.

Sarna, Nahum M. 1989. *Genesis*. JPS Commentaries. Philadelphia: Jewish Publication Society.

Schellenberg, Annette 2009. Humankind as the "Image of God": On the Priestly Predication (Gen 1:26–27; 5:1; 9:6) and Its Relationship to the Ancient Near Eastern Understanding of Images. *TZ* 65:97–115.

Schmidt, Werner H. 1990. *Alttestamentliche Glaube und seiner Geschichte*. 7th ed. Neukirchen-Vluyn: Neukirchener.

Schüle, Andreas. 2005. Made in the "Image of God": The Concept of Divine Images in Gen 1–3. *ZAW* 117:1–20.

———. 2007. Humanity, OT. Pages 907–12 in vol. 2 of *The New Interpreter's Dictionary of the Bible*. Edited by Katherine D. Sakenfeld. Nashville: Abingdon.

———. 2011. Anthropologie des Alten Testaments. *Theologische Rundschau* 76:399–414.

Smith, Mark S. 1990. *The Early History of God: Yahweh and the Other Deities in Ancient Israel*. New York: Harper & Row.

Stendebach, Franz J. 1972. *Der Mensch, wie ihn Israel vor 3000 Jahren sah*. Stuttgart: KBW.

Thompson, Thomas L. 2009. Imago Dei: A Problem in Pentateuchal Discourse. *SJOT* 23:135–48.

Towner, W. Sibley. 2005. Clones of God: Genesis 1:26–28 and the Image of God in the Hebrew Bible. *Int* 59:341–56.

Walker, Christopher, and Michael B. Dick. 1999. The Induction of the Cult Image in Ancient Mesopotamia: The Mesopotamian Ritual. Pages 55–121 in *Born in Heaven, Made on Earth: The Creation of the Cult Image*. Edited by Michael B. Dick. Minneapolis: Fortress.

Walters, Stanley D., ed. 2008. *Go Figure! Figuration in Biblical Interpretation*. Eugene, Oreg.: Pickwick.

Walton, John H. 2006. *Ancient Near Eastern Thought and the Old Testament: Introducing the Conceptual World of the Hebrew Bible*. Grand Rapids: Baker Academic.

Welker, Michael. 1997. Creation and the Image of God: Their Understanding in Christian Tradition and the Biblical Grounds. *JES* 34:436–48.

Westermann, Claus. 1974. *Genesis 1–11*. BKAT. Neukirchen-Vluyn: Neukirchener.
Wildberger, Hans. 1965. Das Abbild Gottes. *TZ* 21:245–59, 481–501.
Wolff, Hans W. 1981. *Anthropology of the Old Testament*. Philadelphia: Fortress. First published 1974.

A Response to Hendrik Bosman's "Figuring God and Humankind: The *Imago Dei* in View of Anthropologies in the Old Testament"

Klaas Spronk

Dear Hendrik,

Your survey of the recent scholarly interpretations of Old Testament texts on humans being created in the image of God is both illuminating and frustrating. You clearly show that we are dealing with different concepts in these texts and also that modern exegetes are far from reaching a consensus in their explanations of these concepts and the way they are related. Therefore, one suspects that it is not likely that anytime soon there will emerge a convincing answer to the question you pose at the beginning: Has the Old Testament any contribution to make to the modern debate on human dignity? In this regard you quote John W. Rogerson, who in his recent book on the theology of the Old Testament also seems to be quite reluctant concerning these matters. Rogerson states that the central question of the Old Testament is posed in Ps 8:4: "What does it mean to be human?" (Rogerson 2009, 171). He states that at first sight the study of the Old Testament itself seems to contribute nothing to the modern discussion on the quality of human life. But then again, the whole of Rogerson's book is an attempt to show that the Old Testament is relevant for today. He invites the reader to consider that the Old Testament view on humanity is something dynamic. Texts on human beings in their relationship to God are not meant to describe a fixed situation but to open new perspectives and to encourage processes of change. In this regard the idea of a person as the image of God plays a central role. Rogerson wants

> to demonstrate the thesis that the more human humans become (whatever is meant by that), the closer they become to what the Old Testament calls the "image of God" (Gen 1:27) and, in what may seem a curious way, the more God and his purposes are realized in the world. (Rogerson 2009, 174)

In his interpretation of Gen 1:26–27, Rogerson rejects the view—as it is usually found in traditional Jewish and Christian theology—that it is meant to say something about the nature of human beings. He follows the view of Claus Westermann who maintains that this passage primarily concerns the divine act of creating humans as objects with whom God can communicate. Following this line, one may say that someone becomes the human being he or she was meant to be in his orher relationship with God. Rogerson (2009, 192), therefore, speaks of the image of God as "an 'empty' concept," "which has to be filled with meaning in the light of human history and what can be learned from it." One may say that the Old Testament time and again testifies to this process. It shows the many trials and errors of humankind on its way to reaching this goal and, even more, God's patience with people and God's perseverance in helping them to fulfill this potential. Without the latter the project would fail. The Bible is full of stumbling blocks to the realization of the vision of a politics of human transfiguration. In order "not to create despair but hope" the Bible speaks

> of possibilities which belong fully to a different world but which may be available in this world—divine forgiveness, divine love and divine grace. These are properties which become most apparent at the point when humans recognize their limitations and weaknesses. Even in an imperfect world they can bring hope and transfiguration. (Rogerson 2009, 195)

Rogerson presents his view in a refreshing and stimulating way—certainly also for our project on human dignity. However, Hendrik, you caution us not simply to use one of the many possible interpretations of Gen 1:26–27. At this point it is important to note an important difference in approach between your essay and the work of Rogerson. You base your observations on a strictly historical-critical analysis of the biblical text, distinguishing between different sources and traditions. Rogerson does not deny the fruits of historical-critical research, but treats the texts as one coherent narrative, the product of cultural memory. One may say that Rogerson suggests that the Priestly tradition has become dominant or that, for us as modern readers in our context, the Priestly tradition is the most relevant of the different voices in the Bible. Within the history of research as you outline it, one may see Rogerson's interpretation as just one of the many possible. I, however, do find a tendency in recent publications towards precisely this view of Rogerson. The latter indicates that his interpretation is in line with the conclusion of Westermann in his monumental commentary on the Book of Genesis. I also find some interesting correspondence with a recent German collection of essays on human dignity (Baldermann 2000). This book, entitled *Menschenwürden* ("human dignity"), in the series *Jahrbuch für Biblische Theologie*, is mentioned neither by Rogerson nor by yourself and certainly deserves our attention.

Like Rogerson, Berndt Hamm and Michael Welker are quite positive about a possible contribution by biblical theology to modern discussions on human dignity. Not only do they state in the preface to the book that in our civilization human dignity is part of the heritage of the Jewish-Christian faith, but they also see an important role for biblical theology in modern discussions about the quality of human dignity:

> Mit der neuzeitlichen Artikulation der Menschenwürde … ist nicht etwas Fremdes auf das Christentum zugekommen, das heikler Integrationsbemühungen in den christlichen Kontext bedürfte. Vielmehr hat hier ein ureigener Impetus jüdisch-christlicher Überlieferungen säkulare Ausdrucksformen und Begründungsweisen gefunden. Sie rufen eine christlich-biblische Theologie zu ihrem Proprium. Indem die christlich-biblische Theologie ihr Proprium auf die neuzeitlichen Problemstellungen hin auslegt, läßt sie sich über traditionelle Begrenzungen hinausführen, übt aber ihrerseits auch Kritik an der rationalistischen Flachheit und moralistischen Engführung moderner Begründungen von Menschenwürde und Menschenrechten. (Hamm and Welker 2000, v–vi)

The contributions on biblical theology and also on church history and systematic and practical theology in this volume demonstrate that this goal, formulated in the introduction, is not beyond reach. In his contribution on the interpretation of Gen 1:26–27 and 9:6, Walter Groß emphasizes that being created in the image of God does not point to what a human is, but to what he or she has to do. Like Rogerson, Groß considers the importance of the repetition in Gen 9:6. Although many things have changed since human beings proved to be imperfect, the assignment given to humans regarding other people and animals remains the same. This apparently also means that humans still have the ability to follow the assignment and can live up to the expectations related to the concept of the image of God, but only if they remain in close relation with this God (Spronk 2007, 198–201).

It is often remarked that the idea of humans being created in the image of God does not seem to play a primary role in what the Old Testament has to say about humanity. Next to the passages in Genesis we find only in Ps 8 an indirect reference to this notion. However, this does not necessarily mean that there is no relation between these texts and others on human dignity in the Old Testament. The study by Rogerson shows that it may be fruitful to relate the concept of the *imago Dei* to biblical stories about humans finding their way by trial and error in the direction that God has pointed out to them. This is also the story of God's reaction to humans who constantly disappoint God.

Genesis 5:1–3 reports that humankind acts as is expected. The qualification of "being made in the image of God" is repeated, and it is added that humans are indeed acting like their creator, namely, in procreating:

> This is the book of the generations of Adam. In the day that God created Adam, in the likeness of God made he him, male and female He created them and blessed them and called them Adam, in the day when they were created. And Adam lived hundred and thirty years, and begat a son in his own likeness, after his image and called him Seth.

This suggests that everything went exactly according to God's plan. It also offers the basic explanation of the expression "image of God." As in Gen 1, it is balanced by the reference that "human" is created "male and female." It indicates that it is only within this combination that "man" can function as the image of God. To this is added in Gen 1:28 the command to "be fruitful, and multiply, and replenish the earth." All this clearly indicates that the expression "being made in the image of God" in the first place points toward the human power of procreation. This is also underlined in Gen 5, which describes how Adam's actions copy those of God. Adam begets a son "in his own likeness, after his image." These are the same words used in Gen 1:26 (in reversed order). In Gen 5:3 this is followed by the same action undertaken by God in verse 2, namely by Adam giving Seth a name.

Genesis 5 seems to indicate that everything is still going according to the order as presented in the description of creation. The only exception is that death has now entered the scene. There is no reference to sin. However, things are indeed different the next time we read about humans as the image of God. This is in Gen 9:1–6 where, after the flood, God blesses Noah and repeats the command to fill the earth:

> God blessed Noah and his sons, and said to them, "Be fruitful and multiply, and fill the earth. The fear and dread of you shall rest on every animal of the earth, and on every bird of the air, on everything that creeps on the ground, and on all the fish of the sea; into your hand they are delivered. Every moving thing that lives shall be food for you; and just as I gave you the green plants, I give you everything. Only, you shall not eat flesh with its life, that is, its blood. For your own lifeblood I will surely require a reckoning: from every animal I will require it and from human beings, each one for the blood of another, I will require a reckoning for human life. Whoever sheds the blood of a human, by a human shall that person's blood be shed; for in his own image God made humankind" (NRSV).

It is clear that the relationship between humans and animals has changed as fear has entered it. Killing has become part of life on this earth. On the one hand God gives humans permission to kill but, on the other hand, this permission is also limited. God again sets the boundaries: human beings are not supposed to kill each other. In this context the reference to humans as the image of God has a different meaning. It does not relay something about the human potential, but places the emphasis on the value of human life and is now also connected with God's commandments. Only in fulfilling these commandments is the image of God safeguarded. With the changes brought about by sin, the concept of humans as the image of God appears to have changed as well. It still testifies to the close relationship between God and humans, but it has become clear that within this relationship choices have to be made, and it is anything but certain whether God can recognize himself in what humans make of their opportunities.

According to Rogerson, the central question posed in the Old Testament is whether the human race can become more human. Can human beings do this by their own efforts? What part does God's loyalty to God's covenant play here? Within this framework, Rogerson makes some interesting remarks regarding the way God is pictured in the book of Judges: as an attempt to express that God "does not give up his project" (Rogerson 2009, 188). Rogerson also elaborates on the story of David, especially in the so-called Court Chronicle (2 Sam 9–20), with its honest portrayal of David as a far from perfect king. According to Rogerson, the latter points to "a breakdown at a decisive point in God's project for the human race through Israel": it is "a betrayal of what is implied in the creation of the human race in the divine image" (Rogerson 2009, 191-92).

It is also possible—in my opinion even preferable—to see this story about David in a more favorable light. Compared to the previous stories in the book of Judges, it is not a breakdown, but a realistic and, therefore, promising example of how humans who are not without sin and who are living in a cruel world can make the best of it in close relation to God. My interpretation is based on the assumption that in its present form the book of Judges is meant as an introduction to the stories in the books of Samuel and Kings that deal with the problems with and the blessings of kingship in Israel and Judah (Spronk 2010). The installation of a king is the answer to a situation in which all respect for human dignity seems to have disappeared. This has become especially apparent in the dreadful story of the brutal murder of a woman in Gibeah (Judg 19). The latter is also a story about a complete lack of hospitality. The clear parallels with the similar story in Gen 19 show that although Sodom and Gomorrah have been destroyed, the sins associated with these cities have not disappeared. The victim is cut into twelve pieces as if she were an animal. Nothing could be further removed from the human being as image of God.

The first attempts at moving away from this low point are not successful. The Israelites become entangled in a civil war that almost eradicates one of their own tribes (Judg 20-21). The refrain in these last chapters of the book of Judges is that there was no king in Israel in these days (Judg 17:6; 18:1; 19:1; 21:25). In the stories that follow, the prophet Samuel at first refuses to give in to the request of the people for a king. The traditional argument against this wish is that God is Israel's king (Judg 8:23). Samuel also uses this line of argument until God commands him to comply with the people's wishes (1 Sam 8:7). Against the background of the concept of humans as image of God, it is a very interesting question whether the king can be seen as God's representative on earth. As you showed in your survey, Hendrik, this was a common notion in the ancient Near East. It also fits in with the way humans are presented as the image of God in Genesis. This is indicated by the fact that it is followed in Gen 1:26 by the command to rule over the animals.

Thus the stories of the kings of Israel—especially Saul and David—may be seen as answering the question whether they, in their function as rulers, can be qualified as the image of God. One finds this question already in Judg 19, which contains a number of allusions to these future kings—note, for instance, the important role of the cities of Jebus and Gibeah, which are later closely related to David and Saul. As may be expected from someone who hails from Gibeah, Saul proves to be not fit for the function of representing God. David, on the other hand, is announced as a "man after God's own heart" (1 Sam 13:14). During his reign, David did not always act according to this illustrious title, but it can also be said that, unlike Saul, he never lost contact with his God. David is not perfect, but it is not in line with the way he is described and remembered in the Old Testament to speak, as Rogerson does, of a failure or even a betrayal of God's intentions for humankind. When Rogerson is right that the *imago Dei* is an empty concept, the stories about David can play a positive role in ongoing attempts to fill it with new meaning.

One may also note the correspondence between the latter and the way the concept of the image of God is related in the New Testament to "the son of David," Jesus Christ. In Col 1:15, for example, Jesus is called "the image of the invisible God, the firstborn over all creation"; and Rom 8:29 describes what awaits the Christian believer, namely "to be conformed to the likeness of his Son, that he might be the firstborn among many brothers." As long as human beings are struggling to reach this lofty ideal, they may be comforted and motivated by seeing it as an empty concept that time and again calls them, notwithstanding their imperfections, to creatively fill it.

With appreciation,
Klaas

References

Baldermann, Ingo, Ernst Dassmann, and Ottmar Fuchs. 2000. *Menschenwürde*. JBTh 15. Neukirchen-Vluyn: Neukirchener.

Groß, Walter. 2000. Gen 1,26.27; 9,6: Statue oder Ebenbild Gottes? Aufgabe und Würde des Menschen nach dem hebräischen und dem griechischen Wortlaut. Pages 11–38 in *Menschenwürde*. Edited by Ingo Baldermann, Ernst Dassmann, and Ottmar Fuchs. JBTh 15. Neukirchen-Vluyn: Neukirchener.

Hamm, Berndt, and Michael Welker. 2000. Vorwort. Pages v–xi in *Menschenwürde*. Edited by Ingo Baldermann, Ernst Dassmann, and Ottmar Fuchs. JBTh 15. Neukirchen-Vluyn: Neukirchener.

Rogerson, John W. 2009. *A Theology of the Old Testament: Cultural Memory, Communication, and Being Human*. London: SPCK.

Spronk, Klaas. 2007. The Human Being as the Image of God and Human Beings Slaughtered in the Name of God: A Biblical Subversion of Ancient and Modern Concepts of Human Dignity. *Scriptura* 95:195–201.

———. 2010. The Book of Judges as a Late Construct. Pages 15–28 in *Historiography and Identity: (Re)formulation in Second Temple Historiographical Literature* (LHBOTS 534). Edited by Louis Jonker. New York: T&T Clark.

The Givenness of Human Dignity: A Response to the Essays of Frits de Lange and Hendrik Bosman

Beverly Eileen Mitchell

Frits de Lange's "The Hermeneutics of Dignity" (and Gerrit Brand's response) and Hendrik Bosman's "Figuring God and Humankind" (and Klaas Spronk's response) provide a stimulating contribution to the ongoing discussion on the nature of human dignity. Not surprisingly, I found many points of convergence with my own thought. Each author also raised issues that were intriguing to me but would require more sustained reflection on my part before I could offer a fully developed response. There was also a small subset of ideas that were discussed that raised serious questions for me, but I will offer a sustained comment on only two. However, before I do so, I feel it is important to set the context for what guides my own thinking on human dignity.

My understanding of human dignity has been developed out of my parallel study of the plight of African Americans under black slavery in the United States and the plight of European Jews during the Holocaust. Despite the particularity of these distinctive contexts, I maintain that foundational theological insights from this study are applicable to all members of the human family. However, I believe that these insights are particularly pertinent to populations throughout the global community who live in conditions in which their dignity is regularly placed in jeopardy.

Two governing principles shape my notions of human dignity. First, what I say is governed by a theological commitment to view matters principally but not solely from the perspective of those whose dignity has been assaulted or has been placed in jeopardy. This perspective keeps human dignity discourse from lapsing into abstraction and irrelevance. If our ruminations regarding human dignity are irrelevant and unhelpful for populations who "live with their backs against the wall," then the value of such ruminations is unsatisfactorily limited (Thurman 1976, 11). Because human beings are rooted in particular socio-historical contexts, discussions regarding what it means to be human and what human dignity is must be understood from within particular social contexts. I privilege the life experiences of the marginalized, the poor, and the disinherited because I believe that what is said and done relative to them reveals more clearly what is at stake when we speak about human dignity.

The second principle regarding discourse on human dignity is that dignity is a graced element of our existence as human beings created in the image of God. Human beings belong to God, for without God we cannot exist. This existence is a gift, an instance of profound grace. This transcendent grounding of our existence, rooted in grace, is the first line of defense against the denial of the intrinsic value and worth of every human being. This transcendent grounding indicates that human life and death are matters under God's jurisdiction. Therefore, no human being or group of human beings has legitimate jurisdiction over these matters. When we usurp divine authority over them, we transgress God's prerogative and tragic consequences ensue.

The notion of humans as beings created in the image of God derives, of course, from the assertion made in Gen 1:26 (Mitchell 2009, 41, 42, 43; Mitchell 2005, 4–5). Hendrik Bosman's discussion of the *imago Dei* in the Old Testament was helpful in highlighting some of the problems associated with trying to fashion a consistent theological anthropology from the Hebrew Scriptures. However, despite the problems associated with the ambiguity and limits of Old Testament texts for a full theological explication of human dignity, I maintain that the biblical story of salvation as depicted in both the Old and New Testaments—beginning with Creation and ending with the Consummation—gives an indication of the value and importance that God has placed upon humans. Despite the entry of sin into the world and the fallenness that has resulted from human capitulation to it, God's gracious commitment to a covenantal relationship with human beings attests to their continuing value and importance in *God's* eyes. Moreover, as Bosman rightly affirms, neither sin (Gen 3) nor the Flood (Gen 6–9) undid the image of God in human beings (45–46). Therefore, as long as the *imago Dei* persists in human beings, the dignity that arises from that divine imprint remains and should be safeguarded. For me, Gerrit Brand's assertion that the "doctrine of the incarnation of Christ confirms the doctrine of creation" underscores the divine intent to safeguard that which was precious and valuable about the human creature despite the devastating intrusion of sin in the good creation (31).

Of particular significance is that whatever dignity that accrues to us as a result of God's divine imprint, its value and worth are things that only God confers. Because all human beings share in that which makes us human, dignity is conferred on us all. The glory or sacred worth that derives from our humanness is not something that we have earned or made ourselves, but something that comes to us from God alone. It is not connected to what we do or fail to do. This dignity is given to all humans, regardless of our abilities, capabilities, or disabilities. It is not mitigated by our economic, social, political status, gender, or any other aspect of our social location that could be used to differentiate one human being from another in a hierarchical way. This dignity is granted to each of us from the beginning of life and follows us to the grave. While it can be obscured, assaulted, hidden, or jeopardized, it remains indestructible. Insofar as this dignity comes from God alone, it cannot be taken away by other human beings. This is why I strongly disagree with Walter Groß who, as Klaas Spronk reports, emphasizes that being created in the image of God does not point to what a person *is*, but to what he or she has to *do* (59). Such a position denies the graced aspect of human dignity and severs it from the *imago Dei*, which is also a graced aspect of what it means to be human.

In light of these two governing principles—concrete discussion of dignity principally from the perspective of the oppressed and the graced nature of human dignity—I will reflect upon two issues that Frits de Lange raised. He asserts that the "rhetoric of human dignity has a strong performative function: *it aims to bring about something*" (emphasis added). He distinguishes between two types of performative discourse relative to human dignity: a discourse on justice and a discourse on flourishing (10). I would like to frame my response to his assertions regarding dignity rhetoric as a performative function and his discussion of the distinction between dignity discourses of justice and discourses of flourishing with a concrete example. If, for example, the discussion on human dignity takes place in the context of protecting the homeless against public policies that ultimately serve to punish them for their misfortune, I could perhaps agree that there is a performative function in such discourse, if it is understood that such a discussion is intended to encourage the safeguarding of the dignity that they already possess as human beings. (The assertion that dignity is something that the homeless already have is true, from my perspective, regardless of the degrading conditions in which many of them find themselves.) However, if the performative function is understood as *granting* them dignity for the sake of justice, I would deny that the nature of dignity discourse in that context aims to impart dignity to the homeless for the sake of justice. The pursuit of justice is a praxis that affirms the presence of dignity in the dehumanized; its pursuit does not impart dignity. The pursuit of justice is predicated on the prior acknowledgement that the dignity already given by God warrants the respect that belongs to human beings *qua human beings*. The fight for justice reflects an acknowledgement that dignity already exists but is being violated.

The second and more substantive issue on which I would comment pertains to de Lange's discussion of the contrast between dignity discourse around justice and dignity discourse around flourishing. He maintains that dignity discourse around justice relates to a shared, general humanity, whereas dignity discourse around human flourishing relates to the individual. Where flourishing is frustrated, the dignity of individuals is endangered, for example, the terminally ill, suffering children, the homeless, the addict, the incontinent elderly suffering from dementia. As de Lange says, "They are suffering, because they are frustrated in being able to lead the kind of life, they had reason to value" (12). In flourishing discourse, concern about human happiness and self-actualization are emphasized. Discussion of human dignity in terms of human flourishing is troubling to me. In this life, given the human condition, flourishing is often an ideal. On this side of the *eschaton*, flourishing, however it might be defined, is a goal that one may or may not reach. Although it is an aspiration that is probably universally desired, the dignity that is granted to us by virtue of our being created in the image of God is not predicated on whether or not we will flourish. It is there whether circumstances permit us to flourish or not. In the Two-Thirds World, where there are multiple obstacles to human flourishing, humans who live under these conditions retain their dignity. Flourishing (or the lack thereof) cannot be a requisite for affirming or denying the presence of dignity. My assertion here does not mean that I disavow the importance of the human desire to flourish, for my own theopolitical commitment to the struggle for justice rests on the belief that the assault on human dignity precludes the opportunity to flourish. However, the inability of individuals or certain populations to flourish, whether because of war, famine, theft of their land, or lack of access to natural resources, does not in any way rob them of their dignity. Rather, it makes their cry against the violation of their dignity that much more urgent.

It is at this point that de Lange's discussion of our tendency to recognize dignity in the very violation of it is apt. When he asserts that "phenomenologically, a reference to dignity sometimes functions as an argument, more often however, it is a cry for justice, an expression of pain" (10), he speaks to a recognition made by moral philosopher Raimond Gaita and philosopher Simone Weil. For Gaita, the violation of our dignity exacerbates any suffering we might experience in our mistreatment (Gaita 2000, 82). For Weil, each of us carries within us a visceral response to the experience of having our humanity denied or our dignity assaulted (McLellan 1990, 274). I have said elsewhere that the dignity that arises out of our being created in the image of God is often most clearly manifested as a bearing witness to the violation in our cries of protest, whether vocal or silent (Mitchell 2009, 4). For me, this inner protest reinforces the notion that even when we view human beings who live in conditions of squalor and dehumanization and fail to acknowledge their dignity, that dignity nevertheless remains. De Lange also makes an interesting observation about the difficulty of defining dignity by way of its violation, when he states, "How hard it may be to give a sound definition of dignity as a concept, the violation of what it stands for goes together with strong feelings of indignation" (10). I think that what mitigates the difficulty of defining dignity is the recognition of its givenness and ever-presence in the first place. Protest or indignation in response to its violation is a warning to the spiritually and/or morally obtuse. An eagerness to recognize the presence of dignity in others from the start should make it easier for us to honor it in others and to avoid the wholesale defacement of the dignity of others sooner rather than later.

De Lange states that the evocation of dignity in discourses on justice functions as an alarm signal, indicating that humanity is in danger. It is only after this that the philosophical theories and religious doctrines give explicit meaning and expression to the notion of dignity. Theory follows life; it comes after the experience (11). But I would argue that if human dignity is properly recognized as God-given and that, consequently, it is something to be viewed as sacred and safeguarded, then the *praxis* of affirming human dignity can actually *preclude* acts of injustice. Affirmation of a dignity already present in the people we encounter can become a safeguard against its violation. Focus on the development of this praxis can reorient dignity discourse in a positive way, because it reinforces the permanent nature of dignity itself. In that way, perhaps, the dignity discourse of justice and the dignity discourse of care, welfare, and flourishing can be viewed as a unified whole.

References

Gaita, Raimond. 2000. *A Common Humanity: Thinking about Love and Truth and Justice*. London: Routledge.

Mitchell, Beverly Eileen. 2009. *Plantations and Death Camps: Religion, Ideology, and Human Dignity*. Minneapolis: Fortress.

———. 2005. *Black Abolitionism: A Quest for Human Dignity*. Maryknoll, N.Y.: Orbis.

Thurman, Howard. 1976. *Jesus and the Disinherited*. Boston: Beacon.

Weil, Simone. 1990. Appendix: On the Human Personality. Page 274 in David McLellan, *Utopian Pessimist: The Life and Thought of Simone Weil*. New York: Poseidon.

Part 2
Engaging the Text

A True Disgrace? The Representation of Violence against Women in the Book of Lamentations and in J. M. Coetzee's Novel *Disgrace*

L. Juliana Claassens

Introduction

The beginning of the book of Lamentations, written after devastating events of 597–587 B.C.E. that saw the city of Jerusalem repeatedly invaded by the mighty Babylonian army, introduces one to a most tragic figure. In Lam 1–2, Jerusalem is personified as a violated woman, a woman invaded, raped, and humiliated. In gruesome detail it tells of the destruction of the walls and protective fortifications around the city and how enemy forces gained entry into her innermost sanctuary, desecrating her secret places. The devastation is described in terms of sexual violence and rape—a metaphor used throughout the prophetic traditions to describe military invasion (cf. Jer 13:22–26; Nah 3:5; Isa 47:1–3).[1]

Many centuries later, in a novel from a very different socio-historical context, one encounters another woman, one who has also been violated and raped, and who lives with the consequences of her humiliation. In *Disgrace* (1999), written by the Nobel laureate J. M. Coetzee, Lucy, the daughter of the disgraced academic David Lurie, is gang-raped by three men in an attack on her smallholding near Grahamstown, South Africa—an attack in which her father also sustains severe injuries after being set on fire. As in the case of Woman Zion, one finds in Lucy a distraught woman

---

1. In this regard, Brad E. Kelle (2008, 104) argues as follows: "Certainly the violation of women as a metaphor fits the destruction of capital cities, for the stripping, penetration, exposure and humiliation of the women is analogous to siege warfare, with its breaching of the wall, entrance through the gate, and so forth."

who refuses to be comforted, and who for a long time refuses to speak about her ordeal.

However horrific the crimes perpetrated against these women, neither are the chief end of the stories. In both instances one sees how violence against women is used by the authors to communicate a larger political and, in the case of Lamentations, theological message. As Frank England (2007, 105, 107) writes regarding the character Lucy Lurie, Coetzee is "inscrib[ing] physical violence upon the body of one of his characters," in the process of "writing a strand of the socio-political reality of South Africa" upon Lucy's violated body. In the book of Lamentations too, the metaphor of rape and violence against women serves as a rhetorical strategy for the prophet to get his audience, the elite men of his society, to pay attention.

In this essay, critical questions will be asked with regard to the effect of using violence against women to deal with a nation's trauma. This will done first by considering what message the authors seek to convey in their use of rape and sexual violence as metaphor for the respective socio-political situations they are addressing. Second, the effect will be considered of such portrayals on readers—in particular, whether the sociopolitical commentary communicated by the sexual violence is a productive means of raising awareness of the prevalent epidemic that tolerates and/or obscures violence against women across ethnic lines in South African society. Do literature and visual representations such as the book of Lamentations and the novel (and film) *Disgrace* serve to counter harmful stereotypes that contribute to a climate in which violence against women is considered the norm? Do they not merely reinforce the reader's or viewer's existing deep-seated perceptions of gender?

The Rape of Woman Zion

Jerusalem is portrayed in most dehumanizing terms in Lam 1–2. Woman Zion is publically humiliated—in verses 8–9 she suffers the ultimate indignity of having her nakedness exposed. The effect of this humiliation is expressed well by Kathleen O'Connor: "her degradation dehumanizes her, as her body becomes an object of shame" (2006, 22).[2]

---

2. Cf. Pamela Gordon and Harold C. Washington (1995, 316), who argue that nakedness does not merely entail "the exposure of the woman's body but ... also the

Numerous allusions are found in the first two chapters of Lamentations to the sexual violation and even rape of Woman Zion. In Lam 1:10, for instance, it is said that the enemy forces "have stretched out their hands over all her precious things"—hand being an euphemism for penis, which is coupled with the notion of "the nations invad[ing]" or entering "her sanctuary." Allan Mintz (1982, 3–4) shows that an equation may be made between the female body and the temple; between genitals and inner sanctuary. He describes the rape imagery as follows:

> So far have things gone that even in the secret place of intimacy to which only the single sacred partner may be admitted, the enemy has thrust himself and "spread his hands over everything dear to her." (1:10; cf. O'Connor 2006, 23)

It is also possible to read the imagery in Lam 1:3 as Woman Zion's being pursued by her attackers and overtaken between narrow places (*bên hammaṣārîm*)—compare KJV's translation, "between the straits," with the more common translation of "in the midst of her distress" (NRSV). The context in which this translation presents itself is indeed one of affliction (*mē'ŏnî*) suffered due to enemy invasion. In this regard, it is noteworthy that the root *'nh* in its *piel* form constitutes the technical term for rape (cf. Deut 21:14; 22:24, 29; Gen 34:2; Judg 19:24, 20:4; 2 Sam 13:12, 14, 22, 32: Lam 5:11). Even though in the *qal* this term means "to be bowed down, afflicted," in *piel* the verb takes the meaning of "to abuse, exploit" and in sexual contexts "to force sexual intercourse upon" (Gordon and Washington 1995, 313). As Deryn Guest argues, "given this context, the pursuit of her and the taking of her between 'narrow confines' may well imply sexual overtaking in a rape context" (1999, 417–18).

Woman Zion is deeply affected by the violence. She strikes a lonely, isolated figure. Weeping day and night, she receives no comfort (Lam 1:1–2; see the refrain repeated in 1:16, 17, 21). In 1:11, she laments: "Look, O LORD, and see how worthless I have become." The effects of the violence committed against her are clear: she suffers physical and mental anguish, as is evident in her claim in Lam 1:13 that God has made her desolate (see the NIV translation of *šōmēmâ*, a term that is also used to describe the

---

pornographic defacement/de-facing of the victim: as the skirt is pulled over her face the woman is dehumanized."

raped Tamar in 2 Sam 13:20, living out her life in the house of her brother as a deflowered, desolate woman without prospects; Guest 1999, 415, 419).

What is even harder to bear than the graphic sexual imagery and the violation experienced by the woman in Lamentations text is the fact that God is responsible for her plight. In 1:13–15, God is made the subject of a series of violent verbs: God sets her bones on fire; yokes her with her transgressions; and treads upon her in a wine press. Kathleen O'Connor (2006, 26) describes this scene as follows:

> His merciless battering leaves her faint and she cannot get up. Her words create a scene of domestic violence in which a powerful angry man beats his wife, hurls her about, and leaves her for dead.[3]

Of course, the portrayal of God in this text relates to some biblical traditions' understanding that assumes a direct link between sin and suffering. Moreover, the metaphor of God as the righteous husband who punishes his wayward, adulterous wife is a prophetic metaphor that, since the days of Hosea (picked up and continued in Jeremiah and intensified even further by the prophet Ezekiel), has been used to deal with difficult questions regarding suffering and the unforeseen trauma brought about by the exile and its aftermath.

In her essay "Hiding behind the Naked Woman," Deryn Guest considers why the author would use this disturbing metaphor to narrate the pain his people experienced after the devastating Babylonian invasion. Guest points out that the "personification of the city as a battered woman has been praised" by many interpreters "as a very useful device whereby a nation may be encouraged to acknowledge their guilt and also their repentance" (Guest 1999, 421). Thus it has been argued that the elite members of society, who are held responsible for the predicament in which Jerusalem finds herself, are cast in the most vulnerable position as a sexually violated and abused woman.[4]

---

3. See Guest 1999, 417, 420. See also the series of violent actions listed in Lam 2:1–9 with God as subject in which God is implicated for making the city vulnerable by destroying its walls, ramparts and gates that had the distinct purpose of keeping invading armies out.

4. See Kelle 2008, 106–8; Ben Zvi 2004, 363–84. The latter article deals with the underlying elements of honor and shame that were key considerations for the prophets' audiences and a significant consideration in understanding their message.

This rhetorical strategy has every intention to shock its audience. It is based upon a number of deeply-embedded gender stereotypes. First, the metaphor of the battered woman/city assumes a link between sin and sexuality, building on beliefs, for example, that women are weak, unfaithful, and inclined to lead men astray by their shameful sexuality. Something of this link between sin and sexuality is evident in the following assertion in Lam 1:8:

> Jerusalem sinned grievously,
> > so she has become a mockery;
> all who honored her despise her,
> > for they have seen her nakedness;
> she herself groans,
> > and turns her face away.

Moreover, in verse 9 it is said that "her uncleanness is on her skirt." Conceivably pointing to her menstrual condition, the reference to "uncleanness" can also refer to evidence of sexual intercourse that continues the association between sin and sexuality that is responsible for Woman Zion's public humiliation (O'Connor 2006, 22).

Second, using the metaphor of sexual violence to describe the downfall of the city assumes and reinforces the notion that women can be restrained or punished for their wanton behavior, "taught a lesson," as expressed by the commonly held notion of putting an "uppity" woman in her place (Guest 1999, 431). Indeed, as Pamela Gordon and Harold Washington point out, "the intrinsic violence of the city-as-woman metaphor is grounded in men's violent control of women in ancient Near Eastern societies" (Gordon and Washington 1995, 318). These stereotypes work together to justify the violence enacted against this woman/city, suggesting that female victims of violent crimes somehow have done something to deserve the treatment that they receive at the hand of their male partners.

In this regard, we see these stereotypes at work in several of the admissions of guilt put in the mouth of Daughter Zion. For instance, in Lam 1:18, Zion admits: "The LORD is in the right, for I have rebelled against his word," and in verse 20 she cries out: "See, O LORD, how distressed I am; my stomach churns, my heart is wrung within me, because I have been very rebellious."

However, as indicated by the title of her essay, Guest believes this rhetorical strategy employed by the author of the book of Lamentations to be deeply disturbing. It is ironic that women, who for the most part were excluded from the political arena, who had no real role in decision-making, are used as the primary vehicle of the metaphor to denote blame and the collapse of the city. The author thus utilizes the bodies of women who suffer physical affliction and the indignity of being publicly exposed to make a political/theological point. The title of Guest's essay suggests that the actual perpetrators are in essence "hiding behind the naked woman," engaging in a process of evading male responsibility. By placing the brunt of the blame upon this personified woman, the Israelite elite distance themselves or even absolve themselves from their actions (1999, 428).

Writing Violence on the Bodies of Women in *Disgrace*

In the South African novel *Disgrace*, the shocking incident regarding Lucy Lurie's rape is found in a larger narrative regarding the sexual exploitations of the aging former Romantics professor who is forced to resign after an illicit affair with one of his students. Dealing with his growing feelings of losing power, David Lurie seeks to come to terms with his increasingly marginalized role in a "rationalized and bureaucratized world," a world in which the Classics and Modern Languages Department has been downsized and Cape Town University now is called Cape Technical University (England 2007, 112).

Closely related to these feelings of being emasculated or even castrated, David Lurie engages in one sexualized encounter after the other. The novel starts with his encounter with the exotic looking prostitute Soraya, who retreats from his life when he, in search of intimacy, draws too close. Shortly after, Lurie harasses one of his students; on more than one occasion forcing sex on the equally exotic and even younger Melanie Isaacs. These incidents cause David to lose his teaching tenure when he refuses to admit before the university disciplinary committee to having done anything wrong.[5]

---

5. Chris N. van der Merwe and Pumla Godobo-Madikizela show how Lurie's sexual relationships with both Soraya and Melanie reveal connotations of rape. Thus, when Soraya breaks off contact, "David Lurie harasses her and becomes a 'rapist' in the sense that he tries to force his will upon her and invade her story." And, in the case of Melanie, the young woman is depicted as "passive throughout" (2008, 19). "In a subsequent encounter, when Melanie tries to resist him, he ignores her resistance and overpowers her," an act of rape (2008, 78–79). See Middleton and Townsend (2009,

From Lurie's sexual encounters it is evident that for him women are objectified, serving but one purpose. This is also evident from his conversation with Melanie when he first asks her to stay the night. When she asks why, his response is: "Because you ought to." Once again when she asks why, he says: "Why? Because a woman's beauty does not belong to her alone. It is part of the bounty she brings into the world. She has a duty to share it" (1999, 16). Within this context of the male gaze and women objectified as sexual objects to be enjoyed even against their will, sexual violence bursts onto the scene. Shortly after arriving on his daughter Lucy's smallholdings in the Eastern Cape (where she grows flowers and vegetables and runs a boarding kennel for dogs), father and daughter are attacked by three men. The attackers violently kill all the dogs, and pour gasoline over Lurie's head and set him alight before proceeding to rape Lucy. This portrayal of rape differs from the depiction of sexual violence in the book of Lamentations, as the rape of Lucy is not described in any detail whatsoever.[6] The rape occurs behind closed doors and all that the reader is privy to is what David Lurie is imagining transpired. However, the suggestion is clear, and in subsequent chapters the effect of the rape is similar to that of the violated woman in Lamentations. Lucy refuses comfort; she is a distraught woman, all forlorn in her disgrace. The effect of the rape is particularly evident in the description offered to us by her father:

> She sits in her housecoat and slippers with yesterday's newspaper in her lap. Her hair hangs lank; she is overweight in a slack unhealthy way. More and more she has begun to look like one of the women who shuffle around the corridors of nursing homes whispering to themselves. (1999, 205)

118–19), who argue that the sexual encounter between David Lurie and Melanie constitutes the novel's first depiction of rape, in addition to the first reference to the term. Lurie is depicted as "the aggressive intruder"; "the intruder who trusts," whereas Melanie is portrayed as "the fragile young woman," who clearly says "no," but to no avail. See also their fascinating account of the rape script that plays itself out in the rest of Melanie and David Lurie's encounters (119–21).

6. Middleton and Townsend note that the silence surrounding Lucy's rape is troubling as is the attempts to narrate what had happened to her. For instance, they note that right after the attack, "neither David nor Lucy has verbalized the word 'rape' yet; it will be many pages, many weeks in narrative time before David does" (2009, 123). Moreover, it seems Lucy refuses "the application of familiar rape narratives," choosing to consider what had happened to her as a "private matter" (1999, 125).

And, earlier on, her father thinks:

> This is what their visitors have achieved; that is what they have done to this confident, modern young woman. Like a stain the story is spearing across the district. Not her story to spread but theirs. They are its owners. How they put her in her place, how they showed her what a woman was for. (1999, 115)

It is only much later that we hear Lucy's voice (albeit it in the voice imagined by its male author) when she speaks out about the rape, saying that she was surprised at their hate (1999, 156). And yet when she finds she is pregnant, Lucy decides to keep the baby—a decision utterly incomprehensible to her father. David Lurie is equally perturbed by Lucy's decision to stay on the farm under the "protective wing" of her neighbor Petrus, who "marries" her in return for her land.

As I noted in the introduction to this essay, the sexual violence narrated in Coetzee's novel is used to communicate some compelling insights regarding the complexities of postapartheid South Africa. When considering the message written on the violated body of Lucy Lurie, two lines of interpretation have been suggested. First, it is noteworthy that *Disgrace* is written in the context of the Restitution of Land Rights Acts, passed in 1994. In this context, it seems that land is equated with the female and that rape becomes a metaphor to denote the dispossession of land. From Petrus's response it seems as if Lucy's rape functions as a way of setting right the wrongs of the past. As Petrus tells David in the following dialogue,

> "Yes I know what happened. But now it is all right."
> "Who says it is all right?"
> "I say." (1999, 138)[7]

It is evident in David Lurie's take on the rape of his daughter that the sexual violation stands for something completely different. As he tells Lucy, "it was history speaking through them ... a history of wrong.... It may have seemed personal but it wasn't. It came down from the ancestors" (1999, 156).

---

7. Van der Merwe and Godobo-Madikizela write that in the novel, "the rapists feel that their raping is justified because it balances the 'rape' of colonialism." And for Petrus, by means of the rape, justice has been restored; Lucy has paid for the sins of the ancestors. To him, "it was a rape to end rapes" (2008, 83–84).

According to England (2007, 111), Coetzee inscribes an act of violence upon the body of Lucy Lurie. This, he argues, "results in an act of reparation more radical than any conceived of by the governing authorities," hence communicating a quite distinct message of restorative justice. Coetzee has Lucy say the following:

> What if ... what if *that* is the price one has to pay for staying on?... They see themselves as debt collectors, tax collectors. Why should I be allowed to live here without paying? (1999, 158)

Violence again breaks into the lives of the Luries when David returns to his apartment in Cape Town. The break-in and rampage in his apartment is described in terms of language that is reminiscent of the sexual violence experienced by his daughter shortly before when, in some sense, his private parts are exposed and his goods taken. He thinks to himself:

> No ordinary burglary. A raiding party moved in, cleaning out the site, retreating laden with bags, boxes, suitcases. Booty; war reparations; another incident in the great campaign of redistribution. (1999, 176)

For Coetzee, the sexual violence in the novel thus serves as a means to consider difficult questions regarding redistribution of property, of restorative justice, particularly as it relates to issues of land and ownership in the new South Africa.

In a second line of interpretation of the message written on the body of women, it seems David Lurie is taught the meaning of forgiveness by witnessing his daughter's response to the rape, when Lucy emerges as a radical example of reconciliation. In this regard, Julie McGonegal (2009, 148) argues that

> *Disgrace* is haunted, and perhaps motivated, by the question of how to absolve guilt after apartheid, how to compensate for the unspeakable horror committed, and how to seek redemption and forgiveness for the atrocities perpetrated.[8]

It further appears that the violence afflicted to the body of Lucy and the accompanying feelings of humiliation and disgrace are used as a metaphor

---

8. Cf. England 2007, 116.

for radical reconciliation. It seems the novel, by means of the metaphor of sexual violence and in particular by means of Lucy's response to the rape, explores interrelated questions of what McGonegal (2009, 171) calls "giving, forgiving, and 'giving up'—the sacrifice that the gift of forgiveness entails." In this regard, McGonegal asks whether Coetzee is "implying that it is only through acts of self-degradation and humiliation that genuine reciprocity and reconciliation can transpire in a society so exceedingly fragmented along racial lines." Such sentiments are clearly expressed by Lucy:

> Becoming nothing: Lucy replies: "Yes, I agree, it is humiliating. But perhaps that is a good point to start from again. Perhaps that is what I must learn to accept. To start at ground level. With nothing. Not with nothing but. With nothing. No card, no weapons, no property, no rights, no dignity. (1999, 205)

Also, in her conversation with David Lurie, Lucy's coworker Bev makes the point that women can be surprisingly forgiving as she assures a deeply concerned David that "women are adaptable. Lucy is adaptable" (1999, 210).

Even though it is vitally important for us to consider questions regarding reconciliation and forgiveness in our postapartheid South African context, it is rather problematic that sexual violence is used as metaphor to communicate this particular message.[9] In a sense sexual violence functions in *Disgrace* much as the rhetorical strategy outlined in

---

9. There has in fact been widespread outrage against this line of interpretation. Derek Attridge quotes Athol Fugard who, apparently without having read the novel, said the following: "We've got to accept the rape of a white woman as a gesture to all of the evil that we did in the past. That's a load of bloody bullshit. That white women are going to accept being raped as penance for what was done in the past? Jesus. It's an expression of a very morbid phenomenon, very morbid" (2004, 164). See also the ANC critique of *Disgrace* before the Human Rights Commission, in which Public Enterprises Minister Jeff Radebe commented that "J. M. Coetzee represents as brutally as he can, the white people's perception of the post-apartheid black man ... It is suggested that in these circumstances, it might be better that our white compatriots should emigrate because to be in post-apartheid South Africa is to be in 'their territory', as a consequence of which the whites will lose their cars, their weapons, their property, their rights, their dignity. The white women will have to sleep with the barbaric black men." Quoted in Van der Merwe and Godobo-Madikizela (2008, 73). For a detailed account of the reception of *Disgrace*, see Peter D McDonald 2002, 321–30.

the book of Lamentations, that is, "hiding behind the naked woman." It seems once more that the true perpetrators in South Africa's tormented past are absolved and those who have sacrificed are asked to sacrifice still more. In this regard, I find England's argument (2007, 114) particularly problematic, especially when he invokes the example of the woman who anointed Jesus in Luke 7:36–50 to argue that Lucy's response to her rape serves as a model of costly self-sacrificial discipleship to which Jesus calls his followers.[10]

I would argue that to use the victimized bodies of women to create a model of self-sacrifice is quite problematic, particularly as such a line of interpretation does little to condemn the all-too-widespread phenomenon of violence against women or to break down the stereotypes embedded in such a metaphor. Particularly for female readers trapped in situations of dehumanization, an interpretation that proposes that they should sacrifice even more is quite troubling and in certain situations even dangerous.

Evoking a Response

What, then, ought our response be to when these two well-crafted works of literature—the book of Lamentations, written in an acrostic pattern where each line of the poem starts with a different letter of the Hebrew alphabet, offering some kind of order in a world where everything has come undone, and *Disgrace,* a brilliant novel by a worthy Nobel Prize winner—use sex and violence to communicate their socio-political commentary to their respective readers?

It is true that one has to acknowledge that both texts use violence against women to narrate, in some sense, the way things are. Society in the time of Lamentations was plagued by violence as devastating enemy attacks inflicted deep wounds on the community. The society that gave expression to *Disgrace* also suffered greatly from apartheid-era violence, and in many areas in the country violent crime is still wreaking havoc.

---

10. England (2007, 116) further argues that "the quest of forgiveness is not without the costly burden of making reparation, because the service to which Jesus charges the Christian does not assert its own rights and privileges but submits to the coming reign of God and pours itself out for the neighbour's good, especially for the good of the poor and outcast." See also Van der Merwe and Godobo-Madikizela, who argue that "Lucy's action is a modern translation of the age-old story of the innocent scapegoat" (2008, 92).

For some readers, the sexual violence and the dehumanizing portrayal of real and imagined women are impossible to bear. Thus, one of the reviewers of *Disgrace* actually described the novel as "carry[ing] a moral weight which is without hope, without the possibility of redemption."[11] And the book of Lamentations tends to evoke some equally strong reactions. Naomi Seidman writes powerfully of her anger at a public reading of Lam 1, and particularly at the way Woman Zion is disgraced and dehumanized, saying:

> My mother sways as she murmurs along, a ready sorrow propelling her words. My own spine is rigid with insult and distance, my thighs clenched with the usual impotent rage. I know full well that I take offense the way a woman might grab a robe to cover herself, and my proud impiety is only a makeshift dam against the insistent words of the reading. (Seidman 1994, 282)[12]

One may well ask what our response to such crude portrayals of gender violence ought to be. Would we not be better off removing *Disgrace* from the literary canon or proverbially ripping these pages from the Bible or "burn[ing] the book of Lamentations" as suggested by Naomi Seidman's reading of this books?

I propose that instead of engaging in violent actions such as "ripping" or "burning" books, one should rather employ in a productive way the strong reactions garnered by the indignity and dehumanization of women written in these two texts. Perhaps these works of literature can be used to raise awareness of the equally disturbing issue of violence against women, as Phyllis Trible (1984, 2) has suggested, "in memoriam"—in memory of the real women who have experienced and continue to experience the brunt of violent actions.[13]

---

11. Beverly Roos Muller's review in *Weekend Argus* of 22 January 2000, quoted in Van der Merwe and Godobo-Madikizela (2008, 74).

12. See also Guest 1999, 441.

13. See also O'Brien 2008, which investigates "challenging" divine metaphors such as God as (Abusing) Husband, God as (Authoritarian Father) and God as (Angry) Warrior and the complex power dynamics underlying these metaphors in their respective socio-cultural contexts. According to O'Brien, reading these prophetic texts—with their often harsh portrayals of patriarchy, hierarchy, and violence against women, children, and neighboring nations—alongside our lives may serve as a window to our own world. Noticing the power dynamics and complex ideologies

I thought about this issue in particular when I watched the movie version of *Disgrace*. I was surprised by the effect the movie had on me: the shock of seeing the male gaze, sexual harassment, and rape all vividly portrayed; the anger at the indignity to which women are subjected and particularly at the fact that we live in a world where our daughters are not safe. This point was driven home particularly well when, after the devastating events in the Eastern Cape that saw his daughter raped and himself the victim of violence, David Lurie, perhaps out of a new sense of contrition, visits Melanie's family in George. During this visit, Lurie once again faces a vision of beauty, this time Melanie's younger sister Desiree. As her name suggests, the younger Desiree is an even greater source of desire.[14]

I wondered whether the people around me in the cinema had the same reaction and whether seeing the movie may also compel them to work toward change or, at the very least, to challenge the negative stereotypes of and dehumanizing behavior towards females in society. I suspect the answer to my question is "yes" and "no." I do think that literature and movies can serve as a powerful tool to start conversations, to raise awareness about issues. However, I would add that in order for people to understand and recognize the prevalence of gender violence in our society, the literature or movie needs to be accompanied by a critical gender analysis. For instance, in a recent class I taught to our postgraduate students at Stellenbosch University on "Gender, Culture, and Scripture," we watched the movie *Yesterday* in order to raise awareness of the link between gender, violence, and HIV/AIDS. One Xhosa-speaking student's response is telling. After the movie, he commented—much to the exasperation of some of his classmates—that the violence perpetrated against the woman in the movie when she went to tell her husband working at the mines about her (and his) HIV status was understandable, given the facts that the woman did not follow the proper channels of communication and that she shamed her husband in front of his coworkers.

---

at work in the biblical text may help the reader to name similar realities in his or her own context.

14. Attridge (2004, 178) notes that Coetzee's visit to the Isaacs family is a step in David Lurie's tentative attempts to make amends, but "his appeal for forgiveness is constantly undercut by the uncontrollable reassertion of desire—he even imagines Melanie and her schoolgirl sister together in bed with him, terming it 'an experience fit for a king!'"

I would thus argue that any employment of literature or media in order to raise awareness of the ongoing dehumanization experienced by women by means of sexualized violence can only serve as a conversation starter, an entry point to a larger conversation on the complex issues surrounding the role of gender in society.

Resisting Dehumanization?

In the final part of my essay, I want to further explore two points in the texts under discussion that have been the focus of this essay and that can inspire us to resist the dehumanization, objectification, and physical abuse of women. I want to argue that in both *Disgrace* and ing the book of Lamentations there are flickers of resistance that may offer help. However, it is up to the reader to lift up, amplify, and expand these roots of resistance into full-fledged resistance.

Guest argues with reference to Lamentations that the hope for the female reader lies in lifting up Women Zion's cry of resistance wherever one finds some signs of this violated woman, owning her pain and so reclaiming something of her dignity. In verse 11, this abused woman addresses God: "Look, O Lord, and see how worthless I have become," and in verse 20, "See, O Lord, how distressed I am."[15] In Lam 2:18–19b, the narrator calls on her to speak up and share her pain:

> Cry aloud to the Lord!
>   O wall of daughter Zion!
> Let tears stream down like a torrent
>   day and night!
> Give yourself no rest,
>   your eyes no respite!
> Arise, cry out in the night,
>   at the beginning of the watches!

---

[15]. Even though Lamentations most likely represents a male viewpoint, Guest (1999, 433–34) proposes that "in Zion/Woman's cries, perhaps we can highlight a suppressed discourse"—a discourse that she describes as a "discourse of anger and indignation—a resistance to her fate." See also Tod Linafelt, who argues that "There is disruption of totality. The Other [Mother] cannot completely be eliminated in any given representational system. The Other survives. The poet's monopoly on the reader is momentarily broken; the one spoken about now becomes the one who speaks" (1997, 222).

Pour out your heart like water
before the presence of the LORD!

It is important to note that these seeds of resistance come from the violated woman herself who, by means of her expression of anger, takes the first steps in resisting her dehumanization. In this regard, Beverly Mitchell (2009 4, 33) notes that one of the first signs that point to the indestructibility of human dignity is "the inner cry of protest"; the fact that each of us "carries within us" what Simone Weil called "a visceral response to the experience of having our humanity denied or our dignity assaulted." Hearing such an outcry and resolving to resist any actions that objectify, harass, and violate women is an important step in resisting the dehumanization of women.

Moreover, one should never fall into the erroneous line of argument that the sexual violence represented in these works of literature is "just" a metaphor. Metaphors always draw their connotations from the suffering of real life women. To use these texts *in memoriam* signifies that one remembers the real women that have served as "inspiration" for using sexual violence to communicate a socio-political or theological message.[16]

Finally, in our commitment to resist dehumanization, every effort should be made to change the way people think and speak about women. It is interesting to note that in the novel *Disgrace,* despite the horrendous multileveled portrayal of violence against women, one does see signs of David Lurie's learning to look differently at women. One should note at the outset that this character development constitutes no dramatic transformation. As Chris van der Merwe and Pumla Godobo-Madikizela (2008, 83) rightly point out, even though David Lurie does exhibit positive change throughout the narrative, "he is only able to take a few small steps."[17]

Moving from being a person who, as Beverly Roos Muller describes him, "appears to not only be incapable of having any mature relationships with women, but more significantly, to be incapable of seeing them as fully co-human"—as evident from his "two divorces, his use and abuse

---

16. It is significant that Gordon and Washington close their essay on "rape as military metaphor" with questions directed at women who have served as the "inspiration" for using metaphor of rape for the broken city (1995, 325). Guest suggests further that in response to this violation, "we should observe an honest silence" (1999, 427).

17. Van der Merwe and Godobo-Madikizela call David Lurie "not a heroic character but rather pathetic" (2008, 83).

of sex workers," and "his hunting of a vulnerable student"—David Lurie, throughout the course of the novel, gradually learns to redirect his gaze, to control his desire, and to view women in a different way.[18]

At first it does not seem as if Lurie is changing. For instance, he is unable to see a connection between the way he had forced sex on his student Melanie (particularly in the second of their three sexual encounters) and what had happened to his own daughter.[19] However, one sees evidence of a change toward the end of the book, when Lurie starts to see his daughter in a different light, as having substance. Her resolve to be "a good mother and a good person" encourages her father to be a good person as well (1999, 216).

David Lurie sees his daughter as "solid in her existence" (1999, 217). He quiet observes her working in the garden, conducting "her ordinary tasks among the flowerbeds." Looking beyond the external beauty of the female subject, Lurie notices that his daughter has attained the beauty of an inner harmony. As Van der Merwe and Godobo-Madikizela suggest, "David ultimately learns to value this kind of beauty, inextricably bound to goodness and inner wholeness, and to appreciate it without attempting to overpower it, as he did with Melanie" (2008, 97).

His relationship with Lucy's coworker Bev (who earlier in the novel served as yet another of his sexual exploits but who was different because she is hardly as pretty or as young as some of his former objects of desire) changes toward the end of the narrative when they become colleagues. David notices Bev's skill in her chosen profession, her kindness to animals, which serves to breaking through David's ill-perceived notion that a woman's only function is sexual. As Van der Merwe and Godobo-Madikizela formulate it:

> His way of thinking about female beauty is one of the old thoughts not fitting for him anymore. Bev, in her compassion for needy humans and animals, has an inner beauty which David learns to appreciate. (2008, 95)[20]

---

18. Beverly Roos Muller's review in *Weekend Argus* of 22 January 2000, quoted in Van der Merwe and Godobo-Madikizela (2008, 74).

19. Lurie reflects as follows on his relations with Melanie: "Not rape, not quite that, but undesired nevertheless, undesired to the core" (1999, 25). See Attridge 2004, 187.

20. See also the opera Lurie is working on, in which he gives up the idea of presenting Byron's lover Theresa as a passionate young woman, and portrays her instead as a "dumpy little widow" (1999, 181) who has lost her physical attraction, but whose

In the cases of both Lucy and Bev, it seems the main character can unlearn harmful stereotypes and learn to look at women in a new way. By redirecting his gaze, he is able slowly to start seeing the women in his life as truly human.

The title of this essay is "A True Disgrace? The Representation of Violence against Women." I want to argue that we are called to proclaim that grace enters into a world of disgrace. Exactly there, where women suffer, and where acts of resistance and the unlearning of harmful stereotypes and negative gender-based behavior are found, one finds signs of grace entering the world.

References

Attridge, Derek. 2004. *J. M. Coetzee and the Ethics of Reading: Literature in the Event*. Chicago: University of Chicago Press.

Ben Zvi, Ehud. 2004. Observations on the Marital Metaphor of YHWH and Israel in its Ancient Israelite Context: General Considerations and Particular Images in Hosea 1.2. *JSOT* 28:363–84.

Coetzee, John M. 1999. *Disgrace*. New York: Viking.

England, Frank. 2007. Lucy Lurie in J. M. Coetzee's *Disgrace*: A Postcolonial Inscription Seeking Forgiveness and Making Reparation. *JTSA* 128:104–16.

Gordon, Pamela, and Harold C. Washington. 1995. Rape as Military Metaphor in the Hebrew Bible. Pages 308–25 in *A Feminist Companion to the Latter Prophets*. Edited by Athalya Brenner. Sheffield: Sheffield Academic Press.

Guest, Deryn. 1999. Hiding Behind the Naked Women in Lamentations: A Recriminative Response. *BibInt* 7:413–48.

Kelle, Brad E. 2008. Wartime Rhetoric: Prophetic Metaphorization of Cities as Female. Pages 95–111 in *Writing and Reading War: Rhetoric, Gender, and Ethics in Biblical and Modern Contexts*. Edited by Brad E. Kelle and Frank Ritchel Ames. Atlanta: SBL Press.

Linafelt, Tod. 1997. Margins of Lamentation, or the Unbearable Whiteness of Reading. Pages 219–31 in *Reading Bibles, Writing Bodies: Iden-*

---

faithful love for the deceased Byron is celebrated by Lurie. As Van der Merwe and Godobo-Madikizela describe this change in Lurie: "David has become more interested in faithful, life-giving love than in youthful beauty and passion" (2008, 96).

tity and the Book. Edited by Timothy K. Beal and David M. Gunn. London: Routledge.

McDonald, Peter D. 2002. Disgrace Effects. *Interventions* 4:321–30.

McGonegal, Julie. 2009. *Imagining Justice: The Politics of Postcolonial Forgiveness and Reconciliation*. Montreal: McGill-Queen's University Press.

Middleton, Kim, and Julie Townsend. 2009. Tenuous Arrangements: The Ethics of Rape in *Disgrace*. Pages 116–37 in *Encountering* Disgrace: *Reading and Teaching Coetzee's Novel*. Edited by Bill McDonald. Rochester, N.Y.: Camden House.

Mintz, Alan. 1982. The Rhetoric of Lamentations. *Prooftexts* 2:1–17.

Mitchell, Beverley E. 2009. *Plantations and Death Camps: Religion, Ideology, and Human Dignity*. Minneapolis: Fortress.

O'Brien, Julia. 2008. *Challenging Prophetic Metaphor: Theology and Ideology in the Prophets*. Louisville: Westminster John Knox.

O'Connor, Kathleen. 2006. *Lamentations and the Tears of the World*. Maryknoll, N.Y.: Orbis.

Seidman, Naomi. 1994. Burning the Book of Lamentations. Pages 278–88 in *Out of the Garden: Women Writers of the* Bible. Edited by Christina Büchmann and Celina Spiegel. London: Pandora.

Trible, Phyllis. 1984. *Texts of Terror: Literary-Feminist Readings of Biblical Narratives*. Minneapolis: Fortress.

Van der Merwe, Chris, and Pumla Godobo-Madikizela. 2008. *Narrating Our Healing: Perspectives on Working Through Trauma*. Cambridge: Cambridge Scholars.

A Response to Julie Claassens's "A True Disgrace? The Representation of Violence against Women in the Book of Lamentations and in J. M. Coetzee's Novel *Disgrace*"

Dorothea Erbele-Küster

Dear Julie,

Thank you for your engaged paper and the unfolding of the victimization of women and for your struggle with (the novel) *Disgrace*.

I must confess to having had mixed feelings when reading the first chapters of *Disgrace* in anticipation of receiving your essay. Why should one read about such lust and concupiscence, and about the sexual adventures of a university lecturer with a student thirty years younger than himself? Was this not simply another story of sexual harassment on a university campus, told from the perspective of the male abuser and, on top of this, in Coetzee's characteristic laconic style?

You may understand, Julie, why I was at first perplexed by exactly how you might bring this androcentric story about a self-centered man into conversation with the female voice crying out in the book of Lamentations. Like you, I was irritated by a Nobel Prize winner's well-crafted descriptions of violence. At the time I did not know, but hoped, that we shared the same feelings on this. One example that comes to mind is when, before his daughter is raped by strangers, the father already casually uses the word "rape" in an outburst in front of her. He seems vexed about the "animal-welfare people," as he calls Lucy's friend Bev Shaw. He mocks their good intentions and deeds by commenting that "everyone is so cheerful and well-intentioned that after a while you itch to go off and do some raping and pillaging" (1999, 73).[1] Such were the thoughts behind my growing curiosity as I awaited the chance to read and respond to your essay.

My letter to you focuses on three points: First I will comment on *Disgrace* and on the way in it deals with human dignity. Second, I will expand further the intertextual reading of *Disgrace* and Lamentations so intriguingly begun by you. My thesis will be that Lamentations may serve as a counter-voice to *Disgrace*. Finally, I will discuss the underlying ethical question of how one can teach and even restore human dignity with the help of a novel such as this.

From Disgrace to Human Dignity

I want to touch on two points: the disputed dignity of animals and the fact that dignity depends on facing the other.

The dignity of animals, which is elaborated on in several books by J. M. Coetzee, comes to the fore in *Disgrace* as well. While staying with his daughter Lucy, the main character David Lurie reluctantly helps with the abandoned dogs. He assists Lucy with their final pain relief and removes their heavy, dead bodies.

> Curious that a man as selfish as he should be offering himself to the service of dead dogs. There must be other, more productive ways of giving oneself to the world.... But there are other people to do these things.... He saves the honor of corpses because there is no one else stupid enough to do it. (146)

In this stupidity of his, Lurie is at his most human. His taking care of the dogs seems one of the random moments in the story when he reveals his humanity and shares his dignity.

In a conversation with her father, Lucy tries to explain why she takes care of animals: "They [the animals] are not going to lead me to a higher life, and the reason is, there is no higher life. This is the only life there is. Which we share with animals ... to share some of our human privilege with the beasts" (74). Ironically, the book depicts human dignity by way of the treatment of animals.

---

1. The word "rape" first appears in the novel in a description of the intercourse between David Lurie and his student Melanie ("Not rape, not quite that, but undesired nevertheless" [Coetzee 1999, 25]). I refer here to n. 17 in your essay, Julie.

Regarding the second point: Part of (the) *Disgrace* concerns the fact that that we do not face the other ("other" in terms of gender or social or ethnic group). I would have liked to have elaborated on how the South African context is reflected in the book. However, as an outsider, I will limit myself to just a few remarks. The representation of violence is incredibly complicated. The former penetrator becomes the penetrated. Lucy belongs to the former colonial power. (In the case of the book of Lamentations, woman Zion did not belong to the colonial power.) As one of the weakest members of the white community, Lucy has to pay the price—as she herself declares in a conversation with her father about the men who raped her: "What if … if *that* is the price one have to pay for staying on?" (158). The idea uttered by the raped woman, that one rape and violation may be counterbalanced by another, is absurd and cruel. Reading such phrases, I painfully and troublingly identified with the woman, while at the same time I was confronted with my own white, European skin.

For me, *Disgrace* is a white, Western, androcentric book. This does not mean that I am confusing the perspective of the main character with that of the author. But the attitudes exposed in the book are the only ones I have at hand from him.

I am also annoyed by the way the novel speaks of postapartheid South Africa—the country and its people. Questions posed by Musa Dube, the biblical postcolonial scholar from Botswana, come to mind: How are foreign people and countries portrayed? How are the journeys to foreign lands justified? (see Dube 2000, especially 97–109). What were the reactions of black South Africans to *Disgrace*?[2] I ask myself the latter question especially since *Disgrace* speaks of black people in a very general way, reproducing existing clichés. David Lurie, though a professor of literature, does not understand a word of Xhosa.[3] He seems to be ignorant of the languages of the other in his own country, and this makes it impossible for him to communicate with them in their mother tongue. The very fact that Lurie is white is emphasized in the second half of the book when he and his daughter are the "only whites" (128) in the house of a black neighbor who is hosting a party.[4] Indeed, the whiteness of the skin becomes visible

---

2. See especially n. 10 in your essay.

3. "She … speaks to the child in what sounds like very halting Xhosa" (81). See the introduction of Ettinger (100).

4. David Lurie talking with Petrus (202): "'This is not the way we do things'. *We:* he is on the point to say *we Westerners.*"

only when we face the other. This is what I am missing in *Disgrace*: the facing of the other!

Lamentations as a Counter-Story to *Disgrace*

I would like now to offer an intertextual reading of the two stories, *Disgrace* and Lamentations, trying to explain my suggestion that Lamentations may be read as a counter-voice to restore the dignity of wo/men. I do this, Julie, in response to your critical stance against Lamentations and *Disgrace* which, according to you (and others), (mis)use the humiliation of female bodies as a metaphor to achieve other ends regarding the political situation in a country, thereby reproducing gender clichés.

The first word in the book of Lamentations is a brief cry of agony: 'êkâ. It is repeated several times. In Hebrew, 'êkâ is the book's title. There could not be a more poignant title, yet it expresses a world of suffering and sorrow. It cannot and need not be translated as if it were an *onomatopoeia*. The Hebrew word/sound 'êkâ can be understood easily in any language: sound and meaning are one.

Israel is portrayed as a woman in Lam 1 (cf. Bail 2004, 62–64; Pham 1999, 37–95). The very fact that a woman is crying here after the destruction of the city of Jerusalem gives a human face to the lament. Zion—the city's population—is portrayed in a female body that mirrors harm and guilt. Note that Lamentations is not a prophetic text in which a woman is accused, as in Ezekiel or Hosea. However, I do agree with you, Julie, that the woman is in a sense blamed for the current situation. Thus I am faced with the question: Why does the lament of a woman about her desolate situation lead to her accusing herself? Is this perhaps what Lucy fears in *Disgrace*?[5] Is this the reason why Lucy does not speak out publically about the rape?

While Lamentations begins with the words of a third-person narrator, one hears from verses 9 and 12 onward the widow herself (interrupted in v. 17). Reading the text we join the lament: "[YHWH] has made me waste/barren. All my days I am displaced/distraught" (v. 13). Compare this with: "I hear Lucy saying 'I am a dead person'" (Coetzee 1999, 161). The last word regarding woman Zion is "haggardness," and at the end "distraught"

---

5. See O'Connor 1992, 178–82, especially 179: "the poem symbolically blames women alone for the destruction of the city, and it teaches disdain for women and for the bodies."

dissipation remains (v. 22): "I am full of groans, my heart is distraught." Again, compare this with one of the last remarks of woman Lucy about her current situation: she is left "with nothing. No cards, no weapons, no property, no rights, no dignity" (205; cf. 158).

Actually, the one who has no weapons[6] disarms herself and maybe finally her father as well. Thus Lucy would disarm the former colonial power from within.

Like you, Julie, I am also irritated by the fact that Lamentations uses cultic terms stemming from the book of Leviticus to blame woman Zion for impurity. However, this comes at the center of verse 17, where a third person, an outsider, describes her situation:

> Zion spreads out her hands
> > She has no one to comfort her;
> YHWH has summoned against Jacob,
> > His enemies all about him;
> Jerusalem has become like a woman in her menstruation (or: like something contaminated).

Thus, even though the city is introduced as a widow and not, as in prophetic texts, as an unfaithful woman (cf. Berlin 2002, 9), her body is stigmatized. It seems as if prophetic accusation and lament interrupt each other. But there is a big difference between the outsider and insider perspectives! When she is seen from the former perspective, her body is contaminated; she is blamed. Where her lament is overheard, she expresses the humiliation to which she has been exposed. The distress and disgrace women have to undergo during and in the aftermath of war come to the fore (Berlin 2002, 7).

In contrast, in *Disgrace* we are spared the details of the humiliating deed. Do we miss this? The woman does not say that she suffered violation. She does not even dare to speak to her father about what has happened to her. She refuses to lament; she simply cannot. When reading the book, I at times feel like her father, David, wanting to ask her: "Why do you try to silence the violent acts perpetrated by the three men?" I have to admit that she would probably respond to me as she did to him: "You do not understand me" (157).

---

6. It is her father who is thinking: "Lucy ought to buy a pistol and a two-way radio, and take shooting lessons" (Coetzee 1999, 113).

I share your critical concerns about using the female body and violence against women to deal with the trauma of a nation. My critique is also informed by the cultural-anthropological work of Mary Douglas (1966), who states that in many societies the (female) body functions as a symbol for society's norms and values. The human body serves as a microcosm that stands for the macrocosm, for the social and religious community. The bodies of woman Zion and of Lucy reflect the traumatic experiences women have undergone. Can we therefore say that Lamentations simply uses or even misuses the female body to depict societal calamities and atrocities? I would like to ask you, Julie: How would you depict the violence women have suffered?

Reading the representations of the violation of female bodies hurts me, my body. How does one then discuss violence without violating again or without justifying violence? As Toni Morrison (1993) comments: "Oppressive language does more than represent violence; it is violence."

I want to pause here. The texts depict the experiences of women—back then in Jerusalem and today. There seems to be no other literary way, then, to describe the distress caused by the catastrophes, other than with the help of the female body. Within these painful reflections, the possibility of a counter-reading tries to form in my mind. Rereading Lamentations after having read *Disgrace* does make a difference. In Lamentations we hear a female voice. The voice cries out: "There is no one who will comfort me." Nevertheless, she *does* lament. This is the empowering strength of Lamentations in the midst of all its fragility: the trauma is not silenced. For me, this is the first step from inhumanity to grace. The woman is empowered (by the text) to cry out in public for the inhumanity she had suffered.

Can Fiction Restore Human Dignity?

Finally, Julie, I come to your burning question: How can fiction restore human dignity? You ask this as a young, white, South African woman engaged in feminist critique. Several points I share with you, even if my context in the Benelux countries is quite different. I agree that there is no direct moral application for a narrative (or a biblical text). You say art may just be a starting point for discussion, and I agree. But what further helps to restore human dignity?

I think we should move toward an ethical understanding of the act of reading itself. As a teacher of biblical studies, I try to empower students to be aware of the contradictions and gaps within narrative structures. You have shown us some of the seeds of resistance in *Disgrace*, and I will add some more.

Rereading a narrative such as *Disgrace* forces one to rethink the (educational) character of literature in general. In modern novels and in biblical stories alike, the main character is often not a moral hero or a paradigm to follow. In *Disgrace* we are confronted with an overdrawn image of a father enclosed in his own sexual affairs. By reflecting upon the ambiguities, one may initiate a self-reflective process. The strangeness of the perspectives may make us aware of the "other" and its fragility (Phillips and Fewell 1997, 1–21). In Lucy's response to her father's speculation about the feelings and motives of the penetrators of the crime against her, she suggests that he should know about it, about sex and men ("You are a man, you ought to know," 158). Later, in an inner conversation, Lurie gradually admits that he can indeed inhabit "the men"—as he calls those who had raped his daughter (159). This is a first step: admitting to being part of the penetrator. The second step is indicated in Lurie's question that sums up his reflection: "The question is, does he have it in him to be the woman?"(160). In other words: am I able to switch sides?

In this sense the androcentric Lurie critically reflects on his own stance, and this leads to what you and I merely dare to hope for: the questioning of deep-seated perceptions of gender.[7] This again underlines the importance of telling the stories of those whose human dignity has been violated. Literature such as the book of Lamentations gives voice to the silenced.

I have thus far argued from within the structure of the story. This can be related to the reader's response and the stance the reader takes: As readers, which protagonists are we going to identify with in a particular story? Depending on our own situation, there are multiple and often contradictory options from which we can choose. In the narratives in Genesis, for instance, First World (Christian and Jewish) women have traditionally identified themselves with Sarai, as opposed to the male focus on Abraham. By contrast, a Third World reader of Gen 16 and 21, such as Elsa Tamez from Costa Rica, finds herself best represented by Hagar, Sarai's antagonist in the story and the one who mirrors her (Tamez's) own experiences of oppression, based not only on her sex but also on her class and ethnicity. Tamez's reading alerts me as a Western female reader to the implicit criticism of Sarai's role that the text contains, namely that her role

---

7. See your introduction to your essay, Julie.

is about consensual hegemony. Genesis 16:6 uses all-too-clear vocabulary to describe Sarai's actions, stating that Sarai "oppressed" her slave Hagar. It is no coincidence that the narrator puts the same root of the word in the angel's mouth when the latter later addresses Hagar in the desert. The angel's assurance that "God has heard [of] your oppression" (Gen 16:11) constitutes serious critique of Sarai's attitude towards Hagar. Ethical awareness, then, arises through an exploration of the multiple points of identification that a story offers, and their points of discontinuity.

I am aware that a critical stance that uncovers the gaps in stories is important. As biblical scholars we should not ask in what way ethical concerns may advance literary theory, but the converse: "How do literary and historical questions advance our understanding of what's at stake ethically in the reading and writing of the Bible?" (Phillips and Fewell 1997, 4).

I strive toward an ethical dimension to the retelling of (biblical) stories (Newton 1995). Aesthetics should reflect ethics. The text itself is the meaning. As the cry of pain (*'êkâ*) in the opening word of Lamentations shows, ethics and aesthetics are not separate paths.

However, ethical rules may also be violated in stories themselves. What is the ethical claim of "texts of terror," to quote the term coined by Phyllis Trible (1984)? In response to this problem, Cheryl Exum distinguishes between the narrative as a literary reflection of (extra-literary) violence, and violence exerted by a text as such, where the text can become a lethal weapon in its own right (Exum 1993, 170–201). It is then up to the analysis to uncover these features in biblical stories.

Even if there is no solution, striving toward a healing memory remains important. In David Lurie's sexual harassment trial, repentance is nowhere to be found. Likewise, there seems to be no healing for Lucy.[8] This fact became all the more painful for me when I was sitting next to you, Julie, listening to your paper. I thus cried out with you: How can repentance and forgiveness be discussed publicly?

As I meditate on the possibilities for restoring human dignity, the conversations I had with my husband Volker Küster while he was writing *God and Terror* come to mind. He cited the colored writer Adam Small: "Only art may contribute to reconciliation." Küster modified this statement by saying, "Art may be a prelude of the wonder of reconciliation and have

---

8. Once, when he asks his daughter for forgiveness, she does not understand and does not even respond (78).

catalytic effects on social and civil processes" (Küster 2008, 37). Reading (biblical) stories may then be a third space where we might try out new ways of behavior. In facing the other—David Lurie starts with Bev and animals—grace becomes visible. Or, as the novel puts it: "The question is, does he have it in him to be the woman?" (160). Are we able to identify with those we have violated?

Lament is a specific way of expressing distress. It takes account of the relational identity of the I-figure and the negotiation of power (Cotrill 2008). Reading and teaching Lamentations as a counter-narrative may help in this.

Let me conclude with the voice of another writer from your homeland—a female voice. Antjie Krog's first collection of poems (1970) is entitled *Dogter van Jefta* (Daughter of Jephthah). In the poem with the same title, a female voice in the first-person singular calls out to God. Krog gives her voice to the voiceless daughter of Jephthah. The literary-autobiographical "I" can now speak because there was a Jephthah's daughter, who could not speak out in the biblical story (see Erbele-Küster 2008).

> Lord God of Jephthah
> Here is my body!
> Here is my Hymen—safe as a retina
> And whole as a green pomegranate.[9]

With that I also thank you, Julie, for raising your voice.

Regards,
Dorothea

References

Bail, Ulrike. 2004. *"Die verzogene Sehnsucht hinkt an ihren Ort": Literarische Überle-bensstrategien nach der Zerstörung Jerusalems im Alten Testament.* Gütersloh: Güthersloher.

---

9. Krog 2000, 13; for original Afrikaans, see Krog 1970, 11. On the meeting at the Protestant Theological University in Kampen, The Netherlands, where mainly Dutch-speaking and Afrikaans-speaking scholars met, I asked Julia Classens to read the poem in the original Afrikaans version.

Berlin, Adele. 2002. *Lamentations*. OTL. Louisville: Westminster John Knox.

Coetzee, John M. 1999. *Disgrace*. London: Vintage.

Cottrill, Amy C. 2008. *Language, Power, and Identity in the Lament Psalms of the Individual*. LHBOTS 493. New York: T&T Clark.

Exum, Cheryl. 1993. Raped by the Pen. Pages 170–201 in *Fragmented Women: Feminist (Sub)versions of Biblical Narratives*. JSOTSup 163. Sheffield: Sheffield Academic.

Douglas, Mary. 1966. *Purity and Danger: An Analysis of the Concepts of Pollution and Taboo*. London: Routledge.

Dube, Musa W. 2000. *Postcolonial Feminist Interpretation of the Bible*. St. Louis: Chalice.

Krog, Antjie. 1970. *Dogter van Jefta*. Cape Town: Human & Rousseau.

Krog, Antjie. 2000. *Down to my Last Skin: Poems*. Johannesburg: Random House.

Erbele-Küster, Dorothea. 2008. Stemmen gesmoord door oorlog en geweld—Jefta's dochter aan het woord (Rechters 11:29–40). *AnBrux* 13:104–13.

Küster, Volker. 2008. *God/Terreur: Een Tweeluik*. Vught: Skandalon.

Morrison, Toni. 1993. Nobel Lecture, 7 December 1993. Online: http://www.nobelprize.org/nobel_prizes/literature/laureates/1993/morrison-lecture.html.

Newton, Adam Z. 1995. *Narrative Ethics*. Cambridge, Mass.: Harvard University Press.

O'Connor, Kathleen M. 1992. Lamentations. Pages 178–82 in *The Women's Bible Commentary*. Edited by Carol A. Newsom and Sharon H. Ringe. Louisville: Westminster John Knox.

Pham, Xuan Huong Thi. 1999. *Mourning in the Ancient Near East and the Hebrew Bible*. JSOTSup 302. Sheffield: Sheffield Academic.

Phillips, Gary A., and Danna Nolan Fewell. 1997. Ethics, Bible, Reading As If. *Semeia* 77:1–21.

Trible, Phyllis. 1984. *Texts of Terror: Literary-Feminist Readings of Biblical Narratives*. Philadelphia: Fortress.

Birth as Creation under Threat?
Biblical-Theological Reflections on
Assisted Reproductive Technologies

Dorothea Erbele-Küster

Introduction

The following arguments are developed against my European context. They were stimulated by my background in Germany, where legal recognition of the inviolability of "human dignity" serves to open up German civil law.[1] Being aware of my context, I asked myself whether the issue of Assisted Reproductive Technologies (ARTs) is something that is restricted to middle- and upper-class (wo)men in neoliberal, social democracies? Are ARTs a luxury limited to such societies? How is the issue perceived by, for example, (wo)men in postapartheid South Africa?[2]

Biblical Anthropology in the Context of ART

Contextual Biblical Ethics

I was asked to reflect on human dignity from the perspective of a biblical scholar. However, in my view this does not imply that dealing with ATRs assigns the role of gatekeeper to biblical ethics. One cannot respond to issues surrounding ARTs by simply appealing to the Bible. Biblical texts represent a diversity of perspectives, which are constantly being reexam-

---

1. As I learned at the conference, the (postapartheid) South African Constitution is based on the concept of human dignity as well.
2. For this reason I am also looking forward to Charlene van der Walt's response to my essay.

ined and judged in light of their (normative and emancipatory) relevance.[3] In the imaginary conversation between scriptural passages and genetic engineering that follows, I will raise some questions that may assist those confronted by human dignity considerations related to ARTs in the areas of theology, ethics, and technology. For such people, biblical texts may serve not as an answer, but as a mirror.

In order to formulate a theological-ethical vision regarding ARTs, one must listen to the stories told, questions raised, and problems faced by men and women, doctors, and researchers challenged by the possibilities and pitfalls of genetic engineering.[4] Only then can biblical and contemporary stories be elucidated from a biblical-theological and biblical-ethical perspective. Narrative and poetic passages that best reflect the fragile nature of human existence are at the forefront here. Questions regarding genetic engineering may change in light of scriptural passages and, conversely, scriptural passages may generate new meanings. The hermeneutical process remains in constant motion. I thus propose a contextual biblical ethics. Within the hermeneutical circle of ethics, one criterion is that the human body is related to the sacred. The latter conviction is based on the so-called purity laws in Lev 11–15 (Eberle-Küster 2008), the heart of the Torah, since in these texts aspects of daily life (such as eating and drinking) and special occasions (such as birth) are connected to the sacred—a connection challenged to a large extent by the commercialization of the body in our own time.

Since creation plays a key role in my argument, I will give a brief outline of how the Hebrew Bible relates birth and creation. This will reveal at the same time aspects of the biblical concept of human dignity as implied in Gen 1, according to which human beings are created in God's image. The creation of the human being implies egalitarian relations. All human beings share a similar relationship with God, constitute the image of God (Gen 1:26–27; Prov 14:13; 22:2), and are bestowed with human dignity.

The expression "birth as creation" shows that there is a mystery behind being human, a mystery with God as its foundation. According to Job 38:4,

---

3. For the double criteria of identity and relevance within the hermeneutic process, see Volker Küster 2001, 26–28.

4. I here draw on personal conversations with mothers and doctors. In addition, I have consulted the following sources: Franklin and Roberts 2006; Huijer and Horstman 2004; Singer and Viens 2008; Mat 2008; and *Assisted Reproductive Technology* 2011.

this mystery concerns respecting human boundaries vis-à-vis God and nature: "Where were you when I laid the foundation of the earth? Tell me, if you have understanding" (NRSV). Referring to creation, God here helps us to gain insight into our own human finiteness as well as into divine infiniteness. The mystery applies to the creation of the human being as well—God has insight even into the unformed fetus (Ps 139:16; see Grohmann 2007, 326).

In the Song of Moses at the end of the book of Deuteronomy (32:18), the people of Israel are reminded that they are born of God: "You were unmindful of the Rock that bore you; you forgot the God who gave you birth." We have in fact lost sight of this. In the quotation from Deuteronomy, general images of creation are supplemented by the concept of birth, connecting the two events. The fundamental human experience of giving birth, and the births of every human being, are drawn upon to describe God's creative acts, and vice versa. Birth is creation; as a corollary, human birth and corporality become important within ethics.

Assisted Reproduction Then and Now

In the ancient Near East people attached value to physiognomic omens, to features, or to physical constitution. People thought they could draw portentous conclusions about the course of pregnancy and parturition by looking at a woman's outward appearance. These are recorded in prognostic sources referring to men's expectations of women (Berlejung 2004, 27–64). Ben Sirach, for example, formulates the pursuit of the best possible offspring from an androcentric perspective: "Seek a fertile field within the whole plain, and sow it with your own seed, trusting in your fine stock" (26:20). Such predictions regarding a child's outward appearance can be read as a distant forerunner of genetic tests for hereditary diseases.

There is currently a debate in the Netherlands on the question of whether embryos developed by IVF (In Vitro Fertilization) may be selected or discarded, for example, based on the presence or absence of the breast cancer gene. This discussion presupposes a mono-causal connection between a particular gene and a disease, while in fact a combination of factors both genetic and environmental influence one's receptivity to the disease (Haker 2002, 116–17). New methods of decoding the genes and thus the health prospects of a fetus by screening the blood of its mother in the tenth week of her pregnancy will undoubtedly have an impact on women's decisions regarding their unborn children (Bahnsen 2011, 31–32).

"Patients" who had undergone genetic testing prior to the implantation of embryos have revealed that what was at stake was exclusion of a particular (lethal) disease in their child. According to a recent study conducted in the United Kingdom, choosing between genes that determine the eye color or something similar was not the issue (Franklin and Roberts 2006, 24, 218–20). However, other uses such as selecting the sex of one's child for social purposes, as it is practiced in India or China, for example, may serve patriarchal and misogynist purposes (Banerjee 2007). If genetic codes are emphasized, one runs the risk of leaving little or no room for development, since genes are understood to determine everything and, as a result, human beings are then reduced to the (pre-natal) past.

Interviews with people who have undergone genetic tests with regard to embryo implantation also reveal the wish of a corporeal relation despite such bodiless conceptions. Future parents wish to be physically near their embryos in the laboratory (cf. Franklin and Roberts 2006, 148–49)—perhaps precisely because reproduction now becomes more and more disconnected from the body. In view of this, the question arises, what are the effects of IVF—practiced for more than three decades now—on sexuality and our awareness of corporality?

ARTs transform not only physical but also social relationships. As summarized in a recent textbook for clinicians, researchers, and bioethicists, the technology "also makes possible the creation of novel social arrangements: postmortem insemination, virgin births, postmenopausal pregnancy, multiple parents, anonymous genetic parents, and embryos conceived at one time being born at different times or to different people" (Mykitiuk and Nisker 2008, 116). These are some of the reasons why some within the feminist movement embrace ARTs for making pregnancy possible for all women, and childless women and men in general find ARTs a source of hope.[5]

A certain amount of control has been possible for some time, even before the development of modern ARTs. To ensure women's and children's survival during pregnancy and birth, medical interventions such as Caesarean sections have been used since antiquity (Dierichs 2002, 139–48; Gourevitch 2004). As we also read in some biblical narratives, surrogate pregnancy was a known phenomenon. According to Gen 16 the socially,

---

5. Julie Claassens addressed this issue suggesting that the possibility to beget a child restores the dignity of (wo)men (cf. as well the response to my essay by Charlene van der Walt).

legally, and economically inferior Hagar, the Egyptian female slave, gives birth to a child for a third party. Abram fathers a child by Hagar. She bears the child vicariously for Sarai, Abram's infertile wife. The pregnancy occurs outside of Sarai's body and inside another woman's body. Sarai can stand neither the pregnant Hagar, nor the child born of her. Hagar, the dependent woman, has no say over her own body. Furthermore, her son will not be accepted as the firstborn and heir. This story, like many modern ones, shows that what is technically and legally possible can often have disruptive effects on people's psyche and entire lives.

Like other critics, I contend that unjust relations are generated by ARTs. In the discussion, therefore, we have to contend with the potential and real effects of genetic engineering and ARTs. One also has to ask who benefits and who profits from that which is technically possible, as economic expectations and motives are not to be neglected. Under political pressure, the possibility of selecting certain genes may also be misused.[6] This may result in ARTs in fact promoting injustice,[7] as equal access to assisted reproduction for everybody "depends on public funding" (Mykitiuk and Nisker 2008, 115).

BEING BORN INTO A COMMUNITY[8]

In biblical narrative texts, the birth of an individual is usually situated within the broader community. It is linked to the importance of a male descendant as the latter is the precondition for the passing on of both one's name and one's property.

In Gen 38, the widow Tamar wants to end her own childlessness and prevent the name of her husband Er, Judah's eldest son, from being effaced. Judah's second-born, Onan, had died after having refused Tamar his seed. Now Judah tries to spare his youngest son the same fate. However, Tamar takes action to beget progeny. She covers her face and positions herself by

---

6. Pollard (2009, 176) warns against the misuse of eugenics.

7. Cf. Katz Rothman 1989. Maura A. Ryan (2001) likewise argues from a Roman Catholic perspective for a social justice-based discussion on reproductive technologies.

8. In contrast to Germany, for example, where births usually take place in clinics, the majority of Dutch women prefer to deliver at home. Here children are literally born within the inner circle, and the local community learns of the event by way of banners put up in the living room announcing, "It's a boy/girl!"

the side of the road. "When Judah [her father-in-law] saw her, he thought her for a harlot ... and said, 'Here, let me sleep with you...'" (Gen 38:15–16, CJPS). Tamar falls pregnant by Judah, the one who wanted to deny her any descendants, and she gives birth to twins.

The steps Tamar took to ensure the survival of her husband's line were both unusual and dangerous. Near the end of the story Judah, who had condemned Tamar's actions (v. 24) before realizing how he was involved in them, declares: "She is more in the right than I" (v. 26). Whereas Judah previously condemned Tamar, he now changes his perception of the issue: It is no longer a legal question in his eyes. He is conscious of a connection between Tamar and himself; he relates his position to hers and vice versa. Having recognized this, he declares that, compared to himself, Tamar had done much better with regard to their community. In the Hebrew text the concept of *ṣedāqâ*, which stands for loyalty toward the community, is used. Biblical texts such as this one usually do not refer to the rights of the individual, but to justice that flourishes in relationships within a community.

The ethical acts in this story are clearly linked to the situation: Tamar's plan is in solidarity with and is aimed at the survival of generations to come. Creating a human being through pregnancy and birth confirms the bonds between successive generations. In Tamar's efforts to beget a child, it becomes clear that private acts do have a communal dimension. The birth of a child transcends the mother's (parents') individual life (lives).

Human (Female) Being and God Cooperating in Creating

Creation is an ongoing process. In fact, the Hebrew Bible uses a specific word that is only applicable to divine creation (*bārā'*, Gen 1). However, creation is also described with reference to cultural concepts such as shaping (as a potter in Gen 2), and with images derived from the experience of pregnancy and birth. The created world is not to be understood as "nature," as something immutable. Humans are called to interact with and in the world; they are "created co-creators."[9] Human creativity is aimed at the life that God has produced. Technical intervention into "nature"/creation is a constitutive element of life itself (see *Assisted Reproduction*

---

9. Philip Hefner introduced the concept of "created co-creator." For a critical evaluation of the concept, see Hefner 2004: "The Created Co-Creator myth is blasphemous, it does indeed bear the seeds of ecological treachery." People often seem to overlook the ambivalence of this concept. See Vander Stichele and Hunter 2006.

Then and Now). The use of technology is a core human capability in order to develop human freedom. It is a means to reach objectives, but it is no objective in itself. Without it, human life would be noncreative.[10] In the acts of the human being, God's creative blessing will emerge (Gen 1:26-28; 4:1). This becomes apparent in every human birth. The opening of the first genealogy in Gen 5:1-3 refers back to the creation of humankind in the likeness of God in Gen 1: Adam brings forth a child in his likeness and image. There thus seems to be an interconnectedness between the genetically-influenced image and the theological promised image of God. The juxtaposition of either God as creator or genetic engineering seems from the perspective of this passage already far too simplistic.

The way in which birth is spoken of tells something about the origin and identity of human beings. In the Hebrew Bible the human being is, for instance, called someone born of a woman (Job 14:1; 15:14; 25:4) or a descendant of a human being (Ps 8:5; Job 16:21; 25:6; 35:8), but also someone born of God (Num 11:12; Deut 32:18). According to biblical literature, human beings are, therefore, of double descent.

On the occasion of the first birth of a human being in Gen 4:1, this double identity of the human being is referred to: "Now the Human knew his wife Eve, and she conceived and bore Cain, saying, 'I have created a person with the help of YHWH'" (Stein 2006). With the cooperation of YHWH, the woman produced a man-child. The verb "to produce/create" (*qānâ*) is used in Gen 14:19 as an epithet for God, creator of heaven and earth. According to Gen 4, the "first" woman acquires a child with the aid of God. Her perception during birth finds expression in her child's name, Cain: the one acquired/created with the aid of YHWH. The ambiguous word *qānâ* (possibly derived from either "to buy" or "to create") expresses in an exceptional way that giving birth is similar to creation. This statement articulates that woman and God cooperate in creating: by giving birth the woman reflects God's creative work. Therefore the question is why, in dogmatic theology, only the technical possibilities of humankind within creation are discussed, and never the corporeal activity of human beings as creative action during conception and birth.[11]

---

10. Cf. Gräb-Schmidt 2005.

11. Many thanks to Karen Sporre of Sweden for commenting on this point and for introducing me to the work of the South African theologian Lyn Holness, who unfolds Mary's giving birth to Jesus and her motherhood as being physical, emotional, and according her will, in mediating the Incarnation.

In the purity laws in Lev 12:2, the female contribution to human beings' origins is emphasized by the use of the causative derivative from "to bring forth seed." Taking this into account, one may translate: "When a woman produces seed and gives birth to a male child." According to a poetic text concerning pregnancy (Ps 139:15), God's acts and those of human beings go hand in hand: "My frame was not hidden from you when I was being made in secret, intricately woven in the depths of the earth." Human beings' origins are described as skillful handiwork. God is the weaver of human dignity (vv. 13, 15). Psalm 139 places the origins in the secret of the depths of the earth. May this sentence from the prayer in Ps 139, therefore, be translated as and associated with a screened-off room, a laboratory? If so, it might read as follows: "My frame was not hidden from you, when I was being made in secret, intricately woven in the depths of the test tube."[12]

Therefore, it seems misleading to me to ask whether the genetically engineered human being can still be called "a creature bestowed with dignity." The question should rather be: What are the criteria for a continuous creation (*creatio continua*) with the human being as subject? In concrete terms: Can birth outside the maternal body not be called birth (anymore)? Phrased differently: Can human beings experience themselves as both *born and made*? (Franklin and Roberts 2008). To conclude, I will set out three implications for the ethical discourse around human dignity of thinking about "birth as creation."

Contextual Biblical Ethics According to "Birth as Creation"

Birth as *Initium*

As explained above, the opportunity for performing creative activities is inherent in all human beings. In and through the gift of beginning something new, in spontaneity and freedom, we re-enact our birth. Philosopher Hannah Arendt characterizes this idea by saying that human beings have

---

12. Frits de Lange refers to the introduction by philosopher Michel Serres to an essay, "L'oef transparent," by scientist Jacques Testart, who states that through IVT human beings lose one of their specific traits, since their beginning lies in the hands of humankind (see Lange 1988).

the capacity to start something new and thus articulate the new beginning that comes into the world with each human being.... With the creation of man [sic] the principle of beginning came into the world (2000, 181).[13]

With birth something new comes into the world. As long as birth means coming into the world and not coming from the world, human beings may realize and enjoy it.[14] This beginning enfeebles old relations and enables reconciliation. Birth breaks up causal connections and allows us to act forgivingly. Thirty or forty years ago, a bioscientist was a "*homo faber* who creates a predictable and material world," but the recombinant DNA technique has thoroughly changed his or her creative power: it resembles acting, a world-changing activity (cf. Huijer 2003, 30).

My question would thus be: Can biotechnological creativity be perceived in a positive sense as something that brings a new beginning, and with it the hope of reconciliation in the world? In view of Arendt's insights on the principle of natality, every human being is a "beginner" (*initium*), and everyone can take the initiative. In light of this, Tamar's action can be read as an exemplary initiative that focuses on the continuity of a communal and just world.

ARTs at birth and during pregnancy should not abrogate the possibility of a new beginning (*initium*). The crucial point is whether reconciliation becomes noticeable. Genetically-engineered changes are not to undermine the understanding that in every birth God's creative act is confirmed. Improvement and renewal of human and world are necessary, but these must happen in such a way that human acts are not contrary to God's acts (Jüngel 2004, 979). The mystery of creation must be reflected in birth. In birth the creative act of God is reenacted. The question is now: How can we experience being a creature bestowed with dignity, which implies perceiving birth/life as gift, while we are also acting creatively (genetic engineering included)?

---

13. For theological interpretations of Hannah Arendt's concept of natality, see Ulrich-Eschemann 2000 and Verhoeven 2003.

14. See the wordplay by Heuser (2002, 33): "Solange Menschen auf die Welt—nicht aus der Welt—kommen [As long as humans come into world and not from the world], geht ihre 'Natur' nicht in einem Gegensatz zu Kultur und Technik auf." For Heuser, however, ARTs do not allow this.

Birth as Relational Event

If technologies are used at birth and during pregnancy, one must bear in mind the manifold relationships that define being human being (man and woman), for example, one's relationship with one's body, with fellow human beings, nature, the worldwide community, and with God. Being born means being interwoven into a "web of relationships" (Arendt 2000, 179). For this reason, I am convinced that there is need for an ethic that emphasizes relationships, rather than a casuistic bioethics (Praetorius 2005).[15] We may then conceive of the possibility of raising children not just as genetic or biological issue, as Mercy Amba Oduyoye has stressed.[16] A perspective based on creation is fundamentally relational and contextual. Bonds between women become distorted through surrogate motherhood, and economically vulnerable women might, for instance, be tempted into becoming egg donors.[17] The question is whether the use of techniques such as ARTs empower all (wo)men or not, and whether they violate human dignity or not (Fabre-Magnan 2007, 307–13).

Ethical discourse often focuses on the independent individual and his or her ability to make autonomous decisions when separated from his or her relations. However, "feminists have long been critical of the claim that simply expanding the number of choices equates with more autonomy" (Widdows 2010, 87).[18] The concept of relational autonomy (MacKenzie and Stoljar 2000), like the (South) African concept *umoja*, is far more helpful.

In fact, the responsibility for producing a healthy child is often placed on women. They find themselves confronted with omnipotent promises of medicine and become exhausted by their efforts to become pregnant with the help of ARTs, which becomes almost a full-time job. The question, furthermore, emerges whether and to what extent a philosophical

---

15. Widdows (2010, 97) puts it as follows: "What feminist ethicists desperately need is a way to value and respect the experience of women seeking to use ARTs and yet to take into account the social and collective import of these decisions."

16. I thank Mary-Ann Plaatjies-van Huffel from Stellenbosch University for reminding me of this point. See Erbele-Küster (2003).

17. Overall 1987, 127: "Surrogate motherhood is not and cannot be a freely chosen 'job' because the practice is such that it recognizes both individuals who can make the choice ... all that is left is what has been described as a 'womb for rent.'"

18. According to Widdows (2010, 87–89), ARTs in the end leave women with the "same old 'choice'" of motherhood.

model of human autonomy is capable of including and integrating both emotional and corporeal experiences, such as are present, for example, in giving birth.[19] This concept of autonomy is also contradictory to the biblical-theological concept of being an infant, because the latter signifies precisely finiteness and relational existence.[20]

In biblical narratives, the beginning of life is seen as relational and as occurring within history. The way in which these stories are told—their narrativity—offers readers the opportunity to retell their own stories (Erbele-Küster 2009). The story of Tamar in Gen 38, and the genealogies in Gen, Ruth 4, and Matt 1, emphasize the social dimensions of birth—the fact that through birth one is admitted into a succession of generations. Furthermore, according to biblical texts, the beginning of life is connected to physical objects, such as semen and the maternal body. This notion is not to be understood as purely biological, but as a reminder of our corporeal existence. Corporeal experiences, such as the relation between mother and the fetus inside her are important. The poetic language employed in the Psalms embraces different dimensions, such as the biological, social, biographical, and theological (Grohmann 2007, 325).

From a perspective based on creation, God's cooperation at the beginning of existence is constitutive to our existence. Prior to the "beginning" of human beings (see Ps 139:15–16), God enters into a relationship with them. This relationship shows that human beings, human heritage, and human tissue are not means toward different ends, and may not be instrumentalized. Otherwise, human dignity is under threat. Against the background of understanding birth as a relational event, human dignity likewise appears to be a relational, and not a static concept.

Birth as Corporeal Experience

Human beings experience and understand the world and themselves via their bodies. This is a crucial presupposition for my argument. The body is likewise central to pregnancy and birth. Some decades ago, coitus was a precondition for conception and birth. That has now changed. This

---

19. As is stressed in the work of the Swedish scholar Kirsten Grønlien Zetterquist. Cf. Sporre 2003.

20. Kohler-Weiß 2009, 223: "Das Lebensverhältnis Schwangerschaft entzieht sich ja gerade unseren begriffslosen Unterscheidungen von Identität und Differenz, Gleichbleiben und Wandel, Zweiheit und Einheit, Selbstständigkeit und Abhängigkeit."

comment is neither meant in a romanticizing way—the sexual act that leads to pregnancy can be involuntary and violent—or in a naturalistic way (suggesting that IVF is against nature). However, it profoundly changes the way in which a human being perceives his or her body and the body of the other, presupposing that it is through and with the body that we live (cf. Marzano 2008). Reproductive techniques (at the far end of which is the issue of an artificial uterus) alienate women from the crucial and specific role bodily experiences play in the development of the fetus.[21]

IVF, genetic selection, and manipulation of embryos are actions that occur *outside* the female body, but that nevertheless make deep inroads into (*inside*) the female body. These technologies are often offered as solutions and promises to childless women, "but the effects on the lives and bodies of women remain undiscussed" (Huijer and Horstman 2004, 243).

As opposed to this, the philosophical and biblical-theological concepts that were outlined here stress that pregnancy is a corporeal experience of being in relationship with others. One only has to think of Rebecca, who feels the twins inside her body (Gen 25:22), or the pregnant Mary, who visits the pregnant Elizabeth. Their encounter leads to the baby's leaping in Elizabeth's womb (Luke 1:39-45).

My plea for taking corporeal relations seriously with regard to pregnancy and birth is not formulated against the background of a creation or natural order argument. It is, in fact, an anthropological argument: corporality is fundamental to being human in everyday life. Conversely, the *imago Dei* may be understood as an embodied presence.[22] From a biblical-theological perspective, ethics will aim at formulating preconditions so that our cognitive, corporeal, and emotional knowledge and experiences remain connected in order that the fragile human body will be neither fragmented nor reduced to mere genes.[23] Some impulses toward a theo-

---

21. Marzano (2008, 110) is assertive regarding the role of the female body: "La relation entre une mère et son enfant pendent une grossesse est quelque chose très particulier que la science et la technique ne pourront jamais recréer." [The relationship between a mother and her child during pregnancy is something very special that science and technology will never be able to recreate.] Widdows (2010, 90–91) mentions this as one argument of feminists rejecting ARTs.

22. I take up here an argument of Robert Vosloo's after the presentation of this essay.

23. The emphasis of Widdows (2010, 94, 98) on embodiment as a key theme—

logical endorsement of corporality are supplied by Lev 11–15. Aspects of daily life, such as food, time, birth, and menstruation are related to God's holiness. In these chapters, a utopia unfolds regarding the relationship between God and the human body. Female and male bodies are not portrayed as mere objects or commercialized. In their relationship with God, humankind comes into being and human dignity flourishes. In the words of the introduction to the Holiness Code in Lev 19:2: "You shall be holy, for I, YHWH, your God am holy."[24]

References

Arendt, Hannah. 2000. *The Portable Hannah Arendt.* Edited by Peter Baehr. London: Penguin.

Assisted Reproductive Technology. Online: http://en.wikipedia.org/wiki/Assisted_ reproductive technology.

Bahnsen, Ulrich. 2011. Früher erkennen. *Die Zeit* 34 (Aug 2011): 31–32.

Banerjee, Kaberi. 2007. Pre-Implantation Genetic Diagnosis and Sex Selection. *IVF.net.* 19 August 2007. Online: http://www.ivf.net/ivf/pre_implantation_genetic_diagnosis_and_sex_selection-o2906.html. Accessed 20 March 2012.

Berlejung, Angelika. 2004. Frau nach Maß: Physiognomische Omina für die Frau als Quellen für Überlegungen zur Mentalität und Kultur der altorientalischen Gesellschaft im 1. Jt. v. Chr. Pages 27–63 in *Sara lacht: Eine Erzmutter und ihre Geschichte.* Edited by Rainer Kampling. Paderborn: Schöningh.

Dierichs, Angelika. 2002. *Von der Götter Geburt und der Frauen Niederkunft.* Mainz: Zabern.

Erbele-Küster, Dorothea. 2003. Rereading the Bible: A Dialogue with Women Theologians from Latin America, Africa and Asia. *Exchange* 32:310–21.

———. 2008. *Körper und Geschlecht. Studien zur Anthropologie von Leviticus 12 und 15.* WMANT 121. Neukirchen-Vluyn: Neukirchener.

---

arguing from a different perspective but along the same lines—opens up new possibilities in this debate.

24. With appreciation to Hanna Tervanotko, of Brussels and Oslo, for our discussions, and to Jos Hoogstede of Kampen for comments and for help with my English.

———. 2009. *Narrativität*. Online: http://www.Bibelwissenschaft.de/wibilex/dasbibellexikon/details/quelle/WIBI/zeichen/n/referenz/37118///cache/e50c6acd68/.

Fabre-Magnan, Muriel. 2007. Dignité. Pages 307–13 in *Dictionnaire du Corps*. Edited by Michela Marzano. Paris: Presses Universitaire de France.

Franklin, Sarah, and Celia Roberts. 2006. *Born and Made: An Ethnography of Preimplantation Genetic Diagnosis*. Princeton: Princeton University Press.

Gourevitch, Danielle. 2003. Chirurgie obstétricale dans le monde Romain: Césarienne et embryotomie. Pages 239–64 in *Naissance et petite enfance dans l'antiquité*. Edited by Véronique Dasen. OBO 203. Göttingen: Academic.

Gräb-Schmidt, Elisabeth. 2005. Die Technik—Unser Leben. Pages 494–509 in *Leben: Verständnis, Wissenschaft, Technik*. VWGTh 24. Edited by Eilert Herms. Gütersloh: Gütersloher.

Grohmann, Marianne. 2007. *Fruchtbarkeit und Geburt in den Psalmen*. FAT 53. Tübingen: Mohr Siebeck.

Haker, Hille. 2002. Der perfekte Körper: Utopien der Biomedizin. *Concilium* 38:115–23.

Hefner, Philip. 2004. The Created Co-Creator Meets Cyborg. Online: http://www.metanexus.net/Magazine/tabid/68/id/8780/Default.aspx.

Heuser, Stefan. 2002. *Menschenwürde: Eine theologische Erkundung*. Ethik im Theologischen Diskurs 8. Münster: LIT.

Huijer, Marli. 2003. Vrijmoedig Spreken: Publieke Gesprekken over Gender en Biotechnologie. *Tijdschrift voor Genderstudies* 2:29–40.

Huijer, Marli, and Klasien Horstman, eds. 2004. *Factor XX: Vrouwen, Eicellen en Genen*. Amsterdam: Boom.

Jüngel, Eberhard. 2004. Schöpfung und Erhaltung 2. Dogmatisch. *RGG* 7:979–80.

Katz Rothman, Barbara. 1989. *Recreating Motherhood*. New York: Norton.

Kohler-Weiß, Christiane. 2009. Von der Gnade geboren zu werden: Eine kleine Theologie der Schwangerschaft. Pages 220–36 in *Kinder haben Kind sein Geboren sein: Philosophische und theologische Beiträge zu Kindheit und Geburt*. Edited by Anette Esser, Andrea Günter, and Rajah Scheepers. Königstein: Ulrike Helmer.

Küster, Volker. 2001. *The Many Faces of Jesus Christ: Intercultural Christology*. London: SCM.

Lange, Frits de. 1988. Kroniek-Ethieken modern voortplantingstechnieken. *GThT* 1:32–41.
MacKenzie, Catriona, and Natalie Stoljar, eds. 2000. *Relational Autonomy: Feminist Perspectives on Autonomy, Agency, and the Social Self.* New York: Oxford University Press.
Marzano, Marcela. 2008. *Penser le Corps.* Paris: Presses Universitaires de France.
Mat, Joke. 2008. Embryoselectie in de Praktijk. 2008. *NRC Handelsblad* (21 June):8–11.
Mykitiuk, Roxanne, and Jeff Nisker. 2008. Assisted Reproduction. Pages 112–20 in *The Cambridge Textbook of Bioethics.* Edited by Peter E. Singer and Adrian M. Viens. Cambridge: Cambridge University Press.
Overall, Christine. 1987. *Ethics and Human Reproduction. A Feminist Analysis.* Boston: Allen & Unwin.
Pollard, Irina. 2009. *Bioscience Ethics.* Cambridge: Cambridge University Press.
Praetorius, Ina, ed. 2005. *Sich in Beziehung setzen: Zur Weltsicht der Freiheit in Bezogenheit.* Königstein: Taunus.
Ryan, Maura A. 2001. *The Ethics and Economics of Assisted Reproduction: The Cost of Longing.* Moral Tradition Series. Washington, D.C.: Georgetown University Press.
Singer, Peter E., and Adrian M. Viens, eds. 2008. *The Cambridge Textbook of Bioethics.* Cambridge: Cambridge University Press.
Stein, David, ed. 2006. *The Contemporary Torah: A Gender-Sensitive Adaptation of the JPS Translation.* Philadelphia: Jewish Publication Society.
Ulrich-Eschemann, Karin. 2000. *Vom Geborenwerden des Menschen. Theologische und philosophische Erkundungen.* Münster: LIT.
Vander Stichele, Caroline, and Alistair G. Hunter, eds. 2006. *Creation and Creativity: From Genesis to Genetics and Back.* Sheffield: Sheffield Phoenix.
Verhoeven, Marijke. 2003. *Boreling en Beginner: Nataliteit bij Hannah Arendt.* Zoetermeer: Boekencentrum.
Widdows, Heather. 2010. The Janus-Face of New Reproductive Technologies: Escaping the Polarized Debate. *IJPT* 4:76–99.

A Response to Dorothea Eberle-Küster's "Birth as Creation under Threat? Biblical-Theological Reflections on Assisted Reproductive Technologies"

Charlene van der Walt

Dear Dorothea,

I want to thank you for your essay and for the privilege of journeying with your compelling argument during the past couple of weeks. However, let me be honest right from the start and say that it has not been an easy journey. I find the subject matter of Assisted Reproductive Technology (ART) a very complex one, mainly because it is not an isolated issue, but relates to issues of poverty, social location, the compromised position of women, the politics of intimate spaces, HIV and AIDS, education, and health care.

The subject matter of your essay is also not something that I have really given much thought. Somehow it has just not been part of my lived reality up to now. My very limited exposure to ARTs has been, on the one hand, within the context of ministry and, on the other, via the isolated experiences of friends struggling to conceive. In both of these contexts, the issue of ARTs had been far removed my own body, so to speak.

However, in reading about and reflecting upon ARTs as they intersect with social contexts, on the one hand, and biblical literature, on the other hand, I became progressively troubled by the issue. I want to highlight two aspects in this regard:

First, right at the beginning of your essay, you ask whether ARTs only concern middle- or upper-class European men and women in liberal social democratic societies—a luxury, as you put it. Your question forced me to reflect upon the realities facing those in the Two-Thirds World and how these relate not only to ARTs, but also to other issues surrounding the options and possibilities of health and medical intervention. These realities, which I will briefly discuss later in this response, are startling.

In reading the stories of women and men and the pain and shame of involuntary childlessness, I became painfully aware of my own position of privilege. Although I am from the Two-Thirds World, I have reaped the benefits of growing up within a previously highly unjust system. I have had the privilege of secondary and tertiary education and I am more or less financially independent because of that education and the opportunities that came with it. Because of my financial independence, I have reasonable control over my relational status, my intimate relationships, and the question of whether or not I would like to have children. My social status and position have very little to do with whether or not I have children and, if I decide to have children and should be unable to do so, I would have access to information regarding ARTs and access to health care, medication, medical intervention, and counseling. These are not circumstances shared by most women in the Two-Thirds World. Therefore, I engage with this subject from a self-conscious perspective of privilege, but nevertheless hope to engage from a position of solidarity with those who suffer from lack of resources, information, opportunities, or autonomy, and with those who experience stigmatization and injustice because of an inability to conceive.

I found your essay troubling or, rather, challenging on a second level, namely with regard to method. My own academic pursuit in the field of biblical scholarship has thus far focused on contextual Bible reading. This approach takes seriously not only the context of the biblical text in terms of the world in which it originated and the intertextual context within biblical literature, but also the contextual realities of modern Bible readers and their unique social locations. Meaning, in terms of this approach, is generated from the creative dialogue between text and reader within a particular context. This creative dialogue is usually rich, dynamic, and surprisingly unpredictable. I think Walter Brueggemann (2011) correctly guesses the reason behind the dynamic nature of this dialogue when he suggests that in this conversation the thick, layered, and conflicting nature of the biblical text is met by thick, layered, and conflicting human beings, speaking from thick, layered, and conflicting contexts. Therefore, it does not really come as a surprise that this is a dynamic conversation. This has been mainly where my own interest in the process of Bible interpretation ended: in the exploration of the creative moment when text and reader meet. Your approach, Dorothea, of contextual biblical ethics now adds a new creative dimension to the equation (a pragmatic consequence, if you will), a moment that I have sorely missed in my own scholarly engagement. I see in the addition of an ethical moment to the conversation the beginning of a new movement. As a result, not only the moment of interaction between the contextually embedded text and reader is paramount, but also the implications of the dialogue. New questions emerge, questions such as: What happens after the conversation? Does it have implications for my life or my lived reality? Does it impact the community in which the dialogue takes place? In this movement a new spiral of engagement potentially exists, because my new lived experience will lead to new questions that will in turn lead me back to the text, hopefully this time with people different from myself. I find this a very helpful moment in the process of contextual Bible reading, especially considering the task of a liberating healing praxis that is inseparable from justice, as Denise Ackermann describes the task of theological engagement in society (Ackermann 1993).

Dorothea, your essay has served as an important mirror reflecting and unmasking my own position of privilege, confronting me with the painful realities of injustice, and challenging me to ponder my own scholarly approach, aims, and goals, and to contemplate the consequences of them. My initial word of thanks is thus a qualified one.

In my response to your essay I want to reflect on ARTs from a Two-Thirds World perspective, first broadly and then by focusing on two separate qualitative studies conducted in the Western Cape in South Africa. A description of the context may pave the way toward a discussion of bioethics from the position of the marginalized, or as Maura Ryan calls it in her discussion of the subject, a bioethic from below. The approach of bioethics from below has some remarkable links with "birth as creation" as presented in your essay. As a final point for reflection I want to bridge the gap between theory and context by identifying some of the resources located within faith communities that can assist in the construction and negotiation of such a bioethic from below.

First, let us consider the realities of infertility and the feasibility of ARTs within a Two-Thirds World context. As Vayena and others outline the problem, infertility and assisted reproduction in the developing world has, until recently, received limited attention at global and regional levels. This has been attributed to two key causes: (1) the widespread perception that infertility is primarily a problem of the developed world and not of developing countries, and (2) the belief that ARTs are technically too demanding for the capacity and expertise available in developing countries, and too costly for their overstretched health care budgets. Furthermore, as a significant proportion of infertility problems in the developing world has been attributed to potentially preventable causes such as sexually transmitted infections (STIs) and postabortion and postpartum infections, the primary response to infertility in these has been a focus on prevention. Although prevention is paramount from the public health perspective, this priority does not address the needs of infertile couples. In many developing countries children are so highly valued that a woman's status is often defined solely in terms of motherhood, with infertility carrying a terrible stigma. Coupled with a lack of access to infertility services, such sociocultural factors exacerbate suffering, worsen health disparities, and cause depression (Vayena et al. 2009, 413).

The compromised position of a woman in such contexts becomes clear right from the start, since a "woman in particular, also commonly suffers from severe negative social consequences such as stigmatization, ostracism, abuse and economic deprivation" (Dyer et al. 2002, 1657). This is mainly because motherhood is such an important component of married women's identity and is important for women's social status (Cooper et al. 2007, 278). Social expectations regarding marriage and children often leave women with very little choice concerning whether they want to have children. This is often the result of the expectations of the intimate partner, leaving infertile women fearing infidelity and abandonment. Furthermore, extended families also attach such social value to married couples having children that childless marriages are perceived as tainting the reputation of the whole family. Hence, married women and those anticipating marriage often feel they would encounter and need to conform to family expectations to produce children (Cooper et al. 2007, 278).

In contexts such as those mentioned above, infertility or inability to have children "can be experienced as [a] deeply painful life crisis and can lead to feelings of loss, grief and anger, feelings of physical powerlessness and loss of control" (Ryan 1994, 196). The inability to produce children can touch on all dimensions of the self: social roles, group identification, relationship with self, body, and family, with life's purpose and meaning. It is thus not surprising that women would pursue other alternatives when faced with the painful personal and social realities associated with infertility.

In 2001, the World Health Organization recognized the above situation in developing countries and recommended that infertility be considered a global health problem. The WHO, therefore, called for more innovative approaches in infertility treatment, such as the development of low-cost ARTs. However, considering the already overstretched health care budgets of many developing countries and the dominant perception that the inability to become pregnant without medical intervention is not always regarded as an illness, it is not surprising that most women in the Two-Thirds World still have no access to ARTs and, when they do, they still cannot afford it.[1] It is thus estimated that ARTs only meet 1 percent of the projected need in the Two-Thirds World (Vayena et al. 2009, 414).

Moving closer to home, I would like briefly to discuss two qualitative research projects conducted in the Western Cape. Dyer, Abrahams, Hoffman, and Van der Spuy (2002, 1657–62) conducted a mixed method inquiry looking into: (a) the knowledge of fertility and the causes of infertility among infertile women in the region; (b) their treatment-seeking behaviors; and (c) their expectations with regards to ARTs. The study was conducted at The Groote Schuur Hospital's infertility clinic in Cape Town, a facility that serves the needs of the Cape Town community. The results of the study highlight the following trends: (1) it is predominantly women who take the initiative to access modern health care as an option for the treatment of infertility, and it often serves as a last resort; (2) these women were willing to "do anything," "do whatever it takes," or "go the whole way" to address their infertility,[2] but most often do not know what exactly the process entails—particularly regarding the low success rate of ARTs especially in the first cycle, the complexity and pain involved in the process, and the costs, consequences, and risks involved; (3) finally, the study also showed that the women lack basic knowledge about sexuality and reproductive health.

When asked whether the women knew why they were infertile, common explanations included: blocked tubes, weak sperm, abnormal menstruation cycles, and previously-used family planning methods. Many women were concerned about a "dirty womb." Women came to the clinic in the hope to be "cleaned" either via medication or a "womb scrape." One woman declared that she might be infertile "because she

---

1. Recent statistics indicate that one cycle of ARTs costs between 2000 and 2700 USD, whereas the average income of a family in Nigeria is between 52 and 62 USD per month (Vayena et al. 2009, 415).

2. One woman stated: "I will do anything. No matter what the cost. I will do everything in my power. I will do what I must do as long as I get a child." The desperate nature of such statements accentuates the vulnerability of these women.

is being punished for having sex before marriage." Nearly half the black women who took part in the study considered evil spirits or witchcraft a possible cause of childlessness.

In light of the findings, the study concluded with an appeal for more efficient sexual and reproductive education as well as for more committed counseling efforts to assist woman in planning for alternative approaches to conception.

A second study, conducted by Cooper, Harris, Myer, Orner, and Bracken (2007, 274–83) considered the reproductive intentions of HIV-positive men and women in South Africa. I found this particularly important research as it brought together the realities of infertility as well as the ever-present realities of the HIV and AIDS pandemic in sub-Saharan Africa.[3] In this region, the majority of HIV-positive individuals are women in their reproductive years. This is not surprising, considering the vulnerable position in which married women find themselves. They often have no choice whether to engage in sexual activity—even when their husbands may be HIV positive or have multiple sexual partners—and are often at risk of becoming victims of sexual abuse and violence. The aforementioned study revealed that a whole set of circumstances—underpinned by personal and intimate partner relations and social factors—determined women's and men's productive desires and intentions. Personal desires, mediated by family and societal expectations, were important influences on reproductive decision-making, and often even outweighed the reality of HIV.

In the Two-Thirds World, the issue of ARTs is embedded in a complex matrix of issues that include poverty; lack of access to information, medical intervention, and counseling; HIV and AIDS; cultural perceptions; and violence. In order to develop an ethical position on ARTs or other biohealth issues, I am convinced that the context that I have just described has to serve as the point of departure. We must start from below, from the position of the poor, the marginalized, and the vulnerable. In this regard I found Maura Ryan's bioethic from below extremely helpful.[4] Due to time

---

3. Approximately 40 million people are currently living with HIV and AIDS worldwide, and sub-Sahara Africa is the epicenter of the epidemic, home to 60 percent of those living with the disease and 75 percent of the global population of HIV-positive women.

4. Maura Ryan is the John Cardinal O'Hara, C.S.C. Associate Professor of Chris-

and scope limitations, I cannot unpack her theory in its totality here. However, I would like to offer some brief remarks in this regard.

A bioethic from below or from the position of the marginalized understands human beings as being part of a community. This principle implies that we cannot isolate infertility from its implications for the community or for society. This principle also critiques the pride of place given to respect for individual autonomy in healthcare decision-making policy recommendations.[5] Within developing countries, society, family, and church assume moral and religious significance. Meaning is created relationally; justice happens within relationships in community.

A bioethic from below not only strives towards the betterment of public healthcare, but also critiques underlying socioeconomic deprivations and inequalities. A bioethic from below speaks out against structural violence by being sensitive to the power connections between different issues that threaten human dignity. Issues of healthcare are thus approached in a holistic way, and take into consideration the systemic realities of human beings.

A bioethic from below begins in narratives from below. Stories, poems, and songs that give voice to those who are silenced are used as the starting point in ethical considerations. Those who do not exist become visible in words and stories as lived and told by them.

Finally, I want to argue that faith communities can be an important resource in the development of a bioethic from below. First, they create spaces for the poor and the marginalized to bring their stories into the conversation with the stories of the biblical text and these thus become contextual Bible reading experiences with an ethical dimension. The power of the narrative is again illustrated in this regard as it becomes a platform for social engagement. Biblical texts function as a reflective surface for the experiences of modern women as they discuss the realities of Bible stories and the ways in which these touch their lives. In this regard I think especially of the story of Tamar in Gen 38, as read from the perspective of an infertile woman; relating stories of lack of agency and powerlessness with

---

tian Ethics at the University of Notre Dame in the U.S. For a comprehensive discussion of a bioethic from below see Ryan 2004 and 2008.

5. To a certain extent genetic and reproductive technologies are a perfect match for modern individualized lifestyles that are characterized by the need, as well as the desire, to plan and to structure the course of one's own life rationally and in accordance with the requirements of modern life.

the actions of Tamar; or, reading the different episodes of the Sarah narrative that outline a woman's struggle to conceive.

Second, faith communities create safe spaces for the language of lament in liturgy. As Denise Ackermann (2004, 52) argues: "Lament is profoundly spiritual but also profoundly political. Lament allows us to speak our pain, to demand justice, to plead forgiveness and to long for change." Thus, the community speaking the language of lament becomes a community that hopes.

Third, faith communities are communities of care creating possibilities for education, counseling, support, and meaning-making. Keeping in mind the contextual picture sketched at the beginning of this response, it is precisely here that the greatest need seems to be with regard to the issue of infertility and ARTs at the grassroots level.

Dorothea, rereading my response I realize that this was perhaps not what you had expected from a biblical scholar, and maybe your expectation would be correct. Maybe a stronger scholarly engagement with the biblical stories would have been more appropriate. But, somehow, my gaze could not shift from those who suffer because of childlessness, from those left behind or left outside because they could not satisfy society's expectations. However, their stories and your contribution of a contextual biblical ethic have again convinced me of the need for a creative conversation between their stories and the stories of the women in the Bible. On both levels, contemporary and biblical, I hear the strong cry for justice, the painful lament, the hopeful prayer, and the comforting song.

May the conversation never end and may we be ever surprised by its unfolding. Best wishes from Stellenbosch.

Charlene

References

Ackermann, Denise. 1993. Liberating the World: Some Thoughts on Feminist Liberation Theology. *Scriptura* 44:1–18.

———. 2004. Tamar's Cry: Re-Reading an Ancient Text in the Midst of an HIV and AIDS Pandemic. Pages 27–59 in *Grant Me Justice! HIV/AIDS and Gender Readings of the Bible (Women from the Margins)*. Edited by Musa W. Dube and Musimbi Kanyoro. Maryknoll, N.Y.: Orbis.

Brueggemann, Walter. 2011. Reading Scripture through Other Eyes. Trinity Institute Lecture delivered at the 41st Annual Trinity Institute

National Theological Conference, New York, January 19–21, 2011. Online: http://www. trinitywallstreet.org/webcasts/videos/conferences-classes/trinity-institute-lectures/ walter-brueggemann.

Cooper, Dianne, Jane Harries, Landon Myer, Phyllis Orner, and Hillary Bracken. 2007. "Life Is Still Going On": Reproductive Intentions among HIV-Positive Women and Men in South Africa. *SSM* 65:274–83.Dyer, Silks J., Naeema A. Abrahams, Margaret Hoffman, and Zephne M. van der Spuy. 2002. Infertility in South Africa: Women's Reproductive Health Knowledge and Treatment-Seeking Behaviour for Involuntary Childlessness. *Human Reproduction.* 17:1657–62.

Ryan, Maura A. 1994. Particular Sorrows, Common Challenges: Specialized Infertility Treatment and the Common Good. Pages 187–206 in *Annual of the Society of Christian Ethics.* Edited by Harlan Beckley. Boston: The Society of Christian Ethics, School of Theology, Boston University.

———. 2004. Beyond a Western Bioethics? *TS* 65:158–77.

———. 2008. Health and Human Rights. *TS* 69:144–63.

Vayena, Effy, Herbert B. Peterson, David Adamson, and Karl-G. Nygren. 2009. Assisted Reproductive Technologies in Developing Countries: Are We Caring Yet? *Fertility and Sterility* 92:413–16.

Human Dignity, Families, and Violence: The New Testament as Resource?

Jeremy Punt

Introduction: Families amidst Violence

Any investigation into the connection between family and violence is from the outset confronted by two almost opposing situations, particularly in a context where biblical texts are deemed to inform the notion of family. On the one hand, the family—defined in various ways and comprising of smaller or larger units of various structural forms—has proven to be a dangerous context for many people. This is attested to, for example, by abused spouses and neglected, maltreated children; it is communicated in personal testimonies, anecdotal reports, and research findings. In the South African context, it is in families where marital partners and children suffer some of the worst forms of physical or psychological abuse, both through active ill-treatment and through similarly destructive neglect. For many families in South Africa, but also elsewhere, the family has proven to be one of the more dangerous contexts which they inhabit daily.[1]

On the other hand, the family and Bible-based family values[2] are often suggested as antidote for a range of contemporary concerns, including loss of identity and purpose, experiences of alienation, and anxiety about declining morals. However, the vastly different socio-historical and ideological settings of families in the first century require circumspection when comparing them with those of modern families. A seemingly

---

1. In South Africa the relatively high prevalence of family murders (generally a father killing his spouse and children before committing suicide) and marital rape in a context of high levels of HIV infections and AIDS are particularly problematic.

2. Both in the senses of the family as social reality and as metaphor in the sense of fictive kinship; the focus here will be on the former.

frivolous matter illustrates the differences in socio-historical context and the nature of families then and now: in the ancient context, "the rich ate in, the poor ate out" (Osiek 1996, 12). The cramped living conditions of the poor, especially in the *insulae* of the cities, mostly did not allow for cooking or food preparation. In short, appeals to the family referred to the New Testament have to be marked by caution. This casts suspicion on claims that the texts provide ready-made blueprints or normative principles for filling out "traditional" family values today.[3]

Concern for appropriate social location and caution about responsible hermeneutics for understanding biblical texts will circumvent conventionalized but often simplistic—and also inappropriate—readings. At the same time, it will allow for a broader appreciation of the biblical texts and for exploring alternative interpretations of and conclusions drawn from the texts, particularly concerning their responsible use in current issues and debates. Before some pointers are formulated for the use of the New Testament in the discussion of human dignity with reference to the link between the family and violence, it is important to understand the scope and reference of families in the texts, within their first-century social location.[4]

Enlisting New Testament Texts?

A number of differences between contemporary and New Testament families frame any more detailed discussion. First, besides differences in com-

---

3. The text-based discussions in Köstenberger 2004 show little understanding of either the early communities following Jesus as part of first-century society, or of the ideological setting of texts, yet they draw "Insights" and "Implications." Barton criticizes the political use of the Bible to sanction traditional family values (Barton 2001, 8–9), but comes close to reaffirming traditional family values as underwritten by the Bible (Barton 2001, 17–36; cf. Barton 1996, 451–62). See Sanders's enlightening comments on the family and the use of biblical notions of the family as important points of debate in the modern "culture wars" (Sanders 2002, 117–28).

4. The widespread use of the term "family" belies the difficulty of defining it. One possible definition is that it refers to "an organized network of socio-economic and reproductive interdependence and support grounded in biological kinship and marriage" (Cahill 2000, x–xi; cf. Thatcher 2007, 4–6). Cf. Moxnes (1997, 14) on universal definitions for family, e.g., "the family is a small kinship structured group with the key function of nurturant socialization" (Reiss in Moxnes 1997, 38 n. 1). Any definition is complicated by the fact that family "is always part of a wider social context and has a cultural meaning" (Moxnes 1997, 15).

position, structure, and purpose, the broader role that households played within society is a distinguishing factor between ancient and modern households. Greco-Roman households were multifunctional. Besides their broader socio-cultural impact, domestic residences had specific political, economic, and religious functions as well. Today's notion of a stable family life as beneficial for the development of wholesome citizens and a healthy society (Moxnes 1997, 14) pales in comparison to the fuller and more complex first-century socio-political setting of the family and its constituent framework and links.

Second, important differences between ancient and modern societies' family structures are located in the former's function and relevance within the total social system, rather than in the composition of the group of people who constituted a family or household (Moxnes 1997, 15). Yet the size and scope of families differed, going beyond the boundaries of the so-called nuclear family.[5] Other family members, associates through work or organization, slaves, tenants, and freedmen and freedwomen regularly formed part of the household (Tsang 2005, 23).[6]

Third, expectations with regard to the roles of family members differed widely from modern sensibilities: children were incorporated into the household and, once accepted, they were played an active role in contributing to it; the head of the household, the *paterfamilias*, was the powerful manager of the household and exercised authority over all its members— even if such absolute authority was often mitigated for legal and practical reasons. Roman society's insistence on reciprocity saw every person in the household as related to others, regulated by uneven power relationships.

Finally, in ancient times a wide spectrum of values was attached to family terminology, attachments that are uncommon today. One example of this is the connection that was often made (even if not exclusively) between children and economics (see, e.g., Frilingos 2000, 93–97). Given these four broad parameters for the discussion, the following important aspects related to the first-century setting of families requires attention.

---

5. "Though the nuclear family certainly existed, it does not seem to have functioned as a social unit in isolation, and therefore, it had no nomenclature" (Osiek 1996, 11).

6. For discussion of an imperially sustained context of dominance and submission, see Johnson (2007, 161–73).

Families and Violence in First-Century Context

Apart from the above thoroughgoing yet surface-level differences in families then and now, there are even more fundamental differences among first-century families in the Roman imperial world. Living conditions of the small, well-off aristocracy differed vastly from those of the majority of the population. In a harsh environment, most people lived poor, vulnerable, and marginalized lives, often undernourished, in unhygienic and violent rural or urban environments. Hostility and violence was natural in the first-century Mediterranean context (Botha 2000, 8–18) since aggression was part of life in the agonistic society to which an analysis of New Testament vocabulary testifies (Desjardins 1997, 63–64; 34).[7] Living in the midst of undesirable standards of safety and sanitation, high child mortality rates and low life expectancy, first-century people also had to deal with high levels of overt violence that was normalized in the ways it was portrayal and practiced (Osiek 2005, 203–8). Violence was an inherent part of the first century; in short, it was a context in which violence was naturalized.

The Central Role of Roman Familia in First-Century Society

The family or household had overriding importance in the formation of a Roman person's identity (Saller 1999, 30–34). In the midst of the competing moral crosscurrents of the first century C.E., a powerful countercurrent to loyalty to the city was found in the laws of family, although those were generally interpreted to be a subset of laws of the city (Meeks 1986, 19–39).[8] In Greco-Roman times, *familia* was central, with different shades of content given to the terms *familia* (family)[9] and *domus* (household),

---

7. The exercise of power meant the ability to exert control over the behavior of others. Thus, power was a highly rated *means* value and a value that facilitated the achievement of core and secondary values (Pilch 1993, 139–43), underscored by the language of patronage and of kinship.

8. The debate in Hellenistic society concerned the tension between justice and nature. With Rome as the universal *polis*, the efficiency of its rule was believed to underwrite its worthiness and validity. It was destined by divine commission to bring nations closer to "one law, eternal and immutable" (Panaetius; Meeks 1986, 19–39).

9. When the jurist Ulpian (*Digest* 50.16.195) distinguishes between people and *res* in describing *familia*, it could, in terms of people, indicate four categories: all those under the *patria potestas* (the power of the father), wife, children, children's children,

the other term increasingly used for family.[10] Claims to agnatic lineage became less tenable in imperial times, granting more respectability to relatives—paternal, maternal, and marital—within the household (Garnsey and Saller 1987, 129).

On the one hand, the danger of stereotypical portrayals, based on contemporary literature reflecting idealized situations, and primarily reflecting concerns of the elite, looms large. A nuanced treatment of such varied family or household components—such as those pertaining to slavery, children, gender, and marriage in discussions of first-century families—is required (Osiek 2005, 208–15).[11] Typical material and ideological patterns or frameworks, such as the image of stark patriarchy as an accurate portrayal of family life in Roman imperial times, were regularly distorted and subverted by the normal social realities of human life and society (Garnsey and Saller 1987, 126). On the other hand, however, the effective transgression of the ideal type clearly did not entail its displacement as paradigm, as indicated by the persistent, widespread continuation of the paterfamilias-family model.

HOUSEHOLD, STATE, AND STABILITY

In Greco-Roman times, household underpinned kingdom, serving as a micro version of the state, the family being the "the seed-bed of the state" (Cicero, *On Duties* 1.53–55). In the Hellenistic-Roman world, it was impossible to separate city and households—Aristotle already considered cities to be constituted by households and all households to be part of a city (Aristotle, *Politics* 1252a–53b; cf. Guijarro 2004, 119). The Roman emperors' desire to ground their power and authority in fatherhood claims relied on the link between empire and household, seeing the empire as

---

adopted children; more broadly, all agnates, that is, those related through the male bloodline (brothers, their children, and their sisters, but not the sisters' children); all related through males to a common ancestor (the *gens* or clan); and the slave staff of the house, farm, or organisation (Garnsey and Saller 1987, 127).

10. While Cicero represents the late Republic notion of family as an agnatic matter of *nomen* (name) and *gens* (clan), Pliny shows how, in the early Empire, *familia* came to mean *domus* where maternal relatives were as well regarded as paternal relatives (Garnsey and Saller 1987, 128–29).

11. Cahill (1996, 141) admits that the legal codes and other normative texts were written by men and reflected an anticipated ideal, perhaps intending to control subversive behavior rather than to provide a historical description of society.

the metaphorical but ultimate household.¹² The household or family functioned as the foundational unit of the state (Green 2001, 92; Hollingshead 1998, 109). While household arrangements and order served as the model for and basis of the empire, their imperial adoption facilitated the assignment of people to specific places and accompanying roles in society.¹³ The household was believed to emulate the city or larger political configuration *in nuce*, as much as the city would not be seen apart from the cosmos—all of which revolved back to the integrity of the human "microcosmic" body and the perceived need to regulate and maintain it according to convention. Therefore, even issues of sex and gender were not mere household concerns, since the potential destabilization of hierarchical household structures extended to the socio-political terrain, where hierarchy was inscribed by imperial power (Martin 1995, xviii, 15–21).¹⁴

A Gendered Understanding of Family or Household

In the first century, the household was a gendered concept, calling up notions of husband and wife, but gendered also as a power-imbued concept, recalling relations between parents and children, and owners and slaves. The household structured and regulated gendered social behavior. Women mostly had a subservient role, yet within the balance of power between men and women/husbands and wives, the notion of *obsequium* as the "obedience" or "compliance" with the will of the other was important (De Marre 2005, 39–50).¹⁵ The institutional nature of slavery and the

---

12. Greek rulers and later Roman emperors used father identity, incorporating priestly responsibilities into fatherly duties on behalf of the imperial household. It was not long before the Roman emperor's public image was understood to be constituted by the threefold authority of political leader, priestly lord, and beneficial head of a communal family (White 1999, 173–206).

13. Human nature was seen as a hierarchically ordered unity. It was also served by the distinction between male and female that provided for procreation, and marriage and "family" provided social continuity and stability (Briggs 2003, 178). Musonius could therefore claim that "whoever destroys human marriage destroys the home, the city, and the whole human race" (Carr and Conway 2008, 292).

14. Household was connected to social stability and slavery. Slaves were controlled by means of punishment, reward, or incentives that sought to stabilize this labor system and thus also the Roman Empire that depended economically upon it (Bradley 1987, 30, 51, 59, 83; Byron 2004, 120–21).

15. Nevertheless, fathers (*patresfamilias*) formally had power over life and death

pervasive presence of slaves played an important part in the formation of identity, roles, and relationships within the household. Slavery impacted elements as diverse as paternal authoritarianism, childbearing, and patterns of sexual behavior (Garnsey and Saller 1987, 128), weaving these and other elements into a tight, gendered web of relations.

The social and political scope and implications of the Greco-Roman household did not exclude the possibility of loving, mutual companionship—insofar as they were coveted first-century values (Dixon 2003, 111–29; Balch and Osiek 1997, 216). Greco-Roman family concerns inevitably provided the socio-historical context for New Testament families and should be taken seriously, but without assuming either a homogenous first-century society or denying New Testament authors' occasional deviation from or improvisation upon conventional norms.

Families or Households in the New Testament

The family or household played an important role in the Jewish world and, albeit in other ways, it retained its prominence in the Greco-Roman world and, therefore, in the early Christian movement.[16] It was, however, a role clouded in ambivalence, as is evident from early Christian texts' compliance to the "family values" of the conventional domestic order of a hierarchical society, amidst expressions anticipating more reciprocity and humaneness toward those of lower esteem. Concern to translate faith in Christ into a new identity and ethos is evident, with even subordinates in stock-in-trade categories such as women, slaves, and children addressed in own right. However, the emphasis on efficient households as the cornerstone of society ensured that the hierarchical framework of society, as the philosophical and political ideal, firmly remained in place, complete with, *inter alia,* patriarchal marriage and slavery (Osiek 2005, 216–17). The consequences of this

---

(*vitae necisque potestas*) of children, that is, to decide whether a newborn would be raised in the household or exposed (Garnsey and Saller 1987, 136–41).

16. The traditions of Israel intermingled with Greco-Roman conventions regarding the family. The family was the basic unit of Israelite culture and society, the basic unit of Israel's stewardship of the land, and the basic unit of its experience and preservation of the covenantal relationship with Yahweh (Sanders 2002, 121). Regardless of other traditions that might have influenced their communities, the terms under which all lived in the first-century Mediterranean world were dictated by Roman law (cf. Osiek 1996, 10).

for discussions of family and for the use of New Testament texts in such discussions now have to be considered, but after a brief word on the contours of the family concept in the texts.

Concepts of Family

Various New Testament documents presume or promote the household, yet at times reconfigure its spatial dimensions as the "household of God" for the early followers of Jesus.[17] Family is expressed by πατρία (Luke 2:4; Acts 3:25; Eph 3:15), and was closely related to the household, expressed by οἶκος or οἰκία (once by οἰκετεία; cf. οἰκεῖος).[18] At times, both πατρία and (more frequently) οἶκος were used to refer to the household in the New Testament.[19] In these texts, constituent elements of the family comprised at least four elements that required the interchangeable use of words such as household (as socio-political structure), kinship (as network of natal ties), marriage (as institution), and interrelations between household members (as system of relations) (cf. Moxnes 1997, 23–36). To avoid confusion between ancient and modern understandings of family,

---

17. New Testament authors were neither unique, nor were they the first to make use of the metaphor of family to describe communities—e.g., Israel is referred to as a household (Amos 5:25; Jer 38:33), and its members as brothers. The Greek notion of members of the same political unit and friends as brothers is also found (Banks 1994, 47–87).

18. A concept narrower than φυλή, but wider than οἶκος, πατρία denotes the "lineage, ancestry" or a "family or tribe" (see Luke 2:4; Acts 3:25; Eph 3:15). According to LSJ, πατρία, which can be translated as "family," "lineage," or "descent," signifies the historical origin of a household, that is, its "patriarch," rather than its present head. The overlapping and polyvalent nature of terminology referring to family and related groups (clan, ethnic group, even nation) is evident in the use of πατριαί in Acts 3:25, quoting the promise to Abraham in the OT; LXX, however, reads "tribes" (φυλαί) in the original promise (Gen 12:3) and "nations" (ἔθνη) when the promise is evoked in Gen 18:18 and 22:18. Similarly, in Luke 2:4 (cf. Luke 1:27; for "house of Israel" see, e.g., Matt 10:6; 15:24; Acts 2:36; 7:42; for "house of Jacob," see Luke 1:33), the words οἶκος (house) and πατρία (lineage) are both used, evidently with similar meanings—the patronymic being the vital point.

19. Οἶκος could refer to the physical household of Stephanas (1 Cor 1:16); the house or structure in which the congregation met (1 Cor 16:19); and the physical but also constructed space of a household (1 Cor 14:35; Osiek 1996, 10).

the ancient Roman household concept is here often a more appropriate way to think about familial issues in the first century.[20]

While Jesus' early followers may have attended the temple as observant Jews according to Acts, the distinctive life of groups following Jesus increasingly shifted to private homes, initiating the intersection between households generally and the household of God. Private homes had obvious advantages for a sect transplanted to cities. On the one hand, households had their own networks of natural connections built upon kinship, friendship, patron-client connections, and affiliations of trade or craft that could assist in proclaiming Christ. On the other hand, households were involved in the larger society of the *polis* in many ways, sometimes leading to conflict (see 1 Cor 8–10) and to the development of complex ways for community members to participate in or abstain from the city's life amidst concern for the protection of the identity and integrity of their faith and community.

DISAVOWING AND CELEBRATING THE FAMILY

New Testament texts display two distinct attitudes toward family or household (cf. Osiek 2005, 217). One set of positions destabilized conventional frameworks and patterns of sexuality and gender (Hanks 2000, 148–49; 177, 182–84; see Punt 2007, 382–98) and in the end spilt over to the family or household as well. Here discipleship was preferred to family ties, and community cohesion to family integrity. The detachment that characterized the portrayal of Jesus and the disciples in the gospels included their detachment from ties to home and family. Since these determined one's identity in a first-century rural culture, this was not a decision undertaken lightly (Meeks 1986, 97–123; cf. Guijarro 2004, 114–15). In the gospel traditions, *no positive* sayings about the goodness of the family were preserved or attributed to Jesus (Osiek 2005, 218).[21] The gospels' sugges-

---

20. The terms for household were used literally, as houses or building structures, as households with people of diverse social ranking (John 5:52; Acts 16:14–15; 16:31–34; 1 Cor 1:16; Phil 4:22), even more broadly of the Christian church as a big spiritual *familia* (1 Tim 5:1–16), and in a general metaphorical way (Luke 11, 17; 12, 39; John 8:35; Heb 3:5–6; see Tsang 2005, 9–11).

21. However, the Synoptics condemned divorce and remarriage and insisted on the honoring of parents; see also the stress on the household in Matt 19–20 (Balch and Osiek 1997, 218).

tion that Jesus, taking his cue from Mic 7:6, anticipated the dissolving of family bonds (cf. Matt 10:35–36 // Luke 12:53) implied the disruption of the household for the sake of the gospel. Jesus re-envisioned the composition and function of household, its social place, and roles, referring to his followers in household terms as brother, sister, or mother, but not as father or wife, in this way avoiding notions of authority, procreation, or patriarchy—the household is queered in the kingdom.[22] Given that the household was an elemental version of the community as a whole, incorporating social structures and institutions from village to people at large, the implications are more wide-ranging than is often admitted.[23] Jesus is portrayed as taking an interest in the family life of others, but he seems to be aloof at best from his own.[24]

Another set of positions suggest that early Christians saw the disavowal or reconfiguration of the family as an impossible ideal, opting rather for retaining the conventional form of family. Early communities following Jesus showed a bias for contemporary household rhetoric reinforced by

---

22. Traditional interpretations have often failed to appreciate the countercultural, radical implications of Jesus' appeal to young men, barren women, and little children to join and thereby to redefine the kingdom of heaven contrary to societal conventions. For Moxnes (2003, esp. 72–90) this transformed household, with its transgression of roles and order, is encapsulated in his saying about himself and his male followers who became "eunuchs for the sake of the kingdom of heaven" (Matt 19:12).

23. Amidst socio-political developments such as Herod Antipas's attempt to establish a new, Greco-Roman-style economy that favored cities and elites, Jesus was depicted as challenging established social boundaries with an alternative social environment for the household.

24. See Hellerman (2007) for an argument that Jesus posited the family model (patrilineal kinship group) in order to break through the restrictive notion of the Jewish *ethnos* ("nationalism" of the time), held intact by Jewish identity markers. While Jesus is portrayed as appreciative of religious requirements regarding the family (e.g., in Matt 15:3–6 // Mark 7:10–12), and sensitive to the needs of and longing for family life in an environment harsh toward the marginalized (e.g., in Matt 9:18–26 // Mark 5:21–43 // Luke 8:40–56; John 4:46–53), his attitude toward his own family was hardly enthusiastic (Luke 2:41–51; Mark 3:31–35), except for one instance of concern for his family as he died (John 19:25–27) (Osiek 1996, 2–6). John 7:5 does offhandedly state that "even his brothers did not believe in him" (cf. Osiek 2005, 218), suggesting that the tension regarding family was deep-set when it came to the Jesus tradition. On the other hand, with familial language of father and son set in a patriarchal framework, the Fourth Gospel extends the family to both the community of faith and the life of God (Balch and Osiek 1997, 219).

religious sanction, as is evident in the Pastoral Epistles and the household codes elsewhere (Bradley 1987, 38; Byron 2004, 127).[25] Potentially liberating notions for the marginalized in society are countered by New Testament portrayals of "household of God" as a decidedly patriarchal space (e.g., in 1 Tim 3:15).[26] Here the household has become a structuring agency for the conduct of community members, theologically based on the life and ministry, death, and resurrection of Jesus (1 Tim 3:16). Discipleship and ministry emerge as key concepts of household-membership, but these are largely reserved for males.[27] Since marriages comprised the ritualization of the honor of two extended families, they generally entailed a union for political or economic reasons. Women were disadvantaged by the patriarchy—at least until they produced a son, enhancing their security and status in the husband's family.[28]

FAMILIES AND THE HOUSEHOLD OF GOD

In the New Testament the metaphorical use of the social family soon reappeared as the family of faith, the community of the faithful.[29] Roman social relations always had a sacred character. This started with the early notions of family and hearth, since both living fathers and dead ancestors were considered sacred.[30] Even when earlier Roman families expanded

---

25. The household code was a regular catechesis describing the mutual duties of members of a Christian household (Col 3:18–4:1; Eph 5:22–6:9; 1 Tim 2:8–15; 5:11–16; 6:1–2; Titus 2:2–10; 1 Pet 2:18–3:7; cf. Balch 1981, 81–109). In the Jerusalem church, according to the narratives in Acts, households were apparently instructed as units (Acts 5:42). Acts ascribes this custom to Paul (Acts 20:20).

26. However, in appealing to the broader New Testament, some scholars argue that "the metaphor of 'the household of God' projects a possible world in which women as well as men are called to full discipleship and ministry in church and community" (West 2004, 169).

27. In 1 Pet 3, there is only a very limited remit extended to men when compared to women in the household code of 1 Tim 3. In 1 Tim 3 it is only v. 7 that prescribes a certain role to men, whereas vv. 8–15 contains instructions for women.

28. However, different forms of marriage meant that occasionally a wife did not find herself under the *manus* (hand/power) of her husband, such as in a marriage based on mutual consent, or when the woman remaining in her father's household (Ferguson 1993, 68).

29. Although a different context, the faithful of God in the Old Testament became known as the household of God.

30. "By his *genius* [creative power or energy], the *paterfamilias* was able to sire

agnatic families into cognatic ones, the sacred obligation to the patron fathers, rooted in the idea of *pietas*, remained.[31] Paul especially describes the community of faith in metaphorical terms as the family of God.[32] In this way he generates and formats a symbolic universe through language, calling into being an anti-structure in which Jesus—as member of both—serves as the link between the family in which God is father and that in which Jesus is the brother of many other brothers and sisters. The connection made between household and church in the New Testament is a strong one[33]—even if the nature of the connections varies from context to context.[34] And, in a context in which believers are described as adopted sons (Rom 8:15–17) or as servants (1 Pet 4:10), referring to the church as household of God (Eph 2:19) or a household of faith (Gal 6:10) is hardly surprising.

The tension in the New Testament between the household *paranesis* and the appeals to discipleship is sometimes addressed by the claim that,

---

children and perpetuate family; he was able to found new life, but always in the context of a founding that has gone on before" (Hollingshead 1998, 106–7).

31. Such considerations were interwoven with a much wider, more complex web of relations and significance. In fact, the entire empire was a network of obligations characteristic of patronage that regulated perceptions of the world and empire by also regulating the activities of communities and individuals in it. Roman social practices were the external manifestations of an intangible morality (e.g., patronage practices within the household), within a holistic perception of the world with Roman religion and Roman society intimately connected. With the social order and the divine order being one and the same for the Romans, the ethics of Roman society were sacred and not negotiable (Hollingshead 1998, 113).

32. Even if Paul's attempts to construe the ἐκκλησία in 1 Corinthians amounts to configuring sanctuary rather than household space (Økland 2004), his use of household metaphors still have to be accounted for.

33. It should be remembered, however, that sometimes only individual members and not whole households joined a community of Jesus followers; e.g., Crispus and Gaius (1 Cor 1:14–16; see 1 Cor 7:12–16, 1 Pet 2:18–3, 16 for the possibility that women (even wives) and other dependants could make their own decisions. See Osiek 1996, 14–15). Tensions still existed, since " the indiscriminate mixing of persons of every age, sex, and social status without proper supervision by appropriate patriarchal authority was perennially suspect, for it threatened the social hierarchy by which power was maintained" (Osiek 1996, 16).

34. Some scholars argue that the basis of Paul's family terminology was the relationship between Jesus (and the believers) and God (Banks 1994, 47–87). See also the recent study by Osiek and MacDonald (2006) on household churches, and in particular the role of women in them.

in the case of the latter, family is not abolished but extended, with the disciples now functioning as a family—much as the church at an early period already started to see itself as surrogate family (cf., e.g., Osiek 1996, 20, 23).[35] However, such readings tend too much toward abstraction and do not consider the reconfiguring of the family through the New Testament's appeals to radical discipleship. Not only is family redefined, but the concept is probably overextended, leaving little of its original connotations intact and barely surviving its metaphorical deployment—the metaphorical deployment of family may have done the church more good than families.

New Testament Families, Violence, and Human Dignity

Given the social location of families in the first century and the ambivalent and varied portrayal of and appeals to family in the New Testament, the question remains: How may New Testament texts serve as resource for reflections on human dignity, family, and violence? A series of responses seems appropriate. First, the several different perspectives on and depictions of the family in the Bible do not bode well for a naive defense of the modern nuclear family. Jesus' subversion of close kinship ties challenges simplistic appeals to biblical family values. Even if such tension is no longer to be found in elaborate patriarchal systems, the persistent tension created by patriarchal attitudes in the community of faith has led many, especially feminists, to call for a radical reinterpretation of the Bible and early Christianity, and to reconceptualize the community of believers as a community of equals (Stuart and Thatcher 1996, 440). In fact, questions are also asked regarding the continuing value of marriage as generally perceived for contemporary times (Ellison 1996) and about the advocacy of the nebulous concept of traditional family values, a discussion that evidently requires caution and restraint.[36] Overrated claims for the family have the tendency

---

35. "The church came more and more to resemble an extended household, characterized by patriarchal leadership, high expectations of cohesiveness, and exclusive claims to honor by some over other members." Later the conceptual shift present in the Synoptics is completed when the church, rather than the household, became the center of allegiance for the faithful (Balch and Osiek 1997, 220; cf. Guijarro 2004, 114–21).

36. According to Thatcher (1993, 16), the argument that appeals to biblical teaching on marriage is inadmissible when slavery is rejected, because the two are "as

to reach the point of becoming idolatrous (Woodhead 1996, 40), with family idealized amidst uncritical allegiance (Harvey 1996, 38).[37]

Second, even if it were possible to assimilate the different New Testament perspectives on family, such an assimilation cannot be made the reigning framework for modern-day thinking about families. At best, interpreters may construe implicit commendations of differing lifestyles in the different New Testament documents that prevent singling out any one authoritative form of behavior. The provisional nature of such construals align well, for example, with Paul's celebration of the diversity constituting the body of Christ, which suggests a multiplicity of community and personal patterns (Good 2007, 1–2).[38] New Testament texts are characterized by tension between the promotion of harmonious relationships within recognized social structures and the subversive challenge to basic human relationships at a social and conceptual level (Osiek 1996, 7–8).[39]

Third, although much energy is (rightly) expended on describing and understanding the first-century context of New Testament texts and topics such as family, the linguistic "setting" of such texts also needs attention. One important aspect is the metaphorical language used. In Pauline texts a range of metaphors focusing on bodily or physical reality and on the family in particular are employed, and these can be interpreted in different ways, reflecting a hierarchical, patriarchal reality, but

---

indissolubly linked as a man and woman are linked in marriage." The same logic is applicable to the argument that traditional family values can be effortlessly harvested from the Bible. See Harvey (1996, 34–39) on the danger of appeals to family values becoming oppressive, partly in becoming a measure to avoid other, related matters (such as lesbigay relationships) and partly in refusing to acknowledge a broader moral berth for such discussions. The lesbigay debate has alerted us to the danger of reading heterosexist assumptions into texts dealing with marriage and to the danger that "the nuclear family of the mid-twentieth century in the industrialised West," can easily be idealized (Germond 1997, 200). Not only homophobia proves to be a particular challenge in contemporary communities of faith, but especially heteronormativity, because of its subtlety, achieved through its perceived and claimed naturalness as well as its deeply ingrained nature.

37. Harvey sees the "unconverted need to receive our identity from the family" at the roots of the idealized model of the family (Harvey 1996, 39).

38. See also Carroll's criticism particularly of the commodification and ideological use of the Bible with regard to the notion of family values (1998, 57–61).

39. The proper model for living lives of love and faithfulness in Christ was not family, but early communities of followers of Jesus, ἐκκλησίαι (Woodhead 1996, 41).

also suggesting intimacy and tenderness. Contemporary interpreting communities need "to choose the moment" in which to interpret these metaphors, whether to align themselves with Paul's authoritarian role or with the dependency that is required of the communities Paul addressed in his letters, but also with regard to the contemporary appropriateness of accompanying attitudes (Polaski 2005, 80–81).

Fourth, the insistence on the conventional nuclear family as the exclusive option for human relationships is not only difficult to defend with appeals to the New Testament, it can also become subterfuge for avoiding wider social engagement on such matters, and for ignoring the need to formulate and consider alternative, morally responsible manifestations of social relationships and unions:

> If family breakdown can be attributable to individual moral weakness, then the contribution of socio-economic conditions to the plight of many families can be bracketed out. If the breakdown can be attributable to the decline of religious faith, then its patriarchal scope can be ignored (Stuart and Thatcher 1996, 439).[40]

In other words, focusing on an idealized family concept can become an excuse for failing to address the bigger issue of human relationships and human dignity in society in a morally sensitive way.

Finally, the structure of the household and different thoughts about it contained the potential for conflict, including moral conflict, and violence among believers.[41] Differences in rank, for example, clashed with an ideal of "equity"—at the time in the sense of proportionality rather than equality.[42] Notwithstanding the notion that any upset in the order

---

40. Critical questions can be raised against "critical familism" as formulated by The Family, Religion, and Culture Project in the USA, headed by Don S. Browning, and its claims that the Bible promotes equal-regard marriage and egalitarian family. The idea that early Christianity moved along a "trajectory" towards "egalitarian marriage" and "servant leadership" is jeopardized by inadequate historical constructions and textual strangeness wrought by sociohistorical placement of texts (Thatcher 2007, 14; 33–42).

41. See Sandnes (1997) on tension between the still patriarchal household and the emerging brotherhood as egalitarian and participatory models in the New Testament. See also Horrell (2001, 293–311) regarding changes in the *form* of authority and power rather than changes from egalitarianism to authoritarianism in the Pauline corpus.

42. Regarding equality in the early house churches, see e.g., Sandnes (1997, 150–

of the home would cause trouble for the whole of society, rituals in the churches implied challenges regarding the conventional roles of women and the system of slavery. It is probably not surprising that second generation leaders harkened back to texts such as those containing the household codes, with women urged to be subject to their husbands, and slaves urged to obey their masters in everything, amidst—or even when it entailed—suffering (Meeks 1986, 19–39; 97–123).

Conclusion

The contemporary practice of lamenting the decline in family morality was already found among the Romans of the Augustan age, as they compared their times with an idealized past (Garnsey and Saller 1987, 126). However, the social location of New Testament families shows that both the claims regarding the constituent elements of family and the notion of the traditional family and concomitant values, are neither neutral nor universal, as is often suggested when these notions are invoked. The value of references to the family and related concepts in the Bible for theologizing is stronger than for moralizing. In other words, the New Testament's contribution regarding family is much more applicable to understanding God's involvement in human lives than to organizing human relationships (Sanders 2002, 117–28). Any use of the New Testament with regard to the family will have to guard against becoming hermeneutically inappropriate, theologically dangerous, or morally restrictive, closing down on possibilities for Christian living (see, e.g., Woodhead 1996, 46). It is important to acknowledge and seek to undo the damage done by the church's oppressive and uncritical collusion, over centuries, in its endorsement of patriarchal, sexist, and marginalizing versions of family life (Barton 1996, 451–62). Such concerns raise many questions: questions of how to unsettle fixed socio-political and socio-economic patterns, theological rationale and justification; questions regarding the place and role of the (continued) use of the Bible in such thinking; questions regarding the valorizing of the family that makes it into "bourgeois idolatry" (Barton 1996, 460); and questions regarding an alternative theological grammar and vocabulary to address body, sexuality, and

---

65). Kinship language did not connote egalitarian relationships, even if ever-present hierarchies were not always precast (cf. Osiek 2009, 147).

marriage, as well as family, gender, and children, in and outside the contexts of families.

References

Balch, David L. 1981. *Let Wives be Submissive: The Domestic Code in 1 Peter*. SBLMS 26. Chico, Calif.: Scholars Press.
Balch, David L., and Carolyn Osiek, eds. 2003. *Early Christian Families in Context: An Interdisciplinary Dialogue*. RMF. Grand Rapids: Eerdmans.
Banks, Robert. 1994. *Paul's Idea of Community*. Rev ed. Peabody, Mass.: Hendrickson.
Barton, Stephen C. 1996. Towards a Theology of the Family. Pages 451–62 in *Christian Perspectives on Sexuality and Gender*. Edited by E. Stuart and A. Thatcher. Grand Rapids: Eerdmans.
———. 2001. *Life Together: Essays on Family, Sexuality and Community in the New Testament and Today*. Edinburgh: T&T Clark.
Botha, Pieter J. 2000. Submission and Violence: Exploring Gender Relations in the First-Century World. *Neot* 34:1–38.
Bradley, Keith R. 1987. *Slaves and Masters in the Roman Empire: A Study in Social Control*. New York: Oxford University Press.
Byron, John. 2004. Paul and the Background of Slavery: The *Status Quaestionis* in New Testament Scholarship. *CBR* 3:116–39.
Cahill, Lisa S. 1996. *Sex, Gender, and Christian Ethics*. New Studies in Christian Ethics 9. Cambridge: Cambridge University Press.
———. 2000. *Family: A Christian Social Perspective*. Minneapolis: Augsburg Fortress.
Carr, David M., and Colleen M. Conway. 2008. The Divine-Human Marriage Matrix and Constructions of Gender and "Bodies" in the Christian Bible. Pages 275–303 in *Sacred Marriages: The Divine-Human Sexual Metaphor from Sumer to Early Christianity*. Edited by M. Nissinen and R. Uro. Winona Lake, Ind.: Eisenbrauns.
Carroll, Robert P. 1998. Lower Case Bibles: Commodity Culture and the Bible. Pages 46–69 in *Biblical Studies/Cultural Studies: The Third Sheffield Colloquium*. Edited by J. C. Exum and S. D. Moore. Gender, Culture, Theory 7. JSOTSup 266. Sheffield: Sheffield Academic Press.
De Marre, Martine E. A. 2005. Arming or Charming: *Obsequium* and Domestic Politics in Roman North Africa. *Akroterion* 50:39–50.

Desjardins, Michel. 1997. *Peace, Violence, and the New Testament.* Sheffield: Sheffield Academic Press.

Dixon, Suzanne. 2003. Sex and the Married Woman in Ancient Rome. Pages 111–29 in *Early Christian Families in Context: An Interdisciplinary Dialogue.* Edited by D. L. Balch and C. Osiek. RMF. Grand Rapids: Eerdmans.

Ellison, Marvin M. 1996. *Erotic Justice: A Liberating Ethic of Sexuality.* Louisville: Westminster John Knox.

Ferguson, Everett. 1993. *Backgrounds of Early Christianity.* 2nd ed. Grand Rapids: Eerdmans.

Frilingos, Chris. 2000. "For My Child, Onesimus": Paul and Domestic Power in Philemon. *JBL* 119:91–104.

Garnsey, Peter, and Richard Saller. 1987. *The Roman Empire: Economy, Society, and Culture.* London: Duckworth.

Green, Joel B. 2001. Crucifixion. Pages 87–101 of *The Cambridge Companion to Jesus.* Edited by M. Bockmuehl. CCR. Cambridge: Cambridge University Press.

Good, Deidre J. 2007. Wrestling Biblically with the Changing Shape of the Family. Online: http://www.ekklesia.co.uk/node/4844/print.

Guijarro, Santiago. 2004. The Family in the Jesus Movement. *BTB* 34: 114–21.

Hanks, Tom. 2000. *The Subversive Gospel: A New Testament Commentary of Liberation.* Translated by J. P. Doner. Cleveland, Ohio: Pilgrim Press.

Harvey, Nicholas P. 1996. Christianity against and for the Family. *SCE* 9:34–39.

Hellerman, Joseph H. 2007. *Jesus and the People of God: Reconfiguring Ethnic Identity.* New Testament Monographs 21. Sheffield: Sheffield Phoenix.

Hollingshead, James R. 1998. *The Household of Caesar and the Body of Christ: A Political Interpretation of the Letters From Paul.* Lanham, Md.: University Press of America.

Horrell, David G. 2001. From ἀδελφοὶ, to οἶκος θεοῦ: Social Transformation in Pauline Christianity. *JBL* 120:293–311.

Johnson, William S. 2007. Empire and Order: The Gospel and Same-Gender Relationships. *BTB* 37:161–73.

Köstenberger, Andreas, with David W. Jones. 2004. *God, Marriage and Family: Rebuilding the Biblical Foundation.* Wheaton, Ill.: Crossway.

Malina, Bruce J., and Jerome H. Neyrey. 1996. *Portraits of Paul: An Archeology of Ancient Personality.* Louisville: Westminster John Knox.

Martin, Dale B. 1995. *The Corinthian Body*. New Haven, Conn.: Yale University Press.
Meeks, Wayne A. 1986. *The Moral World of the First Christians*. LEC. Philadelphia: Westminster.
Moxnes, Halvor. 1997. What Is Family? Problems in Constructing Early Christian Families. Pages 13–41 in *Constructing Early Christian Families: Family as Social Reality and Metaphor*. Edited by H. Moxnes. London: Routledge.
———. 2003. *Putting Jesus in His Place: A Radical Vision of Household and Kingdom*. Louisville: Westminster John Knox.
Økland, Jorunn. 2004. *Women in Their Place: Paul and the Corinthian Discourse of Gender and Sanctuary Space*. JSNTSup 269. London: T&T Clark.
Osiek, Carolyn. 1996. The Family in Early Christianity: "Family Values" Revisited. *CBQ* 58:1–24.
———. 2005. Family Matters. Pages 201–20 in vol. 1 of *Christian Origins: A People's History of Christianity*. Edited by R. A. Horsley. Minneapolis: Fortress.
———. 2009. The Politics of Patronage and the Politics of Kinship: The Meeting of the Ways. *BTB* 39:143–52.
Osiek, Carolyn, and David L. Balch. 1997. *Families in the New Testament World: Households and House Churches*. FRC. Louisville: Westminster John Knox.
Osiek, Carolyn, and Margaret Y. MacDonald, with J. H. Tulloch. 2006. *A Woman's Place: House Churches in Earliest Christianity*. Minneapolis: Fortress.
Pilch, John J. 1993. Power. Pages 139–42 in *Biblical Social Values and their Meaning: A Handbook*. Edited by J. J. Pilch and B. J. Malina. Peabody, Mass.: Hendrickson.
Polaski, Sandra H. 2005. *A Feminist Introduction to Paul*. St Louis: Chalice.
Punt, Jeremy. 2007. Sex and Gender, and Liminality in Biblical Texts: Venturing into Postcolonial, Queer Biblical Interpretation. *Neot* 41:382–98.
Saller, Richard P. 1999. Roman Kinship: Structure and Sentiment. Pages 7–34 in *The Roman Family in Italy: Status, Sentiment, Space*. Edited by B. Rawson and P. Weaver. Oxford: Clarendon.
Sanders, James A. 2002. The Family in the Bible. *BTB* 32:117–28.
Sandnes, Karl O. 1997. Equality within Patriarchal Structures: Some New

Testament Perspectives on the Christian Fellowship as a Brother- or Sisterhood and a Family. Pages 150–65 in *Constructing Early Christian Families: Family as Social Reality and Metaphor*. Edited by H. Moxnes. London: Routledge.

Stuart, Elizabeth, and Adrian Thatcher, eds. 1996. *Christian Perspectives on Sexuality and Gender*. Grand Rapids: Eerdmans.

Thatcher, Adrian. 1993. *Liberating Sex: A Christian Sexual Theology*. London: SPCK.

———. 2002. *Living Together and Christian Ethics*: Cambridge: Cambridge University Press.

———. 2007. *Theology and Families*. CCT. Oxford: Blackwell.

Tsang, Sam. 2005. *From Slaves to Sons: A New Rhetoric Analysis on Paul's Slave Metaphors in His Letter to the Galatians*. SBL 81. New York: Peter Lang.

West, Gerald O. 2004. Taming Texts of Terror: Reading (against) the Gender Grain of 1 Timothy. *Scriptura* 86:160–73.

White, John L. 1999. *The Apostle of God: Paul and the Promise of Abraham*. Peabody, Mass.: Hendrickson.

Woodhead, Linda. 1996. Christianity against and for the Family: A Response to Nicholas Peter Harvey. *SCE* 9:40–46.

A Response to Jeremy Punt's "Human Dignity, Families, and Violence: The New Testament as Resource?"

Magda Misset-van de Weg

Dear Jeremy,

I was initially quite overwhelmed by the task of responding to your essay. Nevertheless, I accepted the challenge and will respond from the perspective of my own social location—Western Europe, understood in the broadest sense possible. It was especially our call for responsible hermeneutics that intrigued me and it is on this theme that I wish to expand. Furthermore, whereas you focused your attention more on the family, my attention will instead be on the element of violence. However, I will start with a general observation.

I noticed that you kept your comments regarding the positive elements of the family to a minimum and I wondered why. Research has after all shown that, in the West, the family is not yet a bankrupt phenomenon, but that it is in fact very much alive (Schaafsma 2010). Concepts such as contact, care, solidarity, and so on are still used with reference to the family. I am also fortunate enough to be able to testify to this from my own experience. However, I am of course also very much aware that there is another side to the coin, namely that family life can also be miserable or at least quite ambiguous—family may, for example, be experienced quite differently in subsequent stages of one's life. Parents can make their children's lives miserable and vice versa. Contrary to the romantic and religious ideal of the family as the cornerstone of society, the warm safe abode, and so on, for many victims of violence the family is a prison (Ganzevoort 2009). Churches communicate and provide a religious basis for the traditional, ideal family, but also for repressive images and concepts, such as traditional beliefs in a God inclined to dominance, subordination of genders or generations, sexism, and discrimination of all kinds (Schwartz 1997, 130).[1] Images of the ideal family are so ingrained into our thinking that they may be one of the reasons why violence perpetrated in the family is often not disclosed. Moreover, the family ideal, and especially emphasis on the desirability of family and thus marriage, creates a backlash of exclusion of, discrimination against, and violence faced by gay and lesbian people and/or those who choose unions that differ from traditional ones. According to the experts, these harsh aspects of family life are not widely discussed.[2] Thus your focus on the possible negative side of the family may, after all, be considered a positive contribution made by your essay, and I will proceed in the same fashion.

Jeremy, in your essay you give a thorough overview of the historical, cultural, and social backgrounds of "the family," its composition, structure, and purpose in New Testament times. You make perfectly clear that the information gleaned from the New Testament adds up to neither neutral nor universal constituent elements that may function either as antidote to contemporary concerns about family life, or as a blueprint for family life and relations in the twenty-first century, not only because of time-bound rules and conventions pertaining to the place, structure, and function of the family in ancient times, but also because the New Testament displays different attitudes toward family or household. I want to dwell upon these attitudes for a moment.

Different Attitudes toward the Family

One of the attitudes toward family in the New Testament that you refer to concerns Jesus' attitude that anticipates the breaking of family ties, as

---

1. In his 2012 New Year message to the Corps Diplomatique at the Vatican, Pope Benedict XVI stated that pride of place goes to the family, based on the marriage of a man and a woman. The family is, according to the pope, not a mere social convention. Rather, it forms the basic structure of society. Policies that undermine the family threaten human dignity and the future of humanity itself (Gezin is gebaseerd op huwelijk tussen man en vrouw, 2012).

2. For reasons why people shy away from "family and violence" as a topic, see Lehner-Hartmann (2009), who suggests that one of the reasons may be that involvement in this topic does not leave one untouched, but traps one in the victim's experience of powerlessness. Unwillingness to become more closely involved with this experience is a natural self-protective reaction.

it appears in texts such as Mark 3:34–35: "And looking at those who sat around him, he said, 'Here are my mother and my brothers! Whoever does the will of God is my brother and sister and mother.'" You conclude, Jeremy, that Jesus is portrayed as taking an interest in and being sensitive to the family life of others, but seems at best to stand aloof from his own. I agree with you that one may detect an antifamily tradition in Mark 3:31–34, Luke 12:51–53, Matt 10:34–46, and other New Testament texts that suggest that Jesus and/or part of early Christian tradition did not support conventional family values, but rather destabilized them, questioning the existing social order. Paul's discourse on the diversity that constitutes the body of Christ seems to corroborate the view that there is not just one type of relationship that each and every relationship should be modeled on (1 Cor 12:12–13; Eph 4). Paul, at least, promotes the freedom to choose between marrying or remaining single—even though the latter is considered the better choice, and thus undermines the priority of the family.[3] However, the question remains: To what extent do these texts really represent a kind of countercultural position? On the one hand, the texts fit well within a framework of an expectation of immanent end times. For this reason, strong family ties, blood relations, and the social institutions of this world mattered much less than the "spiritual Christian family" and the coming of the future and alternative kingdom (Ehrman 2004, 179). On the other hand, change, especially radical social change, does not result in autonomy but always demands new, other, or revised social relations (Cahill 1995, 9). The attitude toward the family ascribed to Jesus also functioned within that framework, that is, as a response to the social and political consequences of joining the Christian community of faith. It could easily amount to loss of identity, family, status, friends, and financial means, and to increased suspicion, harassment, and so on. The emphasis on belonging to the new "spiritual family" was intended to strengthen the resolve of those who had to suffer these consequences. At the same time, however, it brings the family concept back into focus, albeit in an alternative form through the use of metaphors such as "heavenly father," and Christians as the children of God and as one another's mothers, brothers, and sisters.

---

3. See, e.g., 1 Cor 7:39. The same attitude was taken up in the *Acts of Thecla*; see especially ch. 5 on the beatitudes.

In line with this, Christian leaders soon began to structure and regulate both the social family and the household of God (οἶκος τοῦ θεοῦ). This represents yet another attitude towards family, one that can be found especially in the so-called household codes or the οἰκονομία ideology that, though modified, were derived from Greek and Roman models prevalent at the time. The οἶκος τοῦ θεοῦ more explicitly provided its members with some kind of social and religious solidarity, a new "family" and thus a new identity and status—even if, as you rightly point out, it still had a decidedly patriarchal structure and character. The same applies to the social family in which slaves (both male and female), children, and women were to obey and to accept the authority of the *paterfamilias*.[4] Without underestimating the positive function that this οἶκος τοῦ θεοῦ may initially have had, in the long run the family model of relationships and ownership it represents has also furthered a culture of violence and coercion, the effects of which are still palpable today.

In short, the New Testament represents different options with regard to relationships. The fact that the Christian tradition has favored the family model does not mean other options should be excluded. Rather, it includes the option to break with convention and to engage alternatives by making use of the New Testament as a source in a responsible way.

The Surplus Value of the New Testament?

A first step in using the New Testament responsibly is to acknowledge, as you have done, Jeremy, that the Bible reflects and is a product of particular times, contexts, and cultures. Interpreters must look beyond and transcend these realities toward the gospel's life-affirming message (LWF 2002, 8). And, based on the conclusion that the New Testament mirrors different views on the family, we now have the choice—as you also state—not to align ourselves with the physical and/or emotional pressure and the damaging effects of dominant/submissive relationality and positional power over others. Furthermore, the exclusive focus on the idealized nuclear family should not be a subterfuge for avoiding wider social engagement on matters of human relationships and for ignoring the need to formulate

---

4. I am aware of different perspectives and arguments that either sharpen or mitigate the meaning and/or effects of the ὑποτάσσω passages. See, e.g., Martin 1991 and Bauman-Martin 2004.

and consider alternative and morally responsible manifestations of social relationships and unions.

The above sounds plausible, but at least the following questions need to be answered as well: What is the importance and surplus value of a historically and culturally determined artifact such as the New Testament or the Hebrew Bible in validating human dignity and in protesting against any kind of violence? Why do we remain bent on finding guidelines and answers in the Bible or, as Ivone Gebara puts it, on taking the Bible as our possible "ally"? And, how can we unsettle a fixed theological rationale and justification, and why should we?

The past and present importance of the Bible in many Christian countries cannot be underestimated. It lingers—even if transformed—in secular concepts, systems, and institutions. The effect of the Bible on our cultural, political, and personal lives and on the way we think should, therefore, not remain unexamined: "If we do not think about the Bible, it will think [for] us" (Schwartz 1997, 8). Not dealing with the Bible is not an option. Battered women, for example, frequently relate their situation to their religious beliefs, and are reluctant to try to change their situation because they have been taught that resistance to the injustice done to them is unbiblical and unchristian (cf. Thistlethwaite 1989, 303, 305, 306). No authority except that of the Bible itself can challenge these women to look at the Bible differently, to become suspicious of a biblical exegesis that aims at maintaining power over them, or to see that the Bible reveals a God who sides with those who are powerless.

Generally speaking, it can be said that even though many contemporary Christian women (or men for that matter) do not feel the need to emulate behavior that was demanded or propagated 2000 years ago, nor to find biblical proof for their full humanity or equality, many of them—precisely as Christians—are still committed to working with the Bible. As Anne-Louise Eriksson (2004, 50) puts it, "The Bible is *our* heritage, our 'golden bag' given *to us*," it is the resource from which the inspiration to envision and embody justice and to resist domination, subordination, violence, and greed can be drawn. In short, the Bible plays an important role in the quest for meaning and for orienting ourselves in the world, measuring the texts and ideals in the Bible against real life.[5] Therefore, this quest is

---

5. Initiated by the Lutheran World Federation in 2002, *Churches Say "NO" to Violence* is a prime example of encouraging women and men to read biblical texts from a critical point of view so that they (women and men) may reinterpret texts and imagine

not directed at finding an ideal or liberating past, but at revisiting and reinterpreting the past in order to live a good life in the present and to ensure a future (Schwartz 1997, 167). Such an orientation may help victims of domestic violence to realize that violence can never be the price paid for love, but that it destroys love, security, fidelity, and trust, and, therefore, marriage, family and any other relationship itself (cf. also Lehner-Hartman 2009, 121).

The above orientation changes the way one reads the Bible. It allows the reading of the Bible as a symbolic word, as a word that goes beyond itself, that is, beyond even its earlier or original cultural conditioning—"the word read symbolically, allows us to read it by reading ourselves today" and thus to understand ourselves (Gebara 1994, 180). To be sure, in order to avoid texts becoming mirrors of ourselves or our own ideas, interpretations, and evaluations of the sacred texts, we need an interpretive community. We need dialogue and, importantly, responsible hermeneutics. It is to the latter that I will now turn with some thoughts on what I think might constitute such hermeneutics. I emphasize that they are "thoughts," in random order and not according to priority or any kind of system.[6]

Responsible Hermeneutics

For me, responsible hermeneutics foster humility in the sense that no final interpretation or ultimate truth can or should be claimed. As readers take part in the creation of meaning by using their real-life experiences and by asking their own questions, "Truth" will become truths, or stories that illuminate and enrich one another. In such a creative dialogue with the texts based on lived experience, the texts may serve as a possible ally. In this regard, Ivone Gebara has challenged women to take the risk taken by the serpent in Gen 3 to disobey the patriarchal law that demands childish submission and fear. Dare taste the fruit; gluttonously eat it with

---

new relationships between the texts and their experiences, in order to free them from the bondage of conjugal rights that involve rape, coercion, and abusive expectations.

6. I am also not ignorant of the fact that quite different views on responsible hermeneutics are circulating, as a cursory search on the internet will reveal. See, e.g., the following "definition": "Responsible Christian hermeneutics receives the Bible as the infallible, inspired Word of God, and seeks to apply its original meanings to the modern world" (TMM 2011).

relish and passion! For Gebara, the serpent is the key symbol for an evolutionary human journey, a paradigm shift with respect to political, economic, and ecclesial systems. Such a rereading may catalyze the potential to challenge the patriarchal traditions it has served so well (cf. Gebara 1994, 178).

Such an approach will "subvert the dominant vision of violence and scarcity with an ideal of plenitude and its corollary ethical imperative of generosity" (Schwartz 1997, 173). It will thus tap into the visions of bounty and generosity the Bible has to offer. It may mean, for example, reading texts of terror not as endorsements of but as warnings against the terrible cost of drawing the boundaries of identity too aggressively or defensively. Or—to cite another example—it may mean looking from another angle at the Christ hymn in Phil 2:6–11: while still recognizing that the hymn is not free from androcentric elements, one may realize that it is a hymn of communities that also, or possibly even mainly, consisted of slaves and poor people who hungered for bread, life, and justice. These were communities that recognized in their sisters and brothers the face of a Christ who voluntarily shared their fate. They celebrated the crucified Christ who won victory in the midst of oppressive power. These powerless people knew that they shared in a project that transcended their own interests (cf. Schottroff, Schroer, and Wacker 1997, 212–13).

A responsible hermeneutic looks critically at what is right/morally laudable or wrong/morally reprehensible, and meaningful. It will discern what is right because it is right and just and not only because it is found in the Bible. For example, rereading the parable of the Good Samaritan along these lines may serve as a witness to social and political vulnerability and resistance to evil, through care as embodying the divine, and through the expression of prophetic action, the quest for justice, and societal transformation (Rollins 2008).

Such an approach will, furthermore, be sensitive to gendered language and concepts, allowing metamorphoses into new possibilities. Sharon Ringe, for example, has argued that the Fourth Gospel's almost exclusive use of "father" as a metaphor for God has made it a largely alien text for many women readers and for readers whose experiences with their fathers in this world are a far cry from John's loving, caring God. As the term became the principal name (and no longer a metaphor) for God—both in interpretations and in doctrinal affirmations and liturgical practice—this alienation was accentuated. We cannot change the text, but what we can do is to work with clearer statements about what is being signified, so that the texts and their contents may be experienced as locuses of hope and grace. And, we may search for language that fully and clearly expresses the God known as I AM—the way, the truth, and the life (Ringe 1999).[7]

Finally, a responsible hermeneutics aims at allowing people to be freed from the powers that bind them, and at restoring power to those who have been wronged. At this point the essay by Peter Horsfield (1995) on the healing of the Gerasene Demoniac (Mark 5:1–20) serves as a good example.

According to Horsfield, the story has at its roots real life experiences of sickness, or violation of the integrity of a person. This introduces a dimension of something beyond the person coming to affect him or her, something over which the person has no control. This mythologized sense of being used or being taken over by something beyond one's control is central to understanding the existential truth of the story. This truth reveals dynamics that equal the experience of those who have been victims of sexual or domestic violence, often at the hands of those they trusted most. The victims' personal space and bodily boundaries have been invaded, their autonomy has been ignored, their self-worth violated by traumatizing, confusing, and shattering experiences that left them with deep, long-lasting effects.

Many horror stories reflect the main elements of the Markan story. Women survivors of sexual assault, for example, frequently describe their experience as being invaded, possessed, and used. Many of those diagnosed with multiple personality disorder have a history of being severely abused—sexually, physically, or psychologically. As one sufferer testified: "The man who came in the middle of the night and molested me was a shadow ... and as I split him into two, I split myself into two."

The story of the Gerasene demoniac also holds up a mirror to "the bystanders." It is a known fact that those hearing such horror stories become upset and simply do not want to hear or believe them. Too often the survivors are socially or psychologically labeled so that the social impact of what has been reported is contained and neutralized. This also has severe effects on the victim/survivor and frequently results in self-abuse.

We do not know what verbal or non-verbal communication transpired between Jesus and the demoniac. Whatever happened, whatever Jesus

---

7. Since Mary Daly's *Beyond God the Father: Toward a Philosophy of Women's Liberation* (1973), many more publications appeared in which the "muscular Christianity of fathers and grandfathers" is analyzed and criticized, especially the performance model of ownership and conquest that feeds a culture of violence.

communicated to this man, it apparently contained the compassion and confidence that removed divisions, conflicts, and violence, and restored wholeness. That same possibility and reality is often witnessed to by victims/survivors when they encounter someone who embodies those qualities that appear to have been embodied by Jesus (Horsfield 1995, 147).

In short, on the one hand, the narrative of the Gerasene demoniac offers a harrowing picture of the horrors and consequences of any kind of violence done to a human being. On the other hand, the story calls for presence, care, and the courage to listen to the horrifying accounts of abuse so that, by naming the personal and social demons, the victim/survivor can restore faith in the wisdom and power of her or his own spirit. This is redemptive power: the wisdom and power of God incarnate in human life. The value of concepts like redemption, then, need not be forsaken, but can be given meaning in interaction with present day experiences.

Women, men, or children who still wish to resort to the Bible may regain strength from responsible reading of texts that allows experiential truths to be heard and validated, texts and readings that underscore that the Bible is not a word of God when used to justify structures and dynamics of unjust power relations. In this sense, then, the New Testament may indeed serve as a resource, especially for hearing and healing.

Sincerely,
Magda

References

Bauman-Martin, Betsy J. 2004. Feminist Theologies of Suffering and Current Interpretations of 1 Peter 2.18–3.9. Pages 63–81 in *A Feminist Companion to the Catholic Epistles and Hebrews*. FCNT 8. Edited by Amy-Jill Levine and Maria Mayo Robbins. London: T&T Clark.

Cahill, Lisa Sowle. 1995. Sexual Ethics: A Feminist Biblical Perspective. *Int* 49:5–16.

Daly, Mary. 1973. *Beyond God the Father: Toward a Philosophy of Women's Liberation*. Boston: Beacon.

Ehrman, Bart D. 2004. *A Brief Introduction to the New Testament*. New York: Oxford University Press.

Eriksson, Anne-Louise. 2004. Radical Hermeneutics and Scriptural Authority. Pages 47–52 in *Holy Texts: Authority and Language*. YESWTR 12. Edited by Charlotte Methuen, Angela Berlis, Sabine

Bieberstein, Anne-Claire Mulder, and Magda Misset-van de Weg. Leuven: Peeters.

Ganzevoort, Ruard. 2009. Domestic Violence against Children: Pastoral-Theological Reflections. Pages 219–32 in *When "Love" Strikes: Social Sciences, Ethics and Theology on Family Violence*. Edited by Annemie Dillen. Leuven: Peeters.

Gebara, Ivone. 1994. The Face of Transcendence as a Challenge to the Reading of the Bible in Latin America. Pages 172–86 in *A Feminist Introduction*. Edited by Elizabeth Schüssler Fiorenza. Vol. 1 of *Searching the Scriptures*. Edited by Elizabeth Schüssler Fiorenza. London: SCM.

Gezin is gebaseerd op huwelijk tussen man en vrouw [Family Is Based on Marriage between Man and Woman]. 2012. *Trouw* (11 January) De Verdieping 9. Online: http://www.trouw.nl/tr/nl/5009/Archief/archief/article/detail/3114977/2012/01/11/Paus-Gezin-is-gebaseerd-op-huwelijk-tussen-man-en-vrouw.dhtml.

Horsfield, Peter. 1995. The Gerasene Demoniac and the Sexually Violated. Pages 141–50 in *Violence against Women and Children: A Christian Theological Sourcebook*. Edited by Carol J. Adams and Marie M. Fortune. New York: Continuum.

Lehner-Hartmann, Andrea. 2009. Familial Violence against Women as a Challenge for Theology and Ethics. Pages 109–30 in *When "Love" Strikes: Social Sciences, Ethics and Theology on Family Violence*. Edited by Annemie Dillen. Leuven: Peeters.

LWF (Lutheran World Federation). 2002. *Churches Say "NO" to Violence against Women: Action Plan for the Churches*. Geneva: LWF.

Martin, Clarice J. 1991. The *Haustafeln* (Household Codes) in African American Biblical Interpretation: "Free Slave" and "Subordinate Women." Pages 206–31 in *Stony the Road We Trod: African American Biblical Interpretation*. Edited by Cain Hope Felder. Minneapolis: Fortress.

Ringe, Sharon. 1999. Reading Back, Reading Forward. *Semeia* 85:189–94.

Rollins, Victoria. 2008. The Power of Male Violence as Evil: Uses and Abuses of Power in the Shoah and the Silent Genocide of Abused Women. Pages 145–86 in *Weep Not for Your Children: Essays on Religion and Violence*. Edited by Lisa Isherwood and Rosemary Radford Ruether. London: Equinox.

Schaafsma, Petruschka. 2010. Theologische perspectieven op familie en gezin [Theological Perspectives on the Family]. *TTh* 50:342–51.

Schottroff, Luise, Silvia Schroer, and Marie-Teres Wacker. 1997. *Feministische Exegese: Forschungsbeiträge zur Bibel aus der Perspektive von Frauen*. Darmstadt: Primus.

Schwartz, Regina M. 1997. *The Curse of Cain: The Violent Legacy of Monotheism*. Chicago: University of Chicago Press.

Strobel, Regula. 1991. Feministische Kritik an traditionellen Kreuzestheologien. Pages 52–64 in *Vom Verlangen nach Heilwerden: Christologie in feministisch-theologischer Sicht*. Edited by Doris Strahm and Regula Strobel. Fribourg: Edition Exodus.

Thistlethwaite, Susan Brooks. 1989. Every Two Minutes: Battered Women and Feminist Interpretation. Pages 302–13 in *Weaving the Visions: New Patterns in Feminist Spirituality*. Edited by Judith Plaskow and Carol P. Christ. San Francisco: Harper & Row.

TMM (Third Millennium Ministries). 2011. Course Group: Hermeneutics. Online: http://thirdmill.org/seminary/group.asp/vs/gherm.

A Fragile Dignity: Intercontextual Conversation on Scripture, Family, and Violence (On the Essays of Juliana Claassens, Dorothea Erbele-Küster, and Jeremy Punt)

Elsa Tamez

After reading the three essays with your respective responses, my head was whirling with ideas. The diversity of approaches to the topic of dignity, family, and violence, to using the Bible, literature, and the complex problem of Assisted Reproductive Technologies as study resources indicate that we are experiencing a true intercultural dialogue. Intercultural and interdisciplinary dialogues are effective ways to become aware of the problems in other contexts, to learn from them, and to reflect on the facts in a critical and self-critical manner. In this regard, the objective has been achieved. However, you have asked for a third voice, one outside of the European and African context, and I appreciate your invitation.

My voice comes from the three different contexts in which I have lived and with which I maintain continuing relationships: Mexico, Colombia, and Costa Rica. In the contexts of Mexico and Colombia, armed violence, drug trafficking, and femicide are daily occurrences. All one needs to do is to read the newspapers or watch televised news programs to learn about such deaths every day. In Costa Rica, intrafamily violence does not lag far behind. This is a country where the ideal of the traditional family lives only in the minds of people, reinforced by the mass media and by ecclesiastical institutions, but in practice this concept does not exist. Women are the heads of households in more than 60 percent of families. To reflect on the family from another angle, as a social construct, is a theme that urgently needs to be addressed and this involves a process of both deconstruction and reconstruction. Thus, a topic like "fragile human dignity," constantly under threat, is of great importance. That is why I agreed to participate in this dialogue.

My first reaction: In a first reading of the three essays and their respective responses, my impression was that they are not very interrelated and that the topic of fragile human dignity is not very explicit. In my second reading, I observed that, even though they have one point in common—the topic of violence in the family and against women—each of the essays addresses its own particular issue and concern, whether from the perspective of Bible, literature, or the contemporary issue of Assisted Reproductive Technologies. The topic of fragile dignity seems to be taken for granted. The reactions of the biblical and literary analysis of the essays indicate that it is the hermeneutical focus that leads to determined conclusions.

I think the study of the family in the New Testament by Jeremy Punt is excellent. The idea of the nuclear family from the patriarchal perspective is present in society and in churches; it is promoted by the mass media, and by educational and medical institutions. However, in reality things are vastly different. In a context of continual violence, such as that found in Colombia, it is difficult for families to experience ideal family life. Poverty and forced displacement caused by the violence, both in rural and urban areas, deprive people of the possibility of fulfilling the conditions for such ideal family life. The reality of daily life is one of many children and women working in the streets; and of unemployed fathers with no sense of responsibility, spending their days and their energy in what they call "scraping together" something to eat for that day. However, we cannot deny that there remains a sense of family ties and solidarity, not only among families in the classic sense of parents and children, but even more so in extended families, which include grandmothers, elderly aunts and uncles, and neighbors, who stay home to take care of small children and to watch over their few belongings to prevent them from being stolen. Family and community ties are obvious at parties, dances, and in the enjoyment of music. When living together and sharing in these festive moments, one feels the grace of God and human dignity, two inseparable experiences.

In this context we need a liberating biblical hermeneutic that encounters a God in solidarity with humankind. A God who defends the vulnerable and threatened dignity of the poor and marginalized is important; this strengthens the hope and confidence to live life—even in the most miserable of situations—as a gift from God. That is why I believe that knowing that the Bible does not offer an ideal for families—such as the ideal proposed by the ideology of the globalized market—is profoundly liberating. We observe that in the Bible, from Genesis through to Revelation, the concept of family is a social construct. I agree with all of you that there are some ambiguous and oppressive texts in the Bible that reflect the patriarchal ideology of the context of its authors. However, I also agree with Magda Misset-van de Weg that, being alert to these oppressive texts, one can emphasize and reread texts that help to reinforce the dignity of persons. Often our post-colonial and feminist readings, mine included, deconstruct texts but do not reconstruct liberating proposals from them. I believe it is important read texts critically, but it is equally crucial to read in a liberating way those texts that lend themselves to such a reading. The poor and marginalized, those who continually experience hostility in society—even in the church—are looking for liberating elements in scripture; they at least want to feel that God has not forgotten them.

I also read with care and interest the essay about violence against women, analyzed with reference to biblical poetry in the book of Lamentations and the novel *Disgrace* by J. M. Coetzee. I believe the choice of such a method is a very wise one because, as we know, literature and all forms of art are able to represent in narrative or pictorial form the broad structural processes, the social, economic, ecclesiastical, and cultural junctures experienced in specific situations. A novel or work of art may better describe and interpret social realities than a book analyzing economics, politics, or religion. *One Hundred Years of Solitude* by Colombian Nobel Laureate in Literature Gabriel García Marques, for example, relates the history of Latin America through the character of Colonel Aureliano Buendía, who led thirty unsuccessful revolutions. In its strategy of enunciation, the literary form reveals the patriarchal mentality of not only the authors, but also of society as a whole. Another novel by this same Colombian author, *Chronicles of a Death Foretold*, tells of the murder of a man. It deals with a murder that everyone in town knew was inevitably going to be committed, but that no one did anything to prevent. Even though the underlying tone of the novel suggests that it is a tale about the continual assassinations in Colombian society, the world recounted is constructed through the story of a woman who was not a virgin when she married. This fact, classified as shameful in the novel, injures the honor of the groom, which leads him to avenge the loss of his bride's virginity. The name of the young man, mentioned in passing, foretells the assassination of an innocent man, publicly, for all to see. That is the "story," the "anecdote," a reflection of traditional family values, but this anecdote is constructed as a backdrop for the true story of frequent assassinations in the country. It deals with two parallel stories, whose denotative and connotative meanings are intertwined. This also occurs with the feminine metaphors used by the prophets in the book of Lamentations regarding "the bad behavior" of Jerusalem; these are terrible images, but they reflect the common *machista* view of society regarding women. Here, the hermeneutic of suspicion plays a fundamental role in unmasking social and patriarchal violence and affirming that all kinds of violence indeed have a gender. L. Juliana Claassens makes this clear in her analysis. Our task, I believe, is to discover those liberating meanings, even if they are minimal, as Dorothea Erbele-Küster does.

In this intercultural dialogue, geographic location does of course also play a role. However, the greatest distance can be observed in the contexts of the First and Third Worlds with regard to the choice of topics relating to Assisted Reproductive Technologies, which is analyzed very well by Erbele-Küster. The Latin American context is characterized by outrageous inequalities—because of high poverty levels, more than half the population has no access to basic necessities such as food, health, work, and education. Here the first option is to struggle for survival. With regard to reproductive methods, the women's struggle is centered more on the right to decide on how many children they want to have and the legalization of abortion (because of the high number of deaths due to illegal abortions). Women often lose this struggle due to strong opposition from churches, particularly the Roman Catholic Church, which rejects everything that deals with reproductive rights. This reality dominates and postpones any discussion on infertility, leaving only women who have the means to do so in a position to resolve their pain. I really liked the response of Charlene van der Walt, where from Africa, a continent pounded by poverty and AIDS, she does not refuse to discuss the topic, but proposes a starting point of a bioethics from below, that is, from the perspective of the excluded or marginalized.

I have thus far responded a little to each of the essays. However, from my Latin American and Third World context, I believe an analysis of the critical state of the global market system, which in fact governs the planet, is necessary. This system constitutes an economic order in which global market forces and neoliberal policies are imposed on all countries with devastating effects. This can be seen in rising unemployment and growing social inequality. It is also reflected in the world financial crisis, in waves of migration from all and the bankruptcy of some countries, as well as in the cutting back on social welfare and pension programs, and so on. The dignity of persons, including that of indigenous communities, is not taken into account because maximizing profits in the least amount of time and at the lowest possible cost is more important. This has unleashed avarice and the immoral accumulation of wealth—both legal and illegal. This situation, which was already predicted as far back as in the late 1980s, has now reached its limits. It has nurtured social and family violence, delinquency and corruption. Organized crime is no longer limited to involvement in drug trafficking. It now includes human trafficking and dealing in human organs. Furthermore, for the same motive of illicit enrichment, the lack of respect for nature has reached alarming extremes, as can be seen in the growing threat of global warming and its consequences, such as floods, devastating droughts, and the extinction of species. An intercultural dialogue cannot ignore these hidden forces that speed up and intensify all kinds of violence—social and domestic, against women and against nature. As one may study the history of the Roman Empire and its impact on violence and the family, one should also investigate the influence of today's global economic empire/system and the role it plays in the perpetuation of violence against families and women. This reality, which we theologically call structural sin, unites us, and should help us perceive challenges in a more integrated way; it should also help us to reflect on our own complicity and on the possibilities for different ways of living.

When speaking of sin and the disrespect of dignity, it is appropriate to talk about the grace of God and God's relationship with human dignity. With a view to this, I want conclude by sharing some reflections of mine in an unpublished English essay entitled "About Divine Experiences in Human Beings: The Grace of God and Human Dignity." I also do this because, except for in the introduction, the essays I have read say very little about the meaning of dignity in the different contexts.

God's grace and human dignity are mutual expressions, since both refer to God and to human beings. They refer us to the Divine because since creation, and in the constant recreation of its creatures, this has been the source of both grace and human dignity; it also refers to us human beings, because only in the totality of creation and human history until the present is it possible to perceive the grace of God and the dignity of human beings. Moreover, human dignity and divine grace are inseparable, because it is impossible to experience the grace of God and not at the same time to experience human dignity. If there is no experience of human dignity there is an absence of gratitude for God's grace; and if there is human dignity, God's grace is present in some way. Grace empowers people. To feel worthy is to feel this internal flame called grace that not only enlivens, but that also gives one the strength to walk with dignity and to resist adversity that wants to deny the gift of dignity.

Spanish theologian José Ignacio González-Faus (1987, 200) writes that God's image implies the dignity of humans and that this "connotes an element of grandeur and absolute mystery in the other, which demands total respect, impedes radical condemnation and prohibits manipulation." If one accepts this, González-Faus continues, "neither for fear nor for comfort, but for something that is demanded from within, we are confessing that in the mystery of others is the true image of God," which implies, one may add, respect for human dignity.

With this affirmation of González-Faus's view, we pass from the divine experience of human dignity in the subject as we have seen above to the divine experience of recognizing human dignity in the other person. That is, there is an experience of God in recognizing that, like oneself, others are also creatures made in the image of God. This is a confession that emanates from within and that expresses the conviction that "the other" carries the divine mark of human dignity.

For those Christians who take refuge in following Jesus Christ, God's grace becomes the source of this same divine experience of recognizing the other, not just because of his or her human dignity, but also because he or she is a brother or sister and carries the divine mark of being a son or daughter of God. Because grace is poured out in the hearts of believers, they have cried out *Abba!*; not only one person but many, and all of them are sons and daughters of the same *Abba* and have, therefore, also become brothers and sisters of each other.

However, in the concrete world, where life is often threatened and where inequality prevails, such divine experiences are never fully encountered—they are located on the horizon of utopia. According to Enrique Dussel (2003, 281–94), dignity is found from negativity. For him,

> the master who has slaves, the feudal, the metropolitan citizen or the settler, the macho, the owner of capital do not need to affirm their dignity; they presume it, nobody questions it; it is an obvious dimension, given as the starting point. One only cries out for dignity when it has been previously denied; when someone screams for dignity that has been taken from him [sic], or that has never been given or attributed to him.

For Dussel, dignity "is won, its growth is a continual process; it is a movement of dignity."

Dussel is right: in our Latin American context dignity will be evidenced as a struggle to assert it. This is not because intimidated, cowardly spirits are swarming around us, but because the denial of human dignity and thus the perceived absence of God's grace in our context is a constant in our daily lives and in the economic, social, and cultural structures surrounding us. It is impossible to talk objectively about human dignity or the presence of God's grace in the midst of homicidal violence and in the absence of work, food, education, home, or possibility of leisure and freedom. The lack of these vital necessities testifies to a lack of respect for human dignity and the absence of God's grace. Because of this, the experience of full human dignity can never be limited to a feeling of personal satisfaction; it involves a continual struggle for recognition and for the grace of God to be present, as happened in the resurrection of the Crucified One.

From here, human dignity and God's grace cannot be simply proclaimed and accepted by the head and the heart without any kind of historical solidification. Both human dignity and God's grace are divine gifts and challenges to be affirmed. They are vocations, that is, they are divine gifts that need to be lived; they are callings that must be carried out; they are vocations that welcome the challenges of "living with dignity" and of "reflecting the grace of God," and at the same time of recognizing the dignity and grace of God in the other person.

Even in contexts where human dignity and the grace of God are denied, to speak of them as a vocation or calling prohibits any interpretation that may postpone the unusual experience of feeling worthy in the present. In the acts of reappropriating the gifts of human dignity and of struggling for full recognition, one may still walk upright as a worthy person. Job, reduced to extreme misery, to skin and bones, smelly, abandoned, and covered in sores, saw himself walking "as a prince" toward the court of God to defend himself. As such Schökel translates Job 31:35-37 as follow:

> Oh that I had One to hear me!
> Here is my signature, let the Almighty answer me!
> And that I had the indictment which my adversary has written!
> Surely I would carry it upon my shoulder;
> I would bind it unto me as a crown.
> I would declare unto Him the number of my steps;
> As a prince would I go near unto Him.

References

Dussel, Enrique. 2003. Dignity, Denial and Recognition in a Liberation Context. *Concilium* 300: 281–94.

González-Faus, José Ignacio. 1987. *Proyecto de hermano.* Santander: Sala Terra.

Marquez, Gabriel García. 1970. *One Hundred Years of Solitude.* Translated by Gregory Rabassa. New York: Harper & Row.

———. 1982. *Chronicles of a Death Foretold.* Translated by Gregory Rabassa. New York: Knopf.

Part 3
Engaging the Context

Dignity in the Family? Analyzing our Ambiguous Relationship to the Family and Theological Suggestions toward Overcoming It

Petruschka Schaafsma

Introduction

In the present late liberal, Western context, family and human dignity do not exactly make an ideal pair.[1] It is not unusual to find suggestions that the family is precisely a setting in which human dignity is under threat. This idea is illustrative of current general distrust of the family. At present, the family seems to stand for things that are at odds with central late liberal values: family favors its own members; it provides people with fixed roles that hinder equality and free self-development; and it is in a sense a closed phenomenon, and may as such foster values different from generally accepted ones. Apart from this general distrust, which is often latent, there is a lively debate on the consequences of the major and obvious changes in family life that have taken place since the 1960s, such as the increase in divorce, blended families, and cohabitation, decrease in marriages, the understanding of procreation as a "conscious choice," and so on. This debate in particular has turned the topic of the family into a controversial, emotionally charged one. Advocates that welcome the new, democratic

---

1. I use the term "late liberal" in the way in which Brent Waters uses it in his analysis of the history of political thinking on the family. "'Liberalism' denotes a range of convictions and principles asserting the primacy of freedom and autonomy, enabling individuals to pursue their respective visions of the good" (Waters 2007, 61). With MacIntyre, Waters regards Kant's thinking as the origin of modern liberalism, while late liberalism refers to twentieth- and twenty-first-century theorists such as John Rawls and Susan Moller Okin (75–82).

family relationships based on intimate love[2] are opposed to skeptics who emphasize the drawbacks of less stable family relationships built on the fragile commitment of partners. This debate often results in deadlock. At first sight, human dignity seems to be a late liberal topic related to values such as democracy, equality, and authenticity. This fact already indicates human dignity's awkward relationship to the family.

This article proceeds from the general aim of this volume, namely, to draw attention to the contexts in which human dignity may be threatened—in this case, the family. This means entering the topical battleground of the family. In this article I will ask what a theological perspective may contribute to the present discussion of the family in general and its relation to human dignity in particular. I am aware that for the general public the answer to this question may seem obvious: in the present debate on the family, also outside academia, people from a Christian background often feel at home in the camp of the family skeptics who point out the dangers of the democratization of the family. Especially in the United States debate on "family values" that started in the 1980s, dominant Christian perspectives are from conservative voices, such as the "Christian Coalition," and "Focus on the Family" (Browning et al. 1997, 43). This skepticism is accompanied by a longing for and plans toward the revitalization of the traditional concept of family. Within academia as well, theologians often argue from a pro-family perspective, which is usually claimed to be biblical.[3] It is difficult not to hear this argument as one that should outweigh all others and sanction a specific view for the Christian group involved. Obvious as this approach may be, I do not aim at joining the current battle, but at analyzing it from a distance. I will ask, for instance, why the family is, as a matter of course, presented as a Christian good. In order to explain this, the specific role played by biblical references deserves particular attention. I will, however, not take as my point of departure a hardline Christian pro-family view, but rather one that has elements of both late liberal family criticism and current pro-family views, and will explicitly steer a middle course, namely the prominent family research led by Don Browning.[4]

---

2. E.g., Ferry 2007; Giddens 2002, 51–66.

3. Classical Bible passages regarding the family are: Eph 5:23, Col 3:18, 1 Pet 3:1 (on male headship); Matt 19:6–9 (on the prohibition of divorce); 1 Cor 14:34–36 (on silencing women in the church; see Browning 2006, 243–60, 249).

4. Browning is a central figure in recent theological investigations into family. From 1991 to 2003 he led the interdisciplinary research project "Religion, Culture, and

The reason is that such a course seems relevant precisely for our theme of family and human dignity: it is aware of the awkward relationship between the two, but it does not end there. In order to understand and to critically evaluate the specific theological character of this approach, I will compare it with other studies on the family with similar aspirations but without theological or biblical content. Behind this critical analysis of Browning's approach, the general issue at stake is what theology may contribute to current debates on major societal and personal topics.

Don Browning's Defense of the Equal-Regard Family as Biblical

Browning's project aims at constructing the profile of the so-called "equal-regard family" and the necessary conditions for it. It is meant to offer an alternative, liberal and critical, but not leftist, position in the American family debate that had been dominated by rightist pro-family voices. This position should be of special interest to the mainline Protestant churches that had hitherto remained silent in the public debate on family issues. The project is an example of Browning's "fundamental practical theology," which aims at integrating practical theology and theological ethics in order to arrive at a "normative ethic" (Browning 2007, 45).[5]

The starting point of Browning's research is explicitly called the "family crisis," the main symptoms of which are the well-known changes in family life mentioned above, but also the more hidden problems of single parenthood and poverty, or the absence of fathers. That these phenomena indicate a "crisis" is presented as something that goes without saying. Browning adds that Christianity has always been skeptical toward

---

Family," and he published on the issue until his death in 2010. This project resulted in twenty publications, most in The Family, Religion, and Culture Series, edited by Browning and Ian S. Evison. Some years after the end of the project, a book appeared containing central articles by Browning himself from different periods of this project, presenting a good overview of it (Browning 2007; for this formulation of the project see p. 38). Below I refer to only Browning, but he represents the project as a whole and a publication co-authored with others.

5. See the final chapter, which deals with "the relation between practical theology and theological ethics" (2007, 391–408). By integrating the two, Browning wants to avoid any simple scheme suggesting that practical theology applies the theory developed in theological ethics. Discovery of the dialectical relationship between "understanding" and "explanation" reveals the complexity of a combined practical and ethical investigation (2007, 36).

these things (2007, 39).[6] His aim is to address this crisis by formulating a "critical theory" (Browning 2006, 250) that combines the specific starting point of the Christian view with arguments that are convincing to a broader audience. This theory Browning calls "critical familism." Browning summarizes it as a pro-family and pro-marriage view, but one that has a substantial criterion for good family life and marriage, namely "equal regard" (Browning 2007, vii).[7] Equal regard means, briefly, that all family members are respected as being of equal value. They should all be enabled to develop themselves fully (2007, 405). Children should be educated to later build equal regard relationships by themselves. All adults are seen as being equally responsible for their family life. Moreover, families should respect and support one another in caring for their relatives (Browning 1997, 303–4). Good, empathetic communication is crucial for this equal regard love. Critical familism values a more or less traditional family life, mainly by promoting the "intact family," but opposes it insofar as it limits unequal individual self-development, especially in the form of patriarchal structures. Browning explicitly defines equal regard in terms of respecting human dignity:

> Equal regard as we define it, is a strenuous ethic: one respects the selfhood, dignity, of the other as seriously as one expects the other to respect or regard one's own selfhood.... Self and other are taken with equal seriousness in a love ethic of equal regard. This is the meaning of the command, "You shall love your neighbor as yourself (Matt 19:19)" (Browning 1997, 153).[8]

This quotation also reveals the biblical basis Browning claims for the criterion of equal regard. Browning's way of arguing is constantly twofold: what he regards as theological, Christian motivations are mostly put first, but these should continuously be enforced and completed by way of general arguments.

---

6. This is the introductory formulation of the first moment of practical theology, i.e., descriptive theology, which is still "naive and uncritical but still very important."

7. Browning mentions Gene Outka (*Agape: An Ethical Analysis*) as the one who coined the term "equal regard love," but bases himself more on Louis Janssens's natural law elaboration of love, than on Outka, whom Browning lumps with proponents of the neo-Kantian understanding of love (2007, 45; cf. Browning 1997, 275).

8. It is not clear why the Matthew quote is taken from the story of the rich young men and not from Jesus' summary of the whole law in Matt 22:39.

What precisely are the biblical aspects to which Browning refers? First of all, he focuses on the position and role of males in the family (e.g., 1997, 101–28). This is striking because the sanctioning of patriarchy and suppression of women seems the most obvious problem raised by those critical of traditional Christianity in relation to the family. Browning, however, introduces a biblical perspective precisely to criticize both male dominance and lack of male responsibility toward their families. In his view, this critique has been inherent to Christianity from its very origins in the New Testament. It can be found precisely in the texts on the role of men, and the relationship between men and women that have been historically influential in affording Christianity the reputation of being oppressive toward women.[9] This is revealed when these texts are read against their original cultural background, which Browning describes as the Roman-Hellenist honor-shame culture (1997, 129–54; 2007, 43–44, 78–79, 181–86, 293–95; 2003, 59–60, 71–74).[10] This culture relates male honor to male dominance over the household. Male honor could be threatened especially by women causing shame through their sexual promiscuity. However, male extramarital sexual activity was not perceived as a problem. Browning argues that, in comparison to the cultural standards of that time, even the more patriarchal statements in the New Testament imply a less oppressive view (1997, 131–47). This does not mean that all relevant New Testament texts may be lumped together. However, an important difference is observed between the principally egalitarian ideals of the early Jesus movement and the later accommodation of Christian views to the prevailing Aristotelian picture of the family, which qualified egalitarian impulses by the need of women to be led by men.[11] The equal regard love found in the Jesus movement should serve—also in line with the Old Testament

---

9. Browning refers, for instance, to traditional nineteenth-century American interpretations (2007, 399; 1997, 76–98).

10. Here Browning refers to New Testament scholars such as Bruce Malina, Halvor Moxnes, and Karl Sandnes, who built their theories on anthropological studies of the honor-shame culture by J. G. Persistiany, Julian Pitt-Rivers, David Gilmore, and others (2007, 43). See also *Families in the New Testament World* by Osiek and Balch (1997, 38–40), the New Testament studies' contribution to Browning's and Evison's book series "The Family, Religion and Culture." Note that the references to the honor-shame culture are limited in this New Testament study of the family, while they are very prominent in Browning's account.

11. This change is related to the deutero-Pauline and pastoral epistles in particular; that the need to focus on assimilation was felt in the later period confirms the exis-

principle of loving one's neighbor as oneself—as the hermeneutical key to interpreting the classical "male headship" texts. Ephesians 5:23, for example, should be read as being explained in verses 25-33, where husbands are summoned to love their wives as they do their own bodies.[12] Apart from the male problematic, the equal regard principle should also be applied more broadly, that is, to the efforts of both men and women to realize a good family life. In this respect, Browning focuses on the importance of mutuality over against self-sacrifice as basic principle of love (2007, 245-46; 1997, 131, 153).

In Browning's reasoning, the biblical arguments stand beside references to Christian tradition and general ones. As regards the negative evaluation of the current state of the family, he cites sociological theories concerning the colonization of the "lifeworld of face-to-face relations" by the empire of the "technical rationality of the systems world" (Browning 2007, 39).[13] He quotes empirical social scientific research showing that family disruption and in particular the absence of fathers negatively affects both adults and children involved (2007, 40).[14] References to evolutionary psychological insights regarding "kin altruism" are a fixed element in Browning's argument, which he parallels with Thomistic naturalism and sometimes with the Protestant theological doctrine of "orders of creation."[15] According to Browning, Aquinas regards equal regard love as the most "natural" way of living together, something that flourishes in the family as a community of blood relatives. Studies in evolutionary psychology also show that the functioning of families as strong communities of blood relatives helps to integrate males into a structure of relationships instead of letting them simply

---

tence of deviations, in particular a much more egalitarian practice (e.g., 2007, 180-86; Osiek and Balch 1997, 117-23; Browning, 1997, 132-49).

12. Five of these twists in comparison to mainline Aristotelian views are indicated with reference to Ephesians (1997, 144-47).

13. Browning specifically refers to Robert Bellah and Jürgen Habermas regarding the colonization thesis.

14. In all Browning's publications on the family, the social science research to which he refers includes the names of Gary Sandefur and Sara McLanahan. Browning's own project also contained a social science component, with elaborate interviews, from which a model of five representative American families resulted (1997, 8-25).

15. Browning refers to Hamilton's theory of "inclusive fitness" and "kin altruism" from the 1960s and 1970s (cf., e.g., 2007, 73, 119-20, 137-38, 154-93, 205, 335; 2006, 252). He regards a "reconstructed Catholic naturalism" as supplementary to the "classic protestant perspectives on the orders of creation" (2007, 125; cf. 2006, 255-57).

"hang around." Moreover, living together with blood relatives matches the human focus on the survival of not only one's own genes, but also of those who carry one's genes. In Browning's view, evolutionary psychology is able in this way to give a "partial account as to why children of intact biological parents seem, on average, to do better" (2007, 121). Browning indicates that each of these theories has its limits: biology cannot provide us with morality. However, precisely a mix of biblical values, insights from Christian theology, and secular scientific theories is—in his view—the best way to argue theologically in our contemporary situation.

I introduced Browning as an example of a theological approach that combines late liberal values with an appreciation of the family. He argues, on the one hand, that "some features of modernity ... are indeed good for families and worth preserving—for example, more equality for women, better and more universal education, and general higher standards of living and health care" (2007, 42). On the other hand, modernity's individualism and technical rationality threaten the world of human relationships—in particular the family. The solution to this dilemma does not lie with a simple embrace of the intact family. The intact family of earlier times was accompanied by many inequalities to which we do not want to return (1997, 71). Therefore, a selective resistance and support of modernity and the traditional family is needed in the present context.

According to Browning, the above selective approach "followed from the reconstructive and critical hermeneutic retrieval of the marvelous and multidimensional marriage and family tradition of Christianity" (2007, 42-43). However, this remark seems to be at odds with his principle of the mutually-reinforcing use of religious and general theories. Confronted with the mixed character of Browning's arguments, one cannot help but wonder whether the elements derived from Christian views form the real the basis of his choice of other, complementary general theories. Does this basis not consist of generally accepted, late liberal values like equality, respect for human dignity, and free self-development? And is not the interpretation of the biblical texts in fact directed by these values, instead of the other way round? For the claim that insights gained from the Christian tradition have resulted in the critical familism theory of equal regard love to be convincing, it should have been related to other possible interpretations of the Bible texts and other evaluations of the current family life, including conflicting ones. As a result, the specific contribution of the theological perspective does not become clear either.

In order to test the intuition that in Browning's work religious and general arguments are in fact exchangeable and that it lacks a specific theological view, it may be helpful to compare his approach to recent family studies with similar aspirations but without references to Christian tradition or the Bible.

Equal Regard and Its Natural Locus Compared

For this comparison two characteristic aspects of Browning's approach that also relate to our theme of the tension between family and human dignity are reflected upon: his focus on the equality of all family members and the so-called natural character of the intact family as locus of this equal regard love. With regard to the first aspect, a recent study in philosophical ethics specifically on family and parenthood by Michael W. Austin (2007) may function as a parallel to Browning's approach. Austin's starting point is the observation of the increasing plurality of forms of parenthood particularly as a result of improved fertility technologies, an increase in the numbers of blended families, and adoption—all of these also with regard to same sex couples. This new situation raises new ethical and juridical dilemmas, especially regarding practical and financial responsibility for children in the case of broken partner relationships. Moreover, the problem of high rates of abuse within families in general poses the question of criteria for good parenthood (Austin 2007, 1-9). Austin argues that this complex field may be ordered by focusing on the ideal of stewardship, which he takes from environmental ethics. Parents are "stewards" because they have to care for something very precious, namely their children's lives, something which they do not own. Their care is also temporary—one day their children will become stewards of their own lives, that is, autonomous human beings (Austin 2007, 8, 83, 98, 112-16). In this limited period of care, it is important to recognize and satisfy the specific interests of the individuals as family members, such as "psychological well-being, intimate relationships, and the liberty to pursue that which provides meaning and satisfaction in life" (2007, 76). The stewardship ideal aims at satisfying as many interests as possible—of parents, children, and the larger community, including future generations (2007, 6, 8, 32, 59, 66, 75-87, 106, 109, 111). On this basis a small set of *prima facie* parental rights and a larger number of obligations are formulated. Both the goals of rearing children to become autonomous and of satisfying family members' fundamental interests are, according to

Austin, in accordance with our common moral intuition regarding what constitutes a good life.[16]

What reminds one of Browning in Austin's argument is the latter's balancing of individually-oriented values with the value of the family as the solution for the present problems regarding family life. Austin finds the basis for balance in the idea that the family serves specific individual interests that cannot be easily satisfied outside of the family. However, he does not elaborate much on the specific character of the family that shapes these interests, and rather focuses on the necessity of paying equal attention to every family member. The same is true of Browning, who chooses equal regard love as the basic criterion for family life, but then reflects more deeply on the aspect of equality than on the specific character of family love. Both Browning and Austin pay attention to the fact that being a family also entails sacrifice for its members. But this sacrifice is understood as being balanced by the good of the family for the individual and not by the collective good of the family for which one sacrifices oneself. This approach seems quite self-evident against the background of the late liberal assumption of a tension between the family and the respect for individual freedom, equality, and autonomy. The comparison with Austin does not reveal Browning's focus on equal regard as adding something specifically theological.

Browning and Austin differ on the most apparent current locus of tension between family and late liberal values. Austin focuses on the parent-child relationship, whereas Browning deals primarily with the relationships between men and women, or husbands and wives, and the male problematic. Neither scholar accounts for his focus in any detail. Austin's focus seems to follow from his use of primarily legal case studies. The discussion on good parenthood and rights and obligations of parents is also an academic one. In both of them, the most important threats are a too great emphasis on parental rights and the negation of children's moral status, or the opposite, a too great emphasis on parental self-sacrifice for the sake of the children (2007, 11–32, 86, 111). Browning's focus on men and women within the family is first of all simply presented as flowing from his biblical sources. Is it here, then, that one, upon further consid-

---

16. See Austin 2007, 3, 79 ("observation and experience"), 127–28. Apart from the explicit references to this common-sense character particularly at the beginning and the end of Austin's book, his style of reasoning constantly refers to a kind of common experience.

eration, encounters a specifically theological view? Is it a theological perspective that shows that inequality in the men-women relationship is the most urgent family issue? This is not the way Browning argues. He does not even explain why, among all possible Bible texts, he focuses on those dealing with men-women issues. One might assume his selection is influenced by an important aspect of his analysis of the current family crisis, that is, the problem of the absence of fathers. However, this analysis itself builds on social science data. Furthermore, in his interpretation of biblical texts, Browning does not primarily emphasize the responsibility of fathers toward the family life, but rather the general aspects of equality, freedom for women, and love of neighbor. Attention to the topic of fatherly commitment to the family follows mainly from theories of evolutionary psychology, which are related to Aquinas's views. Therefore, a distinguishing theological view is not displayed in this focus on men-women issues. If Browning's central aim is to argue for equal regard, his first task as a Christian theologian is to show that traditional Christianity's contribution to family structures that foster gender inequality can be opposed on the basis of biblical texts and authorities like Aquinas. But, again, this is not how Browning presents his argument. Therefore, its specific theological character does not become clearer in this comparison with Austin.

While there are clear parallels between Browning's and Austin's views on the family with reference to their pleas for equality in the family, the second aspect—intact families as the most "natural" loci for nurturing equal-regard love—does not figure in Austin.[17] Browning bases this "naturalness thesis" on both Aquinas and evolutionary psychology. However, a parallel to this second aspect can be found in Brenda Almond's 2006 philosophical study of the current family issue. She analyzes the current state of the family as one of fragmentation leading to its devaluation. This fragmentation has its origins in the fact that the family's natural character is no longer seen as constitutive of it. This can be observed in four fields of "Western wisdom and technological expertise," namely law, social sciences, medicine, and philosophy and education (Almond 2006, 1–5). There is a "legal deconstruction of the family." Contrary to earlier times, present legislation deprivileges marriage and defines the family in a functional or a

---

17. Austin devotes only a few words to the issue of the specific composition of the family: "It is preferable to have at least one parental figure who is consistently and intimately involved in [the children's] lives, and … a large number of such parental figures is counterproductive" (Austin 2007, 3).

socio-legal instead of a biological way. Medicine contributes to this tendency, most obviously by reproductive technologies that enable nongenetic parenthood. In approaches like feminism, Marxism, and deconstructionism, philosophy influences the debate through strong voices supporting the view of the family as a vehicle of inequality. However, in mainstream philosophy the topic is surrounded by silence. In the domain of education one finds a similar silence, which originates in a downplaying of educational influence on family-related topics such as sex and relationships, and results in an uncritical acceptance of new trends. This analysis of current tendencies already reveals what Almond means by the natural character of the family. First of all, she means that reproduction constitutes the basis of the family. Taking this seriously may lead one to acknowledge a basic right to know one's genetic or biological parents (2006, 96). Marriage is subsequently seen by her as grafted onto this basis of physical reproduction.[18] In addition, Almond refers to natural, innate aspirations with regard to family that are different for men and women.[19] She is not unaware of certain good effects of unlinking family from its natural foundations. But the effect of the current ideology that neglects the natural character and defines it as a legal or social convention is more harmful.

Almond and Browning both think that a reassessment of the natural character of the family may help to solve current problems, because it helps to clarify the importance and value of the family. The dignity of all family members, especially of the most vulnerable ones, the children, is best guaranteed when the naturalness of their relationship is acknowledged and lived in accordance with.[20] Although Browning and Almond do not explicitly say so, the power of this argument of naturalness is of course that it sounds like the self-evident, obvious way to live, more or less objectively, empirically proven. To confirm the natural goodness of the "intact family," they both refer primarily to proof supplied by the social sciences

---

18. "The law that creates marriage ... can be seen as an artificial means of changing what was originally a non-binding and voluntary relationship into the same unrelinquishable category as biological family relationships, like those of parent and child" (Almond, 2006, 40; cf. also 15).

19. Almond 2006, 77–81. Almond briefly refers to evolution psychology as suggesting that women have a direct relationship with their children, while men have a mediated one. She also mentions Carol Gilligan's analyses of the difference between women and men in dealing with moral dilemmas.

20. This is another important element in Almond's reasoning (2006, especially 123–45; see also 17, 55, 68, 101).

showing better results from being raised in an intact family. Like Browning, Almond is aware of the trap of "reasoning from what *is* to what ought to be" (2006, 14; cf. 9). Biology cannot provide us with morality. Nevertheless, it can indicate what "human life at its best could be" and thus it guides us in our judgment of what is good (2006, 14). In this use of "natural facts" Browning and Almond do not differ.

Still, Browning differs from Almond in the weight that is eventually attached to naturalness in clarifying more specifically what families should look like. For Almond, naturalness is in the end a rather broad and, therefore, vague dimension. She aims primarily to show that it has been forgotten in our times and that this leads to problems. Browning, on the other hand, sees the natural—that is, intact—family, as a solution to fundamental human problems. As in his interpretation of biblical material, Browning focuses in his naturalness thesis on the male problematic, while Almond refers in a more general way to problems related to marriage and divorce, artificial reproduction, same-sex parenthood, and so on. As was seen, Browning cites evolutionary psychology to show the problems inherent to mammalian males. Thomas Aquinas is quoted as someone who already long ago acknowledged the naturalistic grounds for matrimony (Browning, 2007, 123). With regard to this specific focus in Browning—on the problems of men compared with those of women—similar remarks can be made as with regard to Austin. In the context of the naturalness thesis, Browning again does not account for why precisely this male aspect of family life should currently be brought to attention. But evolutionary theories and social science data on the consequences of the absence of fathers again seem the most important reason. There are again no signs that this focus would be motivated specifically from a theological perspective. Browning's references to theological doctrines, such as the Roman Catholic natural law tradition and the Protestant concept of spheres or orders of creation, are quite general. One finds formulations such as that God's grace reinforces human commitment, and that a husband should model Christ's love for the church in his commitment to his wife. In the end, the impression is that what matters is that the tenor of Aquinas and evolutionary psychology is the same. Thus, Browning's argumentation seems in line with Almond's option to present the naturalness of the family as a secular theory.[21]

---

21. Almond is well aware that the high esteem of the natural is central to an important philosophical tradition, that of natural law. Although this natural law tradition has been largely elaborated on in a religious framework, Almond wants to

The comparison between the views of Browning, Austin, and Almond clarifies how, behind Browning's emphasis on equal regard, the late liberal difficulty with the family becomes visible. Browning's thesis that living in an intact family is a natural good is underpinned by evolutionary psychology, social science, and ancient authorities such as Aquinas. The focus specifically on the role of males in the family and on the equality between men and women is not accounted for in detail. All these characteristic aspects cannot be seen as informed by theological reasoning in particular. This means the theological character of Browning's research must be found mainly in that it shows that currently accepted values and practices can be related to the Christian tradition, and in particular to the Bible. This is not, however, how Browning himself describes his project: in his account, the Christian and biblical views are foundational. The fact that Browning does not elaborate on why he focuses on specific aspects of the family issue and on particular biblical texts and not on others does not add to the persuasiveness of his reasoning. But more importantly, one may ask whether this theological approach is what is needed in the current family debate.

Theology as Stepping Back and, Informed by the Bible, Constructing Anew

As indicated above, the general question behind this critical analysis of Browning's approach is what theology may contribute to current debates on great societal and personal topics. Browning's contribution may be described as one of harmonizing—that is, showing that modern values are compatible with Christian ones. A critical perspective from modernity on Christianity, or the other way around, is not absent. But the aim is to relate them, and not to play them off against each other, or to use the one to introduce a new, surprising point of view into the other. Is this the theological contribution that is needed in the current family debate? It was seen that the family is a controversial, emotionally charged topic at present, debated by both advocates and skeptics of recent developments in family life. Browning steers a middle course between them. On the one hand, he tries to dispel the late liberal distrust of the family, especially in light of its perceived threat to human dignity. On the other hand, he tries

---

interpret it "in a way that avoids the need to appeal to religious doctrines that can be accepted as a guide only by adherents" (2006, 15). Thus, she hopes to avoid the "contention that resort to religion often brings" (207).

to keep the specifically Christian appreciation of the family in the more or less traditional sense. But who will Browning take with him on this middle course? One may wonder whether the advocates of the democratic family will be convinced by his thesis on the natural good of the intact family. Christian pro-family activists, on the other hand, will not so easily give in to his choice and interpretation of biblical texts. This fate—of not being taken seriously by either side of the debate—seems to befall many so-called liberal, middle-of-the-road theological approaches. However, this does not mean that the left, right, or middle options are the only ones capable of making a contribution—whether theological or not—to the family debate. What seems to be lacking is a more distanced analysis of the debate that investigates what is actually at stake in it. Why are some people spontaneously and wholeheartedly devoted to an ideal of traditional family, while others are allergic to it? It is clear that other sentiments also play a role in this debate, and that it is not just the issue of the family as such that rouses the emotions. Why should theology not step back and engage in such a distanced analysis? I will conclude, therefore, with some suggestions regarding the direction such an analysis may take, and how use of the Bible—in ways differing from Browning's—may contribute to it.

The starting point of such an analysis would be to ask what aspects of human life embodied in the phenomenon of the family are somehow difficult to deal with in our time and what aspects remain attractive. Thus, one may also gain insight into the relationship between human dignity and the family as being an ambiguous one. The difficulties and dangers the family embodies may be described most easily: they have to do with threats to individual freedom and autonomy, to the ability to determine one's own life and norms, to being independent. There are many potential risk factors in the sphere of the family—to mention only a few: one's specific family history; the social class and occupations of one's parents; but also dependent child-parent and parent-child relationships as such; social control among family members; and traditional roles of different family members. Family relationships are characterized by involuntariness, inequality, and irreplaceability. These characteristics go against the grain of autonomy-related values like freedom of choice and equality (especially in relations), and also against the idea that our qualities determine our specific roles and not our simply being "born" into such roles. Finally, these characteristics make the family into a setting of vulnerable relationships in which abuse is more easily possible than in other relationships.

The values of family life that we nevertheless do not want to lose may be indicated by a term that is often prominent in policy documents on family life, namely cohesion. Despite all efforts to encourage people to become free, autonomous individuals, it is clear that it is also important that they should be related to others, or otherwise society falls apart. Cohesion is necessary, not just because of the "exceptional" situation in which we need others to care for and help us, but also for one's upbringing, for learning moral values and codes, and finally also for feeling safe or at home in this world. The family is often presented as the most natural and basic context of learning and living this cohesion, on which society at large subsequently builds. As the most natural context for being connected, it represents the ideal of a safe haven where one should find comfort and consolation, especially in our globalized, too-large world. This attitude toward the family may contribute to a self-isolating, secluded family sphere, which—paradoxically—makes it even more susceptible to the perpetration of abuse.

If this brief indication of some important difficulties and attractiveness of family in our times is correct, the general disquiet regarding the family requires coming to terms with both our fundamental dependence and our longing for comfort in being connected with others. It is here that theology has an important double contribution to make. This contribution lies, first of all, in a reflection on these phenomena of dependence and comfort-in-connectedness. Religion is preeminently a context in which these are practiced. Fundamental to a religious anthropology is that human beings are not self-made but dependent on others for the meaning of their lives, for their happiness. This anthropology is, therefore, always critical of too strong an ideal of autonomy. However, it would also be critical of any easy, insular comfort. This is reflected, for example, in the religious tension between comfort in the present world and eschatological hope in the coming world. It is precisely theologians who may have the task of bringing these hidden aspects of the debate to the fore, because their familiarity with premodern religious sources always implies a critical, comparative perspective on late modernity. They may, therefore, be especially sensitive to the blind spots of the modern framework. But they must also show that coping with these blind spots is never a simple matter of restoring what is made "visible" again. What is needed in the current family debate—apart from this distanced analysis—is a critical construction of *new* meanings that presupposes a deep insight into the context in which theses meanings should function.

Precisely to the purpose of critically analyzing our own context and constructing new meanings for it, biblical texts may make a valuable contribution. This use of the Bible does not regard it as a historical document that reveals the life and thought of early Christians, but as a *Fundgrube* of meanings. For a Christian theologian it may seem self-evident to turn to the Bible for guidance regarding contemporary problems, but taking biblical meanings seriously is of course highly contested in our time. This makes it necessary to give an account of the status of these meanings. For this reason two aspects of the possible value of relating to biblical meanings in our time may be mentioned, both taken from Ricoeur.[22]

Ricoeur characterizes our time as one of forgetfulness *and* restoration. We have forgotten about the sacred that is preeminently visible in the positivist endeavor of speaking in a precise and univocal manner (Ricoeur 1969, 349). However, at the same time, it is a "gift of our 'modernity'" that our thinking can be recharged with the help of "philology, exegesis, phenomenology of religion, and psychoanalysis of language." Remarkably, Ricoeur as a philosopher starts this "filling anew of our language" by studying religious texts via a second naiveté—that is, not the first naiveté of the premodern believer. Since the combination of Greek philosophical reflection and biblical thought characterizes the Western context, Ricoeur turns specifically to biblical texts for his hermeneutical construction. These texts contain a different, literary kind of discourse that gives rise to a different kind of philosophical reflection than that of Western philosophy building on Greek thinking (LaCocque and Ricoeur 1998, ix–xix). Ricoeur characterizes this discourse as "radically nonspeculative and prephilosophical" (1969, 224).[23] This may be a first reason to turn to biblical meanings precisely in the present situation.

---

22. I refer in particular to his early work on the symbolism of evil (1960) and two later articles in Ricoeur 1995, "Philosophy and Religious Language" (35–47), and "Naming God" (217–35).

23. The philosophical value of pre-philosophical expressions is something that Ricoeur already recognized in his early works *Fallible Man* and *The Symbolism of Evil*. In this philosophical investigation of evil, he regards these expressions as providing the key to understanding the more reflected, speculative language of evil. Moreover, they contain a wealth of meanings and a depth that is instructive for philosophy, and which it cannot equal. On the other hand, reflection is necessary to bring clarification and coherence to the darkness and complexity of the pre-philosophical expressions.

A second motivation follows from Ricoeur's reflections on what it means to be a "listener to Christian preaching."[24] In his view, this listening implies a double sense of letting go (*se depouiller*). First of all, the letting go of the knowledge of God in any metaphysical or ontotheological sense. The naming of God should instead arise from the plurality of different modes of discourse of the biblical texts. Secondly, it also requires letting go of the "more subtle and more tenacious pretension" of the strong view of the subject that is implied by Kant's alternative to metaphysics, that is, the subject of transcendental knowledge, which claims insight into the boundaries of human knowledge. "Listening excludes founding oneself.... It requires giving up (*dessaissement*) the human self in its will to mastery, sufficiency, and autonomy." It assumes an "antecedent meaning that has always preceded me." What is characteristic of the biblical meaning is the "naming of God," or having God and God's kingdom as its "referent." This "referential" character of the biblical text should again not be understood in a metaphysical way, or in the sense of Kant's illusion, but as a specific form of "poetic disclosure." Fiction and poetry refer to a "proposed world," or a "being in the world" that is liberated after the "abolition of first order reference," that is, reference to the objective or empirical world (Ricoeur 1969, 42–43). This is "the world of the text." What characterizes biblical texts in comparison to poetic texts in general, is that this world of the texts has a "force of rupture and opening."[25] This force relates to the specific referent of the biblical poetical text—God and God's kingdom—that can never be named in a complete sense in one single image or model, but only in a polyphony of expressions and limit-expressions, which also conflict with each other (1969, 233–34). This elaboration of the attitude of "listening" is what is meant here with a different way of relating oneself to the Bible than the historicizing way of, for example, Browning. It is characterized by a view of the biblical texts as containing a radical form of poetic

---

24. This is how, at the beginning of the article "Naming God," Ricoeur describes his own position as a philosopher relating himself to the Bible. The following is taken in particular from pages 223–24.

25. Elsewhere, in an article on "The Specificity of Religious Language," Ricoeur characterizes "proclamatory sayings, proverbial formulae and parables" of New Testament texts by "intensification, transgression and going to the limit" (Crossan 1975, 107–22). This is an example of the specific character of religious language in comparison to poetic language in general.

disclosure of a possible world that disorients and upsets our discourse and our action (Crossan 1975, 124).

What may such a way of relating to the Bible yield in the case of the family issue? Rather than turning immediately to the texts on family affairs—for instance, honoring one's parents, divorce, male headship, "hating the family"—we may focus on the manifold examples in which the relationship between human beings and God is depicted in terms of family relations: God as father, mother, or husband; Israel as faithless wife or beloved son; the believing community as children of God; or the relation, especially in Luke, between fathers and sons in the light of the view of God as father and Jesus as son.[26] Or one may turn to a parable like that of the prodigal son (Luke 15:11–32), in which family relations are prominent. Analyzing texts like these in relation to our discussion on family and dignity may indeed imply "rupture and opening." An obvious opening thought to which they give rise is that in all of these texts some sense of inequality is present within the relationship, but it is apparently not perceived as problematic. This may confront us with our (late liberal) intuitive concern regarding the equal respect of all family members. Is it equality that is constitutive of human dignity, or may human relationships also imply "healthy" forms of inequality—such as those related to parental care and guidance of children, or children's obedience to parents? If God and human beings are never seen as equals, what does it mean to say that precisely in God's love we are all acknowledged as human beings who should be respected? Why did the prodigal son in the end become son in a new way, which is not so much that of the autonomous and independent owner of his inheritance, and in that sense equal to his father, but that of a man who has lost everything and even receives the sonship as a gift from his father? May we say that the prodigal son's salvation lies exactly in his becoming dependent?

Questions like these invite us to rethink the present seemingly self-evident connection between human dignity and respect for equality and autonomy, and their problematic relation to the family. Moreover, in focusing on metaphors, symbols, and parables the intention cannot

---

26. This focus is very much in line with what Leo Perdue (1997) calls, in one of the books of Browning's research project, "Old Testament theology," distinct from social history: "Throughout its history, ancient Israel's major understandings of God, creation, the nation, the nations, and morality were forged in large part by the social character and experience of the family household. Many of the key metaphors for imagining God, Israel, the land, and the nations originated in the household" (1997, 225).

be to find a clear example of instruction, with its accompanying risk of religiously sanctioning the status quo. Symbols always require interpretation; only in the effort of interpretation will the world of the text reveal itself. Several times, we came across the need to operate carefully and in a distanced way when addressing issues related to the family. The way of relating to the Bible indicated here may contribute to such an attitude, since it allows for the possibility that the biblical meanings may alienate us from our well-known patterns of thinking, and more or less prompts us to reflect on the emotions this may arouse. Biblical literature may supply us with meanings, which may enable us to rethink these topics. That one thinks it is possible to "think anew" is an assumption that expresses belief. But, I would argue, the specific character of the Bible seems to call for this assumption, sometimes even if one would never regard oneself as a believer.

REFERENCES

Almond, Brenda. 2006. *The Fragmenting Family*. Oxford: Clarendon.
Austin, M. W. 2007. *Conceptions of Parenthood: Ethics and the Family*. ASAE. Burlington, Ind.: Ashgate.
Ferry, Luc. 2007. *Familles, Je Vous Aime: Politique et Vie Privée à l'Âge de la Mondialisation*. Paris: XO Éditions.
Giddens, Anthony. 2002. *Runaway World: How Globalization Is Reshaping Our Lives*. London: Profile.
Browning, Don S. 2003, *Marriage and Modernization: How Globalization Threatens Marriage and What to Do about It*. Grand Rapids: Eerdmans.
———. 2006. World Family Trends. Pages 243–60 in *The Cambridge Companion to Christian Ethics*. Edited by Robin Gill. Cambridge: Cambridge University Press.
———. 2007. *Equality and the Family: A Fundamental, Practical Theology of Children, Mothers, and Fathers in Modern Societies*. Grand Rapids: Eerdmans.
Browning, Don S., Bonnie J. Miller-McLemore, Pamela D. Couture, K. Brynolf Lyon, and Robert M. Franklin. 1997. *From Culture Wars to Common Ground: Religion and the American Family Debate*. FRC. Louisville: Westminster John Knox.
LaCocque, André, and Paul Ricoeur. 1998. *Thinking Biblically: Exegetical and Hermeneutical Studies*. Translated by David Pellauer. Chicago: University of Chicago Press.

Osiek, Carolyn, and David L. Balch. 1997. *Families in the New Testament World: Households and House Churches*. FRC. Louisville: Westminster John Knox.

Perdue, Leo G. 1997. The Household, Old Testament Theology, and Contemporary Hermeneutics. Pages 223–257 in *Families in Ancient Israel*. FRC. Edited by Leo G. Perdue, Joseph Blenkinsopp, John Collins, and Carol Meyers. Louisville: Westminster John Knox.

Ricoeur, Paul. 1969. *The Symbolism of Evil*. Translated by Emerson Buchanan. Boston: Beacon. First published in 1960 as *Philosophie de la Volonté II, Finitude et Culpabilité: La Symbolique du Mal*, Paris: Aubier.

———. 1975. The Specificity of Religious Language. In *Paul Ricoeur on Biblical Hermeneutics*. Edited by J. D. Crossan. *Semeia* 4:107–22.

———. 1986. *Fallible Man*. Translated by Charles A. Kelbley. New York: Fordham University Press. First published in 1960 as *Philosophie de la Volonté II, Finitude et Culpabilité: L'Homme Faillible*. Paris: Aubier.

———. 1995. *Figuring the Sacred: Religion, Narrative, and Imagination*. Translated by David Pellauer. Edited by Mark I. Wallace. Minneapolis: Fortress.

Waters, Brent. 2007. *The Family in Christian Social and Political Thought*. OSTE. Oxford: Oxford University Press.

A Response to Petruschka Schaafsma's "Dignity in the Family? Analyzing Our Ambiguous Relationship to the Family and Theological Suggestions toward Overcoming It"

Robert Vosloo

Dear Petruschka,

In your essay you engage in a critical and nuanced way some of the important insights from philosophic-ethical, sociological, and theological studies on the family, including the work of Michael W. Austin, Brenda Almond, and especially Don Browning. Your engagement with these scholars is presented with a clear goal in mind, namely to determine in what way the analysis informed by texts from the Christian tradition, and in particular from the Bible, adds to arguments that seek to offer theological perspectives on the family. It is certainly not easy to say what makes a viewpoint on the topic of the family theological or biblical. You rightly show that values such as equality or equal regard may be supported by drawing on other sources than the Bible or the Christian tradition, and that it is not a straightforward matter to use the Bible for these purposes. Moreover, you also note in your article that the belief that biblical literature may supply us with meanings that might enable us to think anew on topics related to "the family." There is no doubt, however, that any of our contemporary attempts to relate the Bible responsibly to the discourse on the family cannot take any hermeneutical shortcuts, but should seriously consider the type of Ricoeurian "detour" that your essay argues for. Now as we know, detours are most often ambivalent events. As Philip Gardner (2010, 32) perceptively observes:

> Detours are inconvenient and unsettling. They throw us off our course, obliging us to enter an unexpected landscape.... Yet on the other hand, once begun, a detour may prove to be a source of unexpected pleasures.... We may begin to recognize that the setting and the hinterland of our destination is more varied, more diverse than we had before supposed, and that glimpsing it from previous unknown vantage point is to see it in a different light, perhaps even anew.

Detours may indeed be frustrating, since they extend the journey beyond our intent, and the unfamiliarity of the road taken may lead to anxiety. But then again, detours may hold interesting surprises and expose us to new vistas. The type of detour in the discourse on the family that your essay proposes (with its question on the role the Bible actually plays, and what role it should play) is not the easiest road to travel, since it requires the high level of hermeneutical competency reflected in Ricoeur's influential work. In reading your essay I sensed that you felt that, amid the difficulties involved, an engagement with the Bible can also bring something new to the conversation by challenging, for instance, certain of the reductions in the discourse on the family that result from an uncritical acceptance of some of modernity's presuppositions. You suggest that the analysis of biblical texts may disrupt and disorient our discourse in a way that opens up new and creative insights that might enrich the conversation and transform current practices. Throughout your essay you are, however, careful not to dissolve certain tensions in the discourse on the family, and this has prompted me to follow to do the same in my response.

I do not wish to engage directly with your nuanced reading of, for instance, Don Browning's use of the Bible, or some of the very interesting suggestions you make on what the Bible may yield in the conversation on family issues. I can mention, though, that I agree with your claim that the valuable biblical texts on the family are not necessarily only those texts with explicit references to family affairs (such as the texts on honoring one's parents, divorce, male headship, and "hating the family"). Texts that depict, for instance, the relationship between God and humanity in terms of family relations are also extremely important when using the Bible in order to think theologically about the family, and more specifically for attempts to bring "the family" into conversation with the notion of human dignity. In my response I would like to reflect with you on some of the issues you raise in your thought-provoking essay by structuring my remarks around four word pairs, namely "normativity and ambiguity," "autonomy and dependence," "equality and asymmetry," and "home and hospitality." These words point to tension and traction, but it is my hope that in the discourse on the family these tensions will not result in dualisms or dichotomies, but may provide some kind of creative space for responsible speech in a world where human dignity is under threat—perhaps especially in the "safe haven" of the family.

Let me turn to the first word pair: "normativity and ambiguity." In the discussions on "the family" there is the temptation to view a certain understanding of the family as normative. In some Christian circles with a strong focus on "family values," there is often a romanticized and idealized view of the family at work, uncritically seeing the biblical view of the family also reflecting the modern nuclear family. I think that we are rightly challenged today to think in more fluid categories about the family, asking ourselves in the process what exactly we mean by "the family" in light of the greater visibility of single-parent families, blended families, and so on.

Today, many churches also use an idealized concept of the family as part of their marketing strategy, with "family services" and "family churches" becoming very much part of the ecclesial landscape. Therefore, I too feel that we need to problematize the language of the family, deflating in the process the type of normativity that is often uncritically equated with a biblical view on the family. In this regard it would be interesting to reflect more historically on how the modern nuclear family evolved. We should, in addition, highlight certain negative traits that the nuclear family often exhibits today. Notwithstanding the fact that we often hear the remark that it takes a village to raise a child, there is a real danger that the nuclear family can become an enclosed and sect-like unit. In the process it displays many of the ills associated with excessive individualism in our society—the nuclear family itself becoming a kind of inflated individual—and an accompanying forced separation between private values and the public good. Maybe my point can be stated by saying that in many contemporary societies the modern nuclear family is in danger of becoming a hegemonic social force that usurps other forms of communal and public life, or at least that isolates itself from finding a rightful place among other social institutions. When we reflect on "the family" today, we need to affirm the positive side and potential of stable family life—and also of what Browning refers to as "the intact family." In the process we need, moreover, to challenge an overly optimistic appraisal of the family that does not sufficiently integrate the reality of fluidity, ambiguity, and ambivalence.

Given your reference to the way in which biblical literature can disrupt and disorient the discourse on the family, I think one of the features that a theological engagement with the topic of family can bring to the conversation is the fact that it can—and in my view it should—problematize the type of normativity often at work in the plea for a strict and exclusive biological or heterosexual view of the "ideal" family. Given the way biblical texts relativize marriage and family in light of the coming of God's kingdom and the way we receive the gift of being adopted into the family of God, these texts challenge us to think about new family configurations. I would be interested to hear more about how you plan to integrate these ideas into your research.

Petruschka, in your essay you not only critique trust in the traditional family, but also address the distrust of the family, showing that the ambiguous attitude that many Northwesterners have toward the family is a real and urgent problem. However, your essay is less clear on what a theological engagement with the family via biblical texts has to say about the need to challenge the type of fragmentation that fuels violence, as well as how the family can provide stable space for human flourishing.

My second set of remarks relates to the word pair "autonomy and dependence." As mentioned above, you are critical in your essay both of contemporary trust in the traditional family and of distrust of the family stemming from the negative "family experiences" many people have. In addition, you argue that at present this distrust should be understood as a byproduct of the development of liberalism up to the present "late liberal" consensus. Given the Enlightenment-inspired focus on personal freedom and autonomy, the family has become suspect. You also refer to the work of Austin that emphasizes that adults should guide children toward adult autonomy while respecting the autonomy that already belongs to them as children.

Of course, on one level the Enlightenment ideals of autonomy and individual freedom are very important. Most of us in family relationships can at one stage or another identify with the response of one of the characters in Jean Paul Sartre's drama *Huis Clos*: "L'enfer, c'est les Autres" ("Hell is others," 1974, 92). We feel that family members impose restrictions on our individual freedom and autonomy. On the other hand, we are also aware that family relations provide stability and a sense of belonging. It is certainly the case that healthy processes of individuation are needed, but the Enlightenment value of autonomy has a darker side as well. You seem to be conscious of the possible dark side of a one-sided emphasis on autonomy. In your intriguing reference to the parable of the prodigal son, your write:

Why did the prodigal son in the end become son in a new way, which is not so much that of the autonomous and independent owner of his inheritance, and in that sense equal to his father, but that of a man who has lost everything and even receives the sonship as a gift from his father? May we say that the prodigal son's salvation lies exactly in his becoming dependent? (186)

You therefore think that we should challenge the seemingly self-evident connection between human dignity and autonomy. I share this view. You also argue that biblical literature can make an important contribution to the discourse on dependence. In this regard I would like to add that an understanding of our fundamental dependence is not merely limited to childhood. It is not a stage that we outgrow as we reach adulthood. Instead, we should keep in mind that as humans we are, to use Alasdair MacIntyre's phrase, "dependent rational animals" (1999, 5).[1]

MacIntyre's phrase suggests that while we should not disregard the values of individual freedom, rationality, and autonomy, we should keep in mind—even celebrate—the fact that our existence is marked by dependence on others. You rightly point to the fact that coming to terms with the family in our day requires new reflection on dependence and comfort. I would like to hear more on how you think theology may contribute to a richer understanding of dependence, especially in light of the fact that the word "dependence" is itself not unproblematic. In family life, unhealthy forms of dependence are often prevalent, leading some to prefer the term "interdependence." We should therefore ask how dependence relates to reciprocity. Further, can we make a plea for dependence while at the same time affirming the need for authority and individual freedom?

My third set of remarks concerns the word pair "equality and asymmetry." In your essay you not only highlight the seemingly self-evident connection between human dignity and autonomy, but also that between human dignity and equality. From early on in your essay you point to the fact that the contemporary distrust of the family in many circles is the result of the emphasis on the equality of human beings in the one common

---

1. MacIntyre's central thesis in this book is "that the virtues that we need, if we are to develop from our initial animal condition into that of independent rational agents, and the virtues that we need, if we are to respond to vulnerability and disability in ourselves and in others, belong to one and the same set of virtues, the distinctive virtues of dependent rational animals, whose dependence, rationality and animality have to be understood in relationship to each other" (1999, 5).

body of society, with family being a potential threat to this view of equality. You also highlight the way in which Don Browning's defense of the equal-regard family (with equality as criterion for good family life) draws on biblical texts, as well as how Browning links equal regard to human dignity. But you further ask whether this critical criterion of equal regard cannot just as well be formulated on a non-theological basis (as is seen, for instance, in the work of Austin). Nevertheless, the notion of equality is very much at the center of many of the biblically informed theological discussions on the family. While you affirm the emphasis on equality, you also point toward the way in which the Bible can "disorient" the discourse on equality. With reference again to the parable of the prodigal you ask:

> Is it equality that is constitutive of human dignity, or may human relationships *also imply "healthy" forms of inequality*—such as those related to parental care and guidance of children, or children's obedience to parents? If God and human beings are never seen as equals, what does it mean to say that precisely in God's love we are all acknowledged as human beings who should be respected? (186, emphasis added)

I think you are making an important point here, Petruschka, although many people may intuitively feel that the language of "inequality" (even "'healthy' forms of inequality") should be used with utmost care. We should certainly acknowledge the advantages that have resulted from the critique of patriarchy in the family structure and admit to the ways in which patriarchy (often with biblical and theological support) has contributed to a world view that has made the family an unsafe space for many women and children. It is my view that a theological defense of equality is indeed called for and that Christians too have a stake in defending this "liberal" virtue.[2] Attention to biblical texts, however, may inform our discourse on equality in a way that sits uncomfortably with some of the presuppositions of modernity, in the process perhaps pointing toward something similar to what Emmanuel Levinas (1969, 215) calls "the asymmetry of the interpersonal." Therefore, given the fact that the family is an important space for the transmission of values and wisdom, the challenge remains to speak about equality in a way that honors authority without legitimizing malevolent power; to protect role differentiation without enforcing harmful hierarchy; and to affirm tradi-

---

2. For an interesting discussion in this regard, see Bruce Ward 2010, 31–69.

tion without condoning oppressive traditionalism. I would like to hear more of your thoughts on how a hermeneutically responsible use of the Bible in the discourse on the family can navigate the tension between equality and "healthy" asymmetry.

A final word pair that calls for reflection, albeit in a more indirect way, is "home and hospitality." The theme of the conference in Kampen, the Netherlands, where you first read your paper in 2010 was "Human Dignity at Home and in Public," and the first draft of your essay had as its provisional title "No Longer at Home in the Family?" When I read your initial title, I at once thought that one can also speak about the family no longer being "at home." For many families, strained economic circumstances impact heavily on family life. Given long working hours and travel, fathers and mothers are often absent from the home. This results in all kinds of societal ills. Our reflection on the family should not be separated from our reflection on our economic contexts, taking into account the effects of processes related to the complex phenomenon we call globalization. In South Africa, as elsewhere, migrant work is very much part of the social landscape. In apartheid South Africa, this caused great upheaval for families, and today it occurs no less that people work (or are forced to work) in places other than the ones where their families reside. The potentially devastating effects of migrant work on family life should be noted. Furthermore, the realities of poverty and unemployment make "being at home" not about coming home after a long day's work, but a reminder of the inability to be economically active and to provide for one's family. Other examples can be added, but the point is that we cannot reflect on the family without taking cognizance of economic realities, just as we cannot reduce our reflection on family to that.

The word "home" is a fitting description of the space of family life. For most people home has a positive connotation, and we should affirm the idea of home as a locus of enjoyment and comfort. However, we should also qualify our thinking on the idea of home as well. You hint at this when you write in the last paragraph of your essay:

> As the most natural context for being connected, it [the family] represents the ideal of a safe haven where one should find comfort and consolation, especially in our globalized, too-large world. This attitude towards the family may contribute to a self-isolating, secluded family sphere, which—paradoxically—makes it even more susceptible to the perpetuation of abuse. (183)

The idea of the safe home can easily become equated with insular self-sufficiency that hides abuse and does not foster hospitality. Especially when there is the perception that our security is threatened, the home can easily become a retreat from life with strangers and a place that keeps strangers outside the gates.

We can say that the home is a wonderful space of protection and enjoyment. In a way we need the protection of the home (with its walls, doors and windows), but "home" can also function as a fortress or a prison. It is the home that is open to the other that is ethical, and therefore is in the true sense "home." All this is to say that our reflection on the family should take the idea of hospitality (in its broadest sense) seriously and seek to resist an unhealthy isolationism.

In conclusion, Petruschka, let me thank you for your comments and your contribution to responsible theological discourse on the family. We should probably remind ourselves that our reflections, including our theological reflections, will never be able to get a total grip on the mystery of "the family," even if we are continually challenged toward responsible speech and practice. As I read your essay, words from a sermon by Dietrich Bonhoeffer on 1 Cor 2:7–10, preached in London on May 27, 1934, came to mind. In this sermon Bonhoeffer speaks about how those closest to us often present the greatest mystery: "The greatest mystery is not the most distant star; to the contrary, the closer something is to us, the better we know it, the more mysterious it becomes to us" (2007, 361). One may say that there is a link—and not only etymologically—between *Heim* and *Geheimnis*. By not respecting the mystery of the other in family relationships, we might easily legitimize a stifling sense of familiarity and proximity. But without any sense of proximity we remain strangers and may in fact not challenge, but only mirror, the coldness of our consumer society.

Regards,
Robert

References

Bonhoeffer, Dietrich. 2007. *Dietrich Bonhoeffer: London 1933–1935*. DBW 13. Minneapolis: Fortress.

Gardner, Phillip. 2010. *Hermeneutics, History, and Memory*. London: Routledge.

Levinas, Emmanuel. 1969. *Totality and Infinity: An Essay on Exteriority.* Pittsburgh: Duquesne University Press.
MacIntyre, Alasdair 1999. *Dependent Rational Animals: Why Human Beings Need the Virtues.* Chicago: Open Court.
Sartre, Jean-Paul. 1947. *Huis Clos Suivi de les Mouches.* Paris: Gallimard.
Ward, Bruce. 2010. *Redeeming the Enlightenment: Christianity and Liberal Virtues.* Grand Rapids: Eerdmans.

Empowering Those Who Suffer Domestic Violence: The Necessity of Different Theological Imagery

Anne-Claire Mulder

Introduction

In *Proverbs of Ashes* (2001), the North American theologian Rebecca Ann Parker writes about an encounter between a pastor and a woman who once came knocking at her door:

> "Hello pastor, I'm Lucia.... I saw your name on the church sign. You are a woman priest. Maybe because you are a woman you can understand my problem and help me.... I haven't talked to anyone about this for a while ... but I am worried for my kids now. The problem is my husband. He beats me sometimes. Mostly he is a good man. But sometimes he becomes very angry and he hits me. He knocks me down. One time he broke my arm and I had to go to the hospital. But I didn't tell them how my arm got broken." I nodded. She took a deep breath and went on. "I went to my priest twenty years ago. I've been trying to follow his advice. The priest said I should rejoice in my sufferings because they bring me closer to Jesus. He said, "If you love Jesus, accept the beatings and bear them gladly, as Jesus bore the cross." I've tried but I'm not sure anymore. My husband is turning on the kids now. Tell me, is what the priest told me true? (Brock and Parker 2001, 20–21)

Lucia is not the first battered woman ever to have been told that her suffering will bring her closer to Jesus. In my research for this essay I came across many variations of her story from different contexts.[1] These stories reveal a number of recurrent themes, notably the references to biblical ideals such as that man and woman "shall become one flesh," that "what

---

1. Cf. Thistletwaite 1989; Brown and Bohn 1985; Cooper-White 1995.

God has joined together man must not separate," and that marriage is a sacrosanct institution. These stories also reflect the idea that love bears and endures all things, and that, in order to follow Jesus Christ, one has to deny oneself and take up one's cross. The fact that these ideas can be found in certain faith communities in all parts of the world indicates that they indeed form part of the ordinary theology of many Christians.[2] They are handed down by pastors and family members, in sermons and songs, in articles in church magazines and in remarks made during catechesis or pastoral counseling.

It is evident from the exchange referred to above that Lucia—like many other women—intuitively feels that a different theology may exist, one that may enable her to resist or change her situation. Parker affirms Lucia's intuition that God does not want human beings to suffer or to be beaten—and Parker accepts the consequences of this affirmation, namely, that she has to rethink her own theology in light of it. All over the world, feminist liberation theologians like Parker criticize the pernicious effects of the theology of the cross on the lives of those who suffer domestic violence—and not only on them.[3] To counter this dominant theological tradition and to give voice to and translate the hesitantly-formulated theological intuitions of ordinary women and men into theological discourse, these theologians turn to different themes in the Christian theological tradition: among these, the *imago Dei* tradition and a theology of creation in which creation is affirmed and elaborated as "very good." The current essay may be seen as contribution to this developing theological counter-tradition. It takes as point of departure the conviction that words and images have performative power, that they can effect change because they move those who read or hear them.

The starting point for my contribution concerns the question of what theological ideas and images may empower those suffering from domestic violence to change their self-perceptions and situations. To answer this question I will turn to the discourse on human dignity, and specifically to that part of the discourse that emphasizes human dignity as both an inherent quality and a subjective, experiential value of human beings. It

---

2. Jeff Astley (2002, 1) defines ordinary theology as "the theological beliefs and processes of believing that find expression in the God-talk of those believers who have received no scholarly theological education."

3. See Slee 2004, 60–71 for an overview of this critique. See also Strobel 1991, 52–65; Jantzen, 2007.

is therefore important to experience or esteem oneself as someone with dignity. To translate this notion into an image or concept that can speak to the imagination, I will advocate the use of the word "dignitary"—someone who possesses human dignity—to refer to human subjects in general. I will show that this concept is a secular translation of the theological idea that human beings are created in the image of God and are as such bearers of the image of God.

I will, moreover, expand on the image of human dignitaries by connecting it to the growing discourse on "flourishing," as it has developed in human dignity discourse as well as in feminist theology. In both discourses flourishing is used to reflect on what is meant by a life lived with dignity. As such, this conceptual image can support those who fight for self-esteem, since it offers not only an image of being human, but also direction in the process of becoming human: a flourishing subject; a dignitary.

However, before I develop these thoughts and images further, I will give a more elaborated account of the effects of domestic violence on the subjectivity of its victims.

Domestic Violence

Stories similar to that of Lucia are told to social workers, police officers, pastors, and pastoral workers every day by women, children, and sometimes men. Domestic violence is a worldwide and widespread phenomenon that may take on many forms. The term refers to violence between partners in relationships and between ex-partners, and to violence toward children or toward the elderly. It ranges from physical and sexual to emotional or psychological abuse, and may occur in the form of beating, kicking, causing cigarette burns, intimidation, name calling, insults, isolation, stalking, humiliation, rape, forcing another to hand over his or her money or possessions, forcing another to view pornographic videos or to be the object of pornographic videos, and so on (Lutheran World Federation, 2002).

It is very difficult to give a precise figure for the number of victims of domestic violence, because the issue is often surrounded by a wall of silence. Recent research in the Netherlands suggests that about one million persons occasionally suffer from domestic violence, while yearly between 200,000 and 300,000 persons are victims of "evident domestic violence."[4]

---

4. "Evident domestic violence is defined as (1) *serious* forms of physical or sexual

The same research reported that 64 percent of victims older than eighteen are female, 36 percent male, and that 83 percent of offenders are male.

The latter percentage reflects the asymmetry in the societal-cultural relationships between men and women, especially in partner relationships. It shows that the percentage of men who are perpetrators of domestic violence is substantially higher than the percentage of female offenders. This is not only expressed in the percentages of cases of physical and sexual violence, but in particular in the use of emotional or psychological violence by way of controlling and restricting the partner's movements. In literature on domestic violence this behavior is also called "intimate terrorism."[5]

In *Intieme Oorlog* (*Intimate War*), Justine van Lawick interprets this desire to exercise control over the partner as a "perversion of the romantic ideal." When partners in a love relationship seek their own fulfillment in the other, differences between the partners may be effaced on a phantasmatic level. When the reality dawns that the romantic ideal of an almost symbiotic relationship is an illusion, the desire to keep this unity intact at all costs takes the form of a desire to control the other—by force if necessary. Van Lawick situates this ideal at the beginning of the well-known spiral of violence in which violence against the partner grows progressively worse, punctuated by periods of respite (Groen and Van Lawick 2010, 59–60).[6]

The process of effacement referred to above is not a symmetrical one, though. It is hierarchically organized by way of the power of the dominant symbolic order that subordinates women, for instance, because it recognizes only the masculine subject as the subject of discourse. In this way, it also suggests to women that they are nothing on their own, that their task is to assist men in their becoming, and that it is therefore wrong or egotistical for them to love themselves (Irigaray 1993, 66). From this theoretical perspective, the romantic ideal of love can be seen as a continuation of an

---

abuse; or (2) *light* of forms of domestic violence that happen at least ten times a year: among others humiliation, forbidding the partner to leave the house or to speak to someone else at a party, destroying personal objects, threatening to leave the partner" (De Jong 2011, 8, emphasis added].

5. According to the latest Dutch research, 20 percent of perpetrators of domestic violence in the Netherlands fit the profile of "intimate terrorists" (De Jong 2011, 8).

6. The advantage of explaining domestic violence from the perspective of the romantic ideal of (love) relationships is that it also accounts for violence perpetrated in homosexual (love) relationships and between parents and children. In all these cases, differences in the relationship are effaced.

"older" patriarchal, societal, and symbolic arrangement in which the male partner had authority over his female partner, their children, and even other members of the household—a state of affairs that has been sanctioned by religious texts, doctrines, and practices. When Lisa Isherwood argues that most abusers operate from a set of moods and motivations that, although not itself Christian, has its roots deep in Christian culture, she implicitly refers to this symbolic order (Isherwood 2003, 206).[7] The intertwining of this dominant order of discourse with religious discourse becomes apparent in the perceptions of battered women from a Christian background. Recurrent themes in their stories include the following misconceptions:

(1) Marriage is a sacred bond: what God has joined together, no one should separate.
(2) Women are supposed to be meek; claiming rights and/or space for oneself is committing the sin of pride (Thistlethwaite 1989, 305).
(3) A battered woman deserves the violence done to her in one way or the other—for example, as a form of punishment for her "sins." In this way of reasoning the woman is considered to be like Eve, who was the first to sin, and is therefore held responsible for the sins of the world and justly punished by submission and suffering.
(4) In bearing the pain of the violence a woman is imitating Christ, who also suffered because of his love for us. This implies that suffering has a redemptive quality. From the fact that Jesus offered his life and God offered his Son, one may draw the conclusion that "the highest love is sacrifice" (Brock and Parker 2001, 20, 25).

The above perceptions in many ways reflect significant characteristics of the profile of the battered woman as someone who:

- has low self-esteem (theme 2)
- feels responsible for the success of a relationship (theme 1)

---

7. In this text, Isherwood gives a thorough picture of the Christian ideas and practices that are part of the symbolic order from which an abuser operates.

- accepts responsibility for the batterer's actions (theme 3)
- suffers from guilt, yet denies the terror and anger she feels (theme 2), and
- believes that no one except herself will be able to resolve the predicament she finds herself in (Thistlethwaite 1989, 305).

These characteristics may also be understood as the psychological and emotional effects of domestic violence on battered women and their children. Effects such as these often greatly outlast the violent relationship itself. However, the above characteristics can also be understood as the enlargement of the implicit profile in the dominant symbolic order of "woman," as someone whose task it is to feed, support, and assist "man" in all his undertakings.

However, the stories of Lucia and of others in similar situations show that women are not entirely trapped in this profile. Their efforts to change their situations or to leave their abusive relationships indicate an awareness of the fact that what is happening to them and their children is not acceptable. The stories suggest a certain form of resistance against the attacks on their self-esteem as well as the presence of "a survival and quality-of-life spirituality."[8]

In order to make these implicit ideas explicit in ordinary theologies, ethics of survival, and qualities of life, it is necessary to find images or words that touch the imagination of human beings and in particular the imaginations of those who suffer domestic violence, so that they may claim their dignity and reclaim their lives. As I have already indicated, this strategy rests upon the idea that words and images have performative power, that they can effect changes in the imagination that can in turn generate changes in the praxis of subjects. In my view, the word "dignitary" might be such a word, one that appeals to the imagination and can touch and change someone's self-understanding. In the following paragraphs I will elaborate upon this image.

Dignitaries

"Dignitary" is a powerful word that inspires the imagination and can exercise a strong empowering effect on the self-understanding of women and

---

8. The phrase "survival/quality-of-life spirituality" is derived from Williams 1993.

men. Normally the word evokes associations with persons in high places—bishops, court officials, judges—and class distinctions and inequality among human beings. My enthusiasm for the word comes from my own sense of being inspired when I first came across the expression "sechsundeinhalb Milliarden Würdetrager und Würdeträgerinnen" (six and a half billion dignitaries—referring to the number of human beings living on the planet at the time) in a text by the German-Swiss theologian and ethicist Ina Praetorius (2008, 105). The idea of six and a half billion bearers of dignity gripped my imagination and evoked a flood of images: pictures of women walking confidently through the streets; a picture of a woman, bald due to chemotherapy, sitting naked on a hospital bed and looking me—the viewer— straight in the eye; images of men immersed in their work; of children talking amongst themselves … images of human beings who "bear dignity"; individuals who carry a sense of natural self-confidence, persons for whom one uses the biblical expression "very good" (Gen 1:31)—even when they are ill, frail, or old. It was only later that I learned that the word *WürdeträgerIn*[9] is the German equivalent for "dignitary," and that Praetorius aims at playfully unsettling its received meaning by adding phrases such as "six and half billion dignitaries." It suggests that *all* human beings "hold a high rank or office," that they are dignitaries, like bishops, courtiers, and other officials, and should be treated accordingly.

My initial enthusiasm for the word grew when I further explored the many associations called forth by it. The German word *WürdeträgerIn* suggests that a human being "bears or carries dignity." This dignity must be understood as an inherent attribute of what it means to be a human being in this world. Moreover, the word refers implicitly to the first article of the German constitution, which reads that "the dignity of human beings is untouchable."[10] Praetorius describes these bearers of dignity, then, "as persons who are in the world for his or her own sake

---

9. This notation of the feminine version of the word *WürdeträgerIn*—with a capital I—refers to a dignitary of either of the two sexes. It has been introduced by German feminists to change the self-evident practice of using the masculine form of the word as a gender-neutral word.

10. The text of Art. 1, Abs. 1 of the German constitution reads: "Die Würde des Menschen ist unantastbar. Sie zu achten und zu schützen ist Verpflichtung aller staatlichen Gewalt [The dignity of human beings is untouchable. To respect and guard this dignity is the duty of all the force by the state]," quoted in Praetorius 2000, 114–15 nn. 77–78). Praetorius explains that this article refers to the preamble of the Universal Declaration of Human Rights.

and not for an extraneous purpose, unique, and not replaceable by any [other] equivalent"—a description that is indebted to Kant's definition of human dignity.[11] The value of this definition is that it depicts dignity as the freedom to give form to one's own life, and that it implicitly resists an order of discourse that does not respect the uniqueness of an individual or that effaces the irreducible differences between individuals. Although Praetorius (2005) affirms that the love of freedom of the human subject is an important passion, she does not emphasize that human subjects are autonomous. On the contrary, in her work she elaborates on the thesis that human existence is being-in-relation: from the intrauterine beginning to the death a person, he or she is part of a network of relations that nurtures and protects his or her life. Seen from this perspective, to become a dignitary means to negotiate this tension between being-in-relation and being a person who is in the world for her or his own sake.

The idea that human dignity protects the individual subject from the reductive power of discourse highlights another aspect of the notion of dignitary, namely that this inherent attribute also functions as a cloak or wrap that protects the uniqueness of each of the six and a half billion dignitaries. In turn, the words "cloak" and "wrap" evoke the idea of investiture: the ceremony by which someone is invested in a high office or in which honors are bestowed upon someone, often by clothing the person in the insignia of an office.[12] The association with "investiture" also calls forth the idea that dignitaries are approached with respect during the encounter; that their dignity is acknowledged and respected. This idea is embodied in the Universal Declaration of Human Rights, since these rights presuppose that all human beings are dignitaries: invested with dignity.

This elaboration of the layers of meaning of the word "dignitary"— moving from the received meaning of the word toward the "new" meaning I introduce here—illuminates its strong connection with the human dignity and human rights discourse. The power of the word lies in its appeal to the imagination. On the discursive level, its evocative and performative power enables the translation of the theoretical discourse of

---

11. "Würde zu haben bedeutet, um seiner oder ihrer selbst, nicht um fremder Zwecke willen in der Welt zu sein, einzigartig, d.h. nicht durch irgendein Äquivalent ersetzbar" (Praetorius 2000, 122, translation mine).

12. This aspect is clear in the Dutch equivalent of dignitary, *(hoog)waardigheidsbekleder/ hoogwaardigheidsbekleedster*, in which one finds the verb "invest" and the noun "vestment."

inherent dignity to the concrete lives of human beings. The word invites hearers and readers to appropriate this notion and to use it to view or to esteem themselves and others as dignitaries and to behave accordingly. On the level of the individual subject, the word may affect the person who hears or reads it in a way that effects a subtle change in self-esteem. By being offered the possibility of recognizing themselves and others as dignitaries, hearers and readers may be empowered to affirm their power to resist psychological and emotional violence directed toward them.

Thus the word "dignitary" and the phrase "six and a half billion dignitaries" can act as vehicles to transfer the central values of human dignity discourse into the ordinary philosophy and ethics of human beings. The images that they evoke offer human subjects an orientation and a direction to live by, enabling them to appropriate and internalize these values into their self-understanding—"I am a dignitary, I embody human dignity"—as well as to incorporate them into the practices of living together.

Dignitary and the *Imago Dei*

The above project needs to be accompanied by a change in religious imagery, especially in our conceptualization of God, because the images we use of God encapsulate the central values our culture lives by. This statement needs some explanation. It refers to an aspect of human dignity discourse that has not been mentioned yet: the relation between that discourse and the *imago Dei* tradition in Christian theology. Genealogically, the concept of human dignity is intimately connected to the theological idea that human beings are made in God's image. This concept underpins the idea that human beings are valuable in and of themselves. When the *imago Dei* tradition is brought to bear upon the concept of dignitary, the notion becomes even richer in meaning, namely by enabling a definition of dignitary as "a person who holds the high rank or office of representing God in her or his unique life," a creature of whom it may be said that she or he is "very good"—something that is not often affirmed in Christian theology. We have become so used to reading Gen 1 and 2 in light of Gen 3 that the representation of human beings as creatures who are affirmed by God as being very good has retreated into the background. To think of or to esteem oneself as a successful creation of the Creator, as a person holding the high rank of representing God, adds to the empowering effect of the word "dignitary." It suggests that respecting or esteeming oneself, which is a form of love of self, constitutes a form of respecting, esteeming, and thus loving, God. This line of thought may be especially important in restoring the self-esteem of victims of domestic violence, since their self-esteem is often negatively affected by this violence. This thinking constitutes a strong intervention in the age-old discourse in which "Everywoman" is seen as Eve— a morally weak temptress; the scapegoat punished for sin's entrance into the world.

However, for the above effect to occur, it is necessary to introduce feminine images of God into theological discourse. This is necessary because neither the repeated effort to tell women—religious women in particular—that they are dignitaries, nor this intervention in discourse (underlining that they hold the high office of representing God), is enough to help women internalize these ideas when there are no feminine images of God. The inferiority of women in discourse is affirmed by this absence of female God-language. The inability to say God-She can be seen as the ultimate symbol of the degradation of women in and by the dominant order of discourse and its concomitant practices (Mulder 2010, 117). The above analysis illustrates the way in which many cultural systems devalue women. This devaluation is reinforced by the rejection of female God-language as sacrilegious by the majority of traditional Christians, deeply invading women's sense of self. From this perspective, the low self-esteem of battered women may be seen as the ultimate consequence of the perverse effects of this devaluation.

Reflecting on the issue of the gender of God-language, the French philosopher Luce Irigaray (1993, 62) points out that "God" represents the site of the ultimate and absolute of a gender and of a people. She explains that women need a God in the feminine to become autonomous, free, and sovereign—to become a human subject. Irigaray therefore calls on women to image, symbolize, and discuss "the values and qualities that would represent the *female* made 'God'" (1993, 72) so that female subjects can in turn embody this "God" (Mulder 2010).

Irigaray's line of thought is relevant for the concept of dignitary—both in its secular and religious meaning—as well as for my effort to intervene in those discourses that undermine women's self-esteem. Irigaray points out that it is vital for the project of becoming a female subject that the site of the absolute and ultimate also become gendered in the feminine genre (genre referring, first of all, to linguistic gender but also to style, generations, and the female sex). Human perfection needs to be represented and imaged in the feminine, because these representations function as beacons that orient and give direction to the female subject on her road to becoming. When human dignity is a central value in our society and a dignitary is a translation of this value in an image that offers a goal for human becoming, it is important to have representations of this notion in the feminine. Otherwise, internalizing the concept of dignitary as a person who holds the high rank of representing the image of God will not bolster women's self-esteem, but will rather subject them again to an ideal of the masculine gender. It is therefore vital to use female images of God to enable women to internalize the idea that they are dignitaries, and to love themselves through loving God, represented in the feminine genre.

The latter is not a new idea. Three generations of feminist theologians have already discussed the necessity of female God-language. Moreover, many have written poetry and songs in which female God-language is used. All biblical female images for God have been retrieved from oblivion and have been used to enrich our theological understanding of God. I am thinking here, for example, of the retrieval and reinterpretation of the Sophia tradition in the Hebrew Bible and the New Testament by scholars such as Claudia Camp (1985), Elisabeth Schüssler Fiorenza (1995), and Sylvia Schroer (1996). I can also mention Helen Schüngel-Straumann's studies regarding the word *rûaḥ* (1992; 1996, 104–21), Phylis Trible's (1978) and Helen Schüngel-Straumann's (1996, 63–71) elaboration of the word Hebrew word *reḥem*, and Juliana Claassens's 2004 book on the female imagery of nursing to describe God's providence. These examples constitute only a small selection of books addressing the issue of biblical female images of God that have been published by feminist scholars in the last thirty years. The study of the texts of produced by women theologians in history (such as Hildegard von Bingen, Hadewijch or Julian of Norwich, to name but a few) have also broadened the repertoire of representations of God, not to mention the many, many books by feminist systematic theologians. All these images are available to enrich the understanding of the word "dignitary." They await transference into mainstream theological and liturgical practice, so that they can in turn become part of the ordinary theology of the faithful.

Flourishing

In my search for images and metaphors that may act as an inspirational counterincentive to the discourse of self-sacrifice, "flourishing" is the second image I want to introduce. This image is already implicitly present in Rebecca Ann Parker's answer to Lucia's question of whether accepting her beatings would bring her closer to Jesus. Parker answers: "God wants you to have your life, not give it up. God wants you to protect your life and your children's lives" (Brock and Parker 2001, 20). This answer liberates Lucia and offers her a religious legitimation for becoming a person who is in the world for her own sake and that of her children, that is, for becoming a dignitary and for flourishing.[13] It is part of the subjugated knowledge of women and of the ordinary theology of many women pastors. It underlies most feminist theological and philosophical reflections on the nature of God. In the following paragraphs I will give a short overview of the way flourishing is elaborated in feminist theological God-talk.

This God-talk is characterized by an emphasis on movement, on becoming. One can already find this in Mary Daly's thesis that God ought to be seen as the verb *Be-ing*, because it is intransitive and the most active and dynamic of all verbs (Daly 1973, 33–34). In her masterful poetic practice, Daly shows how this verb is part of a range of other verbs, such as be-longing, be-friending and be-coming, thereby liberating it (be-ing) from the way it is usually understood as unmoving and unchanging (Daly 1987).

Luce Irigaray emphasizes *becoming* as a divine characteristic. Becoming, infinitely, is the most valuable goal for the will to live, and is therefore necessary for life. It gives us direction to live life, and hence it is a quality worthy of the predicate "divine." For Irigaray, becoming divine means "realizing the fullness of what we are capable of being" (Irigaray 1993, 61, translation adapted). This picture of "God" is echoed in the sentence "God does not oblige us to anything but to become" (1993, 68, translation adapted) that appeals to the imagination in a way similar to the expression "six billion dignitaries." It offers a different perspective on our obligations as human beings, and as women in particular. It suggests that it is not necessarily a virtue to invest all one's energy in the becoming of others to the point of forsaking oneself, but rather that one follows God in and through realizing the fullness of what one is capable of being, thereby implying that becoming is directed at flourishing.

Grace Jantzen (1998) develops Irigaray's thoughts on becoming further. She connects them with Hannah Arendt's concept of natality and the concomitant emphasis on birth and beginning. Jantzen introduces

---

13. Parker describes how Lucia attends courses to learn a marketable skill and then moves out of the house, away from her husband (Brock and Parker 2001, 21).

"flourishing" as a metaphor that offers direction and orientation to the becoming of "natals," precisely because it evokes this idea of realizing the fullness of what they are capable of being. Jantzen shows that there are ample references to the words "to flourish" and "flourishing" in the Hebrew Bible and to "abundance" in the New Testament. These references witness to the fact that the steadfast love of God for Israel and his creation is a love that is directed at their flourishing. Jantzen, furthermore, refers specifically to a number of passages from the prophets to support her argument. One example is Hos 14:5, 7:

> I will be like the dew to Israel;
>   he shall blossom like the lily,
>   he shall strike root like the forests of Lebanon....
> They shall again live beneath my shadow,
>   they shall flourish as a garden;
> they shall blossom like the vine,
>   their fragrance shall be like the wine of Lebanon.

Jantzen also refers to Zech 9:16–17:

> On that day the Lord their God will save them,
>   for they are the flock of his people....
>   For what goodness and beauty are his!
> Grain shall make the young men flourish,
>   and new wine the young women.

Jantzen's quotes also include texts from wisdom literature, such as Prov 11:28: "Those who trust in their riches will wither, but the righteous will flourish like green leaves"; Prov 14:11: "The house of the wicked is destroyed, but the tent of the upright flourishes"; Ps 92:12: "The righteous flourish like a palm tree." In the New Testament, references to abundance and abundant life take up the theme of flourishing, according to Jantzen. She refers to 2 Cor 9:8: "God is able to provide you with every blessing in abundance, so that by always having enough of everything, you may share abundantly in every good work" and also to John 10:10: "I have come that they may have life, and have it abundantly."

The above are only a few examples of biblical passages that speak of flourishing and of life abundant. When one includes those texts that compare human beings to trees, the number of passages that implicitly speak of flourishing increases. The same applies when one takes words such as "blessed" or "blessing" into account. Moreover, analysis of the images of trees rooted firmly in the soil, of shoots, of fruit, of trees that are beautiful to the eye and the nose illuminate that "flourishing" encompasses the well-being of body and mind, that it is embodied well-being. Such images suggest that attention to the body, and enjoying capabilities that come with embodied existence—including sexuality—are part of the connotations of "flourishing," connotations that are intensified by the notions "abundance" and "being blessed."

When taken together, the above passages point toward an affirmation of becoming, of the goodness of creation. Clothed in utopian language, the prophetic texts suggest hope of transformation of an oppressive present and of well-being and flourishing. They express a spirituality that Delores Williams (1993) has also discerned in the God-talk of African-American women. Anchored in the daily experiences of suffering, this spirituality does not view suffering as perfection or as a practice one chooses. It is rather oriented toward survival and toward realizing some quality of life, an aspect of what one is capable of being—for example, by creating some beauty in and by gardening or quilting.

These biblical texts also paint a picture of the kind of transformation that is hoped for: enough to eat, enough to drink, trees that bear fruit, flocks that are safe, security, peace; bread and roses; "a humble and earthly paradise in the *now*."[14] The power of all these texts lies in the fact that they affect us: they touch our imagination, "our embodied, energizing commitment" (Grey 2000, 50); and they inspire hope: a hope that can "organize energies for action" (57). These texts can result in something exactly because they affect the imaginary of the one who reads or listens. "Flourishing" calls forth a whole range of notions that are entwined with the concept of human dignity. Flourishing, as one's point of departure, will eventually encompass all the human needs as described by Maslow: the need to be nurtured and sheltered, to be safe, and to be respected by others. The importance of the fulfillment of these needs cannot be underestimated. They show that respect for human dignity needs to go hand in hand with critical analyses of social, cultural, religious, economic, and ecological relations within local and global communities. Such analyses will reveal what prevents human beings from realizing their capabilities, the fullness

---

14. This phrase is taken from "A Woman's Creed" published in the Beijing preparatory document and quoted in Grey 2009, 197.

of what they are capable of being. This is the implicit rationale behind the fact that the Lutheran World Federation's document *Churches Say No to Violence against Women* situates domestic and sexual violence against women in the larger context of economic, social, and cultural injustices in the relations between men and women.

The concept of flourishing also calls forth associations with and images of vitality, beauty, and the divine: with plants in bloom, with laughing children, with the lined faces of elderly people, with people singing, playing, walking with joy, creativity, vitality, with wisdom and rest—hence with spirituality. These associations are already present in the biblical texts quoted above. In these texts flourishing is presented as a blessing from God. This gift itself harks back to God's affirmation that creation is very good and to the picture of the Garden of Eden and its abundant life. The flourishing of nature and of human beings can thereby act as a vehicle for the experience of the presence of God in the world, affirmed as creation.

Finally, when flourishing is used explicitly in the context of becoming human and realizing the fullness of what we are capable of being, the word evokes the image of a free and sovereign subject (a dignitary), someone representing the image of God, exactly because of the connotations with well-being, vitality, and beauty that I mentioned before. And, although this image creates its own problems—especially in the context of illness, disability, and end-of-life discourse (Grey 2009, 197–211)—it makes flourishing a powerful, critical notion in the context of domestic violence. It highlights that in a relationships that has turned into intimate wars neither victims nor perpetrators realize what they are capable of being, or live up to the idea that they are dignitaries, persons who are unique and in the world for their own sakes.

Conclusion

The starting point of my reflections was the research regarding the low self-esteem of battered women. Some of these women think that they have somehow deserved this violence perpetrated against them, and others think that suffering is a virtue that brings them closer to God. Therefore, they find it difficult to speak out against their batterer or to leave an abusive relationship. The idea that they themselves are of value, invested with dignity, and in the world for their own sakes and not for some extraneous purpose, that they are unique and irreplaceable, is missing from their self-understanding. Nor is it easy for them to internalize this, because the ordinary discourse and theology they live by reinforce their negative self-image through the absence of images of female subjectivity and of images of God in the feminine, as well as through an overemphasis of the sinful nature of humanity.

I have argued that, in order to empower those who suffer domestic violence, a different moral and theological imagination is necessary. This requires a change toward images that touch and move the creative faculties of human subjects, that affect their self-understanding, and that energize them to act accordingly. Such a change of the imagination can begin by taking up and developing current moral traditions, such as the human dignity tradition. It can, moreover, affirm and develop biblical and theological strands of thought that witness to the goodness of creation and that picture God's salvation in terms of flourishing and well-being. These strands of thought can to some extent be experienced as an articulation of what is already present in ordinary theology and discourse or in the survival/quality of life spiritualities of those who suffer (domestic) violence. These spiritualities must be interpreted as testimonies of a subjugated knowledge of human dignity and justice as indelible part of God's promise for human life as well as of a nebulous understanding of a human subject as created in the image of God.

Based upon these presuppositions, I have presented two images or ideas that are both evocative and affirmative of female subjectivity—and male subjectivity for that matter—notably, the image of the dignitary as representation of a human subject and that of flourishing as horizon of human becoming. Both images adds substance to the idea and notions developed in the human dignity discourse and underpin the strands of thought within that discourse that develop the experiential and existential aspects of the concept. These images also contribute to and intervene in the theological reception of the human dignity discourse, showing that the grounding of human dignity in the *imago Dei* tradition requires a reformulation of our God-talk so that the endless possibilities of being human are not reduced to one model. In my elaboration upon the word "flourishing," I underlined the evocative power of this image. Here I want to add that the strength of the notion of flourishing is that there exists no general or universal program for flourishing—the meaning of flourishing is revealed in the particularity of individual lives or the lives of small groups. This is important, since it recognizes that human beings are forever becoming—forever realizing their humanity in this process of becoming.

References

Astley, Jeff. 2002. *Ordinary Theology: Looking, Listening, and Learning in Theology*. Aldershot: Ashgate.
Brock, Rita Nakashima, and Rebecca Ann Parker. 2001. *Proverbs of Ashes: Violence, Redemptive Suffering, and the Search for What Saves Us*. Boston: Beacon.
Camp, Claudia. 1985. *Wisdom and the Feminine in the Book of Proverbs*, Decatur, Ga.: Almond.
Carlson Brown, Joanne, and Carole R. Bohn, eds. 1985. *Christianity, Patriarchy, and Abuse*. New York: Pilgrim.
Claassens, L. Juliana. 2004. *The God Who Provides: Biblical Images of Divine Nourishment*. Nashville: Abingdon.
Cooper-White, Pamela. 1995. *The Cry of Tamar: Violence against Women and the Church's Response*. Minneapolis: Fortress.
Daly, Mary. 1973. *Beyond God the Father: Toward a Philosophy of Women's Liberation*. Boston: Beacon.
———. 1987. Be-Friending. Pages 199–207 in *Weaving the Visions: New Patterns in Feminist Spirituality*. Edited by Judith Plaskow and Carol P. Christ. San Francisco: Harper & Row.
De Jong, Tim. 2011. Huiselijk Geweld [Domestic Violence]. *Magazine E-quality Matters* 13(1):8. Online: http://www.e-quality.nl/assets/e-quality/publicaties/2011/Matters/EQMatters%2312011.pdf.
Grey, Mary. 2000. *Our Outrageous Pursuit of Hope: Prophetic Dreams for the Twenty-First Century*. London: Darton, Longman & Todd.
———. 2009. *Natality* and *Flourishing* in Contexts of Disability and Impairment. Pages 197–211 in *Grace Jantzen: Redeeming the Present*. Edited by E. L. Graham. Aldershot: Ashgate.
Groen, Martine, and Justine Van Lawick. 2010. *Intieme Oorlog: Over de Kwetsbaarheid van Familierelaties*. [Intimate War: On the Fragility of Family Relations]. Amsterdam: Van Gennep.
Irigaray, Luce. 1993. *Sexes and Genealogies*. Translated by G. Gill. New York: Columbia University Press.
Isherwood, Lisa. 2003. Marriage: Heaven or Hell? Twin Souls and Broken Bones. *FemTheo* 11:203–15.
Jantzen, Grace M. 1998. *Becoming Divine: Towards a Feminist Philosophy of Religion*. Manchester: Manchester University Press.

———. 2007. The Courtroom and the Garden. Pages 29–48 in *Violence against Women in Contemporary World Religion: Roots and Cures*. Edited by Daniel C. Maguire and Sa'ddiya Shaikh. Cleveland: Pilgrim.

Lutheran World Federation. 2002. *Churches Say NO to Violence against Women*. Geneva: LWF.

Mulder, Anne-Claire. 2010. A God in the Feminine: My Arguments to Speak about God-She. Pages 111–24 in *Wrestling with God, En lucha con Dios, Ringen mit Gott*. JESWTR 18. Edited by Lisa Isherwood, Jenny Daggers, Elaine Bellchambers, Christine Gasser, and Ursula Rapp. Leuven: Peeters.

Praetorius, Ina. 2000. Die Würde der Kreatur: Ein Kommentar zu einem neuen Grundwert. Pages 97–139 in *Zum Ende des Patriarchats: Theologisch-politische Texte im Übergang*. Edited by Ina Praetorius. Mainz: Grünewald.

———. 2005. *Handeln aus der Fülle: Postpatriarchale Ethik in biblischer Tradition*. Gütersloh: Gütersloger.

———. 2008. *Gott dazwischen: Eine Unfertige Theologie*. Ostfildern: Grünewald.

Schüssler-Fiorenza, Elisabeth. 1995. *Jesus, Miriam's Child, Sophia's Prophet: Critical Issues in Feminist Christology*. London: Continuum.

Schüngel Straumann, Helen. 1992. *Ruach bewegt die Welt: Gottes schöpferische Lebenskraft in der Krisenzeit des Exils*. Stuttgart: Katholisches Bibelwerk GmbH.

———. 1996. *Denn Gott bin Ich und kein Mann: Gottesbilder im erste Testament feministisch betrachtet*, Mainz: Grünewald.

Schroer, Sylvia. 1996. *Die Weisheit hat ihr Haus gebaut*: Studien zur Gestalt der Sophia in der biblischen Geschriften. Mainz: Grünewald.

Slee, Nicola. 2004. *Faith and Feminism: An Introduction to Christian Feminist Theology*. London: Darton, Longman & Todd.

Strobel, Regula. 1991. Feministische Kritik an traditionellen Kreuzestheologien. Pages 52–65 in *Vom Verlangen nach Heilwerden: Christologie in feministisch theologischer Sicht*. Edited by D. Strahm and R. Strobel. Luzern: Edition Exodus.

Thistlethwaite, Susan. 1989. Every Two Minutes: Battered Women and Feminist Interpretation. Pages 302–13 in *Weaving the Visions: New Patterns in Feminist Spirituality*. Edited by Judith Plaskow and Carol P. Christ. San Francisco, Calif.: Harper & Row.

Trible, Phyllis. 1978. *God and the Rhetoric of Sexuality*. Philadelphia: Fortress.

Williams, Delores S. 1993. *Sisters in the Wilderness: The Challenge of Womanist God-Talk*. Maryknoll, N.Y.: Orbis.

A Response to Anne-Claire Mulder's "Empowering Those Who Suffer Domestic Violence: The Necessity of a Different Theological Imagery"

Mary-Anne Plaatjies van Huffel

Dear Anne-Claire,

Thank you for a thought-provoking essay in which you reflect, in view of ghastly statistics of domestic violence, on the dignity of human persons from the perspective of their creation in the image of God. On the basis of the relationship between the human dignity discourse and the *imago Dei* tradition in Christian theology, as well as the link between the notions of flourishing and human dignity, you argue for a different moral and theological imaginary in order to empower the victims of domestic violence.

As you rightly show, Anne-Claire, domestic violence does cut across boundaries of culture, gender, class, education, income, ethnicity, and age. It also occurs within heterosexual as well as homosexual marriages and relationships (Dissel and Ngubeni 2003). However, statistics show that sexual violence is the primary form of domestic violence in South Africa and that men most often are the perpetrators and women the victims such violence.[1] To a degree, this is expected, since violence against women is also usually an expression of historically unequal power relations between

---

1. By 2006 the official annual number of rapes in South Africa exceeded 55,000. However, unofficially, based on the premise put forward by the National Institute of Crime Rehabilitation that only one in twenty rapes is reported, the figure reaches 494,000 a year. This means that on average approximately one in every 1,300 women can be expected to be raped per day in South Africa. A study by Interpol revealed that South Africa has the highest incidence of rape in the world and that a woman is raped in South Africa every 17 seconds. The study did not include child rape victims. Furthermore, between 28 and 30 percent of adolescents reported that their first sexual

the sexes, and it remains one of the crucial social mechanisms by which women are forced into a subordinate position in many societies.

Related to the latter is the fact that many victims of domestic violence become trapped in a cycle of violence. They are often unable to leave abusive relationships due to social and financial factors. Others may be psychologically trapped—for example, members of the gay and lesbian communities that may have internalized society's prejudices against them to the extent that they come to believe that they deserve to be violated (cf. Lawson 2003). Poverty, stigmatization associated with intimate partner violence, and a lack of trust in the police all exacerbate the situation in South Africa (Dunkle 2004). Furthermore, children, besides suffering lasting emotional effects from exposure to abusive relationships between parents, are often themselves the victims in more direct ways. For instance, there has been a marked increase in child and baby rapes in South Africa since 2001, the violent nature of which often requires extensive reconstructive surgical intervention. An appalling fact is that friends, neighbors, and even family members are the most common perpetrators of the physical, emotional, or sexual abuse of children.[2] Furthermore, since the 1980s, the South African media have been reporting on a startling number of family murders in which both young and old members of a family suffered the extreme consequences of domestic violence.[3] In South Africa, as elsewhere, victims are thus in danger in the primary sphere where they should be the recipients of love, security, and shelter (UNICEF 2000). These incidents increased the conviction of the need to address the problem not only through legislation, but also on a social and moral level.

I think it does help to think of domestic violence in terms of human dignity. There can be little doubt that domestic violence constitutes one of the most pervasive forms of human rights violations. However, human rights are also related to human dignity and in the Universal Declaration

---

experience had been a forced encounter. For South African rape statistics, see *Rape Statistics—South Africa and Worldwide 2011*.

2. Examples that sent shockwaves through South African society were the rape in 2001 of a nine-month-old baby girl by six men between the ages of 24 and 66 after she was left unattended by her mother, and the death of a four-year-old girl after being raped by her father (see Gang-Raped Baby Is "Recovering Well," 2001). The belief among some South Africans that sex with a child or baby might be a cure for HIV or AIDS is another unfortunate factor in the high incidence of child rape in the country.

3. An overview of this phenomenon can be found in Marchetti-Mercer, 2003.

of Human Rights (UNDHR), adopted by the United Nations back in 1948, mention is made of the "inherent dignity" and "equal and inalienable rights" of persons. Domestic violence amounts to the denial of the human rights of its victims (and thus to the denial of their dignity) with regard to their "right to life, liberty and security of person" (UDHR 1948, Article 3) and it is clearly in opposition to Article 5 of the UDHR that forbids, among other things, the "cruel, inhuman, or degrading treatment" of people. Over the years, other international human rights instruments, such as the Convention on the Elimination of All Forms of Discrimination Against Women (CEDAW) (1979), the Convention on the Rights of the Child (CRC) (1989), and the United Nations' Declaration on the Elimination of Violence against Women (DEVAW) (1993) were adopted. All of these instruments affirm the fundamental rights and dignity specifically of women and children. The World Conference on Human Rights (Vienna 1993) explicitly stated that the rights of women and girls are "an inalienable, integral and indivisible part of universal human rights." It is also noteworthy that in DEVAW quite a broad definition of gender-based violence is used, namely:

> Any act ... that results in, or is likely to result in physical, sexual or psychological harm or suffering to women, including threats of such acts, coercion or arbitrary deprivation of liberty, whether occurring in public or private life. Different categories of this crime include: abuse, sexual assault and rape. Abuse can take various forms including economic, emotional, physical or sexual (quoted in Hirschowitz et al. 2000, 1).

Many countries, including South Africa, are cosignatories of these international instruments, but have in many instances also promulgated their own laws and formulated policies that aim at protecting not only the equality, but also the dignity of their citizens, and to which they should be held accountable. In South Africa, these include not only the Constitution for the Republic of South Africa with its Bill of Rights (section 10 of which expressly recognizes the dignity of all people), but also a wide array of other legislation, including the Employment Equity Act, Human Rights Commission Act (1994), Commission on Gender Equality Act (1996), Basic Conditions of Employment Act (1997) and the Employment Equity Act (1998). As is foundational to all of these pieces of legislation, the South African National Policy Framework for Women's Empowerment and Gender Equality also emphasize the importance of human dignity. It is also part of why the South African National Crime Prevention

Strategy (NCPS) (1996) declared the prevention of crimes against women and children a national priority (a status that such crimes continued to enjoy in subsequent national policing strategy documents). This prioritization of these crimes resulted in the setting of mandatory minimum sentences for certain kinds of rape (the Criminal Law Amendment of 1997), the tightening of bail conditions in rape cases (the Criminal Procedure Second Amendment Act of 1997); the National Policy Guidelines for the Handling of Victims of Sexual Offences (1998) and later the Policy Framework and Strategy for Shelters for Victims of Domestic Violence in South Africa (2003). However, most importantly, it resulted in the first ever national legislation in South Africa expressly to address domestic violence, namely the Prevention of Family Violence Act of 1993—the limitations of which were later addressed by the Domestic Violence Act of 1998[4] (Vetten 2005).

The above examples show that the protection of the vulnerable against domestic violence is not only a legal, but also a health, economic, educational, and developmental issue. It is also a human dignity issue and, for Christians and the Christian church, it should also be an issue of faith.

In addition, the discourse on domestic violence is characteristically sexist and biological-essentialist in nature. It is full of patriarchal metaphors and images that are set in fundamental binary opposition to each other: male/female, strong/weak, superior/inferior and reason/emotion. It associates power and domination with everything male, and emotions and service with everything female. This leaves victims of domestic violence feeling inferior and powerless vis-à-vis perpetrators. These biological-essentialist conceptual categories and the patriarchal anthropology behind it need to be deconstructed. We need alternative constructions of masculinity, gender, and identity that can foster non-violence and gender justice. A more congruent holistic understanding of humankind is thus needed. Can the Bible help us in this process?

It has often been noted that the Bible represents God predominately in male images (father, king, judge, etc.), that women are referred to in the Bible much less than men, and when this does happen, women

---

4. The limitations addressed include the vague definition of family violence in the 1993 legislation to broaden the concept to include marital rape, violence perpetrated in nonmarital relationships, and abuse by parents, grandparents, guardians, and anyone residing with the victim.

are often presented in relation to men (Hannah, Esther, Mary, etc.).[5] However, the Bible also uses a few female images to refer to God—for example, as woman (Isa 42:13-14), mother (Isa 49:13-15, Ps 131:1-2), a mother hen (Luke 13:34)—and I totally agree with you, Anne-Claire, that these biblical female images for God await transference into mainstream theological and liturgical practice, so that they can in turn become part of the "ordinary theology of the faithful" (209) You also emphasize the importance of using female images of God to enable women to internalize the fact that they are "dignitaries"—persons possessing human dignity—and to love themselves through loving God, the latter represented in the feminine. In your essay, the word "dignitary" refers to all human subjects, and you try to show that this concept is a secular translation of the theological idea that human beings are created in, and thus bearers of, the image of God. Central to the Christian vision on human life is also the notion that, being created in the image of God (Gen 1:26-27, Gen 5:1, Gen 9:6, Jas 3:9), every human being possesses dignity. I believe that, despite the predominance of men and male metaphors for God in the Bible, this vision should indeed also be a central aspect of our discourse on domestic violence as Christians.

The opening chapter of Genesis relates that humans were created "in God's image" and that upon looking at his creation God saw that it was "very good." Human beings thus have transcendent worth and value that comes from God; this dignity is not based on any human quality, legal mandate, or individual merit or accomplishment. It is an essential part of and a quality intrinsic to being human. Human dignity is inalienable; it can never be separated from other essential aspects of being human. Being created in the image of God can form the basis of a much-needed holistic understanding of humanity, of an inclusive theological anthropology, of a view of the common humanity of all, regardless of gender or race or class. According to Graff (1995, 195), affirming that every human person is created in the image and likeness of God is not enough. We need an understanding of the *imago Dei* that, while respecting gender diversity, clearly does not exalt the latter to a divine value, but also one that recognizes

---

5. Denise Ackermann (1992, 69) reminds us that language has the capacity to constitute social and cultural realities and, according to Elizabeth Johnson (1992, 49, 55), such gender exclusive language about God "supports an imaginative and structural world that excludes or subordinates women," undermining women's self-worth and dignity.

and has clear implications for the idea of human relationality. The phrase "being created in the image of God" is therefore intended to give rise not only to right thinking, but to right relationships, and should thus help in replacing abusive relationships with partnership relationships.

Anne-Claire, you also connect the concept of human "dignitaries" with the "growing discourse on 'flourishing' developed in human dignity discourse as well as in feminist theology" (page 137). By "flourishing" you mean living with dignity, the well-being of mind and body.

According to Douglas Rasmussen (1999, 194), human flourishing is a relatively recent term in ethics, as a more accurate translation of the Greek and Aristotelian *eudaimonia*, commonly translated as *happiness* or *welfare*. Aristotle used *eudaimonia* as a term for the highest human good, living a moral and flourishing life. In Rasmussen's neo-Aristotelian conception, human flourishing is not static, but is a way of living that consists in certain activities (*omne ens perficitur in actu:* flourishing is to be found in action), and it comprises basic or "generic" goods and virtues (such as knowledge, health, friendship, creative achievement, beauty, and pleasure; and such virtues as integrity, temperance, courage, and justice; 1994, 4). According to Rasmussen, human flourishing must be attained through a person's own efforts. As such, it cannot be the result of factors that are beyond one's control. Flourishing does not consist in the mere possession and use of goods, but rather in "a person's taking charge of his [sic] own life so as to develop and maintain those virtues for which he alone is responsible and which in most cases will allow him to attain the goods his life requires" (1994, 4). Therefore, one may also say that in order to create a world in which the human dignity of all is protected, people must learn to act, to conduct themselves as moral agents. Not only the universal and inviolable rights and duties, but also the inherent dignity of each human person created by God should be affirmed and respected, so that all will be able to flourish as God intended. Finally, this also entails the ordering of social institutions toward human fulfillment or flourishing, as well as the protection and affirmation of rights and duties that are the concern of the entire human family.

To summarize: domestic violence violates human dignity and inhibits human flourishing. As such, it also prevents both victims and perpetrators from becoming fully human. When perpetrators dehumanize others, they themselves also become dehumanized in the process. Domestic violence flies in the face of the Christian conviction that human dignity is an inalienable, inherent, and universal consequence of being created in the image of God. The prevention of domestic violence should therefore not only be a primary concern to us, but also our vocation. With this, Anne-Claire, I am sure you agree. Thank you for reminding us of this.

Your co-worker in Christ,
Mary-Anne

REFERENCES

Ackermann, Denise. 1992. Women, Human Rights and Religion: A Dissonant Triad. *JSR* 5:65–82.
Dissel, Amanda, and Kindisa Ngubeni. 2003. Giving Women Their Voice: Domestic Violence and Restorative Justice in South Africa. Paper submitted for the Eleventh International Symposium on Victimology, 13–18 July 2003, Stellenbosch, South Africa. Online: http://www.csvr.org.za/docs/crime/givingwomenvoice.pdf.
Dunkle, Kristin L. 2004. Prevalence and Patterns of Gender-Based Violence and Revictimization among Women Attending Antenatal Clinics in Soweto, South Africa. *AJE* 160:230–39.
Gang-Raped Baby Is "Recovering Well." 2001. *IOL News*, 6 November 2001. Online: http://www.iol.co.za/news/south-africa/gang-raped-baby-is-recovering-well-1.76442.
Hirsowitsch, Ros, Seble Worku, and Mark Orkin. 2000. *Quantitative Research Findings on Rape in South Africa*. Pretoria: Statistics South Africa. Online: http://www.statssa.gov.za/publications/Rape/Rape.pdf.
Johnson, Elizabeth A. 1992. *She Who Is: The Mystery of God in Feminist Theological Discourse*. New York: Crossroad.
Lawson, David M. 2003. Domestic Violence between Same-Sex Partners: Implications for Counseling. *JCD* 81:19–32.
Marchetti-Mercer, Maria C. 2003. Family Murders in Post-Apartheid South Africa: Reflections for Mental Health Professionals. *HSAG* 8:83–91.
Rape Statistics—South Africa and Worldwide 2011. Online: http://www.rape.co.za/index.php?option=com_content&view=article&id=875:rape-statistics-south-africa-a-worldwide-2010&catid=65:resources&Itemid=137.
UNICEF. 2000. Domestic Violence against Women and Girls. Florence: UNICEF Innocenti Research Centre. Online: http://www.unicef-irc.org/publications/pdf/digest6e.pdf.

Universal Declaration of Human Rights (*UDHR*). 1948. Online: http://www.un.org/en/documents/udhr/.

Family and its Discontents: On the Essays of Petruschka Schaafsma and Anne-Claire Mulder

Cheryl B. Anderson

Even at first reading, the articles by Schaafsma and Mulder work well together. Schaafsma's article acknowledges that the human dignity of individual family members may be compromised in the family itself—a problem that Dan Browning's work seeks to address. In turn, Mulder's article develops theological constructs to counter the low self-esteem of battered women. By discussing domestic abuse, Mulder effectively offers one example of how the human dignity of an individual family member can be undermined, just as Schaafsma notes.

Schaafsma evaluates Don Browing's proposals concerning "the equal-regard family" as a way to uphold the dignity of it members. In general, one finds in an equal regard family a relationship between a husband and wife that involves mutual respect and justice considerations, and children who have access to both parents and who learn about justice and mutuality by observing their parents (Miller-McLemore 2004, 52). As Schaafsma rightly observes, Browning's proposals for dignity and mutual respect in the family are similar to secular arguments, and the theological grounding he presents is not as persuasive as it might be. I think that the problem Schaafsma identifies is due to "the middle course" that Browning attempts. His work reflects an attempt to be situated between traditional patriarchal and hierarchical notions of family and the greater variety of groupings that are found today—such as single mothers, same-sex parents, and blended families. Browning's equal regard family may attempt to move away from some of the harshness of traditional patriarchal concepts of family, but he affirms the need for an "intact family," which clearly means a heterosexual couple with their biologically related children.

It seems to me that Browning's supposed "middle course" is not tenable. It is not possible to hold the traditional heterosexual family as normative, yet to think that its abuses will be eliminated simply by suggesting that human dignity be respected within such a family. From my perspective, the crux of the problem can be found in the traditional meaning of "family" or "family values," as expressed in contemporary conservative theological and political circles. In my context, the United States, references to "family values" are usually "coded messages about women and how they should behave in relation to men," and the assumed relationship between men and women is that men should be dominant and women subordinate (Ruether 2000, 3). As the concept of a Christian family developed over time, the appropriate family structure became that of a working husband and a stay-at-home wife. For conservative Christians today, such a familial arrangement is "the revealed norm of the Bible" and "the order of creation," as established by God (Reuther 2000, 11).

However, the need to uphold a traditional hierarchical pattern that privileges men over women does not end there. Basically, that gender paradigm is part of an intricate system of ideologies that serves to justify why one group is privileged and other groups are not:

> There is one superior race: white Western Europeans. There is one exclusively true religion—Christianity—and one right kind of Christian: a born-again evangelical Protestant. There is one right family model: a heterosexual, monogamous marriage with a male breadwinner and a female housewife. There is one right economic system, free-market capitalism, and one chosen nation, the United States of America (Ruether 2000, 206).

Based on these interlocking assumptions and the hierarchical order that they presume, any threats to the heteronormative family, such as same-sex relationships or single mothers, are thought to be inherently "disordered," and therefore to threaten the "foundation of the social order" (Ruether 2000, 173).

Apparently, Browning and his colleagues eliminated same-sex relationships from their discussions of the family for the sake of dialogue across political and theological lines. But by doing that, they left traditional heterosexual norms in place and the interlocking assumptions listed above were left unexamined. Recognizing that such an omission occurred helps one to understand why the theological grounding in Browning's work is not persuasive, as Schaafsma contends. If he had developed more fully the liberative aspects of the biblical and theological tradition, these perspectives might have worked against his upholding the traditional family standard required to maintain support from conservatives.

Furthermore, Browning's proposal is not tenable because the concept of the equal-regard family assumes an employment environment that does not currently exist. In an equal-regard family, each parent can work part-time. But in our free-market capitalism this would mean that neither parent would accrue sick leave, or have retirement or health care benefits—which would be an impossible situation. As Gloria Albrecht (2002, 148–49) argues, there must be a public commitment to women's equality so that workplace and public policies support both men and women who choose to care for dependents. However, such support is difficult to obtain when the traditional theological perspective recognizes only the validity of free-market capitalism and that system rewards those with no responsibilities for dependents.

In addition to addressing the difficulties of creating families where human dignity is respected and individuals within the family flourish, there is another connection between the articles by Schaafsma and Mulder. In Schaafsma's article, the problem that prompted Browning's work is the absence of men as fathers. This absence has resulted in the breakdown of the traditional family structure. The problem that prompted Mulder's analysis is that of intimate partner violence. As we are reminded in her article, domestic violence is a gendered phenomenon, since men are the ones who overwhelmingly commit violent acts against women. Reading these two articles together raises an interesting question: Is the key problem to be addressed that of men's absence from families, or is it that, when present, men have a tendency toward violent behavior? Browning's work does not address the issue of domestic violence; its underlying goal is to bring men back into the home. However, as Bonnie McLemore-Miller writes: "For women and children who have suffered domestic violence or physical or sexual abuse within Christian contexts upholding male authority, soft patriarchy is simply too high a price to pay for maintaining 'stable' family life" (2004, 61).

One should not be surprised that traditional patriarchal authority is associated with violence. In earlier times, for example, it was thought that a wife had a duty to submit sexually to her husband. Thus, any force he needed to use to make her submit in this way was acceptable. In other words, rape within a marriage was not an actionable crime. Even today, some pastors in conservative evangelical circles contend that a husband's beating his wife is not grounds for divorce (unless it occurs "regularly"; see Joyce 2009). Furthermore, traditional gender paradigms encourage male dominance, authoritarian notions of power, and a sharp distinction between the private family and the public arena (perceived to be "the outside world"). Yet those same factors are associated with wife and child beating and the sexual abuse of children (Coontz 1992, 279–80). Obviously, there is some relationship between traditional hierarchical notions of gender and male violence.

To counter the debilitating and demeaning effects of domestic violence on women, Mulder identifies feminine images of God in scripture and proposes their broader use. As an African American woman, I am reminded of the powerful words at the end of Ntozake Shange's groundbreaking choreopoem, "For Colored Girls Who Have Considered Suicide: 'i found god in myself/and i loved her/i loved her fiercely'" (Shange 1977, 63).

Both Schaafsma and Mulder offer scriptural passages and theological constructs that can be used to create and maintain Christian families where all persons can flourish and where human dignity is truly respected. Nevertheless, we cannot begin to understand why it is so difficult for such positive scriptural and theological constructs to take root unless we first examine the interrelated oppressive ideologies that result from current constructions of "family values."

References

Albrecht, Gloria H. 2002. *Hitting Home: Feminist Ethics, Women's Work, and the Betrayal of "Family Values."* New York: Continuum.

Coontz, Stephanie. 1992. *The Way We Never Were: American Families and the Nostalgia Trap.* New York: Basic.

Joyce, Kathryn. 2009. Biblical Battered Wife Syndrome: Christian Women and Domestic Violence. *Religion Dispatches Magazine* (January 22, 2009). Online: http://www. religiondispatches.org/archive/1007/some_pastors_believe_abuse_is_biblical_grounds_for_divorce/.

Miller-McLemore, Bonnie. 2004. A Feminist Christian Theologian Looks (Askance) at Headship. Pages 49–62 in *Does Christianity Teach Male Headship: The Equal-Regard Marriage and Its Critics.* Edited by David Blankenhorn, Don Browning, and Mary Stewart Van Leeuwen. Grand Rapids: Eerdmans.

Ruether, Rosemary Radford. 2000. *Christianity and the Making of the Modern Family*. Boston: Beacon.

Shange, Ntozake. 1977. *For Colored Girls Who Have Considered Suicide/ When the Rainbow Is Enuf*. New York: Collier.

Missing Links in Mainline Churches: Biblical Life Stories and Their Claims in Today's Family Preaching

Ciska Stark

Mapping Churches' Cultural Identity

When Walter Brueggemann describes the situation Christian preaching finds itself in in American culture, he uses the metaphor of *exile* to express the "loss of a structured, reliable, 'world' where treasured symbols of meaning are mocked and dismissed" (Brueggemann 1997, 2). The loss of white, male, Western, and colonial hegemony that affects churches as well as cultures constitutes a limit experience for many Christians. This requires corresponding verbal expressions—for example, in sermons—that can adequately address this situation. Within this context, Brueggemann argues,

> such a consideration is appropriate for preachers precisely because preachers in such a limit experience have an obligation and possibility of being the very ones who can give utterance both to "represent the catastrophe" and to "reconstruct, replace, or redraw" the paradigms of meaning that will permit "creative survival" (1997, 16).

Since worship is seen as a formative practice of faith, it is of primary importance to know whether and how orientations toward meaning and values in worship and preaching correspond to values of human dignity.

In exploring this line of thought, I will focus on preaching in the Protestant Church in the Netherlands (PCN).[1] This essay forms part of

---

1. The establishment of the PCN, the largest Protestant church in the Netherlands, resulted from the unification of the Evangelical Lutheran Church in the King-

a recently set-up research project into preaching practices and styles in churches belonging to this denomination. The goal of the project as a whole is to map current trends in preaching throughout the entire scope of churches. It is done by empirical research into liturgical and preaching materials in order to arrive at an analysis of the content, form, and importance of preaching and the challenges it faces in contemporary culture. This research project is motivated by the rapid changes in the position of the Protestant church in Dutch society today and the changes in communication patterns, both in church and in society. In this article a preliminary analysis of the material gleaned from 15 church services (out of a total of 60) is presented. The focus here is on the following two questions:

- How are fundamental value orientations of human society expressed in the linguistic discourse of the hymns, prayers, and sermons in contemporary church services?
- How are these orientations related to Scripture and dominant culture?

To answer these questions, I will give an outline of the context of the PCN from a broader social perspective. Then I will briefly indicate the growing interest in the experiential and "event" character of church services, and ask what consequences this has for how the Bible is discussed. After an investigation into actual service material with respect to the value orientations in it, I will show how this relates to hermeneutical patterns. Finally, I will evaluate what this reveals in light of the research questions.

SERMONS AND CHURCHGOERS: THE CURRENT SITUATION

According to statistical research, 19 percent of the Dutch population attends a church service or religious celebration at least once a month.[2] For the PCN this means that more than a third of its members attend services

---

dom of the Netherlands, the Reformed Church of the Netherlands, and the Reformed Churches in the Netherlands. In 2009 it had 1.8 million members.

2. Figures for 2008 in *Religie aan het begin van de 21e eeuw* [Religion at the Beginning of the 21st Century], Centraal Bureau voor de Statistiek (CBS) 2009, 42. In the more conservative wing of the church, church attendance is as high as 41 percent; in more liberal wings, church attendance is about 15 percent. These figures seem to be quite reliable. By way of comparison, North American surveys report church atten-

at least once a week and that 63 percent say that they attend church regularly. Who are these people?

Social research shows that members of the PCN do not fit the profile of the average Dutch citizen and believer. Members of the PCN are generally more involved in society than the average Dutch person. This social involvement takes the form of volunteer work, participation in societal life, and providing assistance to others (CBS 2009, 137). In communities where a large number of PCN members and regular churchgoers live, this has a positive effect on social cohesion (CBS 2009, 138). The social engagement of PCN members is also evident in their interest in developments in culture and society. They often subscribe to newspapers and visit museums, and are interested in politics. They show a high appreciation of contact with family—92 percent speak to family members who do not reside with them on a weekly basis (CBS 2009, 138). They also show great commitment to and trust in one another and in a democratic society (CBS 2009, 139). However, it is not clear whether PCN members have contact outside their own group (bridging), or whether they only have contact within their own group (bonding) (CBS 2009, 140).

The above-average involvement of these PCN members in society corresponds to an equally great concern about moral values. They worry about the deterioration of society and the discarding of social conventions, and they view education, the environment, and the disintegration of the population as challenges (CBS 2009, 85). These PNC members also respond with reservation to proposals for the far-reaching liberalization of legislation concerning euthanasia, and they do not find it necessary for shops to be open on Sunday. PCN members are, however, tolerant toward asylum seekers and are predominantly positive with respect to gay marriages. In addition, they think that more money may be devoted to development cooperation with poor countries. If non-religious Dutch people place problems of healthcare high on their agenda, PCN members do not (CBS 2009, 87), since they usually lead sober lifestyles—they smoke and drink less, and engage in more physical activity than the average Dutch person (CBS 2009, 141). They are also predominantly happy people—92 percent claim to feel either happy or very happy (CBS 2009, 141).

---

dance of 40 percent, but it is claimed that surveys in the U.S. tend to overreport this number (Robinson 2011).

With respect to the Bible, 23 percent of the Dutch population indicates that for them scripture constitutes a guide on how to act. The church service is the place where people come into contact with the Bible most, and 76 percent of respondents who attend church weekly also read the Bible. What primarily attracts the latter are the "human experiences" and "fascinating stories" in it (Stoffels 2004).

All in all, a picture emerges here of churchgoers who are responsible, socially involved, and loyal citizens who are extremely committed to one another and to maintaining social cohesion. However, the membership of this group is shrinking quite rapidly. The PCN is losing almost 2.5 percent of its members annually, and church attendance has been dropping for years. There is a clear relation between age and church attendance in the PCN: people above 65 are now the most faithful attendees, and this means that many congregations are aging.

The leadership in the PCN is aware of this problem, and is initiating missionary programs aimed at teaching people to view churches more from "outside in" (cf. PCN 2011). Churches should have a sense of what they have to offer members of society who are seeking meaning. What seems to be of great importance here is that churches realize what fundamental value orientations they present, and what value orientations are therefore communicated in their sermons.

BRICOLAGE, EXPERIENCE AND THE BIBLE

Throughout the last fifty years, polarization in society into clearly distinguished Protestant, Catholic, liberal and other groups has been disappearing. The same thing is happening with the denominational pillars of the traditional churches. Worship has become more dynamic and services have changed in character. If until a few decades ago each denomination had its own more or less fixed liturgy with its accompanying consequences for the use of Bible translations and hymnals and for prayer and preaching traditions, we now find a form of "blended worship" or "bricolage liturgy" being practiced, including within the PCN. In this one finds that different styles and forms of worship alternate within the same congregation or even within the same service (Barnard 2006). Alongside congregations that continue to be guided by the influence of the liturgical movement of the twentieth century, there are also congregations in which "praise and worship" forms an important supplement to a traditional Reformed or Lutheran liturgy. Church music is changing: there are fewer organists, and the praise and worship band is slowly becoming a common sight in traditional orthodox congregations. There is no one dominant liturgical discourse, but a variety of alternating practices that have largely not been reflected upon. Continuity as well as discontinuity is present between actual worship practices and fixed confessional claims (Barnard 2003, 51).

Liturgical and homiletic literature indicates an increase in the perception of the worship service as an event. People attend church as part of their free time in which they simply want to have an experience. As a consequence, the church service is viewed as a high "event" directed at the individual and communal religious experience of the moment. In liturgical studies, this trend is seen as a sign of the liminal character of church ritual, in which fixed forms are exchanged for provisional, temporary, and flexible ones: "In the network society liminality is the norm: flow, instability, transgressions, transformation and metaphors are in the center of society, whereas the stable and structured human interrelatedness has moved to the margin" (Barnard et al. 2012). Worship is no longer tied to fixed identities of denominations, congregations, and individuals.

In homiletics, the emphasis on experience was initially greeted with enthusiasm: there was finally more to the sermon than a catechetically-flavored exegesis, and ministers began once more to pay attention to the old values of rhetoric that were directed not only toward the mind but also toward feelings.

The rise of narrative theology also resulted in a renewed interest in the possibilities of narrativity in preaching. Looking at the audience from a postmodern perspective resulted in an emphasis on the evocative character of preaching. The preacher is now more a facilitator than a proclaimer, teacher, or witness. He or she will be oriented to offering the congregation enough room to be challenged to give their own personal interpretations. The presupposition is, of course, that there is no single unambiguous interpretation of the Bible and even less of a uniform message for the diverse group of churchgoers.

In the meantime, postmodernism and its accompanying relativism seem to have reached its peak, and the call for proclamatory preaching with a clear Christian witness can be heard once more in the Netherlands (Stark 2011; Dekker 2011; Immink 2011). However, this too seems problematic, for what should the content of this witness be? Again the question arises: What value orientation will be communicated, and what is to be the guiding principle in the interpretation of the Bible?

Value Orientations Found in the "Best Practices" of Contemporary Church Services

The research material as a whole—and on which this essay is based—has been supplied by sixty ministers who have each been in ministry for about ten to fifteen years. These ministers also took part in a survey via the internet. For this project we analyzed material from fifteen randomly-chosen church services. The services were not constructed or conducted with a view to the research; rather, the material was sent in afterwards by the ministers as examples of "best practices." Furthermore, these recent services were taken from the entire scope of the PCN, and were conducted by both male and female ministers during the first half of 2011. To analyze the material we used a simplified form of grounded theory.[3] This method corresponds to the idea that new homiletical and hermeneutical models arise in correlation with the practice of preaching itself and, somehow, independently of denominational and theological structures. We used grounded theory together with a preliminary categorization of themes as introduced on the basis of the theoretical framework that was sketched. Each textual and/or conceptual unit was then labeled according to content, and this content was then analyzed more closely in light of specific questions concerning value orientations.

Involvement was a basic category used in this project because involvement was a clear value orientation reflected in the profile of the PCN churchgoers sketched above. The initial themes that were viewed as important were involvement in family (both extended and nuclear) life, the faith community, the coexistence of different groups, politics, education, environment, and health and healthcare. These results will be scrutinized next.

Family Life (Extended and Nuclear)

The theme of family life is prominent in a significant majority of the services analyzed. Without exception, the issue at stake is the importance of family relations—even if people have negative feelings about it. Both positive and negative experiences are discussed. Childhood is referred to in a positive way, revealing paradise-like features in the memories of many

---

3. Using ATLAS.ti 6 (a computer program used in qualitative research or qualitative data analysis); cf. Boeije 2010.

(14).[4] Family life is valued as an opportunity to make life pleasant, for example, "by going on holiday with the family" (4). The hymns used also refer to positive aspects of family life—for example, Ps 133 (11, 15)—and the family features as the place where people give shape to God's call: "in your daily life, your family, your work. Dedicate yourself to this" (15).

Family values also come up when God is thanked explicitly for the birth of a child in whose life the family, relatives, and the congregation are expressly involved, as in the following prayer: "Bless her with a life full of light, in the midst of her family, her father, her mother, and her sister, in the midst of their relatives, in the midst of the congregation" (8). Elsewhere, gratitude is expressed for "children, grandchildren, and great-grandchildren" (3).

The reason for gratitude is not so much for having a family as for belonging to a family circle: "that there are people who let us know we're welcome." In one sermon, this was said:

> I always see it as especially poignantly expressed in the notices that are published in this area whenever a child is born. They say, "Welcome to the family," "Welcome to the gang," "Welcome to the neighborhood." Before you know it, you're included in the group, in a community. And the notices say it all: you're not alone; you belong to our family, our neighborhood, our gang. That's very, very biblical, you could say. To know you're not alone, that you belong to a group, a people, a community (3).

Paying attention to parents within the family is mentioned specifically only once—as figures one identifies with and as those who have gone before one in faith: "Maybe you have come to know people who went before you on the way of faith: a grandmother who prayed for you...." (1)

That family life can have negative sides is also mentioned. There is recognition of "fractures" in the family that suddenly "make you silent" (1). One sermon explicitly refers to victims of incest: "Things can happen to you in your life that cause so much grief and anger, that you can NEVER forgive: abuse, threats, incest, rape, victims of terrorism" (5).

One specific theme that is often found concerns the difficulty of sharing one's faith within the family circle: "That can be hard for us, hard to say something about God, even to your children or grandchildren" (13). Or, elsewhere: "You can be anxious for opportunities to talk about Jesus

---

4. The materials of the church services are numbered 1–15.

in your family or circle of friends. You can understand rejection, social discomfort, and embarrassment" (11). People can feel they are "strangers, odd men out" as a result of this difficulty within their own families "because [they] are called by God" (3).

In one service (15) "family" is the theme of the service as such: "Family of God." In the reading of the law in this service there is the assurance that "we" are children of God, and there is the call to "give our lives for our brothers and sisters" (1 John 3:1, 16–18, 23–25). That sets the tone. The scripture reading is the description of Jesus' mother and brothers searching for him, his dismissal of them, and the rejection that Jesus himself encounters from his fellow villagers in Nazareth (Mark 3:31–35; 6:1–6). The sermon starts with the observation that family relationships are not always "the way you want them." Then the sermon points out that, just as with Jesus, the "water ties" of baptism must be more important than "blood ties":

> It is God's will that we respect our family ties and invest in our relationships with parents, children, brothers, and sisters. But situations can occur in which one has to make a choice. And the question is: What is the decisive factor for you? Blood ties or water ties—the ties of baptism? This sounds quite serious.

Examples of such conflicts are, however, primarily described as practical problems—such as the dilemma of deciding how to spend one's time, and giving priority to the church or to other activities. More serious examples are given later: "For those who want to convert to Christ from Islam in a Muslim country, life can be incredibly hard. In many cases, the family connection is broken, and the family no longer wants anything to do with the convert." This implicitly suggests that the real problems are elsewhere, in Muslim-Christian families.

The Faith Community

In addition to family values, church services remind churchgoers that they belong to a faith community. Loyalty is expected: "Where does your first loyalty lie? With your family, friends, a club to which you belong? Or with Jesus and his spiritual family?" (15). The connection with the faith community not only involves the congregation or worldwide Christianity, but also those who have "preceded us" in faith, such as the witnesses in Heb

11 (1). Solidarity with other living believers is present primarily in prayers. Concern for less privileged people is particularly pronounced: "We pray for the people who have to live in areas where they do not have freedom of speech or where they may not talk openly about their faith" (5). There is also gratitude for belonging to the community: "Let us be able to participate with joy in your [God's] congregation and work on behalf of that community" (11). That the life of a congregation may also result in disappointment is raised only in one service, namely when the congregation "no longer likes" the minister: "what an affliction that can be" and "the church of Christ—that's a wreck now as well and a ramshackle affair" (13). All in all, the interest seems mostly limited to the local community; the global faith community is not brought up very often; ecumenism does not appear to be important.

Co-Existence

The co-existence of various groups in society is an important theme in Dutch politics. The integration of diverse peoples has become a problem, and relations between Muslims and Christians, and between believers and secular citizens, are tense. Nevertheless, one hardly encounters this theme in the services, and when one does, it is only in a general sense. The hymns used then are on responsibility for one another: "offer your neighbor a helping hand" (Hymn 62, Huub Oosterhuis, *Liedboek voor de Kerken* [7]), or on how the purpose of the human being is "to live on [God's] earth where it is good, to live with one another out of his covenant" (Hymn 86, Ad den Besten, *Liedboek voor de Kerken* [8]). One minister cites "the mechanism of repaying evil with evil" (5), and another prays for society where "harsh and merciless judgments are often made about others" (8). In the same service, the concern "for the sake of a world where peoples threaten one another, races hate one another, people outshout one another" is voiced in a *kyrie* prayer (8). In general, the prayer is made that we "bravely and openmindedly travel the road to the neighbor, forgiving, and generously, as Jesus showed us" (11). In another services, even though Rom 12:12-21—which contains concrete references to virtues like compassion, modesty, forgiveness, hospitality, and so on—is read, the minister does not further refer in the sermon or the prayers to the virtues mentioned in the text (12). It seems that social life as such is not raised as a topic anywhere.

Politics

Almost nothing is said about politics in any of the services analyzed—at least not on topics in current political debates. Only in prayers, concerning the famine in Sudan, for example, is it said that this is also a political issue (3, 11). Prayer in connection with the current economic crisis also focuses only on its victims and says nothing about responsibilities. Only in one service does the minister refer in both prayers and sermon to the unequal distribution of money and goods in the world, to the issue of human rights, the threat of fundamentalism, and the difficulty that believers face when the choices they make also have political significance. Subsequently, the prayer in this service is for "all who bear political and administrative responsibility" (10).

Education

Education is not a topic as such in the services. In one service thanksgiving is offered for the opportunity to receive an education (5) and one prayer is said for young people who had to write examinations. Otherwise, when the topic of education does arise, it has to do with learning faith, learning to trust in God (3).

Environment

The environment and environmental sustainability, both socially important themes, do not play a prominent role in the services analyzed. In one sermon the planet is referred to as a garden, but the elaboration of this had to do exclusively with issues of livability in the context of coexistence (4). In one other service the *kyrie* prayer is devoted to "what was to be done now about this world, in which irreplaceable nature and animals are threatened" (10). For the rest, the theme is not addressed in sermons or in prayers.

Health

Healthcare is another theme that does not feature in the services, apart from one instance of thanksgiving for the fact "that we have good health care facilities here" (5). When illness is referred to it happens only in examples and prayers, but challenges regarding matters of health and healthcare and problems resulting from healthcare policies are never raised in sermons.

Additional Values

In addition to the values derived from the social reports, two other important orientations emerge: (1) an emphasis on the negative aspects of the *spirit of the times*; and (2) the importance of *religious identity*. Although these themes converge somewhat with the above, they are explicitly cited and will therefore be dealt in a similar manner here.

The Spirit of the Times

In the material analyzed, preachers call life "busy": "You've been busy" (15); we are "swallowed up by the busyness of everyday" (5). The world is full of temptations that demand one's attention: "you can think of things like hobbies, sports, career, TV, or the internet, money." "Pleasure, striving for maximal pleasure" is in the air (2). Another minister prays that people may to be able to resist all kinds of "temptations that transgress the limits of law, decency, and your commandments" (14).

The world is said to be "chaotic" (8), "it's not getting any better in this world" (9), and it is going "from bad to worse."[5] "Where does this world go from here?"(10). People are well off in the Netherlands, but not in a spiritual sense: "If you ever want to say something about God, people do not seem to listen" (13). Religious awareness is put under pressure: "Life is given to you. But now we live more from demands and things that we find we have a right to" (5). "When things are going well, we think we do not need God so much" (6). The churches are becoming emptier and interest in the world of the spirits is increasing: "Those things are connected," for when the influence of the Christian faith decreases, that void is filled by occultism and spiritism (7).

All in all, it is significant that in quite a few church services the spirit of the times is viewed as negative. Busyness and consumption keep people away from a fundamental sense of dependence on God, and this is seen as a concrete threat even to churchgoers.

Religious Identity

As a kind of antidote to the "negative poison" of the world, the churchgoer should very deliberately develop and express a religious identity. To

---

5. Quotation from "Psalm 14" (*Psalmen voor Nu*, 2005).

allow Jesus into one's heart is a condition for not becoming "lukewarm" in faith (2). One must observe principles that are different from those held by people in one's environment (3), be equipped with the spiritual armor of God, abandon all occult practices (7), not seek any certainty in what human beings offer "but build up one's trust in Christ" (12, 14), and candidly witness to one's faith (11), "even if one ends up alone because of it" (13).

Preliminary Conclusions

With respect to categories of fundamental value orientations that were expected to be important for PCN churchgoers, it turns out that two of them are especially strongly emphasized: belonging to a family and belonging to a faith community. This is striking, given the fact that we live in a very individualistic society where, on the one hand, family matters are largely privatized and excluded from religious interference, and whereas, on the other hand, the expectation that the formative principles of Christian practices should still be based on faithful interpretation of scripture seems to be revived. In the sermons analyzed, family connections are presented as a given for our existence. However, at the same time, the actual relational reality of life in the family context does not really feature. Aspects like divorce, upbringing, finances, domestic violence, sexuality, elderly care, and volunteer work are not mentioned. The value orientations cited are constantly used in a general sense; few concrete ethical dilemmas are discussed, and little instruction is given on how one should to act. It always concerns a basic orientation, an attitude that is important for a Christian. The sermons do refer more to ethos than to ethics (Cilliers 2000, 14, 15, 119). The overall view of family life seems rather naive and not connected to real life and the actual cultural context in which people live.

A new and even striking phenomenon in the Dutch context is that the choice for Christianity by a single individual within a family does feature. This indicates again the extent to which faith has become a private matter in this society, no longer encompassing whole families.

All in all, one may conclude that belonging to a family and faith community, and believing in the search for a Christian identity should be particularly important in sermons. However, exactly these concepts are imprecisely and inadequately worked out. Preachers do not seem to be able to move beyond the level of general observations, concerns, and simplicity. The majority of traditional active attendees do not feel the need for a bridging dialogue with other Christian religious or non-Christian groups in order to be able to deal with new kinds of "otherness." Although there is awareness of global problems and concerns, there does not seem to be any real engagement with these. The sermons reflect an air of a small isolated group in the midst of a hostile world. This reminds one of Brueggemann's comments on "triangulation" theory from the field of pastoral theology to the field of biblical theology and homiletics. He thereby identifies the pastor, the biblical text, and the congregation as three partners in the process of interpreting scripture. What happens in the sermon is that

> the text continues to be present, but it has been usurped by the pastor. Our standard practice is for the pastor to triangulate with the text against the congregation, that is, to make an alliance so that the voice of the pastor and what is left of the voice of the text gang up on the congregation and sound just alike (Brueggemann 2007, 37).

This will have its effects on the attitude of the pastor toward the congregation: "Predictably the third party, the congregation, becomes a hostile, resistant outsider who will undertake reckless, destructive action in such a triangle where one is excluded by the other two." In the sermons analyzed above, either the congregation becomes the hostile outsider and needs to be educated and converted, or the preacher identifies with the congregation and depicts the world outside the congregation as the hostile environment in which a Christian lifestyle and Christian witness are no longer valued and appreciated.

Connecting with the Biblical Text

Now that clarity has been found regarding value orientations, the way these themes are related to the Bible will be explored. For this the division principle of the *Wesleyan Quadrilateral*, which distinguishes four ways by which a theological or, in our case, a homiletical conclusion can be reached, will be used. According to this principle such a conclusion may be reached via one of the following four paths:

- Scripture
- Common Faith Tradition

- Reason
- Experience[6]

This quadrilateral is based upon Wesleyan hermeneutical principles. Alternating principles were dominant at various times in the history of hermeneutics.[7] A central notion in John Wesley's theology was that of the inspiration of scripture through the internal light of the Spirit.[8] This made him recognize sources beyond the literal sense when interpreting scripture. Although the authority of the latter in its literal meaning remained preeminent for Wesley, he also recognized the importance of the common faith tradition, the experience of faith, and reason as corrective and supplementary principles and barriers against interpretations that were too individualistic, mystical, or moralistic.

For research purposes here, the Wesleyan classification is used because of its openness in clarifying what hermeneutical keys ministers prefer with regard to value orientations.

Scripture

An analysis of the research material indicates that the authority of scripture itself is not frequently used as hermeneutical key. The preachers do not legitimate their interpretations in their sermons by way of "prooftexts." They do, however, illustrate their findings with the help of biblical references. The authority of scripture is neither stated beforehand nor questioned in the sermons itself. Preachers seem to trust that reinterpreting scripture will automatically prove its relevance. Only in some sermons is it understood to be so self-evident that the biblical text speaks in the here and now that further arguments about similarities and differences are superfluous. This is particularly true of the more conservative sermons. This leads to shortcutting interpretations—as in a sermon on the Jewish

---

6. For Wesley, the Bible was central, and the other sources were derived from it (Zwiep, 2009, 20).

7. In the early church and up to the Middle Ages, the common faith tradition was dominant. Scripture dominated during Reformation times, reason since the Enlightenment, and experience in the postmodern period (Zwiep 2009, 20; Weeter 2009).

8. "The Spirit of God not only once inspired those who wrote it, but continually inspires and supernaturally assists those that read it with earnest prayer" (Wesley 1948, 794).

exorcists (Acts 19:13–20) where the latter are immediately equated with people today who are involved in occultism, spiritism, and magic.

The Common Faith Tradition

Further analysis shows that the element of "tradition" does not play any explicit role either. Previous exegeses or the normativity of the confessional tradition are not used as hermeneutic keys. One does not find explicit references to concepts of biblical theology or salvation history. If any "tradition" is present, it is in the unspoken self-evidence and relevance of the act of worship and preaching itself. In addition, one finds implicit references to shared values in family life, shared questions, and shared feelings, but no explicit references to locally-dominant language ideologies or shared biblical narratives (Klaver 2011, 223).

Reason and Experience

The emphases on the other factors, namely reason and experience, seem to be more or less equally strong. In general, one may state that the connection between the Bible and the present is made by way of analogy: "Just as then … so now …." One often finds the minister inserting an "equal sign" between a text and its application, moving without a hitch from sketching the biblical situation to the present time. Jesus' familial relationships are a model for ours:

> Rejection. We're good at that. Especially in a village. The negative, sneering attitude of the people in Nazareth was apparently so strong that Jesus couldn't even perform miracles there. If we were clearer on what our negative words can bring about, what kind of walls we can build with them, we would perhaps keep quiet more often (15).

In connections between text and current context such as those above, the bridge seems to be formed by experience. However, in most cases the connection is not called up by evoking and citing the experiences of the churchgoers as such. "Lessons" from scripture are to be learned (1). Rather than being explicitly recalled with the use of applicable feelings and associations, experiences are talked about from a rational perspective. Thus, immediately after the story of Lamech in Gen 4 has been read, the following is said: "Is this not what our society is like? The mechanism of repaying evil with evil is part of the foundation of human society" (5). And in a sermon on the fool who says there is no God (Ps 14), the minister compares, in a rational way, the argument of the psalmist with those of people today (9). Only when speaking in a more general sense about trusting faith is experience itself more frequently brought into the discussion: As David trusted in God when he was in need (Ps 23), so we can also trust in God (1, 6).

Some ministers do make churchgoers aware of the distance between the biblical text and their own time. They, nevertheless, quite easily presuppose a possible identification between the two: "In how far do you feel yourself a stranger on earth, and can you identify with the poet of Ps 119?" (3), and: "The situation in the Bible is never a one-to-one match for the situation in 2011, but is it so strange that we can't find parallels?" (11). Thus, even though differences are noted once in a while, it is primarily the parallels between there and then, and here and now that are mentioned.

Conclusion

From this first analysis of contemporary church services in the PCN, the extent to which these services mirror the fundamental value orientations of the average churchgoer is evident. "Belonging" and "believing" are supposed to be particularly important for loyal church members who attend church services regularly. However, the sermons are not very specific with respect to these value orientations; rather, they refer to a more general religious mentality and ethos, and they refer to biblical texts mostly by way of a presupposed sort of analogy by faith that is not expressly articulated. This undermines the relevance and urgency, as well as the application, of the sermons. The contemporary context is outlined only in general terms, and ethical themes are almost never more closely elaborated on. In the verbal sections of the sermon, the vital contemporary experiential aspect of the church service features in arguments aimed at persuading the listener, instead of being called forth via evocative and open linguistic forms. What seems to be missing in preaching in the mainline PCN is actual space for evocation and concreteness, for ethics and genuine naming of the current situation. This requires a hermeneutic whereby the contextuality of the churchgoers and of scripture can actually be detected in preaching. As Johan Cilliers (2007, 170) states: when preaching is truly naming and addressing the human condition in light of the gospel, it does have a cathartic function and creates a heuristic space for new ways of believing and living one's faith. Since the hermeneutical bridge between scripture and life is mostly crossed by an analogy of experience, it is precisely this analogy that should be critically elaborated in order to construct new forms of incipient theology, based on real life experiences.

REFERENCES

Barnard, Marcel. 2003. Belijden is Vieren: Confessionele en Liturgische Pluraliteit in de Protestantse Kerk in Nederland [Confessing Is Celebrating: Confessional and Liturgical Plurality in the Protestant Church in the Netherlands]. Pages 33–51 in *Protestants Geloven bij bijbel en belijdenis betrokken*. Edited by Marcel Barnard, Luco van den Brom, and Frits de Lange. Zoetermeer: Boekencentrum.

———. 2006. *Liturgie voorbij de Liturgische Beweging* [Liturgy Past the Liturgical Movement] Zoetermeer: Meinema.

Barnard, Marcel, Cas Wepener, and Johan Cilliers. Forthcoming. *Worship in the Network Culture: Liturgical-Ritual Studies—Fields and Methods, Concepts and Metaphors*. Liturgia Condenda 28. Leuven: Peeters.

Boeije, Hennie. 2010. *Analysis in Qualitative Research*. Los Angeles: Sage.

Brueggemann, Walter. 1997. *Cadences of Home: Preaching among Exiles*. Louisville: Westminster John Knox.

———. 2007. *The Word Militant: Preaching a Decentering Word*. Minneapolis: Fortress.

Cilliers, Johan. 2000. *Die Genade van Gehoorsaamheid: Hoe Evangelies is die Etiese Preke wat ons in Suid-Afrika hoor?* [*The Grace of Obedience: How Evangelical Are the Ethical Sermons That We Hear in South Africa?*] Wellington, South Africa: Lux VerbiBM.

———. 2007. Preaching as Language of Hope in a Context of HIV and Aids. Pages 155–76 in *Preaching as a Language of Hope*. Edited by Cas Vos, L. Lind Hogan, and Johan Cilliers. Studia Homiletica 6. Pretoria: Protea.

Centraal Bureau voor de Statistiek (CBS) (Statistics Netherlands). 2009. *Religie aan het Begin van de 21e Eeuw*. Centraal Bureau voor de Statistiek: The Hague/Heerlen, 42. Online: http://www.cbs.nl/NR/rdonlyres/953535E3-9D25-4C28-A70D7A4AEEA76E27/0/2008e16pub.pdf. This can also be accessed at http://www.cbs.nl/nl-NL/menu/themas/vrije-tijd-cultuur/publicaties/publicaties/archief/2009/2009-e16-pub.htm.

Dekker, Wim. 2011. *Marginaal en Missionair* [*Marginal and Missional*]. Zoetermeer: Meinema.
Immink, Gerrit. 2011. *Het Heilige Gebeurt: Praktijk, Theologie en Traditie van de Protestantse Kerkdienst* [*The Holy Event: Practice, Theology, and Tradition of the Protestant Church Service*]. Zoetermeer: Boekencentrum.
Klaver, Miranda. 2011. *This Is My Desire: A Semiotic Perspective on Conversion in an Evangelical Seeker Church and a Pentecostal Church in the Netherlands*. Amsterdam: Pallas Productions. Protestant Church in the Netherlands (PCN). 2011. *30 Kansrijke Missionaire Modelle*. Online: http://www.pkn.nl/missionair/MM30/.
Liedboek voor de Kerken. 1973. Leeuwarden: Jongbloed.
Psalmen voor Nu: Voor niemand Bang [*Psalms for Now: Afraid of Nobody*]. 2006. Zoetermeer: Boekencentrum.
Robinson, B. A. 2011. How Many North Americans Attend Religious Services (and How Many Lie about Going)? In *Religious Tolerance.org: Ontario Consultants on Religious Tolerance*. Online: http://www.religioustolerance.org/rel_rate.htm.
Stark, Ciska. 2011. Duurzaam Preken in een Veranderende Cultuur: Trendbericht Homiletiek [Lasting Preaching in a Changing Culture]. *Handelingen: Tijdschrift voor Praktische Theologie* 3:73–78.
Stoffels, Hijme. 2004. Bijbelbezit en Bijbelgebruik in Nederland [Bible Ownership and Bible Use in the Netherlands]. Online: www.krizzz.nl/files/ Bijbelbezit%20en%20bijbelgebruik%202004.doc.
Weeter, Mark. 2009. *John Wesley vs. John Calvin: Is There a Wesleyan Hermeneutic?* Paper presented at the Doctrinal Symposium on Hermeneutics, World Headquarters of the Wesleyan Church, 5–6 June 2009. Online: http://www.wesleyan.org/bgs/doctrinal_symposium.
Wesley, John. 1948. *Explanatory Notes upon the New Testament*. London: Epworth.
Zwiep, Arie. 2009. *Tussen Tekst en Lezer: Een Historische Inleiding in de Bijbelse Hermeneutiek* [*Between Text and Reader: A Historical Introduction to Biblical Hermeneutics*]. Amsterdam: VU University Press.

A Response to Ciska Stark's "Missing Links in Mainline Churches: Biblical Life Stories and Their Claims in Today's Family Preaching"

Ian Nell

Dear Ciska,

Thank you for the privilege and opportunity to respond in this way to your thought- provoking contribution on the "missing links in mainline churches" as these relate to biblical life stories and their claims in today's family preaching.

In my response I want to take up your central image of "missing links," and structure my letter to you around four of the topics that you address in your essay. The purpose of my letter is to look at possible "missing links" from a South African perspective. In this way I hope to contribute to the issue that you have brought to the table, but also to the overall theme of this volume, namely "human dignity under threat."

- First, I shall remark on the *methodology* that you are using in searching for the missing links.
- Second, will follow some comments on the *context* of sermons and churchgoers in South Africa where these missing links can be found.
- Third, I shall comment on *value orientations* found in church services within the South African Protestant church context, highlighting some of the missing links.
- I shall conclude with a few remarks on the way in which "family preaching" is in itself an important "missing link" in preaching within the South African context.

In a recent essay, Hennie Pieterse, a leading South African homiletics scholar (2010b), discusses different methods of sermon analysis. Pieterse's main argument is that one's leading research question for content analysis of sermons directly influences one's choice of a model for research analysis. He classifies the different analyses according to the following categories:

- The Heidelberg method—with Stellenbosch University's Johan Cilliers as an exponent.
- The Heidelberg method with the use of the Kwalitan computer program.
- The hermeneutical model developed by Vaessen.
- The model for researching the sermon as Word of God as exemplified by your own work.
- The grounded theory model for inductive analysis.

I find it interesting that when Pieterse describes one category, namely, "researching the sermon as Word of God," he cites you as the main exponent of the model with reference to your doctoral research (Pieterse 2005b, 131).

However, considering the method that you use for this contribution, it looks as though there has been a shift from your previous focus toward "grounded theory," and particularly toward a more inductive approach that you call a "simplified form of the grounded theory," according to which you do a preliminary categorization of themes that are introduced on the basis of a specific theoretical framework.

Your study project revolved around the concept of *involvement* as a basic category because

> in this project ... a clear value orientation [was] reflected in the profile of the PCN churchgoers sketched above. The initial themes that were viewed as important were involvement in family (both extended and nuclear) life, the faith community, the coexistence of different groups, politics, education, environment, and health and healthcare. (238)

It is in this regard that I think that you will find an important conversation partner in the research of Pieterse (2010a) on "preaching in the context of poverty." He also makes use of a grounded theory approach in analyzing sermons on poverty that are directed at the poor as audience. He describes this approach as follows:

> This is an abductive approach in the paradigm of social constructionism as developed by Cathy Charmaz in Sociology. I am applying this method of empirical analysis to sermons, in this case sermons on poverty with Matthew 25:31–46 as sermon text.... The process of sermon analysis in its different phases will be discussed as well as the interaction of this bottom-up theory with existing homiletic theories in relation to the research topic. The goal is to update our knowledge contextually in the interaction between praxis and theory with a view to preaching in our context of poverty. (2010a, 113)

When looking for "missing links," I think the use of this research approach (grounded theory) in analyzing sermons in the different contexts (South Africa and the Netherlands) may enrich and contribute to our thinking on human dignity.

Space does not allow going into a statistical analysis of churchgoers in the mainline Protestant churches in South Africa—one can find important research data regarding this in the *South African Christian Handbook 2007–2008* (Symington 2005). I do, however, want to point to a recent publication, *We Need to Talk* (2011), by Jonathan Jansen, Rector of the University of the Free State. In it Jansen offers a short explanation of what he calls his fascination with anger in South Africa. He asks the question: Why are South Africans so angry? In his response, Jansen refers to many examples of the acts flowing from this anger—including murders on farms, strikes, protest marches, turning over of garbage cans in streets, and so on. According to him, there are at least three reasons for this extreme anger, violence, and brutality in South African society:

> First, we may be more traumatised than we think. Because of the longevity and intensity of apartheid brutality, we did not recover. We were the last country in post-colonial Africa to taste freedom and democracy. The sheer duration of colonialism and apartheid over centuries stripped us of our dignity and so much of our humanity.... Second, we internalised the brutality that we had to bear. Burning people inside petrol-filled tires is only possible when the perpetrator has lost his or her own humanity through earlier events.... Third, we did not mourn enough. Mourning the loss of the dead, which is so crucial to many cultures, especially African ones, is fundamental to both personal and societal recovery and transformation. (2011, 5–6)

In the end, according to Jansen, there is only one way out of this political and moral quagmire: we need to talk!

One of the things I think we need to talk about is the importance of *social cohesion*—something you also discuss with reference to the commitment of many churchgoers in the PCN to "maintaining social cohesion" (236).

Social cohesion constitutes another important "missing link" in our South African context. In a recent essay on social cohesion and inclusion in local integrated development plans, Cloete and Kotze (2009, 4) write the following:

> There are a number of reasons why social cohesion has become a concern of national importance. In the post-1994 era, the main challenge to the Government is to resolve the race and class polarizations within the population and to form and build a united nation within a unitary state in which justice and equity are leading values. At the same time, diversity in cultural terms is regarded as an asset that should be preserved. Social inclusion is seen as a necessary condition for achieving a high level of cohesion and, therefore, all members of society, regardless their race, sex, belief, or class are to participate within public affairs and processes.

From the above quotation it becomes clear that the main focus of social cohesion is to increase livelihoods and quality of lives, and in that sense to contribute to the dignity of life. It is also apparent from literature on social cohesion that the latter works with the concept of solidarity in the sense of positive social relationships. In this regard social cohesion is sometimes referred to as the "glue" that binds people together and becomes a deeper-lying positive value worth striving for.

Furthermore, one of the themes you highlight in your essay regards the value orientations you found during your research on the sermons and church services in the PCN. In 2008, Dirkie Smit published an article with the title "Mainline Protestantism in South Africa—and Modernity? Tentative Reflections for Discussion." In the essay he shows the many ways in which

> South African society has come under the impact of Western-type modernisation over the last decade, with the breakdown of apartheid society and the accompanying acceleration of Western-style development. A crucial question concerning religion is accordingly what role religion played and still plays in these processes, and vice versa whether and how religion has been affected and perhaps transformed by them. (2008, 92)

Smit goes on to discuss some of the obvious effects of what he calls this "collapse in modernity" on mainline Protestant and especially Reformed churches. He makes use of three social forms of the church, namely worship in congregational life, in denominations, and in the ecumenical church, and the life of faith of individual believers. The article describes in a nutshell some of the same value orientations you discussed in the central part of your presentation. A comparison between the different aspects involved in the different contexts can provide some more clues to the missing links we are looking for.

In a recent paper Johan Cilliers and I presented at a conference in Berlin on "'Seeking a Safe Haven'—The Impact of Global Religious Transformations on Social Cohesion and Social Development in Different Cultural Contexts" (Berlin, November 25–28, 2010), we look at the interaction between religious and social transformation specifically within Dutch Reformed traditions in South Africa. By making use of Mary Douglas's concept of "the enclave," we propose that a new enclave developed in the Dutch Reformed Church. We describe an enclave—for instance the one that formed around "Afrikaner identity" before and during apartheid—as an entity that

> differentiates itself from other groups in order to create internal cohesion. An enclave is directed against the "other," which could, again in the instance of historical Afrikaner identity, be seen as "other" empires (like the British—during the Boer wars), "other" races (as expressed during apartheid), "other" languages (as exemplified during the so-called "language movement": or "Taalbeweging"), etc. Enclaves often operate with syndromes of anxiety (the "black danger," or the "red, i.e., Roman Catholic danger," etc.) and (often extreme) efforts to maintain the "purity" of the enclave. In typical enclave mentality, you are either "in" or "out." No compromise, no grey areas—things are black and white. (Cilliers and Nell 2011, 4)[1]

---

1. At that time a new Afrikaans TV series called *Hartland* aired on KykNet. It was written by Deon Opperman. The series focused on an extended Afrikaner family and how the individual choices of each of the characters influenced the rest of the family. Themes of forgiveness, the future of the Afrikaner, the complexity of Afrikaner culture, and also identity formation (read "enclave") as well as the sins of the fathers were found in every episode.

Cilliers and I also use the three concepts of stabilization, emigration, and separation to try to explain the triad of activities one finds in the functioning of the enclave that creates the feeling of a "safe haven." We conclude by stating that

> it is difficult, if not impossible, to predict how the future scenario in South Africa will turn out with regard to the development of new enclaves. What is clear in our opinion, however, is that the different churches (denominations) will have to *cross borders* in order to be enriched and guided by the other. We will have to move beyond *denominationalism*, if we hope to have any impact on society. We will have to revisit the *hermeneutical space of the ecumenical church* in order to address societal ills in our country. For it is exactly within this hermeneutical space that we may discover not a self-destructive "stability," but rather our true identity; not a misleading introversion, but rather a vocation (to help transform society); not stigmatization of, and separation from, the other, but rather the experience of facing the other and, in doing so, facing ourselves—and in the end, hopefully, the Other. (2011, 6; emphasis original)

Finally, in the title of your essay you refer to "today's family preaching." Looking at some of the research done by the South African Institute of Race Relations (with project title "First Steps to Healing the South African Family"), one understands why this organization recently published a research paper on "Fractured Families: A Crisis for South Africa" (Holborn and Eddy 2011). The article starts by pointing out that

> family life in South Africa has never been simple to describe or understand. The concept of the nuclear family has never accurately captured the norm of all South African families. Thus when we speak of South African families, we talk not only of the nuclear family, but also of the extended families, as well as care givers or guardians. In South Africa the "typical" child is raised by the mother in a single-parent household. Most children also live in house-holds with unemployed adults. (2011, 1)

From this research it is obvious that many children in South Africa are not growing up in secure environments and in safe families. Many children are affected by the HIV/AIDS pandemic and by poverty. The article concludes by stating:

> This pandemic has resulted in an epidemic of orphanhood and child-headed households, which has left many children having to fend for

themselves.... It is evident that familial breakdown is circular, where children growing up in dysfunctional families are more likely to have dysfunctional families themselves. (2011, 4)

In reflections on instances in which human dignity is under threat, I propose that in considering research on family life in South Africa and in reflecting upon the "crisis in family life," one will find not only some of the most important "missing links," but also some of the most serious threats to human dignity in the country.

Although families within Protestant denominations in South Africa will differ from place to place and according to socio-economic factors, it is obvious that reflecting on "belonging" and "believing" in the PCN might differ considerably from the South African situation. Once again the research by Pieterse may help us to consider ways in which "contextuality" and "ethical themes" are touched upon in—or absent from—sermons.

All in all I want to thank you for putting on the agenda—by way of your research on preaching, family life, and values in the PCN—these issues for reflection and discussion.

Sincerely,
Ian

References

Cilliers, Johan, and Ian A. Nell. 2011. "Within the Enclave": Profiling South African Social and Religious Developments since 1994. *VE* 32, Art. #552. Online: http://dx.doi.org/10.4102.ve.v32i1.552.

Cloete, Peter, and Kotze, Frans. 2009. Concept paper on social cohesion/inclusion in local integrated developmental plans. Commissioned by Department of Social Development, Republic of South Africa.

Holborn, Lucy, and Gail Eddy. 2011. Fractured Families: A Crisis for South Africa. *Johannesburg: South African Institute of Race Relations.* Online: http://www.tshikululu.org.za/fractured-families-a-crisis-for-south-africa/#.UfxD-GRQMrg.

Pieterse, Hennie. 2010a. Grounded Theory Approach in Sermon Analysis of Sermons on Poverty and Directed at the Poor as Listeners. *AcT* 30:113–29. Online: http://www.scielo.org.za/pdf/at/v30n2/v30n2a09.pdf.

———. 2010b. Die keuse van 'n model vir inhoudsanalise van preke oor armoede en aan armes as hoorders [The Choice of a Model for Content Analysis of Sermons on Poverty and to the Poor as Audience]. *In die Skriflig: Festschrift* 44:121–36.

Smit, Dirk. 2008. Mainline Protestantism in South Africa—and Modernity? Tentative Reflections for Discussion. *NGTT* 49:92–105.

Symington, Johann, ed. 2005. *South African Christian Handbook, 2007–2008*. Wellington, South Africa: Tydskriftemaatskappy.

"Household" (Dis)loyalties and Violence in Judges 14 and 15: Dignity of Gendered and Religious "Others" in a Dialogical Theological Praxis

D. Xolile Simon and Lee-Ann J. Simon

INTRODUCTION

Referring to tragic stories, Exum (1992, 8) argues that "the association of good and evil within the divine provides fertile ground for tragic awareness to grow." According to Exum, "telling" and "re-telling" a biblical tragic narrative also makes one knowledgeable and "honest about reality." The process creates openness to "a multivalent, inexhaustible narrative world" of good and evil. In a dialogical theological conversation, it instills a "tragic vision" that contributes to a "fullness of insight into the human condition" (1992, 9). This essay assumes that tensions between loyalties and disloyalties (re)produce the good and the evil, that which upholds and violates human dignity. This occurs within and at the interface between broader cultural (re)productions of social, religious, and theological realities (Wuthnow 1987, 53, 63, 65, 140, 97–185; 2004, 5–6). Households, which include individuals, groups, communities, and nations, interact and (re)produce (dis)loyalties under specific threatening conditions, for example, domestic violence and poverty. Depending on abilities and capabilities, and resources in macro and micro contexts, the (dis)loyalties may actualize or threaten human dignity; they may overcome, instigate, or contribute to conflict and violence. In this essay it is argued that human dignity is under threat when micro and macro contexts impact negatively on the abilities and capabilities of households (individuals or families) to negotiate personal and communal (dis)loyalties and identities. It shows how two women, the woman of Timnah (Judg 14–15) and Susan van der Merwe (the pseudonym of a woman living in a township, Griquatown, in South Africa) renegotiate their (dis)loyalties around personal identities and relationships (micro contexts of families) and communal or collective identities (macro contexts of religions, cultures, class, and gender).

The first two parts of this essay describe and conceptualize the main themes of the dialogical praxis, namely the criteria, conditions, and contexts of human dignity, border-crossings, and household (dis)loyalties. Parts three and four introduce and reflect on aspects of the two case studies from the perspective of (dis)loyalties and border-crossing, exclusion, conflict, violence, destruction, and death. They refer to some similarities and particularities of gender-based violence in households as threats to the human dignity of these two women. Reflection on the cases introduces hints at a dialogical theological praxis that taps into diverse and often conflicting loyalties.

Personal Identity and Social Justice: On Contexts and Conditions of Human Dignity

In a conceptual article, Kelman (1977, 533) describes personal identity and social justice as two fundamental conditions and criteria for understanding and actualizing human dignity in contexts of violence. Personal identity pertains to the dignity of a person and personal freedom (autonomy). Social justice as relational justice deals with the interconnectedness of a person, personal relationships in a community (relationality). The contextual family therapy of Boszormenyi-Nagy and Krasner (1984, 105) emphasizes "relational autonomy," which encompasses both autonomy and relationality, and identity and social justice. An anthropological study by Waldman (on the abovementioned Susan van der Merwe) links and contextualizes key concepts of human dignity. It examines "one woman's attempt to establish independence and autonomy within the context of a community and widespread poverty" (2006, 86). Communal and collective identities of the macro contexts largely regulate and scrutinize how women negotiate personal identities, "individual autonomy and personal relationships" (micro contexts) under socio-economic conditions of poverty and social grants (2006, 85–86). How gendered and religious "others" negotiate relational autonomy depends on contexts, abilities and capabilities, and the tensions between personal and household (dis)loyalties. Iversen (2003) discusses the dimensions of human dignity with regard to identity and relationality in micro contexts, namely under "conditions of intra-house inequality." He defines the substantive and contextual criteria and conditions for human dignity (e.g., personal freedom, choice, and justice) within the framework and approach of Amartya Sen. The praxis-based question deals with

> how Sen's capability approach applies in the context of individuals living together on unequal terms. Intra-household inequality is common in developing countries and often distinctively gendered. In such contexts, the concepts of agency, freedom and choice require special attention and caution. (Iversen 2003, 110)

The criteria, conditions, and micro contexts of human dignity are implied in how Boszormenyi-Nagy and Krasner conceptualize "context" in contextual family therapy. Context means "relational reality" (interconnectedness), relational justice, loyalties, and disloyalties. The approach defines "context ... to convey a highly specific meaning: the dynamic and ethical connectedness—past, present and future—that exists among people whose very being has significance for each other" (Boszormenyi-Nagy and Krasner 1986, 8). Developments of contextual pastoral care, which expand on personal identity, social justice, and human dignity, are significant. In critical engagements with the main schools of family approaches, Boszormenyi-Nagy applies the themes of personal loyalty, trust, responsibility, and relational justice in families and communities. The themes constitute the fourth dimension of a relational reality, namely personal identity and fairness as social justice. The dialogical praxis uses them in a "multilateral dialogue" (see references to dialogue in Martin Buber in Boszormenyi-Nagy and Krasner 1986, 33) to tap into resources and capabilities within and between different households (family, clan, kinship, community, and nation). Thus, as

> an enabling whole, context recognizes the limiting aspects of thinking in terms of family "pathology." Instead, it emphasizes the existence of *resources* in significant relationships that, once actualized, can rechannel hatred into closeness, felt injustice into balance of fairness, and mistrust into trust. In this sense context is inductively defined by the process and flow of relational consequences. (Boszormenyi-Nagy and Krasner 1986, 9; emphasis original)

In the process, "people are helped toward active consideration of the context of justice in the human order, and toward resources of residual trustworthiness" (Boszormenyi-Nagy 1986, 64). The assumption is that narratives of (dis)loyalties shape discourses of personal identity and social justice. As a reflexive and enabling partner in the discourse, the dialogical theologian or pastor relies mainly on qualitative empirical evidence instead of broad assumptions about failures and pathologies of household violence. The ultimate goal of grounding the praxis on resources and capabilities is to understand and guide the productions of personal and communal meanings and identities.

These two dimensions of human dignity guide interreligious and pastoral praxes and programs. The definitions of Kelman and the capability approach offer contextual parameters within which to define and evaluate the nature, scope, goals, and contexts of praxes of human dignity in faith-based and secular institutions and organizations. Personal freedom and social justice are, according to Kelman, two interdependent "and, at least to some degree mutually exclusive" goals. Relational autonomy is a precondition and intermediate goal of praxes that aims at (re-)claiming personal, cultural, and religious identities, and at pursuing social justice. In terms of "systemic discrimination," relational autonomy, loyalties, and human dignity are regulated by chronic unemployment and poverty, on the one hand, and violence and ethnic or religious borders, on the other.

Household (Dis)loyalties and Border-Crossing in Judges 14 and 15

As a fundamental social and religious category in the Old Testament, the concept of the family (a basic and comprehensive kinship term which can include family units, clan, tribes, people, and nation associations and patterns) encompasses this network. The "family household" or "father's household" is the primary social unit, namely "the extended or intergenerational family" or "multiple generations living in the same family" (Drinkard 2001, 485, 487) that cuts across the book of Judges. Smith (2005a, 281) suggests that "the theme of the failure of the family fits within the various levels of this chiastic arrangement" in the following way:

    A. Introduction 1: Israel's Military Compromises (1:1–2:5)
        B. Introduction 2: Israel's Religious Compromises (2:6–3:6)
            C. The Cycles of the Judge Stories (3:7–16:31)
        B. Epilogue 1: Israel's Religious Failures (chs. 17–18)
    A. Epilogue 2: Israel's Moral Failures (chs. 19–21).

However, studies have ignored or downplayed the impact of the networks, relational and intergenerational dimensions of the family on the production of covenantal relationships and (dis)loyalties in Judges. Referring to Samson and the woman of Timnah, Smith summarizes the main problem and proposes alternatives:

> While "the literature on Judges is voluminous" [Connor 1986 in Smith], one theme scarcely touched on in studies on this book is the role of the family. Women in Judges are often examined in relative isolation. These women need to be studied, however, not as stand-alone characters, but within the social context of their families. Also, male characters in Judges should not be studied in isolation, but should be seen in the cultural setting as husbands, fathers, and leaders at various levels who are responsible to prepare the way for the future of Israel in successive generations. (2005a, 279)

Although the theme of family and violence spans the chiastic arrangement of Judges, interpretations need to account for the particularities of contexts, stories, and scenes of household violence. A moralistic interpretation of violence accentuates and generalizes covenantal disloyalty, moral failure, and pathology in the household. Weitzman (2002, 165, 169) claims, for example, that the border-crossing and what Samson "saw" led to "hybridization" (a negative view of interethnic or interreligious marriage) between two nations. It caused the downfall of the households in Judah and Philistine. On the other hand, a dialogical theological approach to border-crossings searches for theological and contextual distinctions (Irvin 1994; Kim 2004). It views the stories in Judg 14 and 15 as cultural productions that select theological, religious, and other resources in communities. The assumption is that border-crossings, like any God-human and human-human interactions, are dynamic. They condition, challenge, threaten, and even subvert personal and communal identities and loyalties of households. In the process, the identities and loyalties are (re)produced through direct and indirect border rhetoric and actions of an interpretative community (Israelites and Philistines) and the narrator of Judges. The encounters, experiences, and conversations of Manoah, his wife, Samson, and the unknown woman of Timnah, to whom multiple identities are assigned—the "young Philistine woman" (Judg 14:1); the "bride" (Judg 14:1); "Samson's wife" (Judg 15:6); a "victim" of violence (Judg 15:6)—form the immediate theological and contextual background to the households and the evolving cycle of conflict and violence.

In Judg 14 and 15, God is "acting behind the scenes" as the cycle unfolds (Gillmayr-Bucher 2009, 699). The narrator of Judges selectively incorporates the relevant aspects of the covenantal relationship into "a double-voiced dialogue" or "polyphonic" voices of conversation partners, including God. Unlike the explicit covenantal loyalties (Judg 2:11–19), Judg 14 and 15 testify to a fading covenantal relationship and loyalty. It is a narrative about a generation and households that do not recognize, know, and acknowledge the God who remains hidden (Judg 14:4, 6, 19; 15:14) up to the last scene (Judg 16). It is important to take note that "the correlation between the activities of the people, their failure to observe God's covenant, and an evaluation and reaction by God" unfolds within implicit Deuteronomistic theological perspectives (Gillmayr-Bucher 2009, 687). Kroeger and Evans (2002, 128) assert that Judges is a theological narrative whereby "the repetitive cycle of blessing, defeat and slavery, restoration and renewed conquest is presented as the result of rebellion against Yahweh's covenant and person." The household narratives in Judg 14 and 15 develop against the background of a loyal and faithful generation in the household of God, for example, the family of Manoah and his wife (Judg 13). On the other hand, the generation of their son, Samson, fluctuates between ethnic, religious, or socio-political loyalties and disloyalties near the borders of Judah and Philistine. It symbolizes the rebellion of covenantal family units and of Israel as a nation.

The tensions between loyalty and disloyalty are produced between two generations and within emerging networks of relationships on and beyond the border of Judah and Philistia. The critical narrative approach of Weitzman explores "the role of storytelling in sustaining the border between the kingdom of Judah and the Philistines in the 'borderlands' of the northern shephelah" (2002, 159). Weitzman refers to evidence that suggests that "the Kingdom of Judah had difficulties controlling the loyalties of the population living along its frontier with Philistia" (2002, 162). Communities regularly crossed the border between Judah and Philistia. More significant relationships were formed than what is often suggested by broad and general theories and grand narratives: the distinctiveness and exclusiveness of the border communities; national hatred; violence; and war between Judah and Philistia. Through ambiguity and control, the "Judahite hegemony" causes mistrust and leads to violence (2002, 163). The scene of the riddle reflects Samson's manipulation of "linguistic ambiguity" (2002, 166). However, we argue that the "father's household" and border-crossing scenes in Judg 14 and 15 are intrinsically part of an evolving cycle of human dignity under threat; of household production of exclusion, violence, and death. The next section introduces three scenes that illustrate the impact of the macro contexts (culture, ethnicity, religion, and language) on the production of household (dis)loyalties that condition, produce, violate, and threaten human dignity.

Household (Dis)loyalties and Macro-Crossing Scenes

The border-crossings of Samson and the encounters with the woman of Timnah end in a cycle of retributive justice instead of relational (covenantal) justice. Retributive justice violates the criteria and conditions of human dignity of the woman of Timnah and the entire households of the Philistines and Israelites. At least three border-crossing scenes in the narrative occur against the background of the macro contexts of the household. They contribute to a negative cycle of exclusion, conflict, and violence, impacting negatively on the woman's ability to negotiate relational autonomy and relational justice.

In the first scene,

> Samson went down to Timnah and saw there a young Philistine woman. When he returned, he said to his father and mother, "I have seen a Philistine woman in Timnah; now get her for me as my wife." (Judg 14:1)

This opening act in the story suggests that ordinary folk often crossed the geographical border between Judah and Philistine. Samson went to Timnah, and saw and became interested in the young woman (Weitzman 2002). Second, the parents' rhetorical question in the second scene seems to be a matter of cultural-ethnic border maintenance (Smith 2005b, 429) instead of a (purely) theological one or covenantal loyalty. "His father and mother replied, 'Isn't there an acceptable woman among your relatives and among all our people? Must you go to the uncircumcised Philistines to get a wife?" (Judg 14:3). The parents do not refer directly to the covenantal imperatives that guided faithful generations of families. Their apparent oppositional and exclusive border rhetoric is informed, produced, and sustained by exclusive ethnic, religious, and national loyalties: "us" and "them"; our people and their people; the "uncircumcised Philistines" and, by implication, the "circumcised" (Israelites). The question and dualities express the ethnic, religious, and national intergenerational loyalties to the "father's household." Covenantal relations maybe implied, but loyalties to the religious and "circumcised" Israelites are contrasted with disloyalties to the profane and "uncircumcised" Philistines. As a judge and leader, one who represents the people of God, Samson knowingly and unknowingly, willingly and unwillingly becomes entangled in the macro intergenerational loyalty conflicts between the Israelites and Philistines.

Third, the riddle scene, "Out of the eater something to eat, out of the strong came something sweet" (Judg 14:14), is a "the turning point in Israel's relation to the Philistines" (Weitzman 2002, 166). Samson poses a riddle that is based on personal and exclusive experiences from the encounter on the way to Timnah. This is not just about a difficult riddle the men of Philistine cannot answer or about cultural miscommunication. Samson manipulates the ambiguity of language to draw boundaries. The boundaries perpetuate and sustain a cycle of mistrust and conflict. They promote disloyalty and perpetuate violence between individuals and their households. The dramatic irony is that while the (dis)loyalties and personal interests cause conflicts, the characters do not know everything. In short,

> the text is full of secrets. The parents do not know about the lion and the honey, the people of Timna do not know the answer to the riddle, Samson does not know that his wife is being pressured by her people. In all this, Samson remains his own man. He claims that his primary loyalty is to his parents rather than his spouse, which is, ironically unknown to him, his wife's position also. (Kroeger and Evans 2002, 141)

The comparative dialogical praxis aims at identifying (possible) contextual and theological factors that influence conversations and responses to the known and unknown events, actions, and (dis)loyalties during border-crossing encounters. Conversations and dialogues are the main instruments of reflection on the representations of encounters with gendered and religious "others" in texts (Judg 14 and 15) or real life encounters today (Waldman 2006).

Household (Dis)loyalties and the Encounter with Susan and the Woman of Timnah

Conditions and resources have shaped attitudes towards gender violence in Sub-Saharan Africa and Ghana (Mann and Tayi 2009). Johnson and Ferraro (2000, 948–63) state that partner violence covers "a broad range of couple relationships." It "cannot be understood without acknowledging important distinctions among types of violence, motives of perpetrators, the social locations of both partners, and the cultural contexts in which violence occurs." The cultural-productive approach makes distinctions to describe human dignity, loyalties, and violence in contexts. Waldman employed an ethnographic approach (participant observation, interviews, etc.) to journey with Susan and tap into her life story and relations within the house and broader context of Griquatown. Waldman uses extracts from the narrative and argues that it is problematic when violence is understood "as essentially male-on-female and domestic violence as something that is confined within the house" (2006, 91).

A series of events and actions testifies to "Susan's desire to situate herself as independent, autonomous and outside the house" (Waldman 2006, 89). Issues of identity, relationship, power, alcohol abuse, and domestic violence constituted a "cycle of conflict and negotiation" between Susan and her husband Karel (2006, 90). These were highlighted during conversations and arguments about, among other things, sharing household responsibilities, freedom of movement, and financial freedom. Karel was working in another town. Hence, Susan looked after the household, but also interacted freely with different people, including Waldman. Waldman focuses on how Susan positioned herself in contrast to different issues within and outside the house, and how Karel responded. For example:

> In contrast to Griqua cultural norms, Susan wanted to situate herself outside of her house and domestic role. She was always willing to accompany me and frequently commented on being seen driving around or walking around town. Susan's husband preferred, however, that she was not drinking soft drinks and socialising outside her home. Other married women, in contrast, entertained me in their homes or gardens, or chatted when we met in town. (Waldman 2006, 88)

Therefore, unlike Judges' representation of the nameless woman of Timnah, Susan of Griquatown is not a mere victim of family or intimate partner violence and socio-economic forces. She is not just a "wounded healer" who responds to physical, emotional, and other forms of abuse at the hand of her husband. Based on extended personal encounters and conversations, Waldman represents her as someone who negotiates her multiple identities and roles amid the challenging macro and changing micro contexts in Griquatown.

The case study of Susan is a reminder of the complexities of household violence and human dignity in contemporary and, by implication, biblical encounters. Waldman employs the themes of "multiple allegiances" and "multiple positioning within society" to describe and evaluate the consequences of intra-household inequalities from the perspective of both personal identities and relational justice in private and public spheres. The themes provide "a means to view domestic violence as contingent upon, or mitigated by, broader societal processes that impinge upon or moderate the behaviour of individuals and spouses" (Waldman 2006, 87). Waldman states,

> Low level domestic and semi-domestic violence permeated the whole of Susan's household, the people with whom they were in daily contact, and indeed all the Griquatown. One witnesses a "domino-effect" in which people's actions reciprocally affected each other and extended beyond one particular house. (2006, 91)

Susan negotiates her personal identity and relationships more adequately amid and despite the domestic violence. Susan is represented "as a daughter, a sister, a wife, a mother and a daughter-in-law" in a Griquatown where many households are affected by unemployment, widespread poverty, and high levels of domestic violence (Waldman 2006, 86). Socio-economic factors influence the actions and responses of Susan and Karel. For example, the disability grant she receives gives her a sense of financial independence, but she also relies on material gifts from Karel. These "structural conditions—of poverty, of insecurity, of unemployment and low wages—affect domestic relations and issues of power" (2006, 89; 91).

Under these conditions Susan keeps her individuality and autonomy and positions herself in the community and its cultural and religious traditions. Despite being unemployed and poor, and despite depending on disability grant, Susan constructs her personal identity within the collective Griqua ethnic, cultural, and religious identities, which include mission Christianity, the Dutch Reformed Mission Church, and Pentecostal Christianity. She is not just another victim of exclusive collective borders and of gender-based violence. Waldman concludes:

> She saw herself as a married woman, who commanded respect, and she carried herself with dignity. In addition, she considered her marriage provided greater opportunities for independence than did conventional feminism. (2006, 97)

How does Judges represent human dignity, personal identity, and relational justice in the texts on the woman of Timnah? The three scenes outlined above set the macro contexts of her encounters with the households from both sides of the border. They act as background and contribute to conflict, violence, destruction, and death. Under conditions of physical threat to herself and her household, she is unable to negotiate and claim personal autonomy, disloyalty, and loyalty to her kin, the Philistines, and her Israelite husband freely. "On the fourth day, they said to Samson's wife, 'Coax your husband into explaining the riddle to us, or we will burn you and your father's household to death. Did you invite us here to rob us?'" (Judg 14:15–17). The accumulation of events, demands, and threats from the Philistines forces her to express (dis)loyalty to her people (the Philistines) and husband carefully. The men threaten her personal identity (life of dignity) and communal identity (Philistine "household" of origin; family and nation). As a desperate response, "Samson's wife threw herself on him sobbing. 'You hate me you don't really love me! You've given my people a riddle, but you haven't told me the answer'" (Judg 14:16).

A question of Exum (1992, 11) as she deals with tragic stories in literature alludes to the complexity of household violence and how it is represented. Is the wife "caught up in a situation not entirely of her own ... making," or is she also responsible, a "guilty victim"? According to Exum, she is a "guilty victim." Kroeger and Evans reach a similar conclusion when they claim that women are comic, stereotypical manipulators in Samson's story (Judg 14:16) and stereotypical victims in the last chapters (Judg 17–21). In the former, we are meant to laugh at Samson, but in the latter we are to shudder at the depth of Israelites sin (2002, 131). For the sake of survival under these conditions, vertical loyalty (to her parents and siblings) becomes much stronger than horizontal loyalty (to Samson and her newly-established family). Contrary to Kroeger and Evans, the woman of Timnah is not a "manipulator" or, according to Exum, a "guilty victim" in the specific scene. She is "the unwitting cause for violence" and "the excuse for acts of violence in the end" (Hackett 2004, 359). In fact, the narrator in Judges presents her as a nameless person and, until just before the threat, as a voiceless woman.

The fact that the woman of Timnah finally speaks and reclaims her loyalty to her people exacerbates the already existing tension and conflict, which is an inevitable dimension of household (dis)loyalties. But her response does not contribute directly to the cycle of household retribution justice and violence. Instead, she and her household are victims of a broader cycle of covenantal, ethnic, and political (dis)loyalties and a series of violent retributions. After her father gives Samson's wife to his friend (Judg 15:2) and "the Philistines went up and burned her and her father to death" (Judg 15:6), Samson burned the fields and vineyards of the Philistines (Judg 15:5). The (dis)loyalties and "ledger of justice" of Samson threaten her human dignity and that of her household. The ledger of justice means that "the revolving slate [*roulerende rekening*] establishes a chain of displaced retributions in families" and generations (Boszormenyi-Nagy and Krasner 1984, 67; emphasis original). Samson is convinced of his personal responsibility for retributive justice. It has disastrous consequences for the Philistine households, including their livestock and fields.

When everything seems to fail and his wife is threatened and "forced" to betray him, "burning with anger he went up to his father's house" (Judg 14:19). Samson takes the ledger of justice to a national level. He claims, "this time I have a right to get even with the Philistines" (Judg 15:3). The ledger of justice turns into a "multigenerational" responsibility for retributive justice (Boszormenyi-Nagy and Krasner 1984, 73, 74). In terms of the household of Judah, Samson is "destructively entitled." The generation of Samson's parents had alternated between unfaithfulness (*ontrou*) and faithfulness (*trou*) to covenantal relations with God. Now the revolving slate is handed down to Samson's generation. As a judge and one who is also accountable, he pays the price on behalf of his people. He is determined to go as far as possible and revenge the death of the woman of Timnah and her immediate household: "I won't stop until I get my revenge on you" (Judg 15:17). He justifies his motivation and action when he asserts, "I merely did to them what they did to me" (Judg 15:11). The cycle of conflict and chain of mutual vengeance moves to the climax when he prays, "O Sovereign Lord, remember me. O God, please strengthen me just once more, and let me get the revenge on the Philistines for my two eyes" (Judg 16:28).

Samson's vindication goes "beyond any measure" (Gillmayr-Bucher 2009, 698). It is a plea of a "tragic" leader and "hero" of Israel who lingers between covenantal loyalty and disloyalty, good and evil, and grace and destruction. Samson symbolizes the theological and contextual realities of (dis)loyalties and violence that threaten the human dignity of the woman of Timnah and households in Judah and Philistia. However, he did not have the last say, for "God's grace, patience, and persistence … was all that kept Israel from self-destruction. To destroy the family would be to destroy the Israel" (Smith 2005a, 284).

Conclusion

A theological praxis of religious plurality and contextual pastoral care should incorporate both realities from real and imaginative encounters with and conversations about household (dis)loyalties, violence and human dignity under threat at the borders. Households draw from the realities as resources that influence their abilities to negotiate their identities and roles. Three initial questions can guide the dialogical conversations in the proposed theological praxis: How is human dignity threatened, actualized, or restored at the intersection of loyalties and disloyalties? How do macro and micro contexts regulate abilities of gendered and religious "others" to (re) claim and negotiate their human dignity in contexts of household violence and poverty? How can these "others" converse and relate personal identities and relational justice to human dignity under concrete conditions of gender-based domestic violence? Although it is beyond the scope of this essay, the praxis should also address the following question: When we converse and "dwell in" the worlds and narratives of the two women, what would be the implications for our (dis)loyalties and the (dis)loyalties of religious and gendered "others" whose human dignity is still under threat today?

References

Boszormenyi-Nagy, Ivan, and Barbara Krasner. 1984. *Invisible Loyalties.* New York: Brunner/Mazel.

———. 1986. *Between Give and Take: A Clinical Guide to Contextual Therapy.* New York: Brunner/Mazel.

Drinkard, Joel F. Jr. 2001. An Understanding of Family in the Old Testament: Maybe Not as Different from Us as We Usually Think. *RevExp* 98:485–501.

Exum, J. Cheryl. 1992. *Tragedy and Biblical Narrative.* Cambridge: Cambridge University Press.

Gillmayr-Bucher, Susanne. 2009. Framework and Discourse in the Book of Judges. *JBL* 128:687–702.

Hackett, Jo Ann. 2004. Violence and Women's Lives in the Book of Judges. *Int* 58:356–64.

Irvin, Dale T. 1994. *Hearing Many Voices: Dialogue and Diversity in the Ecumenical Movement.* Lanham, Md.: University Press of America.

Iversen, Vegard. 2003. Intra-Household Inequality: A Challenge for the Capability Approach? *Feminist Economics* 9:93–115.

Johnson, Michael P., and J. Ferraro. 2000. Research on Domestic Violence in the 1990s: Making Distinctions. *JMF* 62:948–63.

Kim, Kirsteen. 2004. Missiology as Global Conversation of (Contextual Theologies). *Mission Studies* 21:40–53.

Kelman, Hebert C. 1977. The Conditions, Criteria, and Dialectics of Human Dignity. *ISQ* 21:529–52.

Kroeger, Catherine, and Mary J. Kroeger, eds. 2002. *The IVP Women's Bible Commentary*. Downers Grove, Ill.: InterVarsity.

Mann, Jesse R., and Baffour K. Takyi. 2009. Autonomy, Dependence or Culture: Examining the Impact of Resources and Socio-Cultural Process on Attitudes towards Intimate Partner Violence in Ghana, Africa. *JFV* 24:232–335.

Smith, Michael J. 2005a. The Failure of the Family in Judges, Part 1: Jephthah. *BSac* 162:279–98.

Smith, Michael J. 2005b. The Failure of the Family in Judges, Part 2: Samson. *BSac* 162:424– 36.

Van den Berg-Seiffert, Christiane. 2007. Áls de ander anders is … Intercultural contextuele pastoraat. Pages 64–85 in *Uit betrouwbare bronnen: De pastorale praktijk vanuit contextuele optiek*. Edited by Marianne Thans. Zoetermeer: Meinema.

Waldman, Linda.1996. Community, Family and Intimate Relationships: An Exploration of Domestic Violence in Griquatown, South Africa. *ASA* 29:84–95.

Weitzman, Steve. 2002. The Samson Story as Border Fiction. *BibInt* 10:159–74.

Wuthnow, Robert. 1987. *Meaning and Moral Order: Explorations in Cultural Analysis*. Berkeley: University of California Press.

Wuthnow, Robert. 1994. *Producing the Sacred: An Essay on Public Religion*. Urbana: University of Illinois Press.

A Response to Lee-Ann J. Simon and D. Xolile Simon's " 'Household' (Dis)loyalites and Violence in Judges 14 and 15: Dignity of Gendered and Religious 'Others' in a Dialogical Theological Praxis"

Leo Koffeman

Dear Lee-Ann and Xolile,

Reading and studying your contribution was in itself an exercise in border crossing. As a systematic theologian who primarily focuses on ecclesiology, church polity, and ecumenical theology, I felt as if I was entering unknown territory.

Xolile, I realize that "border crossing" is a pivotal category in your discipline, missiology. Our PThU colleague in missiology Mechteld Jansen chose it as the subject of her inaugural professorial inaugural address, describing missiology as a discipline of "theological coaching in situations of border crossing" (Jansen 2008). It is, first of all, missiology that reminds us as theologians of the existence and the function of borders, as well as of the challenges that borders—geographical, cultural, linguistic, religious, and other—pose.

If your contribution were only missiological in nature, I might easily have felt at home. However—and we, of course, owe this primarily to Lee-Ann—it is a truly interdisciplinary contribution in itself. It draws on missiology, biblical theology, and practical theology—with strong input from Boszormenyi-Nagy's view of contextual pastoral care. Therefore, it introduces me to a panorama with which I am not really familiar. I might even say that it gave me an awareness of *otherness*.

This is an experience similar to that of traveling abroad. Crossing borders allows one to meet other people and, maybe most of all, oneself in a new way. The fact that one may experience problems in understanding and communicating does not necessarily lessen the excitement one feels at the end of the day. The opposite might well be true!

So it indeed took some time and energy for me to understand the thrust of your joint contribution, and to start preparing what I hope is an adequate response. Let me try to take a next step in communication with reference to a vital issue you deal with: if people are confronted with violence (or at least with the threat of violence) in situations of "border crossing," how can they maintain their human dignity?

What strikes me in a positive way is, first of all, your view of "human dignity as dialogue-in-context." If I interpret you correctly this means: human dignity is not a general attribute of people worldwide, but it is something that has to be realized—or should I rather say, discovered?—again and again in specific situations and contexts where people are challenged to communicate. In other words, human dignity is relational in nature.

Such people are thus necessarily living in a system, or household, of loyalties and disloyalties, a system where borders play a role—whether the latter are emphasized, neglected, put into perspective, or even crossed. It is in such situations that people are challenged "to situate and negotiate the dignity of religious and gendered 'others' within a transformative theological dialogical praxis," as you state. If I understand you correctly, it is primarily in situating and negotiating the dignity of "others" that one is able to realize—or discover—one's own human dignity.

I was helped by the way you, with reference to Kelman, balance personal identity and social justice as two "fundamental conditions and criteria for understanding and actualizing human dignity in contexts of violence," conditions that should always be seen as complementary. Human dignity is not only a matter of individual freedom or "relational autonomy," and it is not only a matter of relationships in a caring community either. That is where the views of Boszormenyi-Nagy open up new horizons. He defines "context" as a "relational reality." An article published eight years ago by my colleague Rein Brouwer, a practical ecclesiologist, was my first encounter with Boszormenyi-Nagy's contextual approach (Brouwer 2003). Brouwer's article deals with pastors who are in a conflict with their congregation—as unfortunately happens too often. What can be done in such a situation? The first option is a trajectory of individual psychotherapy that suggests that the pastor is the problem.

The second option is system therapy focusing on processes in order to restore a certain balance, if necessary at the expense of the individual pastor. The third—and preferable—option would be a contextual therapeutic approach as suggested by Boszormenyi-Nagy. The latter approach focuses on "the dynamic and ethical connectedness—past, present, and future—that exists among people whose very being has significance for each other." It is this ethical dimension that makes a difference and that is decisive of the quality of relationships. You can see it in the dilemma of "victim versus perpetrator."

I think the latter approach really makes sense. Nevertheless, it also raises quite a view questions. Let me highlight some of the most relevant ones.

First, I have some reservations about with the way you deal with the biblical story of the young woman of Timnah. You state that

> the men threaten her personal identity (life of dignity) and communal identity (Philistine "household" of origin; family and nation). As a desperate response, "Samson's wife threw herself on him sobbing. 'You hate me you don't really love me! You've given my people a riddle, but you haven't told me the answer'" (Judg 14:16).... For the sake of survival under these conditions, vertical loyalty (to her parents and siblings) becomes much stronger than horizontal loyalty (to Samson and her newly-established family). (269)

It seems that, according to you, the woman assumes the position of a victim in order to save her parents and siblings, even if this would endanger Samson. Is this an interpretation, an analysis of the narrative, or is it a moral judgment after all? According to Cheryl Exum, to whom you refer, the woman is a "guilty victim," and it seems to me as if you agree. But was her own life not at stake as well, and first of all? The Philistines threaten her: "or we will burn *you and* your father's household to death"! Not only your father's household, but you as well. Is not she rather a clever agent of keeping the peace by trying to pass on Samson's secret to the Philistines? How could she possibly know that Samson would kill thirty Philistines and in that way would pay his debts, and that a cycle of violent retribution would also lead to the death of her and her father? Indeed, in terms characteristic of the ideas of Boszormenyi-Nagy, "the revolving slate ... establishes a chain of displaced retributions in families and generations." The woman's actions become the source of a violent cycle of retaliation, a dynamic system of force to be considered. That seems to be what happens in such situations. Is this really how it is, or is it something that someone has to be blamed for? If so, who should be blamed? The young woman of Timnah? Samson?

The way I read Boszormenyi-Nagy, it is understandable that an intergenerational imbalance leads to "destructive parentification" and consequently to "destructive entitlement." I am also convinced that an analysis such as this can be of great help in finding a form of therapy, in terms of fostering "multiple allegiances." But what does it say in terms of responsibility?

Second, from this perspective I also wonder what one can say about God in this context. Is it all about an analysis of violence and counter-violence, or about human responsibility? What about God? In a way this concerns the role of theology, as "God-talk."

With Gillmayr-Bucher you say, Xolile and Lee-Ann, that God is involved, "acting behind the scenes." When the story reaches its terribly violent climax, Samson states, "I won't stop until I get my revenge on you" (Judg 15:17). He justifies his motivation and action by saying, "I merely did to them what they did to me" (Judg 15:11). But then, at the end of the Samson narrative as a whole, he prays: "O God, please strengthen me just once more, and let me get the revenge on the Philistines for my two eyes" (Judg 16:28). According to you, this is "a narrative about a generation and households who do not recognize, know, and acknowledge the God who remains hidden (Judg 14:4; 6; 19; 15:14) up to the last scene (Judg 16)." It might be too much to say that Samson's final act of violence seems to receive a kind of divine covenantal blessing through the direct or indirect hand of God in the events. Nevertheless, one has to ask oneself whether this is theology, God-talk with which one can work. Is it not perhaps no more than a disputable interpretation of historical facts or popular legends, a theology we cannot possibly accept anymore? I am aware that this is an extremely difficult question, but in a way it refers to the core of all "theology," and we cannot afford to leave it totally unanswered. How should I understand God's "acting behind the scenes" in the book of Judges, and in the text of the Griqua women Susan?

In other words: What does it mean to deal with situations pertaining to human dignity and domestic violence from a theological perspective?

In a third observation, I want to take a next step in searching for an answer to these questions. It regards another important aspect of your contribution, and of the theory of Boszormenyi-Nagy in the background.

Am I interpreting you correctly, if I say that eventually all—and I mean really *all*, including the possibility of speaking about God—depends on the way people take responsibility in conflict situations? Your contribution draws a depressing picture of "an evolving cycle of human dignity under threat; of household production of exclusion, violence, and death." Time and again you refer to this dynamic: the "evolving cycle of conflict and violence," the "cycle of retributive justice instead of relational (covenantal) justice," the "negative cycle of exclusion, conflict, and violence, impacting negatively on the woman's ability to negotiate relational autonomy and relational justice" (265); the "cycle of mistrust and conflict that promotes disloyalty and perpetuates violence between individuals and their households" (266). However, this cycle also creates possible conditions and spaces for individuals and communities to situate and negotiate the dignity of religious and gendered "others" within a transformative theological dialogical praxis. Thus, the question basically is: What does one do in such situations? Does one negotiate one's own position, for instance as a victim seeking recognition, if not revenge? Or does one indeed negotiate the dignity of religious and gendered "others"?! Does one enhance the cycle of violence and retribution, or does one rather use the "resources in significant relationships that, once actualized, can rechannel hatred into closeness, felt injustice into balance of fairness, and mistrust into trust" (261)?

Fourth, I could not help connecting what I read with the outburst of violence in England at the time I read it. It started in the Tottenham area in London. In our Dutch newspapers and on our talk shows, a discussion immediately ensued about the causes of such outbursts, which seemed to be totally unexpected. Some would refer to the social and economic situation in these areas as a kind of explanation—high unemployment among the youth, poverty, drug and alcohol abuse, lack of perspective, cuts in social care, and so on—what did you expect? Others would emphasize that such situations should never ever be used as an excuse for looting and burning down shops and for the orgy of violence we saw; at the end of the day it is only personal responsibility that counts. One also heard a few stories of people that crossed borders, that tried to keep their brothers or sons from perpetrating such actions, or that reported them to the police afterward in spite of bonds of kinship. Is that what it is finally all about?

Let me summarize the questions that your reflections on Judg 14–15 raise concerning the way we deal with conflict situations now. First, is this biblical narrative more than just a story of what happens in such situations? Is it something someone has to be blamed for? Second, what can we say about God (theo-logically) in such a context? Third, does all not eventually depend on the way people take responsibility in conflict situations?

I assume I owe you a bit more than a series of questions. In his *Church Dogmatics* (IV/3, §72), Karl Barth deals extensively with the mission of the Christian community. However, he begins this paragraph with a challenging exposition on "the people of God in world-occurrence." In that context, Barth raises issues that come very close to what we are dealing with in our exchange. What about the lordship of God over his own people and yet also—crossing borders!—over all peoples? Barth quotes a number of Old Testament texts, especially from the book of Psalms. But immediately afterwards he reminds us:

> To be sure, these statements are not made in terms of historical analysis, but from an eschatological standpoint. Yet all of them look through and beyond the present aspects of world-occurrence to their future and determination which are their true meaning and purpose. And eschatological means supremely realistic. From the standpoint of the history of God with Israel attested in the Old Testament, world-occurrence has not yet to acquire, but already has, this future and determination, and with it its true essence, contradicting, transcending and integrating its present aspect" (Barth 1962, 692).

According to Barth, such recollection of God's rule is certainly the first, decisive, and comprehensive thing that we have to say and continually have to recall theologically in relation to world history. In this context, however, Barth also refers to a well-known Swiss maxim: *Hominum confusione et Dei providentia Helvetia regitur* (Switzerland is governed by the confusion of men and by the providence of God). Human confusion,

> in a way which is most unsettling ... stands before us as an obscurely and even absurdly distinctive reality which we can neither overlook nor deny as such, but which we must clearly grasp in all its inexplicability. The community of Jesus Christ has to do with this distinctive reality. And it will be constantly tempted to wonder whether after all the confusion of man, perhaps against the background of what is if possible an even more dreadful cosmic disorder, is not merely the reality but the inner truth of world-occurrence, with which it has to reckon as the final word in the matter (Barth 1962, 693).

But if it does so, there can be no serious question of a mission of the community into the world and to the world: "As the community of those to whom Jesus Christ has entrusted the word of reconciliation, it cannot possibly understand itself in this way" (Barth 1962, 693).

We will never be able to explain theologically the evolving cycles of conflict and violence. Not even the book of Judges can help us in this respect. However, this in no way diminishes our hope, nor our responsibility.

Thank you, Lee-Ann and Xolile, for raising such important issues.

Leo

References

Barth, Karl. 1962. *Church Dogmatics*. Vol. IV/3. Edinburgh: T&T Clark.

Brouwer, Rein. 2003. "Als één die gerechtigd is tot vertrouwen..." Een door I. Boszormenyi-Nagy geïnspireerde contextueel-ecclesiologische oefening ["As One Entitled to Trust..." A Contextual Ecclesiological Exercise Inspired by I. Boszormenyi-Nagy]. Pages 215–31 in *Praktische Theologie in Meervoud: Identiteit en Vernieuwing [Practical Theology in the Plural: Identity and Renewal]*. Edited by Gerrit Immink and Henk de Roest. Meinema: Zoetermeer.

Jansen, Mechteld M. 2008. God op de Grens: Missiologie als theologische begeleiding bij grensoverschrijding [God on the Border: Missiology as Theological Accompaniment to Border Crossing]. Inaugural address delivered on 8 November 2008, PThU, The Netherlands.

Honor in the Bible and the Qur'an

Gé Speelman

Introduction

On June 22, 2002, a Pakistani woman from the Punjab, Mukhtaran (or Mukhtar) Bibi, was gang-raped. The deed was the result of a conflict between her family and another family in her village, belonging to the Mastoi clan. The Mastoi accused Mukhtaran's twelve-year-old brother of assaulting a woman of their clan (in fact, it seems he had been seen talking to the woman in a field). The boy was therefore kept under lock and key by the Mastoi. In such cases, of conflict between families, Pakistani villagers often have recourse to a local tribal law council, a Panchayat. One possible outcome of conflicts regarding honor is that the family who has offended gives away in marriage one of their women to the offended family.

When Mukhtaran Bibi accompanied her father to plead before the tribal council for the release of her young brother, the Mastoi men, the powerful leading family in her village, started to intimidate her father and her uncle. Then the young men of the Mastoi took the law into their own hands. In Mukhtaran's words:

> When I appeared before the council, one of the elders said that "since the girl has come here, therefore we must pardon her." But suddenly a man stood up and said: "we will rape her."

And so it happened. When the men dragged her away to a neighboring shed, Mukhtaran Bibi testifies, she appealed to one of then, a man she knew, pleading: "Khaliq, I am like a sister to you." She also asked their forgiveness in the name of the Qur'an. However, her appeals fell on deaf ears. After the men had raped her, they sent her away almost naked and she had to walk home amidst the jeering of fellow villagers. This, it was decided, was the way to restore the honor of the Mastoi clan.

It was not expected that Mukhtaran Bibi or her clan, the Tatla, would seek compensation for the rape. Nobody respects a raped woman. She had lost her honor, and for many the only way out for such a woman is to commit suicide. Surprisingly, however, a local imam, Abdul Razzaq, publicly condemned the rapists in his Friday sermon in the mosque. This rape was contrary to the principles of Islam, the imam declared. Mukhtaran Bibi then found the courage to go to court. The case grew in notoriety when a foreign press agency became interested in it, and it became a hotly debated issue both inside and outside of Pakistan (Bowman 2006, 15).

The story of Mukhtaran Bibi is one example of a so-called crime of honor. In the Netherlands as well, migrant women, many from Islamic countries, have been victims of such crimes. Here honor appears to be something women do not own in any positive way, since it is merely something they may lose. In debates on Islam in Western societies, the prevalence of honor crimes is often used as an argument for the incompatibility of Islam with modern Western societies and their values. However, the concept of honor is not coterminous with Islam. It was present in many cultures long before the advent of Islam and still functions in many non-Muslim cultures. Many of its presuppositions go against the principles contained in the Qur'an.

In fact, notions and systems of honor predate all contemporary organized religious systems. Not only Islam, but Judaism and Christianity as well came into being in cultures in which honor systems were already functioning. The more interesting question is how the sacred texts of these religions reflect on honor. The central question in this essay is how honor functions in two narratives from the body of sacred texts of Judaism/Christianity and of Islam. In both narratives honor is connected with the sexuality of women.

Before proceeding, however, one must keep in mind that there are different types of honor. In analyzing both ancient and contemporary honor cultures, it is important to clarify what type of honor is referred to. Only then may one proceed to a discussion, for example, of the narratives of the rape of Dinah and the accusations of adultery against Aisha, and determine how existing cultural notions of honor are treated by the authors of these texts and what roles the female protagonists in the stories play. Finally, the possibility of using these texts to come to a transformed notion of honor as a concept that motivates moral behavior will be explored.

Honor and Respect

In his interesting book on honor among Bedouins in the Sinai Desert, Frank Henderson Stewart analyzes the relationship between honor and respect. He argues that honor is more than a subjective or intersubjective emotion, such as the value I ascribe to my own behavior or the respect I receive from my neighbors. Honor is treated by Stewart's reference group as a kind of possession, a legal entitlement. He comes to the conclusion that "Honor is the right to respect" (Stewart 1994, 21).

What gives people the right to expect respect from their neighbors, their peers, or their superiors? This depends on the situation they are in, the (sub)culture that they share, and the norms and values that operate within the group with which they identify. The saying "there is honor among thieves" expresses the awareness that different subgroups in society may have different criteria to judge who among themselves are entitled to respect. Groups that share a code of honor may create a well-defined system of honor that has repercussions for many other elements of their culture. Honor can be so central that a culture is defined by it. We then speak of an *honor culture*. Although honor cultures are often associated with rural areas, there are modern examples, such as street gangs in major Western cities, where honor systems seem to exist that are in many ways comparable to those in Pakistani villages.

Honor cultures have a few things in common:

- They flourish in small-scale societies, where face-to-face contact is important. Inside the smaller units in such societies (families, streets) there are warm contacts and solidarity. Honor is the collective possession of the group. When the honor of one group member is compromised, all others must react (Peristiany 1961, 11).
- These cultures often do not know a strong outside authority. There is no state with a monopoly on violence and no independent judiciary.
- Between subgroups there exists intense competition for economic resources, because these resources are not stable. One may think of here of movable possessions like herds (Bedouins) or drugs (street gangs), or even land in situations of war or conflict.

- The honor of male members of the group is tied to their ability to use violence. That of female members is connected to their sexual behavior.

Stewart distinguishes between two types of honor. Honor as the right to respect from one's neighbor, the respect that is due to an equal, he calls "horizontal honor" or "negative honor." It is negative because it is the kind of good reputation that one may lose but cannot accumulate. It is what the Romans called one's *fama* or good name. Stewart contrasts this with vertical or positive honor, the respect one may enjoy by being considered superior in light of one's rank or virtuous behavior. This is what the Romans called *honor* (Stewart 1994, 58).

Honor and Women

Stewart calls *fama*—the identity-linked type of honor—"horizontal honor" because he regards it as a type of honor that functions between peers or equals.[1] He shows in his study that this applies to the Bedouin men of the Sinai Desert. However, honor groups (groups in which the same validations of honorable behavior function) are more complex. The men in an honor group may see each other as peers where honor is concerned, but they would certainly not regard women as their peers with regard to honor. In some studies on honor, it is explicitly stated that women literally "have no honor"; they are outside the honor system (Stewart 1994, 82).

And yet, Bedouin women in the Sinai Desert do have definite *perceptions* about honor. In this sense they are also members of the same honor reference group. They share the same honor culture as the men of their community, and they participate in the evaluation of other women and of men in matters of honor. Therefore, I would hesitate to define all members of an honor group as equals or peers. One can at most say that within each honor group that shares the same standards, there are subgroups of peers who judge one another and other groups' members according to some criteria.

When members of one honor group are not peers, it follows that there can be different honor standards for different members of the group. This

---

1. As does Bowman, who sees the honor group as "a society of equals" (Bowman 2006, 4).

is particularly clear for men and women. As Pitt-Rivers states regarding the Mediterranean honor culture: "Male honor faces the outside, female the inside: male honor resides in the valor of the (young) men of the family; they are responsible for the sexual purity of 'their' women" (Pitt-Rivers 1961, 78).[2]

As we saw in the case of Mukhtaran Bibi, honor may be linked to female sexuality. The Mastoi men felt that their honor was compromised because a twelve-year-old boy had been present in the same space as a Mastoi woman. One might think these men prudish, Victorian. One would think they have rather repressed ideas about sexuality. But in an honor culture, the problem is not sex as such. The problem rather is: who has sex with whom? The fact that a mere Tatla boy could be in the presence of one of their women and be left unpunished is what set off the Mastoi men's reaction. Their reaction does not mean that they considered the woman guilty in any moral sense. Western observers of honor crimes often believe that the woman who in some way transgressed against the honor code is perceived as someone guilty of misconduct and that this is the reason she has to be punished; she has "sinned" and should be punished. Yet, if this were so, it is difficult to understand why in many cases women are killed because they had been raped. After all, a woman who did not consent is not responsible for the sexual transgression. She is not guilty of any sins, and yet she is eliminated.

In honor cultures that attach such importance to the sexual purity of women, however, the question of whether the woman consented to the act or not is irrelevant. The intentions of the actors are not the point. In such cultures a woman's sexuality "belongs" to her male guardian (her father, brother, or husband). The dishonor of sexual contact outside of marriage then falls upon such guardians: *they* have been dishonored, no matter whether the woman disobeyed them or whether she was raped. In both cases, it is clear that the guardian is incapable of either controlling or protecting her. The result is the same. Dishonor is less like a fatal disease than like a moral failure (Bowman 2006, 18). In Muhktaran Bibi's case, her father, belonging to a minor and powerless clan, was incapable of protecting her against the males of the dominant Mastoi clan. Therefore,

---

2. I do not share the claim of Pitt-Rivers that there is one universal "Mediterranean honor code" that is shared by different cultures across time and space. However, the distinction he makes between male and female honor holds true for many different contexts.

the expectation was that she would commit suicide, sparing her clan the shame of her prolonged existence.

More Differences within the Honor Group

In many cultures, including the culture of the Pashtuns, negative honor is often connected to the control males extend over the sexuality of the females in their care or under their jurisdiction. If the good name (*fama*) of such a female is jeopardized, the whole family loses its honor. In Pakistan this type of honor is known as '*Izzat*.

Yet another distinction exists. Fredrik Barth, who conducted a very interesting study of Yusufzai Pashtuns who lived in the Swat valley in Afghanistan, found that among the landowners in the region there were two kinds of power. The local landowners could only preserve their property in the lawless country by behaving in a strong, aggressive, and virile manner. They could thus draw as many dependents and followers as possible. Their strength was supported by an acute sense of honor. Any threat to their honor had to be swiftly countered (Barth 2004, 89). Should someone injure them or gossip about their womenfolk—or in the worst case when someone from their family was killed—violent revenge was the only to restore their honor. At the same time, they also competed with other landowners when it came to excessive hospitality and generosity. Anyone staying in the men's house in the village could get food from the house of the chief. All who were dependent on the local landowner would receive food or other gifts at festivals and other occasions (Barth 2004, 91).

So within the group of landowners there was a certain equality when it came to their horizontal honor, but there was also competition to rank as the most hospitable, generous man. This competition, Fredrik Barth points out, was another instrument for them to gain power. The landowner, who had the greatest ability to demand the respect of his dependents in this way, would have a great number of followers who would also defend him in any quarrels with other landowners. Power was closely linked with honor, especially vertical or appraisal-linked honor (Barth 2004, 88–91).

But there was yet another kind of power at work at the same time. In every village, there were groups of descendants of the Prophet Muhammad known as "saints." Some of these saints were landowners in their own right; some hardly possessed any land. Their power was based on their spiritual weight as Sufi leaders (Barth 2004, 92). If local landowning families had a quarrel, the saints would be the ones to intervene and to initiate peace negotiations. The local landowners were in some ways dependent on the local saints, and in exchange they supported them. The power of the saints was not based on their virility and aggression, but on their peace-brokering capabilities and their moral reputation. Whereas the landowners were praised when they were quick to revenge their honor, the local saints were spoken of in terms of their wisdom and wit (Barth 2004, 96–99).

Although some elements of the recognition of honor were the same for saints and landowners (for instance, neither group would tolerate any doubts about the chastity of their women), their *fama* or reputation rested on different foundations. One could offend a landowner by doubting his striking power, but not a saint. However, one might offend a saint by doubting his piety or authenticity. "Many acts which would bring honor to a chief, such as the immoderate display of violence, would be regarded as most inappropriate in a saint, and might seriously harm his reputation" (Barth 2004, 100).

Both the landowners and the saints could acquire the Roman *honor*, that is, they could accumulate an increasingly better reputation among their fellow men, but the type of *honor* would be different. People did not expect excessive hospitality from saints. They would, of course, show charity toward the poor, but what gave them their real reputation was their knowledge and mystical powers (Barth 2004, 101).

Thus, illustrated schematically:

	Negative honor (*fama*) for landowners	Negative honor (*fama*) for saints	Positive honor (*honor*) for landowners	Positive honor (*honor*) for saints
Loss caused by	Unchaste women. Attacks on family.	Unchaste women. Attacks on family. Doubts about piety.	Miserly behavior. Poverty. Lack of supporters.	Lack of wisdom (failed mediation). Lack of piety or sincerity.
Produced by	Virile and violent behavior.	Fasting, praying, moving quietly, and speaking softly.	Generosity.	Diplomatic skills.

In the story of Mukhtaran Bibi one recognizes these two types of power at work. The men of the Mastoi clan, landowners of great repute, acquired power through their ability to humiliate Muhtaran Bibi and her family. However, the local imam Abdul Razzaq countered this with another sort of power and another idea about what was honorable: a moral power, based on his knowledge of the holy Qur'an. Mukhtaran Bibi refers to this alternative view of honor when she appeals to her rapists in the name of the Qur'an.

Honor can thus be afforded to different people in different ways, depending on their role and position in society. Landowners and saints share the same perceptions and standards for honor, the same *honor code*. But they do not apply them to everybody in the same way.

These differing criteria for honor that are at work among Pathans in the Swat Valley are, *mutatis mutandis*, also at work in the story of Dinah and Prince Shechem.

The Story of Dinah

Genesis 34 tells the story of Dinah, the daughter of Jacob and Leah. Dinah is raped by the son and the heir-apparent of the city Shechem near which Jacob had settled and bought land. "And when Shechem the son of Hamor the Hivite, the prince of the land, saw her, he seized her and lay with her and humbled her" (Gen 34:2).[3]

On the face of it, this seems to be a clear case of rape. However, Lynn Bechtel argues that the term '*nh* does not necessarily imply rape. In other parts of the Bible, the term is used for the humiliation derived from inappropriate sexual contact. But what makes particular forms of sexual intercourse shameful is when it occurs outside of community bonding or when there is no prospect of marriage (Bechtel 1994, 24).

In Deut 22:23–24, where a young woman who is bonded has sex with an outsider, the guilty parties must be put to death. The woman has not been raped (she did not cry out), and yet she has been "humbled" ('*nh*). The intercourse is shameful because it threatens the social bonding of the community. In Deut 22:28–29, sexual intercourse occurs without the prospect of marriage. Again, the text speaks of the act "humiliating" ('*nh*) the woman—again no rape, but shameful intercourse. In Deut 22:25–27,

---

3. Translations are from the Revised Standard Version.

a clear case of rape in modern terms is described. Here, however, the term *'nh* is not used. The woman is not "shamed," because she has behaved in the correct manner.[4] After the illicit, and therefore humiliating, sexual act (however humiliating that is for the woman in question), Shechem falls in love with Dinah.[5] He "speaks tenderly to her" and urges his father, King Hamor, to ask on his behalf for her hand in marriage. Jacob hears that his daughter has been defiled (*ṭm'* a cultic term for defilement), but he says nothing, as his sons are out in the fields. When they return, however, they are very indignant and angry about the disgrace (*nəbālâ*) done to their sister: this ought not to happen in Israel.

Meanwhile, Hamor has arrived at Jacob's household. He talks to Jacob and his sons and says:

> The soul of my son Shechem longs for your daughter; I pray you, give her to him in marriage. Make marriages with us; give your daughters to us, and take our daughters for yourselves. You shall dwell with us; and the land shall be open to you; dwell and trade in it, and get property in it. (Gen 34:8–10)

Dinah's brothers give a deceitful answer. They demand that the inhabitants of Shechem be circumcised before they can give their daughters in marriage and marry women from Shechem. When the condition has been met and the men of Shechem are recovering from their wounds, Simeon and Levi, the two full brothers of Dinah, go out, kill all the men, and take their city. They also take their cattle, their women, and children as booty. Jacob is very upset at their act and declares:

> You have brought trouble on me by making me odious to the inhabitants of the land, the Canaanites and the Perizzites; my numbers are few, and if they gather themselves against me and attack me, I shall be destroyed, both I and my household. (Gen 34: 30)

The story of Dinah is a story of revenge for the sexual appropriation of a woman belonging to a different family. In some ways it can be compared

---

4. For a different opinion, see Scholz 2001, 8. However, I find the arguments of Bechtel more convincing, since Scholz mainly uses classical reference books to make her point.

5. The terms used (*dābaq*, *'āhab*, *wayĕdabbēr 'al-lēb*) leave no doubt as to the affection Shechem feels for Dinah (Gunn 1991, 196). I do not agree with the translations for these terms used by Scholz (2001, 7).

to the story of Mukhtaran Bibi. One finds an attempt to solve a dispute between two families (that of Jacob and the clan of Hamor). The solution Hamor seeks would appeal to a gathering of Pakistani mediators in a Panchayat. A marriage, Hamor suggests, should repair the damage done to the honor of Jacob's family. This was the kind of solution that the older members of the Panchayat in Mukhtaran's village also sought. In the case of the Hamor and Jacob clans, it would have prepared the way for future ties between them: marriage bonds and the possibility for the newly-arrived clan to acquire land and property.

The voice of Dinah herself is not heard during the negotiations. She is an entirely passive victim during the whole of the story. Did she resist or did she consent to sex with Shechem? Did she respond to Shechem's "tender speech"? Was she happy with the outcome of the events? Did she rejoice in her brothers' revenge of the offense to the honor of her family? Unlike Mukhtaran Bibi, Dinah is not afforded a chance to speak her mind on the matter. The writer of this narrative is more interested in the interplay between the males around her.

In his description, we see another person who remains passive during most of the proceedings: the head of the clan of Israel, Jacob. Shechem takes steps to acquire a bride; Hamor throws his weight into the negotiations; the sons of Jacob are emotional and angry, deceitful and violent. But Jacob does not do or say anything at all. Hamor, who planned to discuss the issue with Jacob leader to leader, must instead address the full gathering of Jacob's sons.

Is Jacob timid and fearful, a man who dares not act, as verse 5 implies? Or is the writer creating an image of a thoughtful man that does not reveal his inner deliberations?

Jacob only speaks at the end of the story, to his sons Simeon and Levi, who have ruined their clan's chances of settling peacefully among the inhabitants of the region: "You have brought trouble on me by making me odious." Jacob has become "someone who smells bad" (*b'sh*), and this makes him and his clan vulnerable. But his sons have the last word. To them, there was no other outcome to the conflict. Their reply is a rhetorical question ("Should he treat our sister as a harlot?") with only one possible answer.

Now is this a story about honor? The term "honor" is nowhere explicitly used in the story, yet the pattern of events points in that direction. Julian Pitt-Rivers (1977), who devoted a book to this passage of the Bible, certainly thinks so.

The reactions of her father, her brothers, and the father of Shechem stand at the heart of the story. Of course this fits perfectly with existing honor cultures, where women's sexuality is under the guardianship of male relatives. Pitt-Rivers sees the story as the outcome of the debate about exogamy: "the limits of endogamy and exogamy are debated throughout the length of Genesis" (Pitt-Rivers 1977, 154). Although, like other peoples in the Mediterranean, the family of Abraham preferred endogamic marriages, sometimes they were not in a position to object when other men took their women, as in the stories of Sarai and Rebekah, who were also prospective brides of a king of Egypt or of Abimelech (Gen 12:10–20; 20:1–18; 26:7–11). Simeon and Levi's revenge on Shechem reflects the growing power of the clan of Israel. At that time, they were in the position simply to take the women of the local inhabitants without having to suffer giving away their own women to outsiders. This is in line with what Pitt-Rivers sees as the prevailing Mediterranean honor system. When Hamor proposes a future exchange of women, he operates within a farmer's world in which there is basic equality among neighbors—they would have to deal with each other in the future anyway, so they might as well create family relationships with each other. However, Simeon and Levi represent the Bedouin type of honor code in which there is not equality, but a power struggle with winners and losers. The winners can afford to take the women of the other party without giving up their own women in exchange (Pitt-Rivers 1977, 166). In Pitt-Rivers's reading of the story, then, honor functions for the brothers as a zero-sum game: I win honor at the cost of your losing honor.

Mary Douglas gives a different interpretation of this episode. She downplays the role that honor plays in the story. For Douglas, the Hebrew Bible affords no special place to honor, except where the honor of God is concerned. She points out that the term "honor" does not occur in the narrative. The rape (if it is a rape) is instead presented as "defilement," a cultic term often used by the priestly authors who compiled the final version of the book of Genesis. If honor is invoked at all, says Douglas (2004, 28), it is done in an oblique and indirect manner (Douglas 2004, 28).

According to Douglas's interpretation of the narrative, the contrast between the vengeful reaction of Simeon and Levi and Jacob's more conciliatory stance reflects the concern of the authors of the passage. She points out that the final version of Genesis was written during the tense time after the exile, when the question of intermarriage was of the utmost importance, and that this overriding concern colors the story. It is no coincidence, she feels, that the center of Jacob's activities in the Holy Land was Shechem, the major rival of Jerusalem after the exile (Douglas 2004, 29). The priestly writers of Genesis situated Jacob right in the middle of this area, stressing the ancient links between the people of Shechem and the returned exiles. They (the priests) were against the rigid laws imposed by Ezra and Nehemiah against marrying "foreign" women—who were often, in fact, women of related families who had remained in Palestine during the exile, families like the people of Shechem. For them, Hamor's proposal of an exchange of women and a peaceful coexistence was at the heart of the story. Hamor's proposal voiced their own pleas for a more conciliatory attitude toward the inhabitants of Shechem. With the story they claimed, furthermore, that Jacob himself did not object to such an attitude. Although his reaction to the deeds of his sons is sad rather than angry, the fact that he would later disinherit his sons for their violent behavior is telling (Douglas 2004, 31).

In my reading, I follow Douglas. However, I do think the narrative of Dinah is about honor. More precisely, it is a story about the different alternatives open to people in honor cultures if they want to deal with violations of honor.

The sons of Jacob resemble the Pathan landowners described by Fredrik Barth: strong, virile, at all times prepared to resort to violence when the sexuality of "their" women moves out of their control. The irony is that in the biblical story the men are actually not landowners. The landowners in the story are the Shechemites, who offer the sons of Jacob the possibility of joining their class by intermarriage. Hamor is acting in the spirit of the "saints" in a Path society. He could easily have used his power as a landowner to take by force whichever woman his sons fancied. He opts instead for a peaceful solution. Clearly, he is cast into the role of the "good guy" by the writers of the story.

Jacob's reaction is the most ambiguous and, therefore, the most interesting. One might conclude from the story that he sees his role—and thus the role of Israel—as more conciliatory than violent. The way of Simeon and Levi leads to destruction. On the surface Jacob is not much concerned with honor, but one should not forget that for people in honor societies, the loss of honor also leads immediately to the loss of power. This is the meaning behind Jacob's address to his sons: their behavior has exposed him as a deceiver who cannot be trusted. The theme of Jacob's deceptions is constantly referred to in Genesis. Here, however, the irony is that it is not Jacob himself who is the deceitful one. The loss of his *fama* is undeserved.

Jacob reproaches his sons because they have made him lose this reputation as a peacemaker, and he has therefore lost the particular kind of honor for which he strives. This may be because he is simply afraid of the threat the majority population of the region poses for his small group. However, if this were so, the violent act of Simeon and Levi would have been dismissed when it became clear that the other groups around them did not seek revenge. At the end of his life Jacob revisits the issue. He refers to it on his deathbed in Gen 49:5–7, and excludes Simeon and Levi from the ranks of his heirs because of their earlier violent behavior:

> Simeon and Levi are brothers; weapons of violence are their swords. O my soul, come not into their council; O my spirit, be not joined to their company; for in their anger they slay men, and in their wantonness they hamstring oxen (Gen 49:5–6).

For this reason, Judah, the fourth in line among Jacob's sons, is declared his true heir. This means that the concept of honor represented by Simeon and Levi—a concept only too familiar in honor cultures—is disapproved of by the author of Genesis. Instead, the latter presents a concept for which wisdom and mediation between warring parties are central elements.

Honor in Pre-Islamic Poetry and in the Qur'an

In the Qur'an, as in the Bible, honor is not a separate topic discussed at great length. Yet the Qur'an was written for an audience that lived according to a strict honor code. Bichr Farès has studied the honor code among Arabs as it is reflected in pre-Islamic Arabic poetry.

Many terms are found in pre-Islamic poetry that may be connected to honor. The most important are derived from the verb *krm* (*karim, karama, akram*), and from the verbs *'azz* (*'aziz, 'azz, 'izza*) and *'ardh*. The first term, best translated as "generosity," reveals the deepseated link between honor and hospitality. An honorable man is generous to a fault, receives even his worst enemy in his tent, and protects the weak members of the tribe. He shares his possessions with his family and clan. Other important aspects here are one's pride of descent, nobility (*sharaf*) and truthfulness to one's word (*sidq*).

'Irdh is connected with the ability to defend one's honor against false accusations. Nowadays, *'irdh* is connected exclusively with the chastity of the women of the family. However, in olden times there were many more

slurs and gossipy tales that would threaten the honor of a pre-Islamic Bedouin. Finally, *'izza* refers to the virility and courage that make men fight against all odds. According to Farès, the center of honor is *'izza*, the fighting power with which the Bedouin defended the area where he lived and his tribe, taking blood revenge against all who killed a member of his tribe.

One can also distinguish among terms describing positive and negative honor in pre-Islamic poetry:

Honor or positive honor	*Karam*: hospitality, generosity	*Sharf*: nobility of descent	*Sidq*: being true to one's given word
Fama or negative honor	*'Irdh*: chastity of women	*'Izza*: ability to defend against all	

The above terms referring to honor remain in use in the Qur'an, but sometimes in totally different contexts, so that their meaning is in many ways transformed.

Krm was and remains a central qur'anic value. All believers should be *karim*, as God himself is (89:15). The Qur'an itself is often qualified as *karim* (56:77). However, the generosity of believers is no longer something by which they can distinguish themselves, their family, and clan from others. It has become an ethical quality in the individual and his or her relationship to God. Where different clans of old used to ridicule each other and boast of their own *karama*, the Qur'an enjoins them to be united in the faith, and the most *karim* (*akram*) is the person who shows the most *taqwa* (devotion, dedication) to Allah. *Karama* thus becomes a category of faith, not of boasting to one's neighbor (s. 49:13).

Although the chastity of women remains a core value, the Qur'an enjoins men also to be chaste (24:30), making chastity a moral category rather than an element of the honor code. In cases of murder or unintentional killing, the Qur'an does not altogether do away with the possibility of revenge, but it points the way toward alternatives such as payment of blood money and reconciliation (42:40).

Last but not least, the concept that, according to Farès, is the pièce the résistance of the pre-Islamic honor code, the concept of *'izza* (incidentally also the term Pashtun tribesmen use for honor), is criticized as something that stands in the way of religion (2:206). Instead, it is God himself who is the *Azz wa jall*: all power finally rests with God.

In other words, the traditional honor code of the Arabs before the advent of Islam is partly accepted, partly rejected, but on the whole transformed by the Qur'an.

Of course, the revolution in thinking this caused was slow in redirecting the Arab mentality. The first community of Muslims still lived according to the old perceptions of honor. There is, however, an incident in the biography of Muhammad that eloquently describes the change in direction that the Prophet indicated to his followers when it came to insults to their honor. The "Story of the Lie" (sometimes called the "Story of the Necklace") refers to events that took place around the year 628.

The Story of the Lie

For this well-known narrative, I follow the rendition of the Prophet Muhammad's biographer, Ibn Ishaq, in his *Sirat Rasul Allah* (*The Path of the Apostle of God*, Guillaume 1978, 493–99).[6]

This version of the story is told by Muhammad's wife Aisha. She tells that Mohammed once went on an expedition with his army. He took her with him. She traveled in a closed *howdah* on the back of a camel. The army spent the night at an oasis on the way back to Medina. When they broke up camp in the early morning, Aisha was looking for a necklace that she had lost, and was accidentally left behind. The men put her *howdah* on the back of the camel without noticing that she was not inside. When she returned to the camp with her necklace, everybody had gone. However, one soldier named Safwan was late as well. He found Aisha and offered her his camel. The two did not manage reach the army until much later. The sight of Aisha, accompanied by a young man, set the tongues of the soldiers wagging. It was not long before the whole of Medina was gossiping about what might have happened between the two. Aisha tells that she was unaware of the gossip until it had spread far and wide. One of the women with whom she goes out at night tells her about the rumors, and Aisha returns home, crying "until I thought that the weeping would burst my liver" (Guillaume 1978, 495). Her mother comforts her, saying: "Seldom is a beautiful woman married to a man

---

6. The text in the Sahihs runs parallel to the text of Ibn Ishaq; cf. Muhammad Muhsin Khan, Part III, 487 (805), 504–12 (829).

who loves her but her rival wives gossip about her and men do the same" (Guillaume 1978, 495).

The focus of the story then shifts to the reaction of Muhammad when he in turns hears about the rumor. He starts by affirming his trust in Aisha and her family. Subsequently, different voices join in, some rejecting and some affirming the truth of the gossip. Muhammad's next step is to ask the opinion of two of his closest allies, Ali and Usama Ibn Zayd. They differ in their advice. Usama defends Aisha against all slander. Ali, however, declares, "Women are plentiful and you can always exchange one for another."

They then call on Aisha's servant, who testifies on her behalf. Ali gets up and gives the servant girl a violent beating, saying, "Tell the Apostle the truth." The servant girl replies, "I know only good of her. The only fault I have to find with Aisha is that when I am kneading dough and tell her to watch it, she neglects it and falls asleep and the sheep comes and eats it" (Guillaume 1978, 496).

When Muhammad asks Aisha outright, in the presence of her parents, whether anything came to pass between her and Safwan, he says, "Aisha, you know what people say about you. Fear God and if you have done wrong as men say then repent towards God, for He accepts repentance from his slaves" (Guillaume 1978, 496).

Aisha waits for the reaction of her parents, who remain speechless. Then she denies everything in tears. In her words:

> "Never will I repent towards God of what you mention. By Allah, I know that if I were to confess what men say of me, God knowing that I am innocent of it, I should admit what did not happen; and if I denied what they said you would not believe me." Then I racked my brains for the name of Jacob and could not remember it, so I said, "I will say what the father of Joseph said: my duty is to show becoming patience and God's aid is to be asked against what you describe."

At that moment, the Prophet receives a revelation from God, reported in Sura 24:2–19. In this part of the Qur'an, first the punishment of adultery is set at one hundred lashes with a whip for both the offending man and the woman (24:2). The Qur'an then qualifies the punishment of people who falsely accuse "honorable" women (*muhsanat*) of adultery: they are to receive eighty lashes (24:4–5). This is followed by a procedure in undecided cases in which the husband has no witnesses, but is convinced of the truth of his accusations (24:6–10).⁷ The second half (24: 11–19) of the qur'anic passage is devoted to berating people who have spread and believed groundless rumors of adultery. The story of Aisha and this passage of the Qur'an are interwoven, as usually is the case with biographical data about Muhammad.

Here one again encounters a story in which a woman finds herself is in a situation that compromises her reputation for chastity. As we saw, in honor cultures this accusation alone is enough to put the honor of her male relatives at risk. Like Caesar's wife, in such a culture, a woman like Aisha must be above all reproach. Even the fact that people gossip about her is enough to destroy her honor and that of her male relatives. If a woman of the present-day Mastoi clan could not be in a field together with a twelve-year-old boy without compromising the honor of her family, how much less a woman who travels alone for a day in the company of a young man?

The lively story takes its time in representing the reactions of different people in Medina—some attacking Aisha, some defending her. With different clans taking different sides, it is clear that her behavior is a political issue. This may also explain the change in behavior of Muhammad, who first simply denies that anything could have taken place, but later in the story finds it necessary to consult his intimate counselors, Usama and Ali. The rumor cannot be stopped by his simple denial, so there must be some further verification. Ali's reaction is interesting. In many early stories about Muhammad's friends and family, he and his wife Fatima are presented as opposites of Aisha and her family. This may be due to later political developments in which Aisha took an active part in the movement to prevent Ali's *khalifate* (Vecchia Vaglieri 1970, 70). Aisha herself tells the story of the confrontation (as she does the rest of the story), and is clearly an important transmitter of traditions regarding Muhammad, especially where his family life is concerned.

In Aisha's story she, the woman who is accused and threatened, is depicted as a vociferous social actor. She resists what she perceives to be injustice against her by invoking the words of the patient patriarch Jacob (!), and is not surprised when God takes her side. This puts her on par with Mukhtaran Bibi.

---

7. In Num 5:11-31, a procedure for similar cases is sketched.

Another aspect of the story is that it shows the social impact of the stories spread about sexual transgressions, both for the women concerned and for whole communities. It is no wonder that there are diverse attempts at mediation, with different mediators giving different messages. In the end, however, the two people it concerns most, Muhammad and Aisha, must find a way out of the situation.

Muhammad does not accuse Aisha outright. He appeals to her sense of morality. For him this is closely linked to what people owe to God: if Aisha has done something wrong it is something primarily between herself and God. As her parents do not speak up for her, it is Aisha herself who must clarify the matter.

In the pre-Islamic Arabic code of honor, the case would have been clear enough. The chastity of a woman could be tainted by any doubts, and only the most extreme measures would have been enough to restore the honor of both Muhammad and Abu Bakr, Aisha's father. However, with the advent of Islam, other rules applied: although chastity (for men and women) remains important in the Qur'an, it is a matter of personal behavior and personal responsibility, and no longer a matter of collective honor. Had Aisha sinned, it would have been her own transgression she had to face, not the reputation of the men of her family. According to the Qur'an, one is personally responsible for one's behavior (Sura 6:164). One consequence of this moral transformation should be that the sexuality of a woman no longer belongs to her father or husband. Furthermore, Muhammad's reaction may be interpreted in the light of this transformation. He needs to hear from Aisha's own mouth—not from the mouth of her father—what had really happened. In an honor system, what really happened would not be as important as what other people thought had happened.

Muhammad's reaction is in accordance with the way honor operates in the Qur'an. It is still present, but as an individual possession, not a collective possession. Men and women are entitled to respect in recognition of the person they are. Unless their moral behavior contradicts the moral prescriptions of Islam, they have a right to their own *fama* (good name).

The Qur'an pays great attention to the immorality of gossip as a means of robbing honorable women of honor and of their good reputation. Gossip is presented as a crime almost comparable to adultery. Even although Muhammad may have had moments of grave doubt at the time, he still abided by his own principles. He did not assume that the gossip was true, but consulted Aisha on it. If the aim had been the restoration of his honor by vigorous, virile measures, he might have resorted to violence.

However, he showed another way out, a way in accordance with the new views of honor in the Qur'an.

Honor with Dignity

Honor cultures date back to pre-Christian and pre-Islamic times, and persist even after the advent of these religions. From the outset, the Bible and the Qur'an were both addressed to audiences that understood the laws of honor. Both books, however, place some question marks around the unspoken assumptions underlying the honor system.

In the two stories from the Jewish/Christian and the Islamic traditions, damage to the reputation of two women was the immediate cause behind the unfolding of the plot.

Dinah was raped, which constituted a clear loss of her and her family's honor. In the story as it is told in Gen 34, there are alternative solutions to compensate for this loss. Hamor tries to resolve the issue by proposing marriage and an extended peace between the clans involved. Dinah's brothers instead choose violent revenge. In exchange for the rape of their sister, who had been "treated like a whore," they kill the men of Shechem, and presumably rape their women. Their solution to the honor issue is lamented by Jacob, who later also disinherits them. The different options in the story indicate that there are different ways to deal with injured honor in honor cultures. Fredrik Barth shows that this is still the case among Swat Pathans. Violent revenge and mediation by saints are alternative courses of action for people to choose. Likewise, Frank Henderson Stewart reports that Bedouin men in the Sinai Desert often solve their honor conflicts with the help of special mediators, the Manshed (Stewart 1994, 81). Jacob was clearly in favor of such a solution, and for good reason. It would have enabled the peaceful settlement of Israel in the region.

In the story, honor stands behind the more important question of how to deal with Israel's Canaanite neighbors. Should they be treated as equals and allies, or as hostile rivals? The authors of the story indicate a preference for the first option. The relentless pursuit of revenge is the wrong reaction against violated honor. Jacobs's honor does not rest on his ability to seek vengeance, but on his capacity to build peace and to accept mediation. The way out chosen by his sons eventually leads him to declare them unfit to carry the inheritance of Israel on their shoulders.

Although the authors of the biblical story take a critical stance toward this aggressive "honor killing," the story remains deeply problematic for the twenty-first-century reader because of the invisibility of the victims. The woman, who is in name the heroine of the story, remains passive throughout the proceedings. The raped or killed women and men likewise remain in the background.

The story of Aisha is written in a different period. It belongs to a different genre, that of an exegetical tale. And yet it can best be understood against the background of an honor culture in which any slur against the reputation of a woman was disastrous to her family.

Despite having been raised in an honor culture, Muhammad reacts in a moderate and wise manner when his personal honor is at stake. His reaction is in accordance with the way the Qur'an transformed the existing honor culture—from a collective, impersonal view of honor, in which inequality is stressed (men as creatures of honor; women and slaves having no share in honor), to an individualized, ethical view of honor. Here we do hear the voice of the woman involved. She is the narrator, and through her eyes the reader sees the situation develop. Though devastated by the gossip around her, Aisha is presented as dignified and unafraid. She knows she is in the right. As with Mukhtaran Bibi, her sense of her own worth makes her willing to fight for her reputation.

In his book on moral revolutions, Kwame Anthony Appiah argues that honor is of enduring importance, even for modern Western individuals, because the sense of honor ties our morality to our psychological need for recognition (Appiah 2010, xiii). Our need to be respected by others for who we are is a powerful motivator for people to behave in a moral manner. People are motivated to act "honorably" because they do not merely want to be respected; they want to know that they are worthy of respect, that they live up to the expectations of others (Appiah 2010, 16). It is this type of honor, a sense of their own worth as human beings, that motivated Mukhtaram Bibi to go to court, and moved Aisha to be certain that God would take her side.

In this nonhierarchical sense, honor comes very close to dignity. Where each individual is seen as equal in honor and each individual is responsible for her or his personal honor, honor need not contradict dignity. Both Christians and Muslims can discover elements in their valued sacred texts that support such a view of honor.

References

Abou-Zeid, Ahmed. 1961. Honor and Shame among the Bedouins of Egypt. Pages 243–60 in *Honor and Shame: The Values of Mediterranean Society*. Edited by G. Peristiany. London: Weidenfeld & Nicholson.
Appiah, Kwame A. 2010. *The Honor Code: How Moral Revolutions Happen*. New York: Norton.
Barth, Fredrik. 2004. *Political Leadership Among Swat Pathans*. Oxford: Berg. First published 1959.
Bechtel, Lynn M. 1994. What If Dinah Is Not Raped? *JSOT* 62:19–36.
Berger, Peter. 1970. The Obsolescence of Honor. *EJS* 11:39–47.
Bourdieu, Pierre. 1961. The Sentiment of Honor in Kabyle Society. Pages 191–242 in *Honor and Shame: The Values of Mediterranean Society*. Edited by G. Peristiany. London: Weidenfeld & Nicholson.
Bowman, James. 2006. *Honor: A History*. New York: Encounter.
Douglas, Mary. 2004. *Jacob's Tears: The Priestly Work of Reconciliation*. Oxford: Oxford University Press.
Farès, Bichr. 1932. *L'Honneur chez les Arabes avant l'Islam*. Paris: Adrien-Maisonneuve.
Guillaume, Alfred. 1978. *The Life of Muhammad: A Translation of Ibn Ishaq's Sirat Rasul Allah*. Oxford: Oxford University Press.
Gunn, David. 1991: Tipping the Balance: Sternberg's Reader and the Rape of Dinah. *JBL* 110:193–211.
Holt, P. M., Anne K. Lambton, and Bernard Lewis, eds. 1970. *The Cambridge History of Islam*. Cambridge: Cambridge University Press.
Peristiany, John G. 1961. Introduction. Pages 9–18 in *Honor and Shame: The Values of Mediterranean Society*. Edited by John G. Peristiany. London: Weidenfeld & Nicholson.
Pitt-Rivers, Julian. 1961. Honor and Social Status. Pages 19–78 in *Honor and Shame: The Values of Mediterranean Society*. Edited by John G. Peristiany. London: Weidenfeld & Nicholson.
———. 1977. *The Fate of Shechem, or the Politics of Sex: Essays in the Anthropology of the Mediterranean*. Cambridge: Cambridge University Press.
Sahih Bukhari. 1984. Translated by Muhammad Muhsin Kahn. New Delhi: Kitab Bhavan.
Scholz, Susanne. 2001: What "Really" Happened to Dinah: A Feminist Analysis of Genesis 34. *Lectio Difficilior* 2:1–15.
Stewart, Frank H. 1994. *Honor*. Chicago: University of Chicago Press.

Winter, Timothy. 2012. Honour. In *Encyclopedia of the Qur'an*. Edited by Jane Dammen McAuliffe. Leiden: Brill.

A Response to Gé Speelman's "Honor in the Bible and Qur'an"

Yusef Waghid

Dear Gé,

Martha Nussbaum's restatement (2004, 43) of a nineteenth-century concept of honor as a dignified act associated with a person's refusal to flee the malicious acts of violence by an assailant who seeks to take her life or to do her enormous bodily harm reminds me of the bravery of Mukhtar Bibi as she was gang-raped by villagers belonging to the Mastoi clan in a rural Pakistani village in 2002. When you recount the demeaning, vile, and barbaric acts of some people as they enacted an archaic and parochial understanding of Islamic Shari'ah, I am reminded of the courage and dignity with which Mukhtar Bibi narrates the heinous and monstrous crime perpetrated against her by some dogmatic Pakistani patriarchs. In a way, this was the real act of honor: the plea by Bibi to be forgiven, as she was raped by some villagers in reprisal for a crime she did not commit—she merely went to the council of elders to ask forgiveness on behalf of her brother for the latter's act of indecency, that is, his presence in the company of a noble woman belonging to a different tribe. The futile plea of the battered Bibi for restoration, after unreasonable villagers raped her in the name of honor, once again highlights the pre-Islamic beliefs that women and wives are the property of men and that men are superior to women. As you correctly argue, Gé, such ill-conceived notions of "manly honor," equality, and justice are alien to a qur'anic conception of honor. In my response I shall examine your position on honor and offer some ways to rethink the notion of positive honor.

Gé, you remind us that the Qur'an (in Sura 49 verse 13) connects an understanding of honor to the attainment of "faith," more specifically God-consciousness (*taqwa*). Because this verse contextualizes the qur'anic notion of honor, I shall refer to it at length to corroborate your main thesis, which is an individualized ethical view of honor that is incommensurate with violence and retribution:

> O mankind! We have created you from a male and female, and made you into nations and tribes, that you may know one another. Verily the most honorable of you with Allah is that believer who is pious. Verily Allah is All-Knowing, All-Aware. (*Al-Hujjurat*, 13)

In this qur'anic injunction, honor is constituted by the achievement of individual piety. This suggests that honor is connected with an avoidance of humiliation, embarrassment, disgust, and rage. So how can villagers callously rape a woman in defense of restoring the so-called "honor" of a clan or tribe? If honor is a moral desire for the individual to be complete, completely in control, and respected by others, it cannot be linked to denigrating others or to causing them harm. Put differently, honor is an enabling condition that protects people from shame. Following Nussbaum (2004, 223), "a decent or honorable society [and person, as well, I would argue] … would treat its citizens with respect for their human dignity, rather than degrading or humiliating them." Such was the example of the Prophet Muhammad when he respectfully conferred with his spouse Aisha about her situation, rather than condemning or dishonoring her—a point you also raise. You describe such a form of honor as positive honor, namely when a person endeavors to curb her narcissistic rage, and acts to protect people from shame. What you evidently do not explore here is the importance of deliberation in countenancing shame as an individual endeavors to enact or live her honor. In the deliberation between Aisha and the Prophet Muhammad, both offered an account of their reasons, and in turn, their reasons were critically scrutinized. The acceptance of one another's reasons happened as a consequence of the one being persuaded by the other. This is an important moment in showing honor—that is, a person's reasons are taken into critical scrutiny by another, who in turn affords the other an opportunity to adjust or modify her reasons. If deliberation were not to be an important virtue in showing one's honor, how will one make others think about what has happened?

Second, why is honor or the showing thereof so important? The most obvious answer would be that honor protects a person from shame. Like you, Gé, I contend that honor should not (and, I would argue, *cannot*) be associated with violence and antagonism, as that in itself would bring about more violence and dishonor. I do not wish to remain silent on the use of violence for implementing a "negative" form of honor. For me, using violent measures such as discrimination, hate crimes, and indignation in the name of "restoring or defending honor" is in itself a form of criminality. A criminal uses emotions such as fear and anger to cause unimagined human suffering (Nussbaum 2004, 50–51). By implication, negative honor cannot be a form of honor at all, as showing honor is associated with the performance of non-criminal acts—those dignified, respectful, and virtuous measures that, as the Qur'an suggests, can enhance human coexistence (that is, "to know one another" or *li ta arafu*). So the qur'anic reason for showing honor is in order to cultivate an ethical community in which people can live their differences without shamefully violating the otherness of the other. In essence, the very idea of negative honor is obsolete. Honor can only exist if people's commonalities and differences are acknowledged, and if nonviolent, nondiscriminatory ways are found to engender human coexistence.

Although you use salient examples in elucidating "honor with dignity" (and I agree with you), Gé, you do not take us far enough in establishing conditions under which honor can be aspired to. I want to take up this difficult task in the latter part of my response. You accentuate respect and faith as necessary conditions for honor. I concur. However, respect and faith (piety) are not sufficient conditions to further elucidate the notion of positive honor, or honor with dignity. I want to suggest that a positive ethics of care can help us cultivate honor among people in communities. Caring requires a person to do three things: to forgive the unpardonable or unforgivable; to protect the helpless (like Bibi); and to do things that might go against one's grain. Derrida (1997, 33) argues for a view of forgiveness that builds on the premise "that forgiveness must announce itself as impossibility itself ... (and that) it can only be possible in doing the impossible." For Derrida, "doing the impossible" implies forgiving the "unforgivable." In his words, "forgiveness forgives only the unforgivable"—that is, atrocious and monstrous crimes against humanity that might not be conceived as possible to forgive (Derrida 1997, 32). Derrida (1997, 44) explicates forgiveness as "a gracious gift without exchange and without condition." Among crimes against humanity, Derrida (1997, 52) includes genocide, torture, and terrorism. This notion of forgiving the "unforgivable" is spawned by the view that forgiveness is an act without finality—that is, the guilty one who perpetrated the evil is considered capable of repeating the crime without repentance or promise that he or she will be transformed.

Forgiving the "unforgivable" takes into consideration that the crime might be repeated. This makes forgiveness an act (of madness) of the impossible (Derrida 1997, 45). Now, a concept of forgiveness that makes possible the act of forgiving the "unforgivable" makes sense, because if the villagers are not going to venture into forgiving what, according to them, is "unforgivable" (such as the dishonoring of their women), and vice versa, these two different clans of the same community might not begin to connect with each other. Then the process of trying to induce transformation in rural Pakistani society might not even begin to take place. Such a Derridian view of forgiveness is grounded in an understanding that "nothing is impardonable [sic]" (Derrida 1997, 47) and that "grand beginnings" are often celebrated and redirected through amnesia of the most atrocious happenings—even what some would argue to be dishonorable acts. A case in point is South Africa's democracy, which grew out of forgiving "unforgivable" racial bigots who committed heinous crimes against those who opposed the racist state.

In relation to protecting the helpless, I once again draw on Derrida (1997, 20), who argues that every person has a right to universal hospitality without limits. Derrida limits this right to innocent and helpless people (perhaps those not guilty of a major crime) who seek refuge or asylum in another country and who want to escape "bloody vengeance," just as Mukhtar Bibi did. Surely innocent women who are subjected to torture, killing, and rape have the right to be protected. Following Derrida, members of a community cannot be victimized, and their protection is possible, on the grounds that every person is endowed with the status of "common possession of the earth" (Derrida 1997, 20).

Finally, Gé, doing something improbable or going against the grain can be linked to the fact that we are interconnected with others and sometimes have to do things that may strengthen our relations. Cavell's remark that "we are alone, and we are never alone," is a clear indication that one belongs to a particular group (being alone with others, that is, "we") and that, by virtue of being human, one bears an internal relation to all other human beings—especially those who do not belong to the same group or clan, and even those whom we might revile. This internal relation with my fellow citizens does not ignore my answerability to and responsibility for what happens to them, despite our not belonging to the same group. As a member of a particular cultural group in society, I cannot simply impose my views (whether religious or political) on others, for that in itself would deny that there are others in different positions, with different cultural orientations than mine. Doing so would be doing an injustice to the others. But, being answerable to and responsible for what happens to them means that their views are acknowledged, even though I might not be in agreement with them. Rather, one conceives the other from the other's point of view, with which one has to engage afresh (Cavell 1979, 441).

In sum, I have thoroughly enjoyed reading your essay, Gé, and I merely offer a positive ethics of care in support of your plausible argument in defense of honor as dignity.

Regards,
Yusef

References

Cavell, Stanley. 1979. *The Claim of Reason: Wittgenstein, Skepticism, Morality, and Tragedy.* Oxford: Clarendon.
Derrida, Jacques. 1997. *On Cosmopolitanism and Forgiveness.* London: Routledge.
Nussbaum, Martha. 2004. *Hiding from Humanity: Disgust, Shame, and the Law.* Princeton: Princeton University Press.

Fragile Dignity: Family, Honor, Scripture
(On the Essays of Ciska Stark, D. Xolile Simon and Lee-Ann J. Simon, and Gé Speelman)

Monica Jyotsna Melanchthon

I come from a culture that is based on what Eisler (1987) identifies as the *dominator model*, in which difference is "equated with inferiority or superiority ... the ranking of one half of humanity over the other," a system of hierarchy (caste) based on force or the implied threat of force. Difference—male/female, young/old, upper caste/lower caste, rich/poor, fair/dark—are signifiers of superiority and inferiority. As in other dominator cultures, difference is construed as an indication that one must be right, good, or superior, and the other wrong, bad, or inferior, so that those who find themselves in positions of influence and choice, and are attributed power (according to race, caste, class, gender, color, sexual orientation), often use these positions to exploit, ignore, diminish, and control others. Policies, systems, and activities imposed to control others—to deprive them of choice and quality of life—all contribute to the overall fragility and vulnerability of an individual or a community. Frequent doses of violent humiliation and subjugation are constant reminders of their subordinate position in the social order. The result is often a life of endless poverty, stigmatized identity, and denial of rights, which destroys holistic life—God's *shalom* (access to daily nourishment; good health; freedom from enemy menace; a life of dignity in family and community; see Prov 3:16).

These assumptions find expression in families and subcultures; they influence and determine what a man or woman can do and get away with. The Indian culture, lauded for its family values, promotes collectivism and the sacrifice of individualism. Importance is attached to interdependence and the need to preserve harmonious family relationships. This has led to the development of structures like extended family and kinship family groupings within the same household. Life-cycle transitions and discontinuities are managed in the context of rules with regard to authority, continuity, and interdependence. These differ from those of Western families. Hierarchical relationships exist between sexes and between generations. Where kinship systems are highly structured, kinship terms delineate not only an individual's place in the family but also his or her duties and obligations. Concepts of "honor" and "shame" provide coherence, cohesion, and unity to a family and are rigidly maintained.

However, it is also crucial to acknowledge that strong religious underpinnings and scriptural sanction underlie traditions and rules governing family life and sources of family and communal authority. Most interpreters of scripture (both Hindu and Christian) circumscribe and reinforce these traditional and cultural roles of individuals and communities. There is honor, respect, and dignity in "belonging." It is one's *dharma* or "duty" to fit in, to put the interests of the family above one's own, and to avoid any shameful or dishonorable acts that are contrary to the interests of family and caste and their status in society. *Dharma*, the Eternal Way, the totality of social, ethical, and spiritual harmony, orchestrates the whole. Dharma at the same time constitutes the eternal law of the universe as well as the virtuous path of each individual.

Foucault (1980) has pointed out that a dominant discourse functions in such a way as to silence the voices and perceptions of the subjugated narrative. This means that even those of goodwill may not think that particular practices or taken-for-granted behaviors are unjust or exceptionable, unless their system of meaning is disturbed sufficiently by new input to enable them to think and see differently. New socio-economic opportunities, educational advancements, and apparent modernization in India are providing new input that has led to a fractured response to these cultural assumptions, both by upwardly mobile groups and by subjugated groups. Some show defiance. Yet others lead in upholding gender, caste, and community norms and practices. Therefore, a higher economic, educational, or social status has no automatic linkage with enlightened or democratic practices. Both these responses result in fracturing group solidarities and dignities, as well as to hostilities, one feeding the other.

This context has lent to my interest in and appreciation of the reflections offered by the essays of Speelman (responded to by Waghid); Xolile and Lee-Ann Simon (responded to by Koffemann); and Stark (responded to by Nell). All three essays make it clear that "dignity" is fragile, and is not an object to be retrieved, much less a coherent one; neither is it an essential cultural emblem. What has been encouraging and enlightening for me is that in these essays discussions of "dignity" have been laid out and discussed within the *materiality* of sites, rather than with abstract positions. Challenging and thought-provoking, these essays have brought to mind many parallels from the Indian experience, and raised some new questions as well.

The reflections of Speelman and Waghid are particularly appealing because of the juxtaposition of thoughts and texts from diverse religions and cultures, bringing new insights to our understanding of the biblical text and new appreciation for other religious texts and traditions. Gender is a key component in these essays. The crimes committed against Mukhtaran Bibi and Dinah and are akin to the many instances of so-called "honor driven violence" or "honor killing" in India. Such crimes are situated on a continuum of acts of violence that use thoughts and deeds (physical, psychological, and philosophical) to violate, damage, corrupt, manipulate, defile, and rob an individual of life, autonomy, freedom, dignity, bodily integrity, and of true personhood (Kirk-Duggan 2003, 3). It seems that the definition of honor is not straightforward. It can best be defined by way of illustration or paradigmatic examples. In the illustrations and texts used, it is a woman's assigned sexual and familial role as dictated by traditional family, tribe, and caste ideology that defines honor. Hence, any suspicion of illegitimate relationships, rape, or meeting with a person considered an "outsider" would constitute an infringement of family honor. Whether preserved or lost, honor is situated in the bodies of women. Genesis 34 is about family and tribal honor, and the Qur'anic text is about conjugal honor. In both cases, the honor in question (read "male honor" that allows for restriction of women's freedom, and may endorse or require violence against women) is embodied by women. They are the custodians of this honor, and they are bound to safeguard it for the sake of men under threat of punishment, even death. The question for me is how can one neutralize these harmful notions of honor? Welchman and Hossain refer to the decision of Pakistani activists to name the killers and perpetrators of honor crimes against women as "dishonorable," thereby destabilizing the prevailing understandings of honor. They have also considered reformulating it with a notion of honor (as respect, tolerance, inclusivity, and reverence) attributed to women (2006, 7).

How is "honor" understood by women? What constitutes "honor" for them? It has been more or less taken for granted that men and women share common understandings of what constitutes honor, especially since many women also participate in the instigation and perpetuation of honor crimes. If given an opportunity, would women define it differently? What might the repercussions be? While violence is used by the brothers in Gen 34 to reclaim honor, it is avoided in the Qur'anic text through mediation and dialogue. These seem to be suggestions aimed at men. How do women respond to these strategies, violent or otherwise, for retrieval of honor?

Families strive to preserve their group values, identity, and coherence while participating in the challenges and opportunities offered by the broader society. But it is the women who to a large extent are still the carriers of tradition, and who are expected to take on these group-determined norms and to pass them on to their children. Xolile Simon and Lee-Ann Simon's article brings to the fore the fact that facing some of the hurtful, destructive, and sometimes violent or fatal actions that constitute part of the war of between the sexes, cultures, castes, tribes, and communities may spill over into our pleasant, cooperative, or loving relationships with partners, parents, and siblings within the family. Again, women seem to be more affected by this, since they are forced to make choices between the family one is born into and that of one's partner. Like the unnamed woman of Timnah in Judg 14 and 15, many women must constantly negotiate their several identities and loyalties between these two families in the light of larger contextual social, economic, political, and religious realities. What makes it rather agonizing is that their options and choices are limited or are often beyond their control, particularly in contexts where women have had little say in the choice of marriage partners.

Samson's attraction to the woman of Timnah was based on what he saw. He was pleased with her after conversing with her. His parents' hesitant response, reminding him that she was a Philistine, could not deter him from his decision to marry her. When a man desires a woman, neither religion, nor race, nor caste is considered a hindrance. This is reminiscent of the many *dalit* women who are raped and used sexually by upper-caste men despite rules of untouchability. All norms and codes regarding purity and impurity, clean and unclean, are disregarded. Women are susceptible and vulnerable to being used once they have been targeted by the male gaze. Even a woman who behaves with sexual propriety may occasion dishonor by provoking the volatile desire of men. The woman in the Judges narrative seems to have become a pawn in a game between two contending parties—the Israelites and the Philistines! The text also reinforces the notion that foreign women were bad influences and threats to the Israelite community and its established hierarchical order.

However, YHWH seemed happy for other reasons, "for he was seeking a pretext to act against the Philistines. At that time the Philistines had dominion over Israel" (Judg 14:4). Were Samson and the woman of Timnah instruments in the hand of God? It is significant that YHWH seems to be a silent spectator, allowing matters to run their course. Only later in the narrative are we informed that YHWH intervened to assist Samson. However, there was no one to save the woman of Timnah. One more woman is used by males who, in the end, do not care about her, only about what she might represent for them in their power games. The focus in the essays by both the Simons and Koffeman are on the household (dis)loyalties of women. What about the (dis)loyalties of men—in this case, Samson? Why is a man honored for being loyal to his clan, and not a woman, who is loyal to hers? Surely the woman of Timnah was aware of the hostility between the two peoples. She had to use a ruse in order to get the answer to the riddle out of Samson. Would she have done so were she not coerced by her own people? Could she have told Samson the truth, namely that she was under pressure to find the answer to the riddle? Would Samson have understood her plight? If there had been respect, honesty, and trust between the two, could they have together negotiated a peaceable solution?

But, back to God: Was God happy with the manner in which things were progressing? I am challenged by Koffeman's question regarding developing a theological response to violence from this narrative, and wonder whether it is more likely that God was being used by the narrator. God is often referred to as justification for violence, and is also seen as the solution to all human problems, as the *Deux ex machina*, so that we tend to forget that God comes to us in the guise of disturbing questions. God is often silent when we are looking for solutions. "She speaks when we are silent and allow ourselves to be challenged and taught by realities around us" (Wilfred 2008, xii). God speaks through the disturbing and unsettling questions raised by the text. "The presence of God is associated with disquiet regarding the prevailing situation" (xii).

The resistance by oppressed groups, including women, takes place on several levels of response. The subjectivities of women as victims of violence and agents of resistance are constituted through the negotiation of situations that confront them. Violence, domestic or otherwise, frequently becomes the initiating moment of knowledge. What happens is that a "tenuous individualism shapes the female subject's resistance"

(Sunder Rajan 1993, 71). This expression of self comes from within oneself, and there is a transition from "passivity to action, from self as static to self as becoming, from silence to a protesting inner voice and infallible gut" (Belenky 1986, 54). Women's growing reliance on their intuitive processes is an important adaptive move in the service of self-protection, self-assertion, and self-definition. Women become their own authorities. I would like to explore this aspect of a woman's "becoming" in the story of the woman of Timnah.

The Bible witnesses to a God who has identified Godself with those who suffer. Both the essays referred to above and the responses to them either directly or indirectly attest to this. The witness of Christian preaching to this truth and a corresponding praxis can make the present church a community of transformation and hope. But such solidarity is only possible when the church overcomes its own sectarianism and acknowledges the humanity and dignity of all people by working toward breaking down all barriers and divisions between the pure and the impure, between the clean and the "untouchable," between male and female, both inside and outside the church. True to the Asian holistic vision of reality, this solidarity should also extend to all forms of life and to nature in its entirety. There is no hope for humanity without hope for the whole of creation, for the cosmos. Unfortunately, the church has sometimes upheld oppressive cultural values that impinge on the autonomy, freedom, and dignity of individuals instead of challenging them.

Preaching plays a significant role in creating the church and in sending it out into the world to *be* church, the symbol of hope as it accompanies people in their struggles toward dignity and humanity within and outside of the family—also in recognition of and in participation in the saving activity of God and the establishment of God's promised reign. Stark reflects on the fact that within the PCN, "belonging" and "believing" are emphasized without much effort toward addressing the various social and ethical issues confronting the society of which it forms a part. Scripture is used only by way of analogy. The situation of preaching in the PCN is perhaps similar to that in other churches. In India, for example, the text is often interpreted allegorically, and attempts are made to enable the hearer to see his or her own experience as a contemporized form of biblical experience. It has tended to locate the problems of people in the people themselves, thereby passing over the various institutions that promote oppression and damage the autonomy, freedom, and dignity of individuals and communities. This emphasis has neglected and sometimes even excluded the social realm and, therefore, any idea of social salvation. It has impacted the manner in which the church views economics, politics, culture, social relationships, and international affairs.

The sermon is one means by which one may challenge society and the systems within it in light of the Word of God, and provide people with the impetus to commit their lives to the transformation of self and the world, to work along with God in ushering in and bringing to fruition God's reign. Perhaps most preachers share the value orientations of their church members, and hence do not feel compelled to address those missing links that have been identified by Stark. The congregation's determination to be served overrides the gospel's commitment to serve, and the result is a church that is more likely to reflect the nature of secular society and its leniency toward the powers than to be "a community of mission and liberating service in solidarity with those who are at the margins" (Waltmann 1992, 67).

The effectiveness of the ministry of pastors, their value orientations and the chief roles they assume in their work are in many ways tied to their self-understanding—who they are and what they are called to as they carry out their work. Our work as ministers is guided and influenced by the ways we picture ourselves and our roles, and these guiding images prompt us to emphasize certain things instead of others in our work and ministry. We may speak and act in the ways demanded by those images (pastor, preacher, activist or shepherd, guide, evangelist, prophet, facilitator, to name a few). Enmeshed in these organizing metaphors of ministry are convictions and opinions about the nature of ministry, the authority of scripture and the mission of the church; the nature of the world; the human condition and society; and our conceptions of what constitutes the gospel. The same is perhaps true in a more particular sense about preaching. The act and task of preaching is embedded in a larger framework of ministerial self-understanding, and making time to prepare a sermon and to preach it effectively is also ministry. As I was taught in seminary, the time required for the study of scripture is not spent apart from ministry; it is not even done in preparation for ministry. It is ministry! As such it needs to be protected and cherished.

In my estimation, all three essays have offered possibilities and opportunities to cast a critical eye toward my own culture and to see and speak out against harmful gendered and discriminatory practices and relations within my context. Together they make possible a common analysis. They put forth a common agenda for action, and produce a shared framework for understanding and for collective action to address issues related to human dignity and honor-driven violence against both men and women in church and society.

These essays have reminded us of the fact that human dignity is not an abstract concept, but rather needs to be understood more concretely as the manifestation of love, equality, respect, and freedom in human relationships, between male and female. Dignity, a full place among all living things, and full communion with God are guaranteed to all human beings by virtue of two attributes, namely the breath of life and the image of God inherent in every human being. In the call to co-creatorship lies the gracious act of God as well as the definitive prophecy about the nature and vocation of human beings (David 1994, 49). It confers on all people a worth or dignity that no person or system—whether political, economic, or social—can take away. This calling extends to all of humanity. This generous conferring of dignity and calling has its origin and basis in the free and unmerited love of God, which is at the root of all creative activity (Macquarrie 1972, 49).

References

Altmann, Walter. 1992. *Luther and Liberation: A Latin American Perspective*. Translated by Mary M. Solberg. Minneapolis: Fortress.

Belenky, Mary Field, Blythe Mcvicker Clinchy, Nancy Rule Goldberger, and Jill Mattuck Tarule. 1986. *Women's Ways of Knowing: The Development of Self, Voice, and Mind*. New York: Basic Books.

David, Kenith A. 1994. *Sacrament and Struggle: Signs and Instruments of Grace from the Downtrodden*. WCC Mission Series. Geneva: World Council of Churches.

Eisler, Raine. 1987. *The Chalice and the Blade: Our History, Our Future*. San Francisco: Harper & Row.

Foucault, Michel. 1980. *Power/Knowledge: Selected Interviews and Other Writings*. Edited by C. Gordon. New York: Harvester Wheatsheaf.

Kirk-Duggan, Cheryl A. 2003. "Introduction." Pages 1–7 in *Pregnant Passion: Gender, Sex and Violence in the Bible*. Edited by Cheryl A. Kirk-Duggan. Atlanta: Society of Biblical Literature.

Macquarrie, John. 1972. *The Faith of the People of God*. London: SCM.

Sunder Rajan, Rajeshwari. 1993. *Real and Imagined Women: Gender, Culture, and Postcolonialism*. London: Routledge.

Welchman, Lynn, and Sara Hossain. 2006. Introduction: "Honour," Rights and Wrongs. Pages 1–20 in *Honour: Crimes, Paradigms, and Violence against Women*. Edited by Lynn Welchman and Sara Hossain. New Delhi: Zubaan.

Wilfred, Felix. 2008. *Margins: Site of Asian Theologies*. New Delhi: ISPCK.

Reflections on Reflections: Rights, In/Dignity, In/Equality, Faith—The Bible as Universal Medicine?

Athalya Brenner

Disclaimer

This collection is a many-layered conversation on conversations. As the introduction states, it originated in a series of research meetings. The introduction provides pointers to the context and to the main issues discussed; every essay has a response attached to it; groups of essays have their own responses; and I have been asked to reflect on the collection as a whole. In my view the volume's editors as well as its contributors should be commended for this manner of presenting their deliberations. It is the closest possible structure to the actual performance of research events, imitating spoken discourse with comments and annotations, thus truly making the volume into a conversational event. As I see it, my task is to provide the metareflection, a reflection on the whole rather than on the detail. In what follows I will, therefore, comment on the whole volume, on how it serves the objectives it sets out to achieve, and on how it fits together as a cohesive and meaningful collection of conversations, referring to individual essays and responses only in passing.

Approaching my reviewing of the volume as a whole, I started by composing a list of tags of leading words. In other words, I made a list of terms that, in my personal understanding, relate strongly to the issues discussed. I then proceeded by grouping those terms into fields, or semantic zones. After this, I scanned the texts with the help of the computer's PDF search function. The next stage was compiling the statistics relating to specific terms and groups of terms. With the results of this survey—an undeniable influence of the newly-acquired reading habits of the FB age—I felt ready to proceed. For technical reasons, I did not include the sectional responses (by Anderson, Mitchell, Melanchthon, and Tamez) in my survey, although I will refer to them at the end of this review.

THE VOLUME'S TITLE: WHAT IT INCLUDES AND WHAT IT OMITS

The title of this volume, of this conversation, is *Fragile Dignity: Intertextual Conversations on Scriptures, Family, and Violence*. As is to be expected from the title, and as becomes immediately clear from the introduction and the list of contributors, the conversations may be intertextual and also interdisciplinary—the latter in the narrower sense—but they all have a dominant common feature: they are theological conversations, carried out within the framework of academic theological research. Indeed, the terms theology and theological (in various combinations) appear 101 and 165 times respectively in this collection of essays (admittedly, at times in names of institutions, units, and so on). Theology is thus the order of the day, overriding differences in discipline, mostly also differences between North and South.

Furthermore, this academic theological framework is a Christian framework of institutional and individual partners. At the outset this does not necessarily imply that the conversations will be focused on Christian themes related to the issues discussed. However, my survey finds Christian and Christianity appearing 181 times, as against Islam and Muslim (thirty-four times), and Jewish and Judaism (sixteen times). This means that the important topics are pondered from Christian viewpoints. Here are some examples: in Stark and Nell this is the topic. There is an essay by Speelman (with a response by Waghid) about Islam, to be sure, but nothing specific about Judaism beyond using the Hebrew bible/Old Testament for Christian Theology (Bosman and Spronk, Claassens and Erbele-Küster). An exception worth noting is Erbele-Küster on ART, with un-Christianized references to the Hebrew bible; but Van der Walt, who does a good job of presenting ART from a sub-Saharan geographical and class viewpoint, brings her presentation back to the fold by ending with the assurance that faith communities assist, or may or should assist, those in need of ART.

And here, then, is the next point: theology, Christian or otherwise, can be emic or etic. In this conversation it is predominantly emic. In plain words: this is not simply a theological conversation, imposing its assumptions on all disciplines; ultimately it is a faith conversation, a conversation about how a certain faith community, Christian and more specifically of a Protestant hue—be it Northern or Southern, Western, African, or Latino, or whatever—deals or should deal with the topics raised. (De Lange is a good example: beginning with philosophy, ending with Brand's response and with faith). "Faith, faithful" and combinations thereof, including expressions like "faith communities," appear seventy-nine times in the book.

Please do not misunderstand me. There is much to be gained and learned from a collection, such as this one, that is academic, scholarly, Christian, theological, and confessional. Who am I to deny that? However, these contexts produce a certain kind of reflection: a reflection that focuses on God and the Divine as much as it focuses on humans, that insists time and again on the inherent dignity of humans because of their similarity to God, in which the United Nations and its so pertinent Universal Declaration of Human Rights (UDHR, 1948) is mentioned only three times each as a source of human dignity (by Plaatjies van Huffel—*Chapeau, madam!*), whereas the *imago Dei*, "image of God," and similar concepts are referred to more than one hundred thirty times as a source and resource of human dignity. Clearly, then, this conversation is relevant, but its relevance is not universal. By that I mean that it is not as relevant to scholars like me—Jewish and secular, albeit Westernized; or Jewish confessional; or Muslims—who are outsiders to the conversation's umbrella community. In spite of geographical, economic, and other differences, it is relevant for one community. Finally, climactically, theology here metamorphoses into faith. This is undoubtedly a virtue for the writers and their community; it is less so for outsiders who share some identity markers with the book's contributors—scholarship, interests, education, to name a few—but not others.

Images of Human Dignity as Reflections of Biblical Divine Images?

As De Lange so ably demonstrates, as do others, human dignity is a slippery concept. It is at most a premodern if not a totally modern concept, a product of the Enlightenment and its historical unfolding in its definitions and redefinitions. It is totally bound up with the understanding of "human rights" as a given. Compare the Preamble to the UDHR:

> Whereas recognition of the inherent dignity and of the equal and inalienable rights of all members of the human family is the foundation of freedom, justice and peace in the world,
> Whereas disregard and contempt for human rights have resulted in barbarous acts which have outraged the conscience of mankind, and the advent of a world in which human beings shall enjoy freedom of speech

and belief and freedom from fear and want has been proclaimed as the highest aspiration of the common people,

Whereas it is essential, if man is not to be compelled to have recourse, as a last resort, to rebellion against tyranny and oppression, that human rights should be protected by the rule of law,

Whereas it is essential to promote the development of friendly relations between nations,

Whereas the peoples of the United Nations have in the Charter reaffirmed their faith in fundamental human rights, in the dignity and worth of the human person and in the equal rights of men and women and have determined to promote social progress and better standards of life in larger freedom,

Whereas Member States have pledged themselves to achieve, in cooperation with the United Nations, the promotion of universal respect for and observance of human rights and fundamental freedoms,

Whereas a common understanding of these rights and freedoms is of the greatest importance for the full realization of *this pledge,*

Now, Therefore THE GENERAL ASSEMBLY *proclaims* THIS UNIVERSAL DECLARATION OF HUMAN RIGHTS *as a common standard of achievement for all peoples and all nations, to* the end that every individual and every organ of society, keeping this Declaration constantly in mind, shall strive by teaching and education to promote respect for these rights and freedoms and by progressive measures, national and international, to secure their universal and effective recognition and observance, both among the peoples of Member States themselves and among the peoples of territories under their jurisdiction. (http://www.un.org/en/documents/udhr/, emphasis original)

The terms "dignity," "rights," "equality," "human," and "family" are almost interchangeable in the Declaration. There is no mention of divine or biblical origins regarding the above statement or regarding the following, taken from the same official U.N. source, and from which I quote the first four articles:

Article 1:
• All human beings are born free and equal in dignity and rights. They are endowed with reason and conscience and should act towards one another in a spirit of brotherhood.

Article 2:
• Everyone is entitled to all the rights and freedoms set forth in this Declaration, without distinction of any kind, such as race, colour, sex,

language, religion, political or other opinion, national or social origin, property, birth or other status. Furthermore, no distinction shall be made on the basis of the political, jurisdictional or international status of the country or territory to which a person belongs, whether it be independent, trust, non-self-governing or under any other limitation of sovereignty.

Article 3:
- Everyone has the right to life, liberty and security of person.

Article 4:
- No one shall be held in slavery or servitude; slavery and the slave trade shall be prohibited in all their forms.

It would immediately seem apparent that the bible (Hebrew bible/Old Testament and New Testament) can hardly be a source for reflection on human rights, equality, or dignity, in light of the Declaration. To begin with, slavery in the bible is a socio-economic fact: regulated benevolently at times, but accepted nevertheless. Furthermore, physical illness and deformity are causes for ritual rejection, certainly in the Hebrew bible and especially for males and their sex organs (Lev 21:20, Isa 53:3); kings and priests have to be physically wholesome in order to be adequate for their tasks. Unseemly skin disease is a reason for—at least temporary—forced isolation (Lev 13-14; Num 12). Homosexuality is problematic, at least under the Law (Lev 18:22 and 20:13) and possibly in the New Testament as well (Rom 1:26, Matt 8 and Luke 7; Acts 8). On women and children's inferior positions in relation to alpha males much can be said. Equality? Gender positions are so unequal that any other claim is, in both Testaments, at best utopian. And this is even before corporeal punishment, *lex talionis*, or, for instance, capital punishment for fornication by married persons (imagine that in present-day Western societies, although it is still found in some Muslim societies) are considered. All these are presumably regulated by the God of the scriptures and that God's missionaries—although, tellingly, capital punishment is never mentioned in this volume. At our own peril we ignore those nonhumanistic signs in favor of more positive humanistic biblical notions, or gloss over the former as being bound to specific times and places.

In this collection, homosexuality as a source of deficient human dignity is not mentioned; human rights are named twenty-four times, while "human dignity" is mentioned two hundred times ("dignity" alone 460 times); illness, disability, and health count for about forty references. Add to this about twenty references to HIV—surely this sub-Saharan pandemic deserves more serious treatment in this regard? Slaves and slavery are mentioned twenty-five times, but inequality and equality fare much better (more than sixty). I also did not find much written concern for basic tenets of human subsistence, such as food and shelter, as prerequisites for a dignified human existence (but see later my short response to Tamez's response). Are these taken for granted? They should not, certainly not in the global South. Tellingly, in the context of this collection, "household" appears 170 times, but "house" and "houses" only seven times.

On the other hand, there definitely are passages in the Hebrew bible that promote the idea of humans as divine-like. For the moment I am thinking less of Gen 1:26–27 and the end of Gen 3, which are very problematic (in Judaism at least), and more of a passage like Ps 8:6, "that You have made him little less than divine, and adorned him with glory and majesty" (JPS).

Bosman emphasizes that different concepts of *imago Dei* in the scriptures are complex and multivalent, even contradictory. This seems reasonable at first glance. However, at second glance, one wonders: Where does the weight of this image lie? In Christianity, I dare speculate, a notion of similarity is advisable, even necessary. In Judaism, a sense of similarity between the human and the Divine is much less pronounced. What is emphasized is a sense of *reciprocity*, of give-and-take, of cooperation. Hence, human dignity would—even in the confessional sense—spring forth less from a reflected human image of an abstracted divine image, than from the cooperation between the two spheres. Divine glory is not necessarily human dignity in the Hebrew bible.

Finally, in this section and only in passing: there is an insistence in this volume—as in so many others, surely—that the *imago Dei* of the Hebrew bible and/or its historically primary users, the developing ancient Judaisms, is abstracted into the spiritual. References to God's body, body parts, speech organs, other organs, emotions, eroticism and human-like actions such as walking and breathing are immediately transformed and given in metalanguage status or dubbed "metaphorical," with the well-known and well-meaning explanation offered that human language cannot aspire to adequately describe the Divine and that human understanding can neither comprehend nor visualize him (sic). In this regard we may do well to remember that the Hebrew bible does not claim that God has no body, not directly nor comprehensively. What it does claim, as polemics against contemporaneous practices, is that God's body should receive no plastic representation. God is gendered as male (a pity for us feminists!) and mostly behaves as a father—in Judaism as well as in Christianity. The so-called pornoprophetic "marriage metaphor" (for instance, in Hosea, Ezekiel, and Jeremiah), in which God is the husband of the wayward (female) community, assumes gender and sex. This necessitates bodies. Is it a metaphor, an image, a figure of speech only? As we know from modern psycholinguistic theory, there no such thing as "just a metaphor." Vestiges of God's body—be they gendered, eroticized, or whatever—obstinately remain in mainstream orthodox Christianity, inasmuch as they form the base for much Jewish and Christian mysticism. The Hebrew bible's choice to reject esthetically-crippled individuals from officiating and participating in the cult may be related to at least an unconscious assumption that the human body reflects that of the Divine. It is indeed complicated, this religious dialogics veering between the human and the Divine, the concrete and the abstract. No sustained resolution seems possible (on this complexity see Bosman again).

I feel that there is a lesson here. The lesson is to begin with the body. Respect and honor are due to the human body and its needs first, even within the *imago Dei* paradigm. This is where faith concerns and the UDHR can intersect, primarily, on a very concrete level of dignity and respect, that of human subsistence a step or more above survival.

To summarize what has been said thus far: The wish to find resources, support, and empowerment for human rights and dignity in the scriptures is understandable. Nonetheless, it would be fair to state that social equality, care for the disabled and the socially weak (beyond tolerating the Other in our midst, and the poor, and the Other without, all the time keeping them as such), and modern notions of honor (mentioned over 270 times in this collection) as a wished-for characteristic of life are sadly infrequent as life-guiding principles in the Judeo-Christian scriptures; their opposites are much in evidence. This collection of essays deals with ethics, bioethics, morality, God/the Divine (almost 550 times in various combinations) and the human (more than eight hundred times). It does so mostly on a theological, Christian, confessional, abstract and abstracted plane. It enlists for its purpose, the all-important purpose of buttressing the theoretical base of human dignity/rights/equality, the intensely and deeply optimistic idea of human similarity to God, hence human inherent worth. This does not answer the question of human equality fully; it does, however, supply a common theo-philosophical ground for its proponents to proceed. But from here to claim that human rights and dignity are *in the bible* is a considerable and unjustified leap of faith. Let me once again make my position clear. Using the bible to bulwark contemporaneous notions for compassionate purposes and in a responsible fashion as it is attempted here is a praiseworthy project. The bible belongs to all of us. It should be used; it is used (and abused, of course). However, to claim that this or the other is so because it is *in* the bible is not always credible. If you wish to bolster human dignity by claiming it is divinely ordained, by all means do so; in your own name, pointing out the limitations of your approaches to faith—as is almost, but not quite, done here.

Indignity and Inequality: Families, Gender and Violence, or: Begin with the Body, Once Again

There is tacit recognition in this volume that not all human bodies are born equal—although no account is supplied for this inequality, which is inherent in religious systems that have a male god and male functionaries at their center. Violence (mentioned 280 times in the volume) is called a violation of human dignity, and violence in the family ("family" occurring a whopping 607 times but, strangely enough, "family violence" only seven times, although the phenomenon signified is well attested and discussed).

To discuss fertility reproductive techniques as if they were a female problem, or violence against women or children especially, problematizing the availability of the former or its discouragement or encouragement in "patriarchal" faith (read: Christian) societies, is half the story—even in the global North. The other half is the strong notion that patriarchy is divine, that every heterosexual man is potentially a patriarch and thus divine or divine-like, powerful, and authoritative, and that women and children of both genders are at his command. Christianity, like Judaism, favors males; this is the flip side of the *imago Dei* notion, in spite of the exegetical acrobatics produced with regard to Gen 1:26–27: the creation of "them" ("man and woman") in his "image." Such gender hierarchy promotes violence against women; the alpha-male and father notions about the Divine promote the acceptability of violence within the family—most often perpetrated by males on females and children. In that sense, the expression "fragile dignity" in the title of this volume is an inadequate understatement. We are talking the *indignity* of women or children, as a rule, in North and South faith communities and with few exceptions; indignity that results from systemic, built-in scriptural inequality. How can one discuss "identity" as a mark of human dignity ("identity" and "identities" appear fifty-six times in this volume) when the dice is loaded in this way? How can one speak of the personhood of low-class and wrong-gender persons? Indeed, one cannotI wonder how much pastoral care within faith communities can really help here, as Mulder and others optimistically emphasize. Community support for human individuals damaged by human violence can indeed be of great help. In fact, it is indispensable for openly dealing with ensuing problems (physical, mental, and emotional) faced by the victims. However, in the background remains the reality of the three male-headed monotheistic religions, the very faith in which fosters violence against what is conceived of as a [corporeal] non-image of the Divine and the privilege to eradicate the personal liberty, even life, for what is considered as nonpatriarchal (= divinely related). No ad hoc pastoral care within a faith community can negate this basic inequality and its ensuing indignity. The way to begin liberating human bodies of religiously-tolerated family abuse—in the context of this volume, and the communities it represents—is, to my mind, to expose the religious biases that (almost) institutionalize this violence. Some theo-pastoral work is necessary here to cut perpetrators down to size—perhaps more so than affording comfort to the sufferers. The sufferers have other legal and formal remedies to appeal to, and should certainly be encouraged to do so; the perpetrators, it seems to me, would need religious re-education and counsel that would strip them of their self-perceived quasi-divine status. I would like to disagree with Mulder here: "God as mother" occurs so seldom and far between in the bible that this image, a weak one, is hardly enough solace for violated women.

Additional Reflections: Earth and Identity

When I think about human dignity and human rights, I immediately think of Gen 1–5 and beyond, and of the idea that human control over the world implies taking care of the earth or land (Gen 1). Another way of expressing this is to accept that humans and land are closely connected, as is especially clear in Gen 2, where the first human male is fashioned out of clay (by God's hands, no?) as much as he receives divine breath.

This description signifies that ecology is a concern invented long before our time. It also implies that earth, land, territory is a human preoccupation. In this volume "earth" is mentioned twenty-eight times, whereas "creation" is mentioned eighty-eight times—"ecology" is not mentioned once. This adequately reflects the authors' own preoccupations. The perception I would like to add here is that most humans are driven by a strong relationship to the land: from the necessity for shelter—a basic human right for us—to the ownership of land and the conquest of territory. Family, house, and land are realities and symbols for human dignified existence in the Hebrew bible: see for instance Ps 1: dignified is the man who has all these, in serenity. Since much human dignity is connected with the earth, it makes sense to conserve the earth's dignity by not abusing it. This can clearly be a theological preoccupation when discussing human dignity.

A Short Response to Respondents

The responses I have seen, those parts of the conversation that add additional and welcome dimensions to clusters of conversations (individual essays and responses), are mostly supportive and take the discussion further in a critical way. Let me summarize them by quoting in short from each the passages I deemed the most essential.

In the final paragraph of her response, Anderson writes:

> Both Schaafsma and Mulder offer scriptural passages and theological constructs that can be used to create and maintain Christian families where all persons can flourish and where human dignity is truly respected. Nevertheless, we cannot begin to understand why it is so difficult for such positive scriptural and theological constructs to take root unless we first examine the interrelated oppressive ideologies that result from current constructions of "family values."

As I have tried to convey, this is mildly put and should perhaps be redefined as "family faith values," especially but not only Christian, as they shape disrespectful, dysfunctional families. I join this critique and, with Tamez, I am happy to see Punt presenting considerations about the possibilities of upholding other scriptural family constructs.

Operating from her own Indian context, Melanchthon contributes to the conversation by taking up a stance of cultural relativism. In the second to last paragraph of her response to the Hebrew bible and Qur'an family violence essays (by Speelman and Waghid), she writes:

> In my estimation, all three essays have offered possibilities and opportunities to cast a critical eye toward my own culture and to see and speak out against harmful gendered and discriminatory practices and relations within my context. Together they make possible a common analysis.

They put forth a common agenda for action, and produce a shared framework for understanding and collective action to address issues related to human dignity and honor-driven violence against both men and women in church and society.

Further, as per her mandate to respond to Stark and Nell, Melanchthon deals with preaching, sermons, the church, and the use and abuse of the Bible. Mitchell's final paragraph summarizes her response as follow:

> But I would argue that if human dignity is properly recognized as God-given and that, consequently, it is something to be viewed as sacred and safeguarded, then the *praxis* of affirming human dignity can actually *preclude* acts of injustice. Affirmation of a dignity already present in the people we encounter can become a safeguard against its violation.

This is a faith response that is extremely optimistic in its positing faith before and above justice and injustice. I rest my case.

Tamez is unequivocal:

> In this intercultural dialogue, geographic location does of course also play a role. However, the greatest distance can be observed in the contexts of the First and Third Worlds with regard to the choice of topics relating to Assisted Reproductive Technologies, which is analyzed very well by Erbele-Küster. The Latin American context is characterized by outrageous inequalities—because of high poverty levels, more than half the population has no access to basic necessities such as food, health, work, and education. Here the first option is to struggle for survival. (162)

Tamez continues this welcome regard for basics, especially bodily basics, when she writes about the global market system that limits human rights and dignity. Her equation of human dignity, satisfied human needs, and fulfilled rights seems to this reader very much to the point. But then Tamez returns to the faith issue:

> God's grace and human dignity are mutual expressions, since both refer to God and to human beings. They refer us to the Divine because since creation, and in the constant recreation of its creatures, this has been the source of both grace and human dignity; it also refers to us human beings, because only in the totality of creation and human history until the present is it possible to perceive the grace of God and the dignity of human beings. (163)

This is a faith confession. I cannot see how it connects with Tamez's previous material and geo-economic analysis. Nevertheless, her contribution is in the reference to divine grace instead of the divine image. Once again, however, should not humans be respected, do they not have inherent dignity, or should they not have it, simply because they are *human*, as a pragmatic attitude, as a live-and-let-live attitude? This is what it is all about, is it not? (In this volume "life" is mentioned more than two hundred times; "death," in spite of the fact that a sizeable portion of the text concerns physical violence, is referred to only twenty-four times.)

To Conclude: An Alternative Perhaps?

Deuteronomy 6:5 demands:

> You shall love the LORD your God with all your heart and with all your soul and with all your might. (JPS)

And in Lev 19:18b:

> Love your fellow as yourself: I am the LORD. (JPS)

Both Hebrew bible passages are joined to produce the basic tenets for life, as attributed to Jesus in Mark 12:29–31. In Matt 19:16–19, and in Rom 13:8–9, "Love your fellow as yourself" is joined to the second part of the Decalogue (Exod 20 = Deut 5), the so-called negative commands that regulate human societies, and said by Jesus and Paul respectively to encapsulate true faith in the true God and his innate goodness, to be reflected in well-regulated human society.

The Hebrew verb that is used in both Deuteronomy and Leviticus, *'ahabh*, is universally translated as "love." However, in the Hebrew, as the New Testament authors must have clearly understood, the verb's semantic range is wider than the English "love." Besides "love" and "desire," it also includes the commitment to act or not to act according to respect owed towards other humans and one's decisions—as in Ruth's "love" for Naomi (Ruth 4:15), and the Hebrew slave's "love" for his master, wife, and children so that he is prepared to forego his personal freedom (Exod 21:5). In all these instances the meaning of "love" is proper, responsible civic behavior.

"Love your fellow as yourself" is considered by most the scriptural reference behind the following story. The Elder Hillel, the head of the Sanhedrin in the last century B.C.E., was pestered by a Gentile who wanted to convert to Judaism while learning the whole Torah very quickly, while "standing on one leg." Hillel eventually complied and said to him, in Aramaic: "*What is hateful to you do not do to your fellow*; this is the whole Torah. The rest is interpretation; go and study" (*b. Šabb.* 31a; paraphrase mine).

This is the whole Torah. Might it perhaps be a potentially shared secular and confessional alternative, looking for human dignity and rights in human survival concerns rather than in a speculative human-divine similarity or reflection?

I want to thank the contributors to and discussants in this volume for making me think about the topics you raised and for asking me to respond to your concerns. When you converse about the biblical texts, on the texts, on the many facets of biblical faith as you understand it, I immediately become engaged. When you move into promoting your own faith, as buttressed by your own readings, you lose me. I am not trying to depreciate your faith and confessional practice concerns as being irrelevant. Your concerns are highly relevant for the communities you are part of and share in. However, they are much less so for the likes of me, even though we too share a community, that of biblical scholars. Ultimately, methodologically, academic research in religion and theology is or should be about beliefs within the texts and the texts those beliefs utilize, not about how to believe and what to believe in. Connections between scholarly work, on the one hand, and preaching and ministry on the other, have been established and reestablished for millennia. Perhaps it is time to think about the boundaries between these two cultural zones, to be crossed and recrossed, but boundaries nevertheless?

Contributors

Cheryl B. Anderson is Professor of Old Testament at Garrett-Evangelical Theological Seminary in Evanston, Illinois. She is also an ordained elder in the United Methodist Church (Baltimore-Washington Conference). She is the author of *Women, Ideology, and Violence: Critical Theory and the Construction of Gender in the Book of the Covenant and the Deuteronomic Law* (T&T Clark, 2004); and *Ancient Laws and Contemporary Controversies: The Need for Inclusive Biblical Interpretation* (Oxford University Press, 2009). Her current research interests involve contextual and liberationist readings of scripture in the age of HIV and AIDS.

Hendrik Bosman is Professor of Old Testament in the Faculty of Theology, Stellenbosch University, where he teaches courses on Old Testament wisdom and prophetic texts and the context and reception of the Old Testament. Recent research projects focused on the book of Exodus as a narrative concerning origin and migration; cultic memories of the exodus and the negotiation of identity; the reception of the exodus in African contexts of resistance against colonialism; and the fear of the Lord and theological ethics in the book of Deuteronomy.

Gerrit Brand, until his untimely death on March 4, 2013, was senior lecturer in systematic theology at Stellenbosch University. After his studies at the University of Pretoria, he obtained his doctorate from Utrecht University in the Netherlands, followed by a postdoctoral fellowship in the Department of Philosophy at Stellenbosch University. His publications include *Speaking of a Fabulous Ghost* (Peter Lang, 2002), academic articles, his blog (DinkNet), popular writings, and columns for the journals *Maandblad Zuid-Afrika, Streven,* and *Kerkbode*. At the time of his death, he was the editor of the theological journal *NGTT* and coeditor of Sol Iustitiae, the online discussion forum of the Stellenbosch Faculty of Theology.

Athalya Brenner is Emerita Professor of Hebrew Bible/Old Testament at the Universiteit van Amsterdam, and currently teaches Biblical Studies at Tel Aviv University. She is the editor of *A Feminist Companion to the Hebrew Bible*, first and second series (19 volumes). Her research interests are biblical poetics and philology, feminist criticisms, and cultural studies as applied to biblical studies.

L. Juliana Claassens studied in South Africa and the U.S.A. (Ph.D., Princeton Theological Seminary) and taught at St. Norbert College in Green Bay, Wisconsin, Baptist Theological Seminary in Richmond, Virginia, and Wesley Theological Seminary in Washington, D.C. Since 2010 she has been Associate Professor of Old Testament with a research focus on human dignity in the Faculty of Theology, Stellenbosch University, South Africa. Her works include *The God Who Provides: Biblical Images of Divine Nourishment* (Abingdon, 2004) and *Mourner, Mother, Midwife: Reimaging God's Liberating Presence in the Old Testament* (Westminster John Knox, 2012).

Dorothea Erbele-Küster is professor in the Faculteit voor Protestantse Godgeleerdheid/Brussels, where she teaches Old Testament and Hebrew. Until 2012 she taught Old Testament at the Protestant Theological University in Kampen, Netherlands. She did her Ph.D. on literary theory and the Psalms (*Lesen als Akt des Betens,* Neukirchen-Vluyn, 2001). She also authored a book on gender and purity issues: *Körper und Geschlecth: Studien zur Anthropoligie von Leviticus 12 und 15* (Neukirchen-Vluyn, 2008).

Rev. Leo J. Koffeman is Professor of Church Polity and Ecumenism at the Protestant Theological University in Amsterdam, and Extraordinary Professor of Systematic Theology and Ecclesiology in the Faculty of Theology, Stellenbosch University, South Africa. His publications include *Het Goed Recht van de Kerk: Een Theologische Inleiding op het Kerkrecht* (Kok, 2009), and *In Order to Serve* (forthcoming).

Frits de Lange is Professor of Ethics at the Protestant Theological University, the Netherlands, and Extraordinary Professor in Systematic Theology and Ecclesiology at Stellenbosch University, South Africa. He teaches courses in theological ethics and the ethics of care, with a special interest in the elderly. His most recent publication is *In Andermans Handen: Over Flow en Grenzen in de Zorg* [*In Someone Else's Hands: Flow and Limits in Care*], 2011.

CONTRIBUTORS

Monica Jyotsna Melanchthon taught in India for many years before joining the United Faculty of Theology, MCD University of Divinity in Melbourne, Australia, where she teaches Old Testament Studies. She is an ordained minister in the Andhra Evangelical Lutheran Church, India, and is strongly committed to and has written on issues of gender, caste, scripture and ecumenism. Melanchthon also serves as secretary to the Society of Asian Biblical Studies.

Magda Misset-van de Weg is lecturer at the Protestant Theological University in Kampen, the Netherlands, and teaches New Testament and Biblical Theology. Her research interests include the position of women in the New Testament and in early Christian literature. Misset-van de Weg is coeditor, with Alberdina Houtman and Albert de Jong, of *Empsychoi Logoi: Religious Innovations in Antiquity. Studies in Honour of Pieter Willem van der Horst* (Brill, 2008).

Beverly Eileen Mitchell is Professor of Historical Theology at Wesley Theological Seminary in Washington, D.C., where she teaches courses in theology, church history, and African American religious history. Among her major publications are *Black Abolitionism: A Quest for Human Dignity* (Orbis, 2005) and *Plantations and Death Camps: Religion, Ideology, and Human Dignity* (Fortress, 2009).

Anne-Claire Mulder is University teacher and Associate Professor for Women's and Gender Studies Theology at the Protestant Theological University. She has published *Divine Flesh, Embodied Word: "Incarnation" as a Hermeneutical Key to a Feminist Theologian's Reading of Luce Irigaray's Work* (Amsterdam, 2006) She has written, among other pieces, "An Ethic of the In-Between: A Condition of Possibility of Being and Living Together," in New Topics in Feminist Philosophy of Religion: Contestations and Transcendence Incarnate (ed. Pamela Sue Anderson; Dordrecht, 2010). Her most recent publication is "Divine Wo/men Are Dignitaries: Seven Billion of Them Walk in Dignity and Flourish," *Feminist Theology* (21 [2013]: 232–43).

Ian Nell is Associate Professor of Practical Theology at Stellenbosch University, where he also coordinates the Master of Divinity and Licentiate programs in the faculty. He coauthored *Draers van die waarheid: Nuwe Testamentiese Visies vir die Gemeente* [*Messengers of Truth: New Testament*

Visions for the Congregation] (Buvton, 2002) and published various of articles on teaching of practical theology and ministry, the most recent being "Blended Learning: Innovation in the Teaching of Practical Theology to Undergraduate Students" in *Practical Theology in South Africa (PTSA)*, forthcoming.

Mary-Anne Plaatjies-van Huffel is a senior lecturer in the Faculty of Theology, Stellenbosch University, where she teaches church polity and church history. She holds two doctorates, one in systematic theology and one in church polity. Among her most recent publications are: "Control, Secede: Vested Rights and Ecclesiastical Property" (*Studia Historicae Ecclesiasticae*, 2011); "The Institutionalization of Christian Women's Organizations: From Docile Recipients to Agents of Change" (*Studia Historicae Ecclesisticae*, 2011); and "Church Polity and Church Governance in the Dutch Reformed Mission Church (1881–1915)" (*NGTT,* 2011).

Jeremy Punt is Professor of New Testament in the Theology Faculty at Stellenbosch University, South Africa. He works on hermeneutics and critical theory in New Testament interpretation past and present, focusing on the Pauline letters. His recent publications include "Hermeneutics in Identity Formation"; "1 Corinthians 7:17–24: Identity and Human Dignity amidst Power and Liminality" (*Verbum et Ecclesia*, 2012); and "Violence in the New Testament and the Roman Empire: Ambivalence, Othering, Agency" (in *Coping with Violence in the New Testament*; Brill, 2012).

Petruschka Schaafsma is lecturer in ethics at the Protestant Theological University in Amsterdam. After her Ph.D. on the theme of evil (*Reconsidering Evil: Confronting Reflections with Confessions*; Peeters, 2006), her current research focuses on religion and philosophical anthropology. She is currently working on the possibilities of the criticism of autonomy and interest in dependency as a possible way to reassess the relationship between human beings and the divine in religion. This research led to an interest in the theme of the family as a concrete context to study human beings in the tension between autonomy and dependence.

David Xolile Simon is a Senior Lecturer in Missiology and Science of Religions in the Department of Practical Theology, Faculty of Theology, Stellenbosch University, South Africa.

Rev. Lee-Ann Simon is a Minister of Religion in the Uniting Reformed Church of Southern Africa, Elsies River Congregation, Western Cape, South Africa. Rev. Simon specializes in Contextual Pastoral Care (HIV and AIDS).

Gé Speelman is Assistant Professor of Religious Studies at the Protestant Theological University, Amsterdam. Amongst her many publications in the field of interreligious hermeneutics is *Een kleine Koran: Hulp bij het Zelfstandig Lezen van de Koran aan de Hand van de Tweede Soera* [*A Little Qur'an*], with Karel Steenbrink (Narratio, 2011); and, on interreligious marriages, *Keeping Faith: Muslim-Christian Couples and Interreligious Dialogue* (Meinema, 2001).

Klaas Spronk is Professor of Old Testament at the Protestant Theological University, Amsterdam. His research focuses on biblical theology and contextual exegesis. He is presently working on a commentary on the book of Judges. Among his recent publications are "Judging Jephthah: The Contribution of Syntactic Analysis to the Interpretation of Judges 11:29–40," in *Tradition and Innovation in Biblical Interpretation: Studies Presented to Professor Eep Talstra on the Occasion of His Sixty-Fifth Birthday* (Brill, 2011); and "The Book of Judges as a Late Construct," in *Historiography and Identity: (Re)formulation in Second Temple Historiographic Literature* (T&T Clark, 2010).

Ciska Stark is Associate Professor of Liturgy and Homiletics at the Protestant Theological University, Amsterdam, the Netherlands. Her research topics include contemporary preaching practices, lay preaching, and the development of methods of sermon analysis. She has worked as a minister in the Protestant Church in the Netherlands and as lecturer in the Mennonite Seminary in Amsterdam, where she also served as rector.

Elsa Tamez is one of the principal initiators and developers of the feminist perspective in Latin American Liberation Theology. She is currently Emerita Professor and former director at the Latin American Biblical University, San José, Costa Rica. She is the author of various books, including *Amnesty of Grace: Justification by Faith from a Latin American Perspective* (Abingdon, 1993; Spanish version, 1991) and *Struggles for Power in Early Christianity: A Study of the First Letter to Timothy* (Orbis, 2007; Spanish version, 2005).

Charlene van der Walt recently completed a two year postdoctoral fellowship exploring the reading strategies of contemporary Bible readers. An ordained minister in the Dutch Reformed Church, she also is a part-time lecturer at the Faculty of Theology, Stellenbosch University, and is responsible for a special focus Master's project on the intersection of gender, health, and theology in the African context. Van der Walt is also researcher for Inclusive and Affirming Ministries (IAM), an organization promoting dialogue on issues of diversity in faith communities.

Robert Vosloo is Associate Professor of Church History in the Department of Systematic Theology and Ecclesiology at the Faculty of Theology, Stellenbosch University, South Africa. His research interests include questions related to memory and historiography, twentieth-century South African church history, and the life, theology, and legacy of Dietrich Bonhoeffer. He is coeditor with Len Hansen and Nico Koopman of *Living Theology: Essays Presented to Dirk J. Smit on his Sixtieth Birthday* (Bible Media, 2011).

Yusef Waghid is Professor of Philosophy of Education in the Department of Education Policy Studies and former Dean of the Faculty of Education at Stellenbosch University. His most recent books are *Education, Democracy, and Citizenship Reconsidered: Pedagogical Encounters* (Sun Media Press, 2010) and *Conceptions of Islamic Education: Pedagogical Framings* (Peter Lang, 2011).

www.ingramcontent.com/pod-product-compliance
Lightning Source LLC
Chambersburg PA
CBHW031705230426
43668CB00006B/108